THE COLLECTED PLAYS OF
W. SOMERSET MAUGHAM

VOL. II

By W. SOMERSET MAUGHAM

LIZA OF LAMBETH
MRS. CRADDOCK
THE MOON AND SIXPENCE
OF HUMAN BONDAGE
THE TREMBLING OF A LEAF
ON A CHINESE SCREEN
THE PAINTED VEIL
THE CASUARINA TREE
ASHENDEN
THE GENTLEMAN IN THE PARLOUR
CAKES AND ALE
THE FIRST PERSON SINGULAR
THE NARROW CORNER
AH KING
ALTOGETHER (*Collected Short Stories*)
DON FERNANDO
COSMOPOLITANS
THEATRE
THE SUMMING UP
CHRISTMAS HOLIDAY
THE MIXTURE AS BEFORE
BOOKS AND YOU
UP AT THE VILLA
STRICTLY PERSONAL
THE RAZOR'S EDGE
THEN AND NOW
HERE AND THERE (*Collection of Short Stories*)
CREATURES OF CIRCUMSTANCE
CATALINA
QUARTET (*Four Short Stories with Film Scripts*)
TRIO (*Three Short Stories with Film Scripts*)
ENCORE (*Three Short Stories with Film Scripts*)
A WRITER'S NOTEBOOK

The Collected Plays

VOL. I: LADY FREDERICK
         MRS. DOT
         JACK STRAW
         PENELOPE
         SMITH
         THE LAND OF PROMISE

VOL. 2: OUR BETTERS
         THE UNATTAINABLE
         HOME AND BEAUTY
         THE CIRCLE
         THE CONSTANT WIFE
         THE BREADWINNER

VOL. 3: CÆSAR'S WIFE
         EAST OF SUEZ
         THE SACRED FLAME
         THE UNKNOWN
         FOR SERVICES RENDERED
         SHEPPEY

THE COLLECTED
❖ PLAYS ❖

of

W. SOMERSET
MAUGHAM

VOL. II

WILLIAM HEINEMANN LTD
MELBOURNE :: LONDON :: TORONTO

THE COLLECTED PLAYS
FIRST PUBLISHED 1931
REPRINTED   1952

PRINTED IN GREAT BRITAIN
AT THE WINDMILL PRESS
KINGSWOOD, SURREY

THE COLLECTED PLAYS OF W. SOMERSET MAUGHAM

—

OUR BETTERS

THE UNATTAINABLE

HOME AND BEAUTY

THE CIRCLE

THE CONSTANT WIFE

THE BREADWINNER

PREFACE

THE three plays following are placed in the order in which they were written. *Our Betters*, though it was not acted in London till 1923, and then only with a scene at the end of the second act altered to suit the exigencies of the Lord Chamberlain, was written in Rome at the beginning of 1915. When at last it was produced I extracted a certain amount of discreet amusement from such of the critics as found in it a development of characteristics that they had discovered in plays produced before but written much later. I may add in passing that in this edition I have reverted to my original version. It was more probable and I do not see that it was more shocking. In the few years that have passed audiences have become used to greater frankness, and if the play were ever revived I have little doubt that the word *slut* used by one of the characters, which made the spectators on the first night gasp with horror, would now fail entirely to express the speaker's indignation. *The Unattainable* was produced under the name of *Caroline*, and it gave Irene Vanbrugh the opportunity for one of the best performances of her distinguished career. I had a somewhat unusual experience with this play. I wrote it in Geneva during the autumn of 1915. It was engaged in work for the Intelligence Department which the Swiss authorities did not approve of, and my predecessor had had a nervous breakdown owing to the strain it put upon his temperament, more sensitive than mine, to break the law; my colleague at Lausanne had lately been sent to prison for two years. I did not know how political prisoners were treated and I had no notion whether, should such an unpleasant fate befall me, I should be allowed pens and paper. I hated the idea of leaving the play unfinished, and I knew it would be very difficult to take it up again after a long interval. It was a great relief to me when I wrote the last line. I sent it to London, and it was put into rehearsal at once. I had written the whole play up to a great comic scene in the last act, a scene of mistaken identity in the classic manner, which in imagination had very much amused me; and, indeed, it was on my exuberant description of this scene that Irene Vanbrugh had accepted the play. I managed to get a few days' leave and went to London for the final rehearsals. The date was fixed for production. Things were very well advanced. The caste was word-perfect. I sat through the first two acts and was not dissatisfied; the play seemed to have come through very much as I had seen it in my mind's eye, but I was awaiting the scene which I expected to prove the climax of the comedy. A very good actor, George Tully, had been engaged to play in it. The persons concerned started. They went through it and they acted it very well. To my dismay I discovered that it did not amuse me at all. Here was a pretty kettle of fish! It took up two-thirds of the last act, and it was to lead up to it that the first two acts had been devised. It seemed to me that there was but one thing to do. I waited till the rehearsal was finished and then, telling Dion Boucicault, who was producing it, that this would not do at all, asked him to give me twenty-four hours, took the script home and rewrote the last act. I left out the scene that had so much disappointed me, and with it the character that George Tully was to act. The play now offered to the reader is the result. I do not know that it is an author's business to point out to his readers the defects of his work, but if I were a critic I should perhaps feel it my duty to make the observation that the play really is finished by the end of the first act. What follows might have very well been left to the imagination of the audience.

The same stern critic might make the same objection to *Home and Beauty*, the third play in this volume, and in each case the answer might be given, in extenuation, that a certain number of diverting scenes do what is possible to atone for the failure to adhere to the strict canons of drama.

Home and Beauty was written in a sanatorium during the last winter of the war. I had escaped a Swiss prison, but the work I was engaged in had much exposed me to the rigours of a singularly bad winter and I had contracted tuberculosis of the lungs. This had been aggravated by a sojourn in Russia, and when on the seizure of power by the Bolsheviks I was obliged to come back to England, I was feeling very sorry for myself. It was impossible then to go to Davos or St. Moritz, so I went to Scotland. It was a very pleasant life at Nordrach-on-Dee. I was sent to bed every day at six o'clock, and an early dinner gave me a long evening to myself. The cold, windless night entered the room through the wide-open windows, and with mittens on my hands so that I could comfortably hold a pen, it was an admirable opportunity to write a farce. For *Home and Beauty* pretends to be no more. I never had an opportunity of seeing it, but I believe it made people laugh very much. Some of the critics called it cruel and heartless. I should not have thought it was. It was written in the highest possible spirits. It was intended to amuse.

So, for the matter of that, where the other two plays. The reader of the previous preface to this edition of my plays will not be surprised at my confession that I think this is the business of a comedy. To my mind it is not a work of edification, though it should be a work of art, and if it castigates the follies of the moment that is by the way and only in so far as this no doubt laudable process occasions laughter. The object is the entertainment of the audience, not their improvement.

I am conscious that my plays are classed by the learned who write books on the drama and contribute articles to encyclopædias as commercial theatre, and it is true that on the whole the managers have made money out of them and I have kept the wolf some distance from my door.

The difficulty of the drama as an art lies for the most part in its dependence on the audience. An audience is a crowd and art as we know has nothing to do with the multitude.

The working classes, absorbed in the daily effort of providing for the needs of the body, have little energy left over to cultivate the disinterested emotions of art. The upper classes know nothing of it and care less. They feign sometimes an interest in it when fashion suggests such a pose as a social distinction. Great ladies then cultivate those occupied with the arts as in former times they kept buffoons. An interest in art is found, if in any class at all, most commonly perhaps in the middle ranks of society. A German observer of this country has stated that it is almost exclusively confined to the northern and western suburbs of London. Even here it must be rare, for it needs not only a natural instinct, which is uncommon, but an elaborate cultivation. That the two are necessary is shown by the fact that a true feeling for one of the arts by no means entails feeling for the others: a man may have admirable taste in pictures and none at all in literature or music. The appeal of the arts then is to the very few.

But the drama cannot do with that. It must address itself equally to the working man in the gallery and to the gilded youth in the stalls. It must interest the stock-jobber who reads nothing but *The Financial Times* and the elderly spinster whose soul is sweet with memories of Italy and Greece. Attempts have been made from time to time to separate the various classes of playgoers. It has been suggested that certain plays should be written with the idea of attracting a limited, intellectual section, rather than the public at large; but the attempts have failed, as indeed an elementary acquaintance with the philosophy of the subject would have shown was inevitable; and the difficulty still remains to move, amuse and entertain an audience composed of persons with every variety of education and intelligence. It would be impossible if the audience consisted simply of the aggregation of individuals, but the play forms it into a distinct organism with characteristics peculiar to itself. It seems obvious that the audience is as much part of the play as the words and their interpreters. I read once a French

criticism in which the theory was advanced that the reading
of a play was the only test of its merit: on the stage one was
influenced by the skill of the actors, the elaborateness of the
setting and the emotions of one's fellow spectators. I think
this is nonsense. The play that is read differs not at all from
that monstrous product, once fashionable, the novel in
dialogue. A play exists without an audience as little as a
colour without a spectator. If plays have maintained
through the many centuries since the drama arose "in a rude
and unpremeditated manner" from the worship of Dionysus,
certain main traits, it is owing not to the imitativeness of the
dramatists, but to the unaltered characteristics of the crowd.
I do not know if the psychology of the audience is capable of
change, but it is clear from the most casual study of dramatic
works since Æschylus that no great change has taken place in
it hitherto.

The audience has a collective soul. It feels, reacts, and
thinks differently from what each member of it, taken
separately, would do. It is emotional rather than intellectual, and this gives it homogeneity; for however unlike
men are by their intelligence, their passions are the same.
The audience is on a lower level of civilisation than the
persons of which it is composed, and it may be for this
reason that the theatre is a generation behind the culture of
the age. The opinions, ideas and beliefs which are suggested
to an audience are accepted or rejected in the mass, un-
critically, and are considered either as absolute truths or as
absolute errors. An audience can only receive ideas when
they are placed before it in their simplest form, and even
then only when they agree with its own instinctive convic-
tions.

An audience demands sympathy, which I take to be no
more than direction of interest; for it is well-known that a
sympathetic character need not be a virtuous one. It has a
moral code which, according to the time, may be stricter or
more lax than that of the individual. At the present moment,
in England at all events, it is shocked by things that would

not shock the individual, though under the reign of Charles II, when probably the general morality was little different from what it is now, it accepted conduct which would have outraged him. It is emotional, but at the same time has more commonsense than the individual. It has its own theories of life which do not always coincide with life as known by the individual. Though swayed by impulse it does not believe in it on the stage. The individual can hardly have failed to notice that the actions of men are much influenced by their passions, but an audience insists that they shall be influenced only by reason. It demands much stronger motives than are demanded in real life. For example, it so often happens that men throw themselves into the water to save a perfect stranger from drowning that the newspapers seldom trouble to announce the fact; but on the stage if you made someone do anything of the kind the spectators would shrug their shoulders and say: These things don't happen. You could only make the occurrence probable by giving at least three overwhelming personal reasons for such a piece of fool-hardiness. An audience has also racial characteristics. The English are not a sexual nation and you cannot easily persuade them that a man will sacrifice anything important for love. I do not think an English audience, notwith-standing the prestige of Shakespeare, ever really accepts the story of Antony and Cleopatra as credible. It is this difference of attitude towards sexual passion that makes foreign plays so improbable to us.

It is clear that the dramatist's business is with the audience as an organic whole and not with the persons who make it up. As soon as they leave the theatre and go about their separate affairs they cease to be an audience and he has no further concern with them. This reduces sensibly the didactic efficiency of the drama, on account of which writers have from time to time been attracted to the stage; for if the individual is so much inclined to hypnotic suggestion that he cannot shake off the emotions he has felt when his personality was fused in that of the audience, he is not a safe person to be trusted alone, and should promptly be shut up in an asylum.

The acute reader of the foregoing remarks will see at once that they reduce dramatic criticism to a logical absurdity. I wish for the sake of those who follow this calling that I could have concealed the fact from him. But the deduction is too obvious. The critic trains himself not to be influenced by the passions of the people who surround him, but in so doing he does not see the play which they see. His rôle is to keep free from the contagion of the audience. But the audience is so much part of the play that you cannot judge it unless you are the audience. He aims at holding aloof from popular clamour, but it is only by popular clamour, the thrill that passes through the house, the excitement of propinquity, that the play exists. Only one form of criticism is logically reasonable. If a critic were so sensitive to the emotion about him that he could feel it in all its subtlety and if he had at the same time the power to stand outside himself and note his sensations, his criticism would be, to the playwright at least, exceedingly useful. But I suppose that a man with such gifts would in these democratic days rule empires rather than write dramatic criticism.

I beg the reader not to think that these remarks were designed to take the bread out of the mouths of that body of honest, industrious, long-suffering and conscientious men who make their living by judging the current drama. It was not indeed till I had set down in black and white my reflections on the nature of an audience that it occurred to me that I had incidentally demonstrated the futility of dramatic criticism. Nothing was further from my intention. We greatly need in England a critic of authoritative position who would be capable of restating the limitations of the various arts, who had the culture and the knowledge of life to point out to those who overstepped the boundaries that they were attempting the impossible, and whose philosophical attainments were sufficient to explain why the direction they were taking must lead to confusion.

For want of this the creators of art are at sixes and sevens. They do not know exactly what they want to do nor what they can do. Sculptors seek to imprison the momentary gesture in imperishable bronze, musicians describe events, poets paint landscapes, essayists write poems in prose (and what detestable, pretentious stuff), novelists write treatises of sociology, and dramatists reason.

It can hardly be denied that at the present time the drama of England is poor. The reason given for this is that the cost of production has so increased that managers hesitate to give new authors a hearing. I do not think this is a fact. The bills of the London theatres are no longer filled by well-established authors, as they were when first I began writing plays, but by authors who were till recently unheard of. The experimental theatres have given them an opportunity they never had before and the dearth of plays is such that the managers will seize with alacrity upon anything that shows a likelihood of attracting an audience. The way is open to the dramatist. He has only to take it. I think it is much more probable that the poverty of British drama is due to the fact that the playwrights have been influenced by false theories to adventure in a field which the nature of the drama forbids and for which they are temperamentally unfitted. They have been told that they must raise the theatre from the depths to which it has sunk. They have been implored to produce something that the intelligent man can see without loss of self-respect. They are on the whole a modest, sincere lot of men, anxious to do their best, and they have honestly tried to comply with the demands made on them.

A few pages back I acknowledged, I hope with becoming modesty, that my plays must be classed as commercial drama, but I did not stay to consider exactly what that signifies. It is of course a term of depreciation. It describes a play which is a source of profit to the manager and the author and thus one which the public is willing to go and see for at least a hundred nights. It infers a lack of artistic merit. It is not immediately obvious why a play that people do not want to see is more artistic than one they do. If commercial success is the test a certain difficulty arises. It appears that Bernard Shaw was a commercial dramatist when he wrote *St. Joan* and an artist when he wrote *Back to Methuselah*. What are you going to think of *Man and Superman*? When it was first written it was very distinctly uncommercial: did it cease to be a work of art when it was produced by Robert Lorraine and everyone concerned made a great deal of money out of it? "Commercial" plays often fail too, four out of five is, I believe, the average; and the reasons for their failure are generally plain. I will enumerate them: a theme that does not interest, poor characterisation, faulty construction, verbose and heavy dialogue. Now it is a very strange thing, but if you examine the plays which are deliberately uncommercial and whose failure the judicious grieve at, you will find they suffer from one or all of these defects. In short the "uncommercial" theatre is uncommercial not because of its merits but because of its faults. A "commercial" play is commercial because of its merits.

It is an error to suppose that the writer of this sort of play writes only to make money. A very small experience of the profession of letters teaches you that to write with this end is folly. It is like happiness which is best achieved by not aiming at it. You earn most money when you write merely to please yourself. Of course you need not go out of your way to make things difficult. You are not likely to attain domestic felicity if you give your wife a black eye and knock your children about, nor will you earn substantial royalties if you write a play about the incestuous relations of a family of mental deficients. But now the intelligent reader sits up and takes notice. That is what we want, he cries, that is the theatre of ideas. All right. Let us leave the commercial theatre and talk of the theatre of ideas.

Ideas appeal to reason. But when you appeal to the reason of an audience you are faced with the difficulty that all its members are not on the same level of culture. A discussion on the shape of the planet cannot be of entrancing interest to those who are already acquainted with the glorious fact that the earth is round. Many writers, when they had produced a play of ideas, have been disappointed to find that a large part of the audience was bored stiff and that the critics only sneered. Stale ideas are no more palatable than stale fish. The fact is that ideas do not grow on every gooseberry bush. I suppose that no one knows exactly why the dramatist can say things in such a way and so present actions that they hold an audience. I can only surmise that it is a rare knack with which he is lucky enough to be born. Experience has shown that it cannot be taught. He must have besides a gift for observation, some literary instinct and a considerable knowledge of the world. It is a good deal to ask that he should be an original thinker as well. His mind moves naturally in the concrete. He grows confused when he has to deal with the abstract, and the nature of his intelligence forces him to see the instance rather than the theory.

But even if a dramatist were by a lucky chance to conceive an idea that was both original and momentous what could he do with it? He could only illustrate it. His play would be like those bad movies in the days of the silent film when the story was told you in captions and the pictures served only to put before your eyes what you already knew. That is to waste the possibilities of the medium. Nor, I suggest, is dialogue the best way of presenting ideas. I do not suppose anyone has used it to better purpose than Plato, but take any one of his dialogues and notice how exasperating it is, once you are interested in the argument, to be held up by the give and take of conversation.

"You will grant, my dear Polemarchus, that a physician is useless to persons in sound health."

"Certainly."

"And a pilot to persons on shore."

"Yes."

"Is the just man, also, useless to those who are not at war?"

"I do not quite think that."

"Then justice is useful in time of peace too, is it?"

"It is."

"And so is agriculture, is it not?"

"Yes."

"That is to say, as a means of acquiring the fruits of the earth."

"Yes."

"And further, the shoemaker's art is also useful, is it not?"

"Yes."

"As a means of acquiring shoes, I suppose you will say."

"Certainly."

Does one not wish he would cut the cackle and come to the 'osses? For my part I prefer ideas to be presented to me with lucidity and succinctness. I do not want to be persuaded to accept the thinker's thought by his art; I want to be convinced by his logic.

The reader must not do me the injustice of supposing that I believe there is no room for thought in the theatre. The more intelligent a dramatist is the better will be his plays. I suggest merely that ideas, new or old, as such, are no concern of his. He must translate them in terms of emotion. He must feel them before they can affect his audience. And what has feeling to do with ideas? The appeal of ideas is to the reason and reason is occupied with truth. But the drama is occupied only with verisimilitude. And what, if you please, is the dramatist going to do when truth is on one side and dramatic effect on the other? I can tell you. If he is a dramatist he will let truth go to the devil (should he be of a scrupulous nature perhaps consoling himself with some fine phrases about the higher truth of art), but if he is a philosopher he will let his play go hang. And that will be the end of his play.

Nor is the drama even a good vehicle for propaganda. I may think that the administration of the dole is very stupid and by choosing characters and instances to prove my case I can make out a scandalous state of things. But I have proved nothing. But choosing other characters and other instances I can show exactly the opposite. And such odd things happen in the theatre that a writer can never be sure that the moral he inculcates will emerge from the circumstances he displays. John Galsworthy wrote *Justice* to show the evils of the prison system and because he was a very able dramatist wrote an interesting and moving play, but what he actually showed was the efficiency with which society eliminates the unfit. The didactic writer may load his dice, but he can never be certain that he will throw sixes every time.

Prose drama is one of the lesser arts, like woodcarving or dancing, but so far as it is an art at all its purpose is to afford delight. I do not think it can usefully concern itself with the welfare of humanity or the saving of civilisation. I am afraid certain critics will say that I am cynical and hold the theatre in contempt. I am afraid of this because they have said it before and critics (like the rest of us) often repeat themselves. I do not think this is so. It may be (and this I do not assert but throw out as a suggestion) that I have naturally good taste and that my conception of the art I practised is the correct one. In the eighteenth century, poets were didactic and wrote long poems on agriculture, astronomy, bee-keeping, forestry and suchlike subjects. They were much praised for doing so. Now we are all agreed that they were in error. When we want to know about such things we consult a text-book. We do not want out poets to impart information or to inculcate the principles of morality. It may be that in a little while people will think that the drama will do best to confine itself to what it can best do. This in my opinion is to give pleasure by telling a story, delineating character, and by stirring the emotions or causing laughter.

The Anglo-Saxon race has always looked upon the artist with misgiving. They have never accepted him as a serious person and now that the spread of education has enabled

writers to move out of Grub Street, this want of consideration is irksome to them unless they have a sense of
humour or a happy indifference to the opinion of their
fellows. Writers consequently are apt to claim moral
intentions and pedagogic ends. They seek respectability by
adopting a portentous attitude. I think it is a pity. So far as
the dramatists are concerned too many, who might write
very good, workmanlike plays, thus waste their talents.
And the English have a cruel sense of humour. I think they
never laugh so much as when they destroy an artist by
turning him into a prophet.

I have little to say of the three last plays in this volume.
The Circle is generally thought the best play I have written. I
have always thought that the device suggested by Clive
Champion-Cheney to his son to prevent Elizabeth running
away not very happy. I should have liked at that point a
more substantial and dramatic invention. *The Constant
Wife* was a failure in London. It was a great success in
America, in the foreign countries where it has been produced
and even in the provincial towns in England in which it has
been from time to time acted. Where it has been successful
it has been much praised by the critics. Not of course
because they were influenced by its success, but because
a play consists of the words, the production and the
audience; and the failure of one of the parties concerned may
make the difference between a good play and a bad one.

OUR BETTERS

A COMEDY
in Three Acts

CHARACTERS

Lady Grayston

Duchesse de Surennes

Principessa della Cercola

Elizabeth Saunders

Arthur Fenwick

Thornton Clay

Fleming Harvey

Anthony Paxton

Lord Bleane

Pole

Ernest

The action of the play takes place at Lady Grayston's house in Grosvenor Street, Mayfair, and at her husband's place in Suffolk, Abbots Kenton.

OUR BETTERS

THE FIRST ACT

SCENE: *The drawing-room at* LADY GRAYSTON'S *house in Grosvenor Street, Mayfair. It is a sumptuous double room, of the period of George II., decorated in green and gold, with a coromandel screen and lacquer cabinets; but the coverings of the chairs, the sofas and cushions, show the influence of Bakst and the Russian Ballet; they offer an agreeable mixture of rich plum, emerald green, canary and ultra-marine. On the floor is a Chinese carpet, and here and there are pieces of Ming pottery.*
It is about half-past four, early in the season, and a fine day.
When the curtain rises, from the street below is heard the melancholy chant of the lavender man.

> Won't you buy my sweet lavender?
> Sixteen blue branches for a penny.
> If you buy it once,
> You'll buy it twice,
> For it makes your clothes
> Smell very nice—
> Sweet-scented lavender.

BESSIE SAUNDERS *comes in. She is a very pretty American girl, of twenty-two, with fair hair and blue eyes. She is dressed in the latest mode. She wears a hat and gloves, and carries a bag. She has just come in from the street. She has in her hand a telephone message, and going over to the telephone she takes up the receiver.*

BESSIE: Gerrard 4321. Is that the Berkeley? Put me

through to Mr. Harvey, please. Fleming Harvey, that's right. [*She listens and smiles.*] Yes. Who d'you think it is? [*She laughs.*] I've just got your telephone message. Where have you sprung from? That's fine. How long are you staying in London? I see. I want to see you at once. Nonsense. This very minute. Now just jump into a taxi and come right away. Pearl will be in presently. Ring off, Fleming. No, I will not ring off first. [*A pause.*] Are you there? How tiresome you are. You might be half-way here by now. Well, hustle.

> [*She puts down the receiver and begins to take off her gloves.* POLE, *the butler, comes in with a bunch of roses.*

POLE: These flowers have just come for you, miss.

BESSIE: Oh! Thank you. Aren't they lovely? You must give me something to put them in, Pole.

POLE: I'll bring a vase, miss.

> [*He goes out. She buries her face in the flowers and inhales their fragrance. The* BUTLER *enters with a bowl filled with water.*

BESSIE: Thank you. You're sure they *are* for me? There's no label.

POLE: Yes, miss. The person who brought them said they was for you, miss. I asked if there wasn't a card, and he said no, miss.

BESSIE:[*With a faint smile.*] I think I know who they're from. [*She begins to arrange the flowers.*] Her ladyship hasn't come in yet, has she?

POLE: Not yet, miss.

BESSIE: D'you know if anyone is coming in to tea?

POLE: Her ladyship didn't say, miss.

BESSIE: You'd better prepare for fifteen, then.

POLE: Very good, miss.

BESSIE: I was being funny, Pole.

POLE: Yes, miss? Shall I take the paper away, miss?

BESSIE: [*With a slight sigh of resignation.*] Yes, do, will you? [*The telephone bell rings.*] Oh, I forgot, I switched the telephone on here. See who it is.

    [POLE *takes up the receiver and listens, then puts his hand over its mouth.*

POLE: Will you speak to Lord Bleane, miss?

BESSIE: Say I'm not at home.

POLE: Miss Saunders hasn't come in yet. I beg pardon, my lord. I didn't recognise your lordship's voice. [*A pause.*] Well, my lord, I did hear them say there was a private view they thought of going to at the Grosvenor. You might find Miss Saunders there.

BESSIE: You needn't elaborate, Pole.

POLE: I was only making it more convincing, miss. [*Listening.*] I think so, my lord. Of course, I couldn't say for certain, my lord; they might have gone out to Ranelagh.

BESSIE: Really, Pole!

POLE: Very good, my lord. [*He puts down the receiver.*] His lordship asked if you was expected in to tea, miss.

POLE: Is there anything else, miss?

BESSIE: No, Pole, thank you.

    [*He goes out. She finishes arranging the flowers. The door is flung open and* LADY GRAYSTON *comes in, followed by* FLEMING HARVEY. PEARL—LADY GRAYSTON —is a handsome, dashing creature, a woman of thirty-four, with red hair, and a face outrageously painted. She is dressed in a Paris frock, but of greater daring both in colour and cut than a Frenchwoman would wear.* FLEMING *is a nice-looking young American in clothes that were obviously made in New York.*

PEARL: My dear Bessie, I've found an entirely strange young man on the doorstep who says he is a cousin.

BESSIE: [*Giving him her hands enthusiastically.*] Fleming.

FLEMING: I introduced myself to Lady Grayston. She drove up just as they were opening the door. Please reassure your sister, Bessie. She looks upon me with suspicion.

BESSIE: You must remember Fleming Harvey, Pearl.

PEARL: I've never set eyes on him in my life. But he looks quite nice.

BESSIE: He is.

PEARL: He's apparently come to see you.

FLEMING: I rang up five minutes ago and Bessie ordered me to come round right away.

PEARL: Well, make him stop to tea. I've got to telephone. I've suddenly remembered that I've asked twelve people to dinner.

BESSIE: Does George know?

PEARL: Who is George?

BESSIE: Don't be absurd, Pearl. George—your husband.

PEARL: Oh! I couldn't make out who you meant. No, he doesn't know. But what's much more important, the cook doesn't know either. I'd forgotten George was in London. [*She goes out.*

BESSIE: George generally dines out when Pearl is giving a party, because he doesn't like people he doesn't know, and he seldom dines at home when we're alone, because it bores him.

FLEMING: It doesn't sound as if Sir George enjoyed many of the benefits of home life.

BESSIE: Now let's sit down and make ourselves comfortable. You are going to stay to tea, aren't you?

FLEMING: It's not a beverage that I'm in the habit of imbibing.

BESSIE: When you've been in England a month you won't be able to do without it. When did you land?

FLEMING: This morning. You see, I've lost no time in coming to see you.

BESSIE: I should think not. It *is* good to see someone straight from home.

FLEMING: Have you been having a good time, Bessie?

BESSIE: Wonderful! Since the beginning of the season, except when Pearl has had people here, I've been out to lunch and dinner every day, and I've been to a ball every night, generally two and sometimes three.

FLEMING: Gee!

BESSIE: If I stopped now I'd drop down dead.

FLEMING: D'you like England?

BESSIE: I adore it. I think it's too bad of dad never to have let me come over to London before. Rome and Paris are nothing. We're just trippers there, but here we're at home.

FLEMING: Don't get too much at home, Bessie.

BESSIE: Oh, Fleming, I never thanked you for sending me the roses. It was perfectly sweet of you.

FLEMING: [*With a smile.*] I didn't send you any roses.

BESSIE: Didn't you? Well, why didn't you?

FLEMING: I hadn't time. But I will.

BESSIE: It's too late now. I naturally thought they were from you, because Englishmen don't send flowers in the same way as American boys do.

FLEMING: Is that so?

[*There is a slight pause.* BESSIE *gives him a quick look.*

BESSIE: Fleming, I want to thank you for that charming letter you wrote me.

FLEMING: There's no occasion to do that, Bessie.

BESSIE: I was afraid you might feel badly about it. But we'll always be the greatest friends, won't we?

FLEMING: Always.

BESSIE: After all, you were eighteen when you asked me to marry you, and I was sixteen. It wasn't a very serious engagement. I don't know why we didn't break it off before.

FLEMING: I suppose it never occurred to us.

BESSIE: I'd almost forgotten it, but when I came over here I thought I'd better make everything quite clear.

FLEMING: [*With a smile.*] Bessie, I believe you're in love.

BESSIE: No, I'm not. I tell you I'm having a wonderful time.

FLEMING: Well, who sent you the roses?

BESSIE: I don't know. Lord Bleane.

FLEMING: You're not going to marry a lord, Bessie?

BESSIE: Have you any objection?

FLEMING: Well, on first principles, I think American girls had better marry American men, but then I happen to be an American man.

[BESSIE *looks at him for a moment.*

BESSIE: Pearl gave a dinner party last night. I was taken in by a cabinet minister, and on the other side of me I had an ambassador. Just opposite was a man who'd been Viceroy in India. Madame Angelotti dined with us, and she sang afterwards, and a lot of people came on from an official dinner in their stars and ribands. Pearl looked superb. She's a wonderful hostess, you know. Several people told me they would rather come here than to any house in London. Before Pearl married George Grayston she was engaged to a boy who was in business in Portland, Oregon.

FLEMING: [*Smiling.*] I see you're quite determined to marry a lord.

BESSIE: No, I'm not. I'm keeping an open mind on the subject.

FLEMING: What d'you mean by that?

BESSIE: Well, Fleming, it hasn't escaped my notice that a certain noble lord is not unwilling to lay his beautiful coronet at my feet.

FLEMING: Don't talk like a novelette, Bessie.

BESSIE: But it feels just like a novelette. The poor dear is trying to propose to me every time he sees me, and I'm doing all I can to prevent him.

FLEMING: Why?

BESSIE: I don't want to refuse him, and then wish I hadn't.

FLEMING: You could easily make him ask you again. Women find that so simple.

BESSIE: Ah, but supposing he went right away to shoot big game in Africa. It's what they do, you know, in novelettes.

FLEMING: I'm reassured about one thing. You're not in the least in love with him.

BESSIE: I told you I wasn't. You don't mind my saying all this to you, Fleming?

FLEMING: Gracious, no; why should I?

BESSIE: You're sure you don't feel sore at my throwing you over?

FLEMING: [*Cheerfully.*] Not a bit.

BESSIE: I am glad, because then I can tell you all about the noble lord.

FLEMING: Has it occurred to you that he wants to marry you for your money?

BESSIE: You can put it more prettily. You can say that he wants to marry me with my money.

FLEMING: And is that a prospect that allures you?

BESSIE: Poor dear, what else can he do? He's got a large place to keep up, and he simply hasn't a cent.

FLEMING: Really, Bessie, you amaze me.

BESSIE: I shan't when you've been here a month.

[PEARL *comes in*.

PEARL: Now, Bessie, tell me all about this strange young man.

BESSIE: He's quite capable of telling you about himself.

PEARL: [*To* FLEMING.] How long are you staying?

FLEMING: A couple of months. I want to see something of English life.

PEARL: I see. D'you want to improve your mind or d'you want to go into society?

FLEMING: I suppose I couldn't combine the two.

PEARL: Are you rich?

FLEMING: Not at all.

PEARL: It doesn't matter, you're good-looking. If one wants to be a success in London one must either have looks, wit, or a bank-balance. You know Arthur Fenwick, don't you?

FLEMING: Only by reputation.

PEARL: How superciliously you say that!

FLEMING: He provides bad food to the working classes of the United States at an exorbitant price. I have no doubt he makes a lot of money.

BESSIE: He's a great friend of Pearl's.

PEARL: When he first came over because they turned up their noses at him in New York, I said to him: My dear Mr. Fenwick, you're not good-looking, you're not amusing, you're not well-bred, you're only rich. If you want to get into society you must spend money.

FLEMING: It was evidently in the nature of a straight talk.

BESSIE: We must do what we can for Fleming, Pearl.

PEARL: [*With a chuckle.*] We'll introduce him to Minnie Surennes.

FLEMING: Who in the world is she?

PEARL: The Duchesse de Surennes. Don't you remember? She was a Miss Hodgson. Chicago people. Of course, they're nobody in America, but that doesn't matter over here. She adores good-looking boys, and I daresay she's getting rather tired of Tony. [*To* BESSIE.] By the way, they're coming in this afternoon.

BESSIE: I don't like Tony.

PEARL: Why not? I think he's charming. He's the most unprincipled ruffian I ever met.

FLEMING: Is Tony the duke?

PEARL: What duke? Her husband? Oh no, she divorced him years ago.

BESSIE: I think Fleming would like the Princess much better.

PEARL: Oh, well, he'll meet her here to-day, too.

BESSIE: She was a Miss van Hoog, Fleming.

FLEMING: Is she divorced too?

PEARL: Oh no, her husband's an Italian. It's very difficult to get a divorce in Italy. She's only separated. She's quite nice. She's one of my greatest friends. She bores me a little.

> [POLE *comes in to announce* THORNTON CLAY *and then goes out.* THORNTON CLAY *is a stout American with a bald head and an effusive manner. He is somewhat overdressed. He speaks with a marked American accent.*

POLE: Mr. Thornton Clay.

CLAY: How d'you do?

PEARL: You're the very person we want, Thornton. An entirely strange young man has suddenly appeared on my doorstep, and says he's my cousin.

B

CLAY: My dear Pearl, that is a calamity which we Americans must always be prepared for.

BESSIE: I won't have you say such things, Mr. Clay. Fleming is not only our cousin, but he's my very oldest friend. Aren't you, Fleming?

PEARL: Bessie has a charming nature. She really thinks that friendship puts one under an obligation.

FLEMING: Since you're talking of me, won't you introduce me to Mr. Clay?

PEARL: How American you are!

FLEMING: [*Smiling.*] It's not unnatural, is it?

PEARL: Over here we haven't the passion that you have in America for introducing people. My dear Thornton, allow me to present to you my long-lost cousin, Mr. Fleming Harvey.

CLAY: It's so long since I was in America that I almost forget, but I believe the proper answer to that is: Mr. Fleming Harvey, I'm pleased to make your acquaintance.

FLEMING: Aren't you an American, Mr. Clay?

CLAY: I won't deny that I was born in Virginia.

FLEMING: I beg your pardon, I thought from the way you spoke . . .

CLAY: [*Interrupting.*] But, of course, my home is London.

PEARL: Nonsense, Thornton, your home is wherever there's a first-class hotel.

CLAY: I went to America seven years ago. My father died and I had to go and settle up his affairs. Everyone took me for an Englishman.

FLEMING: That must have gratified you very much, Mr. Clay.

CLAY: Of course, I haven't a trace of an American accent. I suppose that was the reason. And then my clothes.

[*He looks down at them with satisfaction.*

PEARL: Fleming wants to see life in London, Thornton. He can't do better than put himself under your wing.

CLAY: I know everyone who's worth knowing. I can't deny that.

PEARL: Thornton calls more countesses by their Christian names than any man in town.

CLAY: I'll get him cards for some good balls, and I'll see that he's asked to one or two of the right parties.

PEARL: He's good-looking, and I'm sure he dances well. He'll be a credit to you, Thornton.

CLAY: [*To* FLEMING.] But, of course, there's really nothing I *can* do for you. At Lady Grayston's you are in the very hub of society. I don't mean the stuffy, old-fashioned society, that goes about in barouches and bores itself stiff, but the society that counts, the society that figures in the newspapers. Pearl is the most wonderful hostess in London.

PEARL: What *do* you want, Thornton?

CLAY: In this house, sooner or later, you'll meet every remarkable man in England except one. That is George Grayston. And he's only remarkable because he's her husband.

PEARL: [*With a chuckle.*] I might have known you were only saying a pleasant thing in order to make the next one more disagreeable.

CLAY: Of course, I can't make out why you never ask George to your parties. Personally I like him.

PEARL: That's all the nicer of you, Thornton, since he always speaks of you as that damned snob.

CLAY: [*With a shrug of the shoulders.*] Poor George, he has such a limited vocabulary. I met Flora della Cercola at luncheon to-day. She told me she was coming to tea with you.

PEARL: She's getting up a concert in aid of something or other, and she wants me to help her.

CLAY: Poor Flora, with her good works! She takes philanthropy as a drug to allay the pangs of unrequited love.

PEARL: I always tell her she'd do much better to take a lover.

CLAY: You'll shock Mr. Harvey.

PEARL: It won't hurt him. It'll do him good.

CLAY: Did you ever know her husband?

PEARL: Oh yes, I met him. Just the ordinary little Dago. I cannot imagine why she should ever have been in love with him. She's an extraordinary creature. D'you know, I'm convinced that she's never had an affair.

CLAY: Some of these American women are strangely sexless.

FLEMING: I have an idea that some of them are even virtuous.

PEARL: [*With a smile.*] It takes all sorts to make a world.

> [POLE *enters to announce the* DUCHESSE DE SURENNES, *and then goes out.*

POLE: The Duchesse de Surennes.

> [*The* DUCHESSE *is a large, dark woman of forty-five with scarlet lips and painted cheeks, a woman of opulent form, bold, self-assured and outrageously sensual. She suggests a drawing of a Roman Emperor by Aubrey Beardsley. She is gowned with a certain dashing magnificence, and wears a long string of large pearls round her neck. During the conversation* POLE *and two footmen bring in tea, and place it in the back drawing-room.*

PEARL: My dear, how nice of you to come.

DUCHESSE: Isn't Tony here?

PEARL: No.

DUCHESSE: He said he was coming straight here.

PEARL: I daresay he's been delayed.

DUCHESSE: I can't understand it. He telephoned a quarter of an hour ago that he was starting at once.

PEARL: [*Reassuringly.*] He'll be here presently.

DUCHESSE: [*With an effort over herself.*] How pretty you're looking, Bessie. No wonder all the men I meet rave about you.

BESSIE: Englishmen are so shy. Why don't they rave *to* me?

DUCHESSE: They'll never let you go back to America.

PEARL: Of course, she's never going back. I'm determined that she shall marry an Englishman.

CLAY: She'll make a charming addition to our American peeresses.

PEARL: And there'll be another that you can call by her Christian name, Thornton.

BESSIE: I wish you wouldn't talk as if I hadn't a word to say in the matter.

CLAY: Of course, you've got a word to say, Bessie—a very important one.

BESSIE: Yes, I suppose?

CLAY: Exactly.

PEARL: Pour out the tea, darling, will you?

BESSIE: Surely. [*To* CLAY.] I know you don't share Fleming's contempt for tea, Mr. Clay.

CLAY: I couldn't live a day without it. Why, I never travel without a tea basket.

FLEMING: [*Ironically.*] Is that so?

CLAY: You Americans who live in America . . .

FLEMING: [*Under his breath.*] So queer of us.

CLAY: Despise the delectable habit of drinking tea because you are still partly barbarous. The hour that we spend over it is the most delightful of the day. We do not make a business of eating as at luncheon or dinner. We are at ease with ourselves. We toy with pretty cakes as an excuse for conversation. We discuss the abstract, our souls, our morals; we play delicately with the concrete, our neighbour's new bonnet or her latest lover. We drink tea because we are a highly civilised nation.

FLEMING: I must be very stupid, but I don't follow.

CLAY: My dear fellow, the degree of a nation's civilisation is marked by its disregard for the necessities of existence. You have gone so far as to waste money, but we have gone farther; we waste what is infinitely more precious, more transitory, more irreparable—we waste time.

DUCHESSE: My dear Thornton, you fill me with despair. Compton Edwardes has cut me off my tea. I thought he was only depriving me of a luxury, now I see he's depriving me also of a religious rite.

FLEMING: Who in heaven's name is Compton Edwardes, that he should have such influence?

PEARL: My dear Fleming, he's the most powerful man in London. He's the great reducer.

FLEMING: Gracious! What does he reduce?

PEARL: Fat.

DUCHESSE: He's a perfect marvel, that man. Do you know, the Duchess of Arlington told me he'd taken nine pounds off her.

PEARL: My dear, that's nothing. Why, Clara Hollington gave me her word of honour she'd lost over a stone.

BESSIE: [*From the tea-table.*] Anyone who wants tea must come and fetch it.

[*The men saunter over to the next room, while* PEARL *and the* DUCHESSE *go on with their conversation.*

DUCHESSE: Who is that nice-looking young man, Pearl?

PEARL: Oh, he's a young American. He pretends to be a
cousin of mine. He's come to see Bessie.

DUCHESSE: Does he want to marry her?

PEARL: Good heavens, I hope not. He's only an old friend.
You know the funny ways they have in America.

DUCHESSE: I suppose nothing is really settled about Harty
Bleane?

PEARL: No. But I shouldn't be surprised if you saw an
announcement in the Morning Post one day.

DUCHESSE: Has she enough money for him?

PEARL: She has a million.

DUCHESSE: Not pounds?

PEARL: Oh no, dollars.

DUCHESSE: That's only eight thousand a year. I shouldn't
have thought he'd be satisfied with that.

PEARL: People can't expect so much nowadays. There
won't be any more enormous heiresses as there were in
your time. Besides, Harry Bleane isn't such a catch as all
that. Of course, it's better to be an English baron than an
Italian count, but that's about all you can say for it.

DUCHESSE: Of course she'll accept him?

PEARL: Oh yes, she's crazy to live in England. And as I tell
her, it's quite pleasant to be a peeress even now.

DUCHESSE: What on earth can have happened to Tony?

PEARL: My dear, he's not likely to have been run over by a
motor-bus.

DUCHESSE: I'm not afraid of motor-buses running over him;
I'm afraid of him running after Gaiety girls.

PEARL: [Drily.] I should have thought you kept a very sharp
eye on him.

DUCHESSE: You see, he hasn't got anything to do from
morning till night.

PEARL: Why doesn't he get a job?

DUCHESSE: I've been trying to get him something, but it's so difficult. You've got such a lot of influence, Pearl. Can't you do something? I should be so grateful.

PEARL: What can he do?

DUCHESSE: Anything. And as you know he's very good-looking.

PEARL: Does he know French and German?

DUCHESSE: No, he has no gift for languages.

PEARL: Can he type and write shorthand?

DUCHESSE: Oh, no. Poor dear, you can hardly expect that.

PEARL: Can he do accounts?

DUCHESSE: No, he has no head for figures.

PEARL: [*Reflectively.*] Well, the only thing I can see that he'd do for is a government office.

DUCHESSE: Oh, my dear, if you only could manage that. You can't think what a comfort it would be for me to know that he couldn't get into mischief at least from ten to four every day.

> [POLE *announces* TONY PAXTON. TONY *is a handsome youth of twenty-five, in beautiful clothes, with engaging manners and a charming smile.*

POLE: Mr. Paxton.

PEARL: Well, Tony, how is life?

TONY: Rotten. I haven't backed a winner or won a rubber this week.

PEARL: Ah well, that's the advantage of not having money, you can afford to lose it.

DUCHESSE: [*Bursting in.*] Where have you been, Tony?

TONY: I? Nowhere.

DUCHESSE: You said you were coming straight here. It doesn't take twenty-five minutes to get here from Dover Street.

TONY: I thought there wasn't any hurry. I was just hanging about the club.

DUCHESSE: I rang up the club again, and they said you'd gone.

TONY: [*After a very slight pause.*] I was downstairs having a shave, and I suppose they never thought of looking for me in the barber's shop.

DUCHESSE: What on earth did you want to be shaved for at half-past four in the afternoon?

TONY: I thought you'd like me to look nice and clean.

PEARL: Go and get Bessie to give you some tea, Tony; I'm sure you want it after the strenuous day you've had.

[*He nods and walks into the inner room.*

PEARL: Minnie, how can you be so silly? You can't expect to keep a man if you treat him like that.

DUCHESSE: I know he's lying to me, there's not a word of truth in anything he says: but he's so slim I can never catch him out. Oh, I'm so jealous.

PEARL: Are you really in love with him?

DUCHESSE: He's everything in the world to me.

PEARL: You shouldn't let yourself be carried away like this.

DUCHESSE: I'm not cold-blooded like you.

PEARL: You seem to have a passion for rotters, and they always treat you badly.

DUCHESSE: Oh, I don't care about the others. Tony is the only one I've ever really loved.

PEARL: Nonsense! You were just as much in love with Jack Harris. You did everything in the world for him. You taught him to wear his clothes. You got him into society. And the moment he could do without you he chucked you. Tony will do just the same.

DUCHESSE: I'm not going to be such a fool this time. I'm going to take care he can't do without me.

PEARL: I can't imagine what you see in him. You must know that . . .

DUCHESSE: [*Interrupting.*] There's very little I don't know. He's a liar, a gambler, an idler, a spendthrift, but in his way he is fond of me. [*Appealingly.*] You can see he's fond of me, can't you?

PEARL: He's so much younger than you, Minnie.

DUCHESSE: I can't help it. I love him.

PEARL: Oh, well, I suppose it's no good talking. As long as he makes you happy.

DUCHESSE: He doesn't. He makes me miserable. But I love him. . . . He wants me to marry him, Pearl.

PEARL: You're not going to?

DUCHESSE: No, I won't be such a fool as that. If I married him I'd have no hold over him at all.

> [*Enter* POLE *to announce the* PRINCESS DELLA CERCOLA. *She is a tall, thin woman of thirty-five, with a pale, haggard face and great dark eyes. She is a gentle, kind creature, but there is something pathetic, almost tragic, in her appearance. She is dressed, though very well, and obviously by a Paris dressmaker, more quietly than the* DUCHESSE *or* PEARL. *She has not only wealth, but distinction.*

POLE: Princess della Cercola.

> [*Exit.* PEARL *gets up to receive her. They kiss.*

PEARL: Darling!

PRINCESS: D'you hate me for coming to bother you? I ran up because I know how difficult you are to catch. [*Kissing the* DUCHESSE.] How are you, Minnie?

DUCHESSE: Don't ask me for a subscription, Flora. I'm so poor.

PRINCESS: [*Smiling.*] Wait till I tell you what it's for, and then you'll remember that you had a father called Spencer Hodgson.

DUCHESSE: [*With a little groan.*] As if I wanted to be reminded of it!

PEARL: You're so absurd, Minnie. You should make a joke of the pork. I always tell people about father's hardware store, and when I haven't got a funny story to tell about it, I invent one.

PRINCESS: You've made your father quite a character in London.

PEARL: That's why I never let him come over. He couldn't possibly live up to his reputation.

[FLEMING HARVEY *comes forward from the inner room.*

FLEMING: I'm going to say good-bye to you.

PEARL: You mustn't go before I've introduced you to Flora. Flora, this is Mr. Fleming Harvey. He's just come from America. He probably carries a six-shooter in his hip-pocket.

FLEMING: I'm told I mayn't say I'm pleased to make your acquaintance, Princess.

PRINCESS: When did you land?

FLEMING: This morning.

PRINCESS: I envy you.

FLEMING: Because I landed this morning?

PRINCESS: No, because a week ago you were in America.

DUCHESSE: Flora!

FLEMING: I was beginning to think it was something to be rather ashamed of.

PRINCESS: Oh, you mustn't pay any attention to Pearl and the Duchesse. They're so much more English than the English.

PEARL: I notice you show your devotion to the country of your birth by staying away from it, Flora.

PRINCESS: Last time I was in America it made me so unhappy that I vowed I'd never go there again.

DUCHESSE: I was there ten years ago, when I was divorcing Gaston. I hadn't been in America since my marriage, and I'd forgotten what it was like. Oh, it was so crude. Oh, it was so provincial. You don't mind my saying so, Mr. Harvey?

FLEMING: Not at all. You're just as American as I am, and there's no reason why among ourselves we shouldn't abuse the mother that bore us.

DUCHESSE: Oh, but I don't look upon myself as American. I'm French. After all, I haven't a trace of an American accent. To show you how it got on my nerves, I almost didn't divorce Gaston because I thought I couldn't bring myself to stay in America long enough.

PRINCESS: It's not because it was crude and provincial that I was unhappy in America. I was unhappy because after all it was home, the only real home I've ever had, and I was a stranger.

PEARL: My dear Flora, you're being very sentimental.

PRINCESS: [*Smiling.*] I'm sorry; I apologise. You're a New Yorker, Mr. Harvey?

FLEMING: I'm proud of it, madam.

PRINCESS: New York's wonderful, isn't it? It has something that no other city in the world has got. I like to think of Fifth Avenue on a spring day. The pretty girls in their smart frocks and neat shoes, who trip along so gaily, and all the good-looking boys.

DUCHESSE: I grant you that; some of the boys are too lovely for words.

PRINCESS: Everyone is so strong and confident. There's such an exaltation in the air. You feel in the passers-by a serene and unshakable belief in the future. Oh, it's very good to be alive in Fifth Avenue on a sunny day in April.

FLEMING: It's good for an American to hear another American say such pleasant things about his country.

PRINCESS: You must come and see me, and you shall tell me all the news of home.

PEARL: How high the newest building is, and how much money the latest millionaire has got.

FLEMING: Good-bye.

PEARL: Have you made friends with Thornton Clay?

FLEMING: I hope so.

PEARL: You must get him to give you the address of his tailor.

FLEMING: Aren't you pleased with my clothes?

PEARL: They're very American, you know.

FLEMING: So am I.

[THORNTON CLAY *comes forward. The* DUCHESSE *strolls over to the inner room and is seen talking with* BESSIE *and* TONY PAXTON.

PEARL: Thornton, I was just telling Mr. Harvey that you'd take him to your tailor.

CLAY: I was going to suggest it.

FLEMING: My clothes are not at all a success.

PEARL: Who d'you go to? Stultz?

CLAY: Of course. He's the only tailor in London. [*To* FLEMING.] Of course he's a German, but art has no nationality.

FLEMING: I'm pleased at all events to think that it's a German tailor who's going to make me look like an Englishman.

[*He goes out.* THORNTON *makes his farewells.*

CLAY: Good-bye, Pearl.

PEARL: Are you going? Don't forget you're coming down to Kenton on Saturday.

CLAY: I won't, indeed. I adore your week-end parties, Pearl. I'm so exhausted by Monday morning that I'm fit for nothing for the rest of the week. Good-bye.

[He shakes hands and goes out. As he is going, POLE opens the door to announce LORD BLEANE. He is a young man, very English in appearance, pleasant, clean and well-groomed.

POLE: Lord Bleane.   [*Exit.*

PEARL: Dear Harry, how nice of you to come.

BLEANE: I'm in absolute despair.

PEARL: Good heavens, why?

BLEANE: They're sending a mission to Rumania to hand the Garter to some bigwig and I've got to go with it.

PEARL: Oh, but that'll be very interesting.

BLEANE: Yes, but we start to-morrow, and I shan't be able to come down to Kenton on Saturday.

PEARL: When do you come back?

BLEANE: In four weeks.

PEARL: Then come down to Kenton the Saturday after that.

BLEANE: May I?

PEARL: You must go and break the news to Bessie. She was so looking forward to your visit.

BLEANE: D'you think she'll give me some tea?

PEARL: I have no doubt, if you ask her nicely.

                               [*He goes over to the inner room.*

PRINCESS: Now I've got you to myself for two minutes. You will help me with my concert, won't you?

PEARL: Of course. What do you want me to do? I'll make Arthur Fenwick take any number of tickets. You know how charitable he is.

PRINCESS: It's for a very good cause.

PEARL: I'm sure it is. But don't harrow me with revolting stories of starving children. I'm not interested in the poor.

PRINCESS: [*Smiling.*] How can you say that?

PEARL: Are you? I often wonder if your philanthropy isn't an elaborate pose. You don't mind my saying that, do you?

PRINCESS: [*Good-humouredly.*] Not at all. You have no heart, and you can't imagine that anyone else should have.

PEARL: I have plenty of heart, but it beats for people of my own class.

PRINCESS: I've only found one thing really worth doing with all this money I have, and that is to help a little those who need help.

PEARL: [*With a shrug.*] So long as it makes you happy.

PRINCESS: It doesn't, but it prevents me from being utterly miserable.

PEARL: You make me so impatient, Flora. You've got more money than you know what to do with. You're a princess. You've practically got rid of your husband. I cannot imagine what more you want. I wish I could get rid of mine.

PRINCESS: [*Smiling.*] I don't know what you've got to complain of in George.

PEARL: That's just it. I shouldn't mind if he beat me or made love to chorus girls. I could divorce him then. Oh, my dear, thank your stars that you had a husband who was grossly unfaithful to you. Mine wants me to live nine months of the year in the country and have a baby every five minutes. I didn't marry an Englishman for that.

PRINCESS: Why *did* you marry him?

PEARL: I made a mistake. I'd lived all my life in New York. I was very ignorant. I thought if you were a baronet you must be in society.

PRINCESS: I often wonder if you're happy, Pearl.

PEARL: Do you? Of course I'm happy.

PRINCESS: An ambassador told me the other day that you were the most powerful woman in London. It's very wonderful how you've made your way. You had nothing very much to help you.

PEARL: Shall I tell you how it was done? By force of character, wit, unscrupulousness and push.

PRINCESS: [*Smiling.*] You're very frank.

PEARL: That has always been my pose.

PRINCESS: I sometimes think there's positive genius in the way you've ignored the snubs of the great.

PEARL: [*With a chuckle.*] You're being very unpleasant, Flora.

PRINCESS: And there's something very like heroism in the callousness with which you've dropped people when they've served your turn.

PEARL: You're driving me to the conclusion that you don't altogether approve of me.

PRINCESS: On the other hand I can't help admiring you. You've brought all the determination, insight, vigour, strength, which have made our countrymen turn America into what it is, to get what you wanted. In a way your life has been a work of art. And what makes it more complete is that what you've aimed at is trivial, transitory and worthless.

PEARL: My dear Flora, people don't hunt in order to catch a fox.

PRINCESS: Sometimes, doesn't it make you rather nervous, when you're sitting on the top of your ladder, in case anyone should give it a kick as he passes?

PEARL: It'll want more than a kick to topple my ladder over. D'you remember when that silly woman made such a fuss because her husband was in love with me? It wasn't till I only just escaped the divorce court that the duchesses really took me up.

[*The* DUCHESSE *comes forward with* TONY PAXTON.

DUCHESSE: We really must be going, Pearl. I expect my masseur at six. Compton Edwardes told me about him. He's wonderful, but he's so run after, if you keep him waiting a moment he goes away.

PEARL: My dear, do be careful. Fanny Hallam got herself down to a mere nothing, but it made her look a hundred.

DUCHESSE: Oh, I know, but Compton Edwardes has recommended to me a wonderful woman who comes every morning to do my face.

PEARL: You are coming to my ball, aren't you?

DUCHESSE: Of course we're coming. Yours are almost the only parties in London where one amuses oneself as much as at a night club.

PEARL: I'm having Ernest to come in and dance.

DUCHESSE: I thought of having him one evening. How much does he charge for coming in socially?

PEARL: Twenty guineas.

DUCHESSE: Good heavens, I could never afford that.

PEARL: What nonsense! You're far richer than I am.

DUCHESSE: I'm not so clever, darling. I can't think how you do so much on your income.

PEARL: [*Amused.*] I'm a very good manager.

DUCHESSE: One would never think it. Good-bye, dear. Are you coming, Tony?

TONY: Yes.   [*She goes out.*

TONY: [*Shaking hands with* PEARL.] I've not had a word with you to-day.

PEARL: [*Chaffing him.*] What are we to do about it?

PRINCESS: I *must* get Minnie to go to my concert. Minnie.
                    [*She goes out.* TONY *is left face to face with* PEARL.

TONY: You're looking perfectly divine to-day. I don't know what there is about you.

PEARL: [*Amused, but not disconcerted.*] It is nice of you to say so.

TONY: I simply haven't been able to take my eyes off you.

PEARL: Are you making love to me?

TONY: That's nothing new, is it?

PEARL: You'll get into trouble.

TONY: Don't be disagreeable, Pearl.

PEARL: I don't remember that I ever told you you might call me Pearl.

TONY: It's how I think of you. You can't prevent me from doing that.

PEARL: Well, I think it's very familiar.

TONY: I don't know what you've done to me. I think of you all day long.

PEARL: I don't believe it for a minute. You're an unprincipled ruffian, Tony.

TONY: Do you mind?

PEARL: [*With a chuckle.*] Shameless creature. I wonder what it is that Minnie sees in you.

TONY: I have all sorts of merits.

PEARL: I'm glad you think so. I can only discover one.

TONY: What is that?

PEARL: You're somebody else's property.

TONY: Oh!

PEARL: [*Holding out her hand.*] Good-bye.

[*He kisses her wrist. His lips linger. She looks at him from under her eyelashes.*

PEARL: It doesn't make you irresistible, you know.

TONY: There's always the future.

PEARL: The future's everybody's property.

TONY: [*In an undertone.*] Pearl.

PEARL: Be quick and go. Minnie will be wondering why you don't come.

> [*He goes out.* PEARL *turns away with a smile.* BESSIE *and* LORD BLEANE *advance into the room.*

PEARL: Has Harry broken the news to you that he can't come down to us on Saturday?

> [*The* PRINCESS *comes in.*

PRINCESS: I've got my subscription.

PEARL: I kept Tony up here as long as I could so as to give you a chance.

PRINCESS: [*With a laugh.*] That was really tactful.

PEARL: Poor Minnie, she's as mean as cat's meat. [*With a glance at* BESSIE *and* LORD BLEANE.] If you'd like to come down to the morning-room we can go through my visitors' book and see who'll be useful to you.

PRINCESS: Oh, that would be kind of you.

PEARL: [*To* BLEANE.] Don't go till I come back, will you? I haven't had a word with you yet.

BLEANE: All right.

> [PEARL *and the* PRINCESS *go out.*

BESSIE: I wonder if you sent me these flowers, Lord Bleane?

BLEANE: I did. I thought you wouldn't mind.

BESSIE: It was very kind of you.

> [*She takes two of the roses and puts them in her dress.* BLEANE *is overcome with shyness. He does not know how to begin.*

BLEANE: D'you mind if I light a cigarette?

BESSIE: Not at all.

BLEANE: [*As he lights it.*] D'you know, this is the first time I've ever been alone with you. It was very tactful of Lady Grayston to leave us.

BESSIE: I'm not sure if it wasn't a trifle too tactful.

BLEANE: I was hoping most awfully to have the chance of getting a talk with you.

> [*The song of the lavender is heard again in the street.* BESSIE *welcomes the diversion.*

BESSIE: Oh, listen, there's the lavender man come back again. [*She goes to the window and listens.*] Throw him down a shilling, will you?

BLEANE: All right. [*He takes a coin from his pocket and throws it into the street.*

BESSIE: I seem to feel all the charm of England in that funny little tune. It suggests cottage gardens, and hedges, and winding roads.

BLEANE: My mother grows lavender at home. When we were kids we were made to pick it, and my mother used to put it in little muslin bags and tie them up with pink ribbon. And she used to put them under the pillows of one's bed and in all the drawers. Shall I ask her to send you some?

BESSIE: Oh, that would be such a bother for her.

BLEANE: It wouldn't. She'd like to. And you know, it's not like the lavender you buy. It knocks spots off anything you can get in shops.

BESSIE: You must hate leaving London at this time of year.

BLEANE: Oh, I'm not very keen on London. [*Making a dash for it.*] I hate leaving you.

BESSIE: [*With comic desperation.*] Let's not talk about me, Lord Bleane.

BLEANE: But that's the only topic that occurs to me.

BESSIE: There's always the weather in England.

BLEANE: You see, I'm off to-morrow.

BESSIE: I never saw anyone so obstinate.

BLEANE: I shan't see you again for nearly a month. We haven't known one another very long, and if I hadn't been going away I expect I'd have thought it better to wait a bit.

BESSIE: [*Clasping her hands.*] Lord Bleane, don't propose to me.

BLEANE: Why not?

BESSIE: Because I shall refuse you.

BLEANE: Oh!

BESSIE: Tell me about the part of the country you live in. I don't know Kent at all. Is it pretty?

BLEANE: I don't know. It's home.

BESSIE: I love those old Elizabethan houses that you have in England with all their chimneys.

BLEANE: Oh, ours isn't a show place, you know. It's just a rather ugly yellow brick house that looks like a box, and it's got a great big stucco portico in front of it. I think the garden's rather jolly.

BESSIE: Pearl hates Abbots Kenton. She'd sell it if George would. She's only really happy in London.

BLEANE: I don't know that I was so particularly struck on Bleane till I was over in France. When I was in hospital at Boulogne there didn't seem much to do but to think about things. . . . It didn't seem as if I *could* get well. I knew I should if they'd only let me come home, but they wouldn't; they said I couldn't be moved. . . . It's rather bleak in our part of the country. We've got an east wind that people find a bit trying, but if you've been used to it all your life it bucks you up wonderful. In summer it can be awfully hot down there, but there's always something fresh and salt in the air. You see, we're so near the marshes. . . . It was only just across the water, and it seemed such an awful long way off I ain't boring you, am I?

BESSIE: No. I want you to tell me.

BLEANE: It's a funny sort of country. There are a lot of green fields and elm trees, and the roads wind about— it's rotten for motoring; and then you have the marshes, with dykes in them—we used to jump them when we were boys, and fall in mostly; and then there's the sea. It doesn't sound much, but I felt it was the most ripping thing I knew. And then there are hop-fields—I forgot them—and the oast-houses. They're rather picturesque, I suppose. I expect it's like the lavender to you. To me it's just England.

> [BESSIE *gets up and walks towards the window. In the distance is heard the melancholy cry of the lavender man.*

BLEANE: What are you thinking about?

BESSIE: It must be very wonderful to feel like that about one's home. I've never known anything but a red stone house in Nineteenth Street. As soon as dad can get a decent offer for it we're going to move further up town. Mother has a fancy for Seventy-Second Street, I don't know why.

BLEANE: Of course, I know it couldn't mean the same to a girl that it means to me. I shouldn't expect anyone to live there always. I can be quite happy in London.

BESSIE: [*With a smile.*] You're determined to do it?

BLEANE: If you *could* bring yourself to marry me, I'd try and give you a good time.

BESSIE: Well, I suppose that's a proposal.

BLEANE: I've never made one before, and it makes me a bit nervous.

BESSIE: You haven't said anything that I can answer yes or no to.

BLEANE: I don't want to say anything that you *can* answer no to.

BESSIE: [*With a chuckle.*] Let me say that I'll think it over, may I?

BLEANE: I'm going away to-morrow.

BESSIE: I'll give you an answer when you come back.

BLEANE: But that won't be for four weeks.

BESSIE: It'll give us both a chance to make up our minds. After all, it *is* rather a serious step. You may come to the conclusion that you don't really want to marry me.

BLEANE: There's no fear of that.

BESSIE: You're coming down to Kenton for the week-end after you get back. If you change your mind send Pearl a wire putting yourself off. I shall understand, and I shan't be in the least hurt or offended.

BLEANE: Then it's good-bye till then.

BESSIE: Yes. And . . . thank you very much for wishing to marry me.

BLEANE: Thank you very much for not refusing me outright.
[*They shake hands and he goes out. She walks over to the window to look at him, glances at the watch on her wrist, and then leaves the room. In a moment* POLE *shows in* ARTHUR FENWICK. *He is a tall, elderly man with a red face and grey hair.*

POLE: I'll tell her ladyship you're here, sir.

FENWICK: That'll be very good of you.

POLE *goes out.* FENWICK *takes a cigar from his case, and the evening paper from a table, and settles himself down comfortably to read and smoke. He makes himself very much at home.* PEARL *comes in.*

PEARL: Aren't Bessie and Harry Bleane here?

FENWICK: No.

PEARL: That's very strange. I wonder what can have happened.

FENWICK: Never mind about Bessie and Harry Bleane. Give me your attention now.

PEARL: You're very late.

FENWICK: I like to come when I stand a chance of finding you alone, girlie.

PEARL: I wish you wouldn't call me girlie, Arthur. I do hate it.

FENWICK: That's how I think of you. When I'm present at one of your big set-outs, and watch you like a queen among all those lords and ambassadors and bigwigs, I just say to myself, She's my girlie, and I feel warm all over. I'm so proud of you then. You've got there, girlie, you've got there.

PEARL: [*Smiling.*] You've been very kind to me, Arthur.

FENWICK: You've got brains, girlie, that's how you've done it. It's brains. Underneath your flighty ways and that casual air of yours, so that one might think you were just enjoying yourself and nothing more, I see you thinking it all out, pulling a string here and a string there; you've got them in the hollow of your hand all the time. You leave nothing to chance, Pearl, you're a great woman.

PEARL: Not great enough to make you obey your doctor's orders.

FENWICK: [*Taking the cigar out of his mouth.*] You're not going to ask me to throw away the first cigar I've had to-day?

PEARL: To please me, Arthur. They're so bad for you.

FENWICK: If you put it like that I must give in.

PEARL: I don't want you to be ill.

FENWICK: You've got a great heart, girlie. The world just thinks you're a smart, fashionable woman, clever, brilliant, beautiful, a leader of fashion, but I know different. I know you've got a heart of gold.

PEARL: You're a romantic old thing, Arthur.

FENWICK: My love for you is the most precious thing I have in the world. You're my guiding star, you're my ideal.

You stand to me for all that's pure and noble and clean in womanhood. God bless you, girlie. I don't know what I should do if you failed me. I don't believe I could live if I ever found out that you weren't what I think you.

PEARL: [*With her tongue in her cheek.*] You shan't, if I can help it.

FENWICK: You do care for me a little, girlie?

PEARL: Of course I do.

FENWICK: I'm an old man, girlie.

PEARL: What nonsense! I look upon you as a mere boy.

FENWICK: [*Flattered.*] Well, I expect a good many young men would be glad to have my physique. I can work fourteen hours on end and feel as fresh as a daisy at the end of it.

PEARL: Your vitality is wonderful.

FENWICK: I sometimes wonder what it is that first drew you to me, girlie.

PEARL: I don't know. I suppose it was the impression of strength you give.

FENWICK: Yes, I've often been told that. It's very difficult for people to be with me long without realising that— well, that I'm not just the man in the street.

PEARL: I always feel I can rely on you.

FENWICK: You couldn't have said anything to please me better. I want you to rely on me. I know you. I'm the only man who's ever understood you. I know that, deep down in that big, beating, human heart of yours, you're a timid, helpless little thing, with the innocence of a child, and you want a man like me to stand between you and the world. My God, how I love you, girlie!

PEARL: Take care, there's the butler.

FENWICK: Oh, damn it, there's always the butler.

[POLE *comes in with a telegram and a parcel of books.*

PEARL: [*Taking the telegram and glancing at the parcel.*] What's that, Pole?

POLE: They're books, my lady. They've just come from Hatchard's.

PEARL: Oh, I know. Undo them, will you? [POLE *cuts open the parcel and takes out a bundle of four or five books.* PEARL *opens the telegram.*] Oh, bother! There's no answer, Pole.

POLE: Very good, my lady.

[*Exit.*

FENWICK: Is anything the matter?

PEARL: That fool Sturrey was dining here to-night, and he's just wired to say he can't come. I do hate having my parties upset. I'd asked ten people to meet him.

FENWICK: That's too bad.

PEARL: Pompous owl. He's refused invitation after invitation. I asked him six weeks ago this time, and he hadn't the face to say he was engaged.

FENWICK: Well, I'm afraid you must give him up. I daresay you can do without him.

PEARL: Don't be a fool, Arthur. I'll get hold of him somehow. He may be Prime Minister one of these days. [*She reflects a moment.*] I wonder what his telephone number is. [*She gets up and looks in a book, then sits down at the telephone.*] Gerrard 7035. If he comes once because I force him to he'll come again because he likes it. This house is like the kingdom of heaven: I have to compel them to come in. . . . Is Lord Sturrey in? Lady Grayston. I'll hold the line. [*Making her voice sweet and charming.*] Is that you, Lord Sturrey? It's Pearl Grayston speaking. I just rang up to say it doesn't matter a bit about to-night. Of course, I'm disappointed you can't come. But you must come another day, will you? That's very nice of you. How about this day week?

Oh, I'm sorry. Would Thursday suit you? Oh! Well, how about Friday? You're engaged every evening next week? You are in demand. Well, I'll tell you what, get your book and tell me what day you are free.

FENWICK: You're the goods, girlie. You'll get there.

PEARL: Tuesday fortnight. Yes, that'll suit me beautifully. 8.30. I'm so glad you chose that day, because I'm having Kreisler in to play. I shall look forward to seeing you. Good-bye. [*She puts down the receiver.*] This time I've got him. The ape thinks he understands music.

FENWICK: Have you got Kreisler for Tuesday fortnight?

PEARL: No.

FENWICK: Are you sure you can get him?

PEARL: No, but I'm sure you can.

FENWICK: You shall have him, girlie. [*She takes the books that* POLE *brought in and puts them about the room. One she places face downwards, open.*] What are you doing that for?

PEARL: They're Richard Twining's books. He's coming to dinner to-night.

FENWICK: Why d'you trouble about authors, girlie?

PEARL: London isn't like New York, you know. People like to meet them over here.

FENWICK: I should have thought your position was quite strong enough to do without them.

PEARL: We live in a democratic age. They take the place in society of the fools whom kings kept about their courts in the middle ages. They have the advantage that they don't presume on their position to tell one home truths. They're cheap. A dinner and a little flattery is all they want. And they provide their own clothes.

FENWICK: You litter up your house with their rotten books

PEARL: Oh, but I don't keep them. These are on approval. I shall send them all back to the bookseller to-morrow morning.

FENWICK: Pearl, you're a little wonder. When you want to go into business you come to me and I'll take you into partnership.

PEARL: How is business?

FENWICK: Fine! I'm opening two new branches next week. They laughed at me when I first came over here. They said I'd go bankrupt. I've turned their silly old methods upside down. He laughs longest who laughs last.

PEARL: [*Reflectively.*] Ah, I can't help thinking that's what my dressmaker said when she sent me in my bill.

[*He gives a slight start and looks at her shrewdly. He sees her blandly smiling.*]

FENWICK: Girlie, you promised me you wouldn't run up any more bills.

PEARL: That's like promising to love, honour, and obey one's husband, the kind of undertaking no one is really expected to carry out.

FENWICK: You naughty little thing.

PEARL: It's Suzanne—you know, the dressmaker in the Place Vendôme. The war has dislocated her business and she wants to get her money in. It isn't very convenient for me to pay just at present. It's rather a large sum. [*She gives him a sheaf of typewritten documents.*]

FENWICK: This looks more like a five-act play than a bill.

PEARL: Clothes are expensive, aren't they? I wish I could dress in fig-leaves. It would be cheap, and I believe it would suit me.

FENWICK: [*Putting the bill in his pocket.*] Well, I'll see what I can do about it.

PEARL: You are a duck, Arthur. . . . Would you like me to come and lunch with you to-morrow?

FENWICK: Why, sure.

PEARL: All right. Now you must go, as I want to lie down before I dress for dinner.

FENWICK: That's right. Take care of yourself, girlie, you're very precious to me.

PEARL: Good-bye, dear old thing.

FENWICK: Good-bye, girlie.

[*He goes out. As he goes to the door the telephone rings.* PEARL *takes up the receiver.*

PEARL: You're speaking to Lady Grayston. Tony! Of course I knew your voice. Well, what is it? I'm not at all stern. I'm making my voice as pleasant as I can. I'm sorry you find it disagreeable. [*She gives a chuckle.*] No, I'm afraid I couldn't come to tea to-morrow. I shall be engaged all the afternoon. What is the day after to-morrow? [*Smiling.*] Well, I must ask Bessie. I don't know if she's free. Of course I'm not coming alone. It would be most compromising. A nice-looking young man like you. What would Minnie say? Oh, I know all about that. . . . I didn't promise anything. I merely said the future was everybody's property. A sleepless night. Fancy! Well, good-bye. . . . Tony, do you know the most enchanting word in the English language? Perhaps.

[*She puts down the telephone quickly, and the curtain falls.*

END OF THE FIRST ACT

THE SECOND ACT

The Scene is a morning-room at Abbots Kenton, the Graystons place in the country. It has an old-fashioned, comfortable look; nothing is very new; the chintzes are faded. Three long french windows lead on to a terrace.

It is after dinner, a fine night, and the windows are open.

The women of the party are sitting down, waiting for the men; they are PEARL *and* BESSIE, *the* DUCHESSE DE SURENNES *and the* PRINCESS DELLA CERCOLA.

PRINCESS: You must be exhausted after all the tennis you played this afternoon, Minnie.

DUCHESSE: Not a bit. I only played four sets.

PRINCESS: You played so vigorously. It made me quite hot to look at you.

DUCHESSE: If I didn't take exercise I should be enormous. Oh, Flora, how I envy you! You can eat anything you choose and it has no effect on you. And what makes it so unfair is that you don't care about food. I am a lazy and a greedy woman. I never eat any of the things I like, and I never miss a day without taking at least an hour's exercise.

PRINCESS: [*Smiling.*] If mortification is the first step in sanctity, I'm sure you must be on the high road to it.

PEARL: One of these days you'll give up the struggle, Minnie, and, like Flora, take to good works.

DUCHESSE: [*With immense decision.*] Never! I shall lie on my death-bed with my hair waved and a little rouge on my cheeks, and with my last breath murmur: Not gruel, it's so fattening.

PEARL: Well, you'll have more serious tennis to-morrow. Harry Bleane plays much better than Thornton.

DUCHESSE: It was very tiresome of him not to come till it was just time to dress.

PEARL: He only got back from Rumania yesterday, and he had to go down to see his mother. [*With an amused glance at her sister.*] Bessie asked me not to put him next her at dinner.

BESSIE: Pearl, you are a cat! I do think it's hateful the way you discuss my private affairs with all and sundry.

DUCHESSE: My dear Bessie, they've long ceased to be your private affairs.

PEARL: I'm afraid Bessie misses her opportunities. Just before he went to Rumania I left them alone together, and nothing happened. All my tact was wasted.

BESSIE: Your tact was too obvious, Pearl.

DUCHESSE: Well, do be quick and bring him to the scratch, my dear. I'm growing tired of people asking me, Is he going to propose or is he not?

BESSIE: Don't they ever ask, Is she going to accept him or is she not?

DUCHESSE: Of course, you'll accept him.

BESSIE: I'm not so sure.

PRINCESS: [*Smiling.*] Perhaps it depends on the way he asks.

PEARL: For heaven's sake, don't expect too much romance. Englishmen aren't romantic. It makes them feel absurd. George proposed to me when he was in New York for the Horse Show. I wasn't very well that day, and I was lying down. I was looking a perfect fright. He told me all about a mare he had, and he told me all about her father and her mother and her uncles and her aunts, and then he said: [*Imitating him.*] Look here, you'd better marry me.

PRINCESS: How very sudden.

PEARL: Oh, I said, why didn't you tell me you were going to propose? I'd have had my hair waved. Poor George, he asked *Why?*

DUCHESSE: The French are the only nation who know how to make love. When Gaston proposed to me he went down on his knees, and he took my hand, and he said he couldn't live without me. Of course I knew that, because he hadn't a cent, but still it thrilled me. He said I was his guiding star and his guardian angel—oh, I don't know what! It was beautiful! I knew he'd been haggling with papa for a fortnight about having his debts paid; but it was beautiful.

PRINCESS: Were you quite indifferent to him?

DUCHESSE: Oh, quite. I'd made up my mind to marry a foreigner. People weren't very nice to us in Chicago. My cousin Mary had married the Count de Moret, and mother couldn't bear Aunt Alice. She said, If Alice has got hold of a Count for Mary, I'm determined that you shall have a Duke.

PEARL: And you did.

DUCHESSE: I wish you could have seen the fuss those Chicago people made of me when I went over last. It was hard to realise that I used to cry my eyes out because I wasn't asked to the balls I wanted to go to.

PRINCESS: Still, I hope Bessie won't marry any man she doesn't care for.

PEARL: My dear, don't put ideas in the child's head. The French are a much more civilised nation than we are, and they've come to the conclusion long ago that marriage is an affair of convenience rather than of sentiment. Think of the people you know who've married for love. After five years do they care for one another any more than the people who've married for money?

PRINCESS: They have the recollection.

PEARL: Nonsense! As if anyone remembered an emotion when he no longer felt it!

DUCHESSE: It's true. I've been in love a dozen times, desperately, and when I've got over it and look back, though I remember I was in love, I can't for the life of me remember my love. It always seems to me so odd.

PEARL: Believe me, Bessie, the flourishing state of father's hardware store is a much sounder basis for matrimonial happiness than any amount of passion.

BESSIE: Oh, Pearl, what is this you've been telling people about dad selling bananas?

PEARL: Bananas? Oh, I remember. They were saying that Mrs. Hanley used to wash the miners' clothes in California. That and her pearls are taking her everywhere. I wasn't going to be outdone, so I said father used to sell bananas in the streets of New York.

BESSIE: He never did anything of the kind.

PEARL: I know he didn't, but I thought people were getting rather tired of the hardware store, and I made a perfectly killing story out of it. I had a new Callot frock on and I thought I could manage the bananas.

DUCHESSE: A most unpleasant vegetable. So fattening.

> [*The men come in.* THORNTON CLAY, ARTHUR FEN-
> WICK, *and* FLEMING. PEARL *and* BESSIE *get up.*

BESSIE: You've been a long time.

DUCHESSE: Where is Tony?

CLAY: He and Bleane are finishing their cigars.

DUCHESSE: Well, Mr. Harvey, are you still enjoying life in London?

CLAY: He should be. I've got him invitations to all the nicest parties. But he will waste his time in sight-seeing. The other day—Thursday, wasn't it?—I wanted to take him to Hurlingham, and he insisted on going to the National Gallery instead.

C

PEARL: [*Smiling.*] What an outrageous proceeding!

FLEMING: I don't see that it was any more outrageous for me than for you. I saw you coming in just as I was going out.

PEARL: I had a reason to go. Arthur Fenwick has just bought a Bronzino, and I wanted to see those in the National Gallery.

DUCHESSE: I think it's much more likely that you had an assignation. I've always heard it's a wonderful place for that. You never meet any of your friends, and if you do they're there for the same purpose, and pretend not to see you.

FLEMING: I certainly only went to see the pictures.

CLAY: But, good heavens, if you want to do that there's Christie's, and there you *will* meet your friends.

FLEMING: I'm afraid you'll never make a man of fashion out of me, Thornton.

CLAY: I'm beginning to despair. You have a natural instinct for doing the wrong thing. D'you know, the other day I caught him in the act of delivering half a bagful of letters of introduction? I implored him to put them in the waste-paper basket.

FLEMING: I thought as people had taken the trouble to give them to me, it was only polite to make use of them.

CLAY: Americans give letters so carelessly. Before you know where you are you'll know all the wrong people. And, believe me, the wrong people are very difficult to shake off.

FLEMING: [*Amused.*] Perhaps some of my letters are to the right people.

CLAY: Then they'll take no notice of them.

FLEMING: It looks as though the wrong people had better manners than the right ones.

CLAY: The right people *are* rude. They can afford to be.

I was a very young man when I first came to London, and I made mistakes. All of us Americans make mistakes. It wanted a good deal of character to cut people who'd taken me about, asked me to dine, stay with them in the country, and heaven knows what, when I found they weren't the sort of people one ought to know.

PEARL: Of course, one has to do it.

DUCHESSE: Of course. It shows that you have a nice nature, Thornton, to worry yourself about it.

CLAY: I'm curiously sentimental. Another of our American faults. I remember when I'd been in London two or three years, I knew pretty well everyone that was worth knowing, but I'd never been asked to Hereford House. The duchess doesn't like Americans anyway, and she'd been very disagreeable about me in particular. But I was determined to go to her ball. I felt it wasn't the sort of function I could afford to be left out of.

PEARL: They're very dull balls.

CLAY: I know, but they're almost the only ones you can't go to without an invitation. Well, I found out that the duchess had a widowed sister who lived in the country with her two daughters. Lady Helen Blair. My dear, she was a very stuffy, dowdy woman of fifty-five, and her two daughters were stuffier and dowdier still, and if possible, older. They were in the habit of coming up to London for the season. I got introduced to them, and I laid myself out. I took them to the play, I showed them round the Academy, I stood them luncheons, I gave them cards for private views, for a month I worked like a Trojan. Then the duchess sent out her invitations, and the Blair girls had half a dozen cards for their young men. I received one, and, by George, I'd earned it. Of course, as soon as I got my invitation I dropped them, but you know I felt quite badly about it.

DUCHESSE: I expect they're used to that.

CLAY: A strangely tactless woman, Lady Helen Blair. She wrote and asked me if I was offended about anything because I never went near them.

PEARL: I wish those men would come, and then we could dance.

DUCHESSE: Oh, that'll be charming! It's such good exercise, isn't it? I'm told that you dance divinely, Mr. Harvey.

FLEMING: I don't know about that. I dance.

DUCHESSE: [*To the* PRINCESS.] Oh, my dear, who d'you think I danced with the other night? [*Impressively.*] Ernest.

PRINCESS: Oh!

DUCHESSE: My dear, don't say, Oh! like that. Don't you know who Ernest is?

PEARL: Ernest is the most sought after man in London.

PRINCESS: You don't mean the dancing-master?

DUCHESSE: Oh, my dear, you mustn't call him that. He'd be furious. He isn't a professional. He gives lessons at ten guineas an hour, but only to oblige. He's invited to all the best dances.

FLEMING: One of the things that rather surprised me at balls was to see all these dancing-masters. Do English girls like to be pawed about by Greeks, Dagos and Bowery toughs?

CLAY: You Americans who live in America, you're so prudish.

DUCHESSE: Believe me, I would go to *any* dance where there was the remotest chance of meeting Ernest. It's a perfect dream to dance with him. He showed me a new step, and I can't get it quite right. I don't know what I shall do if I don't run across him again very soon.

PRINCESS: But why don't you let him give you a lesson?

DUCHESSE: My dear, ten guineas an hour! I couldn't possibly afford that. I'm sure to meet him at a dance in a day or two, and I shall get a lesson for nothing.

PEARL: You ought to make him fall in love with you.

DUCHESSE: Oh, my dear, if he only would! But he's so run after.

[BLEANE *and* TONY PAXTON *come in from the terrace.*

DUCHESSE: At last!

TONY: We've been taking a stroll in the garden.

PEARL: I hope you showed him my tea-house.

BESSIE: It's Pearl's new toy. You must be sure to admire it.

PEARL: I'm very proud of it. You know, George won't let me do anything here. He says it's his house, and he isn't going to have any of my muck. He won't even have new chintzes. Well, there was an old summer-house just over there, and it was all worm-eaten and horrid and tumble-down, what they call picturesque, but it was rather a nice place to go and have tea in as it had a really charming view; I wanted to pull it down and put up a smart Japanese tea-house instead, but George wouldn't hear of it, because, if you please, his mother— a peculiarly plain woman—used to sit and sew there. Well, I bided my time, and the other day, when George was in London, I pulled down the old summer-house, got my Japanese tea-house down from town, put it up, and had everything finished by the time George came back twenty-four hours later. He very nearly had an apoplectic stroke. If he had I should have killed two birds with one stone.

BESSIE: Pearl!

PRINCESS: I don't know why you've furnished it so elaborately.

PEARL: Well, I thought in the hot weather I'd sleep there sometimes. It'll be just like sleeping in the open air.

FENWICK: These young people want to start dancing, Pearl.

PEARL: Where would you like to dance, in here with the gramophone, or in the drawing-room with the pianola?

BESSIE: Oh, in the drawing-room.

PEARL: Let's go there then.

BESSIE: [*To* CLAY.] Come and help me get the rolls out.

CLAY: Right you are.

> [*They go out, followed by the* DUCHESSE *and* PEARL, TONY, FENWICK, *and* BLEANE.

FLEMING: [*To the* PRINCESS.] Aren't you coming?

PRINCESS: No, I think I'll stay here for the present. But don't bother about me. You must go and dance.

FLEMING: There are enough men without me. I'm sure Thornton Clay is a host in himself.

PRINCESS: You don't like Thornton?

FLEMING: He's been very kind to me since I came to London.

PRINCESS: I was watching your face when he told that story about the Hereford ball. You must learn to conceal your feelings better.

FLEMING: Didn't you think it was horrible?

PRINCESS: I've known Thornton for ten years. I'm used to him. And as you say yourself, he's very kind.

FLEMING: That's what makes life so difficult. People don't seem to be good or bad as the squares on a chessboard are black or white. Even the worthless ones have got good traits, and it makes it so hard to know how to deal with them.

PRINCESS: [*Smiling a little.*] You don't approve of poor Thornton?

FLEMING: What do you expect me to think of a man who's proud of having forced his way into a house where he knew he wasn't wanted? He reckons success by the number of invitations he receives. He holds himself up to me as an example. He tells me that if I want to get into society, I must work for it. What do they think of a man like Thornton Clay in England? Don't they despise him?

PRINCESS: Everywhere, in New York just as much as in London, there are masses of people struggling to get into society. It's so common a sight that one loses the sense of there being anything disgraceful in it. Pearl would tell you that English society is a little pompous; they welcome a man who can make them laugh. Thornton is very useful. He has high spirits, he's amusing, he makes a party go.

FLEMING: I should have thought a man could find some better use for his life than that.

PRINCESS: Thornton has plenty of money. Do you think there is any point in his spending his life making more? I sometimes think there's too much money in America already.

FLEMING: There are things a man can do beside making money.

PRINCESS: You know, American wealth has reached a pitch when it was bound to give rise to a leisured class. Thornton is one of the first members of it. Perhaps he doesn't play the part very well, but remember he hasn't had the time to learn it that they've had in Europe.

FLEMING: [Smiling.] I'm afraid you don't think me very charitable.

PRINCESS: You're young. It's a real pleasure to me to know a nice clean American boy. And I'm so glad that you're not going to be dazzled by this English life that dazzles so many of our countrymen. Amuse yourself, learn what you can from it, take all the good it offers you and go back to America.

FLEMING: I shall be glad to go back. Perhaps I ought never to have come.

PRINCESS: I'm afraid you're not very happy.

FLEMING: I don't know what makes you think that.

PRINCESS: It's not very hard to see that you're in love with Bessie.

FLEMING: Did you know that I was engaged to her?

PRINCESS: [*Surprised.*] No.

FLEMING: I was engaged to her before I went to Harvard. I was eighteen then, and she was sixteen.

PRINCESS: How very early in life you young people settle things in America!

FLEMING: Perhaps it was rather silly and childish. But when she wrote and told me that she thought we'd better break it off, I discovered I cared more than I thought.

PRINCESS: What did you say to her?

FLEMING: I couldn't try to hold her to a promise she gave when she was a schoolgirl. I answered that I sympathised and understood.

PRINCESS: When did this happen?

FLEMING: A couple of months ago. Then I got the chance to go over to Europe and I thought I'd come to see what was going on. It didn't take me long to tumble.

PRINCESS: You're bearing it very well.

FLEMING: Oh, the only thing I could do was to be pleasant. I should only have bored her if I'd made love to her. She took our engagement as an amusing joke, and there wasn't anything for me to do but accept her view of it. She was having the time of her life. At first I thought perhaps she'd grow tired of all these balls and parties, and then if I was on the spot I might persuade her to come back to America with me.

PRINCESS: You may still.

FLEMING: No, I haven't a chance. The first day I arrived
she told me how wonderful she thought this English
life. She thinks it full and varied. She thinks it has
beauty.

PRINCESS: That sounds rather satirical.

FLEMING: Pearl has been very nice to me. She's taken me
about, I've driven with her constantly, I've sat in her
box at the opera, I'm her guest at the moment. If I
had any decency I'd hold my tongue.

PRINCESS: Well?

FLEMING: [*Bursting out impetuously.*] There's something in
these surroundings that makes me feel terribly uncomfortable. Under the brilliant surface I suspect all kinds
of ugly and shameful secrets that everyone knows and
pretends not to. This is a strange house in which the
husband is never seen and Arthur Fenwick, a vulgar
sensualist, acts as host; and it's an attractive spectacle,
this painted duchess devouring with her eyes a boy
young enough to be her son. And the conversation—
I don't want to seem a prude, I daresay people over
here talk more freely than the people I've known; but
surely there are women who don't have lovers, there
are such things as honour and decency and self-restraint.
If Bessie is going to remain over here I wish to God
she'd marry her lord at once and get out of it quickly.

PRINCESS: D'you think she'll be happy?

FLEMING: Are they any of them happy? How can they
expect to be happy when they marry for . . . [*The*
PRINCESS *gives a sudden start, and* FLEMING *stops short.*]
I beg your pardon. I was forgetting. Please forgive me.
You see, you're so different.

PRINCESS: I'm sorry I interrupted you. What were you
going to say?

FLEMING: It wasn't of any importance. You see, I've been
thinking it over so much that it's rather got on my

nerves. And I haven't been able to tell anyone what I
was thinking about. I'm dreadfully sorry.

PRINCESS: You were going to say, how can they expect to
be happy when they marry for a trumpery title? You
thought, they're snobs, vulgar snobs, and the misery of
their lives is the proper punishment for their ignoble
desires.

FLEMING: [*Very apologetically.*] Princess.

PRINCESS: [*Ironically.*] Princess.

FLEMING: Believe me, I hadn't the smallest intention of
saying anything to wound you.

PRINCESS: You haven't. It's too true. Most of us who
marry foreigners are merely snobs. But I wonder if it's
all our fault. We're not shown a better way of life. No
one has even hinted to us that we have any duty towards
our own country. We're blamed because we marry
foreigners, but columns are written about us in the
papers, and our photographs are in all the magazines.
Our friends are excited and envious. After all, we are
human. At first, when people addressed me as Princess,
I couldn't help feeling thrilled. Of course it was
snobbishness.

FLEMING: You make me feel a terrible cad.

PRINCESS: But sometimes there've been other motives, too.
Has it ever occurred to you that snobbishness is the
spirit of romance in a reach-me-down? I was only
twenty when I married Marino. I didn't see him as a
fortune-hunting Dago, but as the successor of a long
line of statesmen and warriors. There'd been a pope in
his family, and a dozen cardinals, one of his ancestors
had been painted by Titian; for centuries they'd been
men of war, with power of life and death; I'd seen the
great feudal castle, with its hundred rooms, where they
had ruled as independent sovereigns. When Marino
came and asked me to marry him it was romance that

stood in his shoes and beckoned to me. I thought of the palace in Rome, which I had visited as a tripper, and where I might reign as mistress. I thought it was splendid to take my place after all those great ladies, Orsinis, Colonnas, Gaetanis, Aldobrandinis. I loved him.

FLEMING: But there's no need to tell me that you could never do anything from an unworthy motive.

PRINCESS: My husband's family had been ruined by speculation. He was obliged to sell himself. He sold himself for five million dollars. And I loved him. You can imagine the rest. First he was indifferent to me, then I bored him, and at last he hated me. Oh, the humiliation I endured. When my child died I couldn't bear it any longer; I left him. I went back to America. I found myself a stranger. I was out of place, the life had become foreign to me; I couldn't live at home. I settled in England; and here we're strangers too. I've paid very heavily for being a romantic girl.

[BESSIE *comes in.*

BESSIE: Really, Fleming, it's too bad of you to sit in here and flirt with the Princess. We want you to come and dance.

[*The* PRINCESS, *agitated, gets up and goes out into the garden.*]

BESSIE: [*Looking after her.*] Is anything the matter?

FLEMING: No.

BESSIE: Are you coming to dance, or are you not?

FLEMING: I had quite a talk with Lord Bleane after dinner, Bessie.

BESSIE: [*Smiling.*] Well?

FLEMING: Are you going to accept the coronet that he's dangling before your eyes?

BESSIE: It would be more to the point if you asked whether I'm going to accept the coronet that he's laying at my feet.

FLEMING: He's a very nice fellow, Bessie.

BESSIE: I know that.

FLEMING: I wanted to dislike him.

BESSIE: Why?

FLEMING: Well, I don't think much of these English lords who run after American girls for their money. I expected him to be a brainless loafer, with just enough cunning to know his market value, but he's a modest, unassuming fellow. To tell you the truth, I'm puzzled.

BESSIE: [*Chaffing him.*] Fancy that!

FLEMING: I think it's a low-down thing that he's doing, and yet he doesn't seem a low-down fellow.

BESSIE: He might be in love with me, you know.

FLEMING: Is he?

BESSIE: No.

FLEMING: Are you going to marry him?

BESSIE: I don't know.

FLEMING: I suppose he's come here to ask you?

BESSIE: [*After a short pause.*] He asked me a month ago. I promised to give him an answer when he came back from Rumania. . . . I'm in a panic. He's waiting to get me alone. I was able to be quite flippant about it when I had a month before me, but now, when I've got to say yes or no, I'm so jumpy I don't know what to do with myself.

FLEMING: Don't marry him, Bessie.

BESSIE: Why not?

FLEMING: Well, first, you're no more in love with him than he is with you.

BESSIE: And then?

FLEMING: Isn't that enough?

BESSIE: I wonder if you realise what he offers me. Do you know what the position of an English peeress is?

FLEMING: Does it mean so much to be called Your Ladyship by tradesmen?

BESSIE: You donkey, Fleming. If I marry an American boy my life will be over; if I marry Harry Bleane it will be only just beginning. Look at Pearl. I could do what she's done; I could do more, because George Grayston isn't ambitious. I could make Harry do anything I liked. He would go into politics, and I should have a salon. Why, I could do anything.

FLEMING: [*Dryly.*] I don't know why you should be in a panic. You've evidently made up your mind. You'll have a brilliant marriage with crowds outside the church, your photograph will be in all the papers, you'll go away for your honeymoon, and you'll come back. What will you do then?

BESSIE: Why, settle **down.**

FLEMING: Will you break your heart like the Princess because your husband has taken a mistress, or will you take lovers like the Duchesse de Surennes, or will you bore yourself to death like Pearl because your husband is virtuous, and wants you to do your duty?

BESSIE: Fleming, you've got no right to say things like that to me.

FLEMING: I'm sorry if I've made you angry. I had to say it.

BESSIE: Are you quite sure that it's for my sake you don't want me to marry Lord Bleane?

FLEMING: Yes, I think it is. When you broke off our engagement I didn't blame you. You wouldn't have done it if you'd cared for me, and it wasn't your fault if you didn't. When I came over I saw that I could expect nothing but friendship from you. You must do me the justice to acknowledge that during this month I haven't given the smallest sign that I wanted anything else.

BESSIE: Oh, you've been charming. You always were the best friend I've had.

FLEMING: If in a corner of my heart I kept my love for you, that is entirely my affair. I don't know that it puts you to any inconvenience, and it pleases me. I'm quite sure that I'm only thinking now of your happiness. Go back to America, and fall in love with some nice fellow, and marry him. You'll have all my best wishes. Perhaps your life won't be so brilliant or so exciting, but it will be simpler and wholesomer, and more becoming.

BESSIE: You're a dear, Fleming, and if I said anything disagreeable just now, forgive me. I didn't mean it. I shall always want you to be my dearest friend.

[LORD BLEANE *enters from the terrace.*

BLEANE: I was looking for you everywhere. I wondered where you'd got to.

[*There is a moment's pause.* FLEMING HARVEY *looks from* BESSIE *to* BLEANE.

FLEMING: I really must go and dance with the Duchesse or she'll never forgive me.

BLEANE: I've just been dancing with her. My dear fellow, it's the most violent form of exercise I've ever taken.

FLEMING: I'm in very good condition.

[*He goes out.*

BLEANE: Blessings on him.

BESSIE: Why?

BLEANE: Because he's left us alone. Ask me another.

BESSIE: I don't think I will.

BLEANE: Then I'll ask you one.

BESSIE: Please don't. Tell me all about Rumania.

BLEANE: Rumania is a Balkan State. Its capital is Bucharest. It has long been known for its mineral springs.

BESSIE: You're in very high spirits to-night.

BLEANE: You may well wonder. Everything has conspired to depress them.

BESSIE: Oh, what nonsense!

BLEANE: First I was in England **thirty-six** hours before I had a chance of seeing you; secondly, when I arrived you'd already gone up to dress; then, when I was expecting to sit next you at dinner, I was put between Lady Grayston and the Princess; and, lastly, you made me pound away at that beastly pianola when I wanted to dance with you.

BESSIE: Well, you've survived it all.

BLEANE: What I want to point out to you is that if notwithstanding I'm in high spirits, I must have a most engaging nature.

BESSIE: I never dreamt of denying it.

BLEANE: So much to the good.

BESSIE: The man's going to propose to me.

BLEANE: No, I'm not.

BESSIE: I beg your pardon. My mistake.

BLEANE: I did that a month ago.

BESSIE: There's been a change of moon since then, and no proposal holds good after the new moon.

BLEANE: I never knew that.

BESSIE: You've been down to see your mother.

BLEANE: She sends you her love.

BESSIE: Have you told her?

BLEANE: I told her a month ago.

> [BESSIE *does not speak for a moment; when she answers it is more gravely*.]

BESSIE: You know, I want to be frank with you. You won't think it disagreeable of me, will you? I'm not in love with you.

BLEANE: I know. But you don't positively dislike me?

BESSIE: No. I like you very much.

BLEANE: Won't you risk it then?

BESSIE: [*Almost tragically.*] I can't make up my mind.

BLEANE: I'll do all I can to make you happy. I'll try not to make a nuisance of myself.

BESSIE: I know quite well that I wouldn't marry you if you weren't who you are, and I'm afraid I know that you wouldn't marry me if I hadn't a certain amount of money.

BLEANE: Oh, yes, I would.

BESSIE: It's nice of you to say so.

BLEANE: Don't you believe it?

BESSIE: I suppose I'm a perfect fool. I ought to play the game prettily. You see, I know that you can't afford to marry a girl who isn't well-to-do. Everyone knows what I have. Pearl has taken good care that they should. You wouldn't ever have thought of me otherwise. We're arranging a deal. You give your title and your position, and I give my money. It's a commonplace thing enough, but somehow it sticks in my throat.

[BLEANE *hesitates a moment, and walks up and down thinking.*]

BLEANE: You make me feel an awful swine. The worst of it is that some part of what you say is true. I'm not such a fool that I didn't see your sister was throwing us together. I don't want to seem a conceited ass, but a fellow in my sort of position can't help knowing that many people think him rather a catch. Mothers of marriageable daughters are very transparent sometimes, you know, and if they don't marry their daughters they're determined it shan't be for want of trying.

BESSIE: Oh, I can quite believe that. I have noticed it in American mothers, too.

BLEANE: I knew it would be a good thing if I married you. I don't suppose I should have thought about you if I hadn't been told you were pretty well off. It's beastly now, saying all that.

BESSIE: I don't see why.

BLEANE: Because after a bit I found out I'd fallen in love with you. And then I didn't care if you hadn't got a bob. I wanted to marry you because—because I didn't know what to do without you.

BESSIE: Harry!

BLEANE: Do believe me. I swear it's true. I don't care a hang about the money. After all, we could get along without it. And I love you.

BESSIE: It's very good to hear you say that. I'm so absurdly pleased and flattered.

BLEANE: You do believe it, don't you?

BESSIE: Yes.

BLEANE: And will you marry me?

BESSIE: If you like.

BLEANE: Of course I like. [*He takes her in his arms and kisses her.*]

BESSIE: Take care, someone might come in.

BLEANE: [*Smiling and happy.*] Come into the garden with me.

> [*He stretches out his hand, she hesitates a moment, smiles, takes it, and together they go out on to the terrace.*
> *For a moment the music of a one-step is heard more loudly, and then the* DUCHESSE *and* TONY PAXTON *come in. She sinks into a chair fanning herself, and he goes over to a table, takes a cigarette, and lights it.*

DUCHESSE: Did you see? That was Harry Bleane and Bessie. I wondered where they were.

TONY: You've got eyes like a lynx.

DUCHESSE: I'm positive they were hand in hand.

TONY: It looks as if she'd worked it at last.

DUCHESSE: I don't know about that. It looks as if he'd worked it.

TONY: She's not such a catch as all that. If I were a peer I'd sell myself for a damned sight more than eight thousand a year.

DUCHESSE: Don't stand so far away, Tony. Come and sit on the sofa by me.

TONY: [*Going over to her.*] I say, I've been talking to Bleane about two-seaters.

DUCHESSE: [*Very coldly.*] Oh!

TONY: [*Giving her a look out of the corner of his eye.*] He says I can't do better than get a Talbot.

DUCHESSE: I don't see why you want a car of your own. You can always use one of mine.

TONY: That's not the same thing. After all, it won't cost much. I can get a ripper for just over twelve hundred pounds, with a really smart body.

DUCHESSE: You talk as though twelve hundred pounds were nothing at all.

TONY: Hang it all, it isn't anything to you.

DUCHESSE: What with the income tax and one thing and another, I'm not so terribly flush just now. No one knows the claims I have on me. Because one has a certain amount of money one's supposed to be made of it. They don't realise that if one spends it in one way one can't spend it in another. It cost me seven thousand pounds to have my house redecorated.

TONY: [*Sulkily.*] You said I could buy myself a car.

DUCHESSE: I said I'd think about it. I wasn't under the impression that you'd go and order one right away.

TONY: I've practically committed myself now.

DUCHESSE: You only want a car so that you can be independent of me.

TONY: Well, hang it all, you can't expect me to be tied to your apron-strings always. It's a bit thick if whenever I want to take a man down to play golf I have to ring up and ask if I can have one of your cars. It makes me look such an ass.

DUCHESSE: If it's only to play golf you want it, I'm sure anyone would rather go down to the links in a comfortable Rolls-Royce than in a two-seater.

[*A silence.*

TONY: If you don't want to give me a car, why on earth did you say you would?

DUCHESSE: [*Putting her hand on him.*] Tony.

TONY: For goodness' sake don't touch me.

DUCHESSE: [*Hurt and mortified.*] Tony!

TONY: I don't want to force you to make me presents. I can quite well do without a two-seater. I can go about in omnibuses if it comes to that.

DUCHESSE: Don't you love me?

TONY: I wish you wouldn't constantly ask me if I love you. It is maddening.

DUCHESSE: Oh, how can you be so cruel to me!

TONY: [*Exasperated.*] D'you think this is quite the best place to choose to make a scene?

DUCHESSE: I love you with all my heart. I've never loved anybody as much as I love you.

TONY: No man could stand being loved so much. D'you think it's jolly for me to feel that your eyes are glued on me whatever I'm doing? I can never put my hand out without finding yours there ready to press it.

DUCHESSE: I can't help it if I love you. That's my temperament.

TONY: Yes, but you needn't show it so much. Why don't you leave me to do the love-making?

DUCHESSE: If I did that there wouldn't be any love-making.

TONY: You make me look such a fool.

DUCHESSE: Don't you know there's nothing in the world I wouldn't do for you?

TONY: [*Quickly.*] Well, why don't you marry me?

DUCHESSE: [*With a gasp.*] I can't do that. You know that I can't do that.

TONY: Why not? You could still call yourself Duchesse de Surennes.

DUCHESSE: No; I've always told you nothing would induce me to marry.

TONY: That shows how much you love me.

DUCHESSE: Marriage is so middle-class. It takes away all the romance of love.

TONY: You simply want to have your freedom and keep me bound hand and foot. D'you think it's jolly for me to know what people say about me? After all, I have got some pride.

DUCHESSE: I'm sure we shall be able to get you a job soon, and then no one will be able to say anything.

TONY: I'm getting fed up with the whole business; I tell you that straight. I'd just as soon chuck it.

DUCHESSE: Tony, you don't mean to say you want to leave me. I'll kill myself if you do. I couldn't bear it, I couldn't bear it. I'll kill myself.

TONY: For God's sake, don't make such a row.

DUCHESSE: Say you don't mean it, Tony. I shall scream.

TONY: After all, I've got my self-respect to think of. It seems to me the best thing would be if we put a stop to the whole thing now.

DUCHESSE: Oh, I can't lose you. I can't.

TONY: No one can say I'm mercenary, but hang it all, one has to think of one's future. I shan't be twenty-five for ever. I ought to be settling down.

DUCHESSE: Don't you care for me any more?

TONY: Of course I care for you. If I didn't, d'you think I'd have let you do all you have for me?

DUCHESSE: Then why d'you make me so unhappy?

TONY: I don't want to make you unhappy, but really sometimes you are unreasonable.

DUCHESSE: You mean about the car?

TONY: I wasn't thinking about the car then.

DUCHESSE: You can have it if you like.

TONY: I don't want it now.

DUCHESSE: Tony, don't be unkind.

TONY: I'm not going to take any more presents from you.

DUCHESSE: I didn't mean to be unreasonable. I'd like you to have the car, Tony. I'll give you a cheque for it to-morrow. [*Coaxingly.*] Tell me what the body's like.

TONY: [*Sulkily.*] Oh, it's a torpedo body.

DUCHESSE: You'll take me for drives in it sometimes?
> [*He turns round and looks at her, she puts out her hand, he thaws, and smiles engagingly.*

TONY: I say, you are awfully kind to me.

DUCHESSE: You do like me a little, don't you?

TONY: Of course I do.

DUCHESSE: You have a good heart, Tony. Kiss me.

TONY: [*Kissing her, pleased and excited.*] I saw an awfully jolly body in a shop in Trafalgar Square the day before yesterday. I've got half a mind to get the people who made your body to copy it.

DUCHESSE: Why don't you get it at the shop you saw it at? My people are terribly expensive, and they aren't any better than anybody else.

TONY: Well, you see, I don't know anything about the firm. I just happened to catch sight of it as I was passing.

DUCHESSE: What on earth were you doing in Trafalgar Square on Thursday? I thought you were going to Ranelagh.

TONY: I was put off. I hadn't got anything to do, so I thought I'd just slope round the National Gallery for half an hour.

DUCHESSE: That's the last place I should have expected you to go to.

TONY: I don't mind having a look at pictures now and then.

> [*A sudden suspicion comes to the* DUCHESSE *that he was there with* PEARL, *but she makes no sign that he can see.*

DUCHESSE: [*Blandly.*] Did you look at the Bronzinos?

TONY: [*Falling into the trap.*] Yes. Arthur Fenwick bought one the other day at Christie's. He paid a devil of a price for it too.

DUCHESSE: [*Clenching her hands in the effort to hide her agitation.*] Oh?

TONY: I do think it's rot, the prices people pay for old masters. I'm blowed if I'd give ten thousand pounds for a picture.

DUCHESSE: We'll go to the National Gallery together one of these days, shall we?

TONY: I don't know that I want to make a habit of it, you know.

> [PEARL *and* THORNTON CLAY *come in. During the conversation the* DUCHESSE *surreptitiously watches* PEARL *and* TONY *for signs of an intelligence between them.*

PEARL: I've got great news for you. Bessie and Harry Bleane are engaged.

DUCHESSE: Oh, my dear, I'm so glad. How gratified you must be?

PEARL: Yes, I'm delighted. You must come and congratulate them.

CLAY: Above all we must congratulate one another. We've all worked for it, Pearl.

TONY: He hadn't much chance, poor blighter, had he?

PEARL: We're going to have one more dance, and then Arthur wants to play poker. You must come.

CLAY: [*To the* DUCHESSE.] Will you dance this with me, Minnie?

DUCHESSE: I'd like to.

> [CLAY *gives her his arm. She throws* TONY *and* PEARL *a glance, and purses her lips. She goes out with* CLAY.

PEARL: You haven't danced with me yet, Tony. You should really pay some attention to your hostess.

TONY: I say, don't go.

PEARL: Why not?

TONY: Because I want to talk to you.

PEARL: [*Flippantly.*] If you want to whisper soft nothings in my ear, you'll find the one-step exceedingly convenient.

TONY: You're a little beast, Pearl.

PEARL: You've been having a long talk with Minnie.

TONY: Oh, she's been making me a hell of a scene.

PEARL: Poor thing, she can't help it. She adores you.

TONY: I wish she didn't, and you did.

PEARL: [*With a chuckle*]. My dear, it's your only attraction for me that she adores you. Come and dance with me.

TONY: You've got a piece of hair out of place.

PEARL: Have I? [*She takes a small glass out of her bag and looks at herself. As she does so* TONY *steps behind her and kisses her neck.*] You fool, don't do that. Anyone might see us.

TONY: I don't care.

PEARL: I do. Arthur's as jealous as cats' meat.

TONY: Arthur's playing the pianola.

PEARL: There's nothing wrong with my hair.

TONY: Of course there isn't. You're perfectly divine to-night. I don't know what there is about you.

PEARL: You're a foolish creature, Tony.

TONY: Let's go in the garden.

PEARL: No, they'll be wondering where we are.

TONY: Hang it all, it's not so extraordinary to take a stroll instead of dancing.

PEARL: I don't want to take a stroll.

TONY: Pearl.

PEARL: Yes?

> [*She looks at him. For a moment they stare at one another in silence. A hot flame of passion leaps up suddenly between them, and envelops them, so that they forget everything but that they are man and woman. The air seems all at once heavy to breathe.* PEARL, *like a bird in a net, struggles to escape; their voices sink, and unconsciously they speak in whispers.*

PEARL: Don't be a fool, Tony.

TONY: [*Hoarsely.*] Let's go down to the tea-house.

PEARL: No, I won't.

TONY: We shall be quite safe there.

PEARL: I daren't. It's too risky.

TONY: Oh, damn the risk!

PEARL: [*Agitated.*] I can't!

TONY: I'll go down there and wait.

PEARL: [*Breathlessly.*] But—if they wonder where I am.

TONY: They'll think you've gone up to your room.

PEARL: I won't come, Tony.

TONY: I'll wait for you.

> [*As he goes out,* ARTHUR FENWICK *comes in.* PEARL
> *gives a slight start, but quickly recovers herself.*

FENWICK: Look here, I'm not going on pounding away at that wretched pianola unless you come and dance, Pearl.

PEARL: [*Exhausted.*] I'm tired, I don't want to dance any more.

FENWICK: Poor child, you look quite pale.

PEARL: Do I? I thought I'd put plenty of rouge on. Am I looking revolting?

FENWICK: You always look adorable. You're wonderful. I can't think what you see in an old fellow like me.

PEARL: You're the youngest man I've ever known.

FENWICK: How well you know the thing to say to please me!

> [*He is just going to take her in his arms, but instinctively
> she draws back.*

PEARL: Let's play poker now, shall we?

FENWICK: Not if you're tired, darling.

PEARL: I'm never too tired for that.

FENWICK: You don't know how I adore you. It's a privilege to be allowed to love you.

PEARL: [*Sure of herself again.*] Oh, what nonsense! You'll make me vain if you say things like that.

FENWICK: You do love me a little, don't you? I want your love so badly.

PEARL: Why, I dote on you, you silly old thing.

> [*She takes his face in her hands and kisses him, avoids his
> arms that seek to encircle her, and goes towards the
> door.*

FENWICK: Where are you going?

PEARL: I'm just going to my room to arrange my face.

FENWICK: My God, how I love you, girlie! There's nothing in the world I wouldn't do for you.

PEARL: Really?

FENWICK: Nothing.

PEARL: Then ring for Pole and tell him to set out the card-table and bring the counters.

FENWICK: And I was prepared to give you a sable coat or a diamond tiara.

PEARL: I much prefer chinchilla and emeralds.

FENWICK: [*Taking her hand.*] Must you really go and arrange your face?

PEARL: Really!

FENWICK: Be quick then. I can hardly bear you out of my sight. [*He kisses her hand.*

PEARL: [*Looking at him tenderly.*] Dear Arthur.

    [*She goes out.* FENWICK *rings the bell. Then he goes on the terrace and calls out.*

FENWICK: Thornton, we're going to play poker. Get them to come along, will you?

CLAY: [*Outside.*] Right-ho!

                      [POLE *comes in.*

FENWICK: Oh, Pole, get the card-table ready.

POLE: Very good, sir.

FENWICK: And we shall want the counters. Let's have those mother-o'-pearl ones that I brought down last time I was here.

POLE: Very good, sir.

    [*The* PRINCESS *comes in.* POLE *proceeds to bring a card-table into the centre of the room and unfolds it. He gets a box of counters out of a drawer, and puts them on the table.*

FENWICK: Pearl has just gone to her room. She'll be here in one minute.

PRINCESS: [*Looking at the preparations.*] This looks like more dissipation.

FENWICK: We were going to have a little game of poker. I don't think we ought to play very long, Pearl is looking terribly tired.

PRINCESS: I don't wonder. She's so energetic.

FENWICK: She does too much. Just now when I came in she was quite white. I'm really very uneasy about her. You see, she never spares herself.

PRINCESS: Fortunately she's extremely strong.

FENWICK: She has a constitution of iron. She's a very wonderful woman. It's very seldom you meet a woman like Pearl. She's got a remarkable brain. I've frequently discussed business with her, and I've been amazed at her clear grasp of complicated matters. I owe a great deal to her. And she's good, Princess, she's good. She's got a heart of gold.

PRINCESS: I'm sure she has.

FENWICK: She'll always do a good turn to anybody. She's the most generous, the most open-handed woman I've ever met.

> [*The* DUCHESSE *comes in as he says these words.*

DUCHESSE: Who is this?

FENWICK: We were talking of our hostess.

DUCHESSE: I see.

> [*She has her bag in her hand; when the others are not looking she hides it behind a sofa.*

FENWICK: I have no hesitation in saying tnat Pearl is the most remarkable woman in England. Why, she's got half the Cabinet in her pocket. She's very powerful.

DUCHESSE: I have often thought that if she'd lived in the reign of Charles II she would have been a duchess in her own right.

FENWICK: [*Innocently.*] Maybe. She would adorn any sphere. She's got everything—tact, brains, energy, beauty.

DUCHESSE: Virtue.

FENWICK: If I were the British people, I'd make her Prime Minister.

PRINCESS: [*Smiling.*] You're an excellent friend, Mr. Fenwick.

FENWICK: Of course, you've heard of her hostel for young women alone in London?

DUCHESSE: [*Sweetly.*] Yes, there was a great deal about it in the papers, wasn't there?

FENWICK: That's a thing I've always admired in Pearl. She has a thoroughly modern understanding of the value of advertisement.

DUCHESSE: Yes, she has, hasn't she?

FENWICK: Well, believe me, she conceived the idea of that hostel, built it, endowed it, organised it, all on her own. It cost twenty thousand pounds.

DUCHESSE: But surely, Mr. Fenwick, you paid the twenty thousand pounds. Pearl hasn't got sums like that to throw away on charity.

FENWICK: I gave the money, but the money isn't the important thing. The idea, the organisation, the success, are all due to Pearl.

DUCHESSE: It has certainly been one of the best advertised of recent philanthropic schemes.

> [THORNTON CLAY, BESSIE, BLEANE *and* FLEMING *come in.*

CLAY: We're all dying to play poker.

FENWICK: The table is ready.

BESSIE: Where is Pearl?

FENWICK: She's gone to her room. She'll be back in a minute.

> [*They gather round the table and sit down.*

BESSIE: You're going to play, Princess?

PRINCESS: Oh, I don't think so, I'll look on. I'm going to bed in a minute.

BESSIE: Oh, you must play.

    [*The* PRINCESS *smiles, shrugs her shoulders and approaches the table.*

FENWICK: Leave a place for Pearl.

DUCHESSE: You must leave one for Tony, too.

CLAY: What's he doing?

DUCHESSE: He'll be here presently.

FENWICK: Shall I give out the counters? What would you like to play for?

PRINCESS: Don't let it be too high.

DUCHESSE: How tiresome of you, Flora! I think I'm in luck to-night.

FENWICK: We don't want to ruin anyone. Shilling antes. Will that suit you?

PRINCESS: Very well.

FENWICK: [*To* CLAY.] The whites are a shilling, Thornton, reds two, and blues five bob. Mr. Harvey, you might count some out, will you?

FLEMING: Sure.

    [*The three of them start counting out the counters.*

DUCHESSE: Oh, how stupid of me, I haven't got my bag.

FENWICK: Never mind, we'll trust you.

DUCHESSE: Oh, I'd rather pay at once. It saves so much bother. Besides, I hate not having my bag.

PRINCESS: One always wants to powder one's nose if one hasn't got it.

DUCHESSE: Bessie dear, I left it in Pearl's new tea-house. Do run and fetch it for me.

BESSIE: Certainly.

BLEANE: No, I'll go.

BESSIE: You don't know the way. I can go through the bushes. It's only twenty yards. You stop and count out the counters.

[*She goes out.*

FENWICK: There's five pounds here. Will **you** take them, Princess?

PRINCESS: Thank you. Here's my money.

DUCHESSE: I'll give you my fiver as soon as Bessie brings my bag.

CLAY: How on earth came you to leave it in the tea-house?

DUCHESSE: I'm so careless. I'm always leaving my bag about.

FLEMING: Here's another five pounds.

PRINCESS: What beautiful counters they are!

FENWICK: I'm glad you like them. I gave them to Pearl. They've got her initials on them.

CLAY: Let's have a hand before Pearl comes. Lowest deals.

[*They all cut.*

FLEMING: Table stakes, I suppose?

FENWICK: Oh yes, it makes it a much better game.

CLAY: Your deal, Fenwick.

FENWICK: Ante up, Princess.

PRINCESS: I beg your pardon.

[*She pushes forward a counter.* FENWICK *deals. The others take up their cards.*

FENWICK: Two shillings to come in.

FLEMING: I'm coming in.

BLEANE: I always come in.

FENWICK: I oughtn't to, but I shall all the same. Are you going to make good your ante, Princess?

PRINCESS: I may just as well, mayn't I?

FENWICK: That's how I've made a fortune. By throwing good money after bad. Would you like a card?

PRINCESS: I'll have three.

[FENWICK *gives them to her*.

CLAY: The Princess has got a pair of deuces.

FLEMING: I'll have one.

[FENWICK *gives it to him*.

BLEANE: One never gets that straight, Harvey. I'll take five.

FENWICK: That's what I call a real sport.

CLAY: Nonsense. It just means he can't play.

BLEANE: It would be rather a sell for you if I got a flush.

CLAY: It would, but you haven't.

[FENWICK *has given him cards and* BLEANE *looks at them*.

BLEANE: You're quite right. I haven't.

[*He flings them down. Through the next speeches the business with the cards follows the dialogue*.

FENWICK: Don't you want any cards, Duchesse?

DUCHESSE: No, I'm out of it.

CLAY: I'll have three. I thought you were in luck.

DUCHESSE: Wait a minute. You'll be surprised.

FENWICK: Dealer takes two.

CLAY: Who bets?

PRINCESS: I'm out of it.

CLAY: I said it was a pair of deuces.

FLEMING: I'll bet five shillings.

CLAY: I'll take it and raise five shillings.

FENWICK: I suppose I must risk my money. What have I got to put down? Ten shillings?

FLEMING: There's five shillings, and I'll raise you five shillings more.

CLAY: No, I've had enough.

FENWICK: I'll take you and raise you again.

FLEMING: Very well. And once more.

FENWICK: I'll see you.

> [BESSIE *comes in. The* DUCHESSE *has been watching for her.* BESSIE *is excessively disturbed.*

DUCHESSE: Ah, there's Bessie.

FENWICK: [*To* FLEMING.] What have you got?

DUCHESSE: Did you find my bag?

BESSIE: [*With a gasp.*] No, it wasn't there.

DUCHESSE: Oh, but I remember distinctly leaving it there. I'll go and look for it myself. Mr. Fenwick, will you come with me.

BESSIE: No, don't—you can't go into the tea-house.

PRINCESS: [*Surprised.*] Bessie, is anything the matter?

BESSIE: [*In a strained voice.*] The door of the tea-house is locked.

DUCHESSE: Oh, it can't be. I saw Pearl and Tony go in there just now.

> [BESSIE *suddenly hides her face and bursts into a flood of tears.*

PRINCESS: [*Starting to her feet.*] Minnie, you devil! What have you been doing?

DUCHESSE: Don't ask what I've been doing.

FENWICK: You must be mistaken. Pearl went up to her room.

DUCHESSE: Go and look for her. . . .

> [FENWICK *is about to start from his chair. The* PRINCESS *puts her hand on his shoulders.*

PRINCESS: Where are you going?

DUCHESSE: I saw her.

> [*For a moment there is a pause.*

CLAY: [*In an embarrassed way.*] Well, we'd better go on with our game, hadn't we?

[*The* PRINCESS *and* BLEANE *are bending over* BESSIE, *trying to get her to control herself.*

FLEMING: That was your money, Mr. Fenwick.

FENWICK: [*Staring in front of him, with a red face and bloodshot eyes, under his breath.*] The slut. The slut.

    [*The* DUCHESSE *takes her bag from behind the cushion, gets out the stick for her lips, and her mirror, and begins to paint them.*

CLAY: You'd better deal, Fleming. The Princess won't play, I expect.

DUCHESSE: Deal me cards. I want to play.

CLAY: Bleane, come on. We'd better go on with our game. Take Bessie's chips.

    [BLEANE *comes forward.* FLEMING *deals the cards. A stormy silence hangs over the party, broken only by the short speeches referring to the game; they play trying to relieve the tension. They are all anxiously awaiting* PEARL, *afraid she will come, knowing she must, and dreading the moment; they are nervous and constrained.*

CLAY: Your ante, Bleane.

    [BLEANE *puts forward a counter. The cards are dealt in silence.*

CLAY: I'm coming in.

    [FENWICK *looks at his cards, puts forward a couple of counters, but does not speak.* FLEMING *puts forward counters.*

FLEMING: D'you want a card?

BLEANE: Three, please.

CLAY: Two.

FENWICK: [*With an effort over himself.*] I'll have three.

    [FLEMING *deals them as they ask. Just as he has given* FENWICK *his,* PEARL *comes in, followed by* TONY. TONY *is smoking a cigarette.*

                                      D

PEARL: Oh, have you started already?

FENWICK: [*Violently.*] Where have you been?

PEARL: I? My head was aching a little and I went for a turn in the garden. I found Tony composing a sonnet to the moon.

FENWICK: You said you were going to your room.

PEARL: What are you talking about?

> [*She looks round, sees the* DUCHESSE's *look of angry triumph, and gives a slight start.*

DUCHESSE: Once too often, my dear, once too often.

> [PEARL *takes no notice. She sees* BESSIE. BESSIE *has been staring at her with miserable eyes, and now she hides her face.* PEARL *realises that everything is discovered. She turns coolly to* TONY.

PEARL: You damned fool, I told you it was too risky.

END OF THE SECOND ACT

THE THIRD ACT

The SCENE *is the same as in the last act, the morning-room at
Kenton.*

*It is next day, Sunday, about three in the afternoon, and the sun is
shining brightly.*

The PRINCESS, THORNTON CLAY *and* FLEMING *are sitting
down.* FLEMING *lights another cigarette.*

PRINCESS: Is it good for you to smoke so many cigarettes?

FLEMING: I shouldn't think so.

CLAY: He must do something.

PRINCESS: Perhaps you can get up a game of tennis later on.

FLEMING: It's very hot for tennis.

CLAY: Besides, who will play?

PRINCESS: You two could have a single.

CLAY: If we only had the Sunday papers it would be
something.

PRINCESS: You can hardly expect them in a place like this.
I don't suppose there are many trains on Sunday.

CLAY: I wonder if dinner is going to be as cheerful as
luncheon was.

FLEMING: Did Pearl send any explanation for not appearing
at luncheon?

PRINCESS: I haven't an idea.

CLAY: I asked the butler where she was. He said she was
lunching in bed. I wish I'd thought of that.

PRINCESS: I'm afraid we were rather silent.

CLAY: Silent! I shall never forget that luncheon. Minnie
subdued—and silent. Tony sulky—and silent. Bessie

79

frightened—and silent. Bleane embarrassed—and silent. Fenwick furious—and silent. I tried to be pleasant and chatty. It was like engaging the pyramids in small-talk. Both of you behaved very badly. You might have given me a little encouragement.

FLEMING: I was afraid of saying the wrong thing. The Duchesse and Bessie looked as if they'd burst into tears on the smallest provocation.

PRINCESS: I was thinking of Pearl. What a humiliation! What a horrible humiliation!

FLEMING: What d'you think she'll do now?

CLAY: That's what I'm asking myself. I have an idea that she won't appear again till we're all gone.

PRINCESS: I hope she won't. She's always so sure of herself, I couldn't bear to see her pale and mortified.

CLAY: She's got plenty of courage.

PRINCESS: I know. She may force herself to face us. It would be a dreadful ordeal for all of us.

FLEMING: D'you think she's feeling it very much?

PRINCESS: She wouldn't be human if she weren't. I don't suppose she slept any better last night than the rest of us. Poor thing, she must be a wreck.

FLEMING: It was a terrible scene.

PRINCESS: I shall never forget it. The things that Minnie said. I couldn't have believed such language could issue from a woman's throat. Oh, it was horrible.

CLAY: It was startling. I've never seen a woman so beside herself. And there was no stopping her.

FLEMING: And with Bessie there.

PRINCESS: She was crying so much, I doubt if she heard.

CLAY: I was thankful when Minnie had the hysterics and we were able to fuss over her and dab her face and slap her hands. It was a very welcome diversion.

FLEMING: Does she have attacks like that often?

CLAY: I know she did when the young man before Tony married an heiress. I think she has one whenever there's a crisis in the affairs of her heart.

FLEMING: For goodness' sake, Thornton, don't talk about it as if it were a joke.

CLAY: [*Surprised.*] What's the matter, Fleming?

FLEMING: I think it's abominable to treat the whole thing so flippantly.

CLAY: Why, I was very sympathetic. I wasn't flippant. Who got the sal volatile? I got the sal volatile.

FLEMING: [*With a shrug of the shoulders.*] I daresay my nerves are a bit on edge. You see, before, I only thought things were rather queer. It's come as, well, as a shock to discover exactly what the relations are between all these people. And what I can't very easily get over is to realise that I'm the only member of the party who doesn't take it as a matter of course.

CLAY: We shall never make a man of the world of you, Fleming.

FLEMING: I'm afraid that didn't sound very polite, Princess. I beg your pardon.

PRINCESS: I should have few friends if I demanded the standard that you do. I've learned not to judge my neighbours.

FLEMING: Is it necessary to condone their vices?

PRINCESS: You don't understand. It's not entirely their fault. It's the life they lead. They've got too much money and too few responsibilities. English women in our station have duties that are part of their birthright, but we, strangers in a strange land, have nothing to do but enjoy ourselves.

FLEMING: Well, I thank God Bleane is a decent man, and he'll take Bessie out of all this.

[*The* DUCHESSE *comes in. Unlike the* PRINCESS, **who is in**
a summer frock, suitable for the country, *the* DUCHESSE
wears a town dress and a hat.

PRINCESS: You've been changing your frock, Minnie.

DUCHESSE: Yes. I'm leaving this house in half an hour. I'd
have gone this morning, if I'd been able to get away. I
always thought it a detestable hole, but now that I've
discovered there are only two trains on Sunday, one at
nine, and the other at half-past four, I have no words to
express my opinion of it.

CLAY: Yet you have an extensive vocabulary, Minnie.

DUCHESSE: I've been just as much a prisoner as if I'd been
shut up with lock and key. I've been forced to eat that
woman's food. I thought every mouthful would choke
me.

PRINCESS: Do keep calm, Minnie. You know how bad it is
for you to upset yourself.

DUCHESSE: As soon as I found there wasn't a train I sent
over to the garage and said I wanted to be taken to
London at once. Would you believe it, I couldn't get a
car.

CLAY: Why not?

DUCHESSE: One of the cars went up to town early this
morning, and the other is being overhauled. There's
nothing but a luggage cart. I couldn't go to London in a
luggage cart. As it is I shall have to go to the station in it.
I shall look ridiculous.

CLAY: Have you ordered it?

DUCHESSE: Yes. It's to be round at the door in a few
minutes.

CLAY: What on earth can Pearl have sent the car up to
London for?

DUCHESSE: To show her spite.

PRINCESS: That's not like her.

DUCHESSE: My dear, she's been my greatest friend for fifteen years. I know her through and through, and I tell you that she hasn't got a single redeeming quality. And why does she want to have the car overhauled to-day? When you're giving a party the least you can do is to see that your cars are in running order.

PRINCESS: Oh, well, that was an accident. You can't blame her for that.

DUCHESSE: I only have one thing to be thankful for, and that is that she has had the decency to keep to her room. I will be just. It shows at least that she has some sense of shame.

CLAY: You know, Minnie, Pearl has a good heart. She didn't mean to cause you pain.

DUCHESSE: Are you trying to excuse her, Thornton?

CLAY: No, I think her conduct is inexcusable.

DUCHESSE: So do I. I mean to have nothing more to do with her. It's a judgment on me. I disliked her the first time I saw her. One should always trust one's first impressions. Now my eyes are opened. I will never speak to her again. I will cut her dead. I hope you'll tell her that, Thornton.

CLAY: If that's a commission you're giving me, it's not a very pleasant one.

PRINCESS: Will you let me have a word or two with Minnie?

CLAY: Why, of course. Come along, Fleming.

    [CLAY *and* FLEMING HARVEY *go into the garden.*

DUCHESSE: My dear, if you're going to ask me to turn the other cheek, don't. Because I'm not going to. I'm going to do all I can to revenge myself on that woman. I'm going to expose her. I'm going to tell everyone how she's treated me. When I was her guest.

PRINCESS: You must take care what you say for your own sake, Minnie.

DUCHESSE: I know quite enough about her to make her position in London impossible. I'm going to ruin her.

PRINCESS: What about Tony?

DUCHESSE: Oh, I've finished with him. Ah! I'm not the kind of woman to stand that sort of treatment. I hope he'll end in the gutter.

PRINCESS: Don't you care for him any more?

DUCHESSE: My dear, if he was starving, and went down on his bended knees to me for a piece of bread, I wouldn't give it to him. He revolts me.

PRINCESS: Well, I'm very glad. It distressed me to see you on those terms with a boy like that. You're well rid of him.

DUCHESSE: My dear, you needn't tell me that. He's a thorough wrong 'un, and that's all there is about it. He hasn't even had the decency to try and excuse himself. He hasn't even made an attempt to see me.

PRINCESS: [*Gives her a quick look.*] After all, he never really cared for you. Anyone could see that.

DUCHESSE: [*Her voice breaking.*] Oh, don't say that, Flora. I couldn't bear it. He loved me. Until that woman came between us I know he loved me. He couldn't help loving me. I did everything in the world for him. [*She bursts into tears.*]

PRINCESS: Minnie. My dear, don't give way. You know what a worthless creature he is. Haven't you any self-respect?

DUCHESSE: He's the only man I've ever loved. I could hardly bear him out of my sight. What shall I do without him?

PRINCESS: Take care, here he is.

[TONY *comes in. He is startled at seeing the* DUCHESSE. *She turns away and hurriedly dries her tears.*

TONY: Oh, I beg your pardon. I didn't know anyone was here. I was looking for some cigarettes.

> [*He stands there awkwardly, not knowing whether to go or stay. The* PRINCESS *looks at him reflectively. There is a moment's silence. Then she shrugs her shoulders and goes out. He looks at the* DUCHESSE *who stands with her back to him. He hesitates a moment, then, almost on the tips of his toes, walks over to the cigarettes, fills his case, takes another look at the* DUCHESSE, *and is in the act of tip-toeing out of the room when she stops him with her question.*

DUCHESSE: Where are you going?

TONY: Nowhere in particular.

DUCHESSE: Then you'd better stay here.

TONY: I thought you wished to be alone.

DUCHESSE: Is that why you've kept away from me all day?

> [*He sinks sulkily into an armchair. The* DUCHESSE *finally turns round and faces him.*

DUCHESSE: Haven't you got anything to say for yourself at all?

TONY: What's the good of talking?

DUCHESSE: You might at least say you're sorry for the pain you've caused me. If you'd had any affection for me you wouldn't have done all you could to avoid me.

TONY: I knew you'd only make a scene.

DUCHESSE: Good heavens, you surely don't expect me not to make a scene.

TONY: The whole thing's very unfortunate.

DUCHESSE: Ha! Unfortunate. You break my heart and then you say it's unfortunate.

TONY: I didn't mean that. I meant it was unfortunate that you caught us out.

DUCHESSE: Oh, hold your stupid tongue. Every word you say is more unfortunate than the last.

TONY: It's because I knew you'd take offence at everything I said that I thought the best thing I could do was to keep out of the way.

DUCHESSE: You're heartless, heartless. If you'd had any decent feeling you couldn't have eaten the lunch you did. But you munched away, munched, munched, munched, till I could have killed you.

TONY: Well, I was hungry.

DUCHESSE: You oughtn't to have been hungry.

TONY: What are you going to do about it?

DUCHESSE: About your appetite? Pray to God your next mouthful chokes you.

TONY: No, about the other.

DUCHESSE: I'm going to leave this house this afternoon.

TONY: D'you want me to come, too?

DUCHESSE: What d'you suppose it matters to me whether you go or stay?

TONY: If you go I shall have to go, too.

DUCHESSE: You ought to start soon then. It's four miles to the station. I shall be obliged if you will not get in the same carriage as me.

TONY: I'm not going to walk. They can run me down in a car.

DUCHESSE: There's nothing but a luggage cart, and I'm going in that.

TONY: Isn't there room for me?

DUCHESSE: No.

TONY: When d'you want me to move out of my flat?

DUCHESSE: What has that got to do with me?

TONY: You know very well that *I* can't pay the rent.

DUCHESSE: That's your look-out.

TONY: I shall go to the colonies.

DUCHESSE: That's the very best thing you can do. I hope you'll have to break stones, and dig, and paint—with lead paint. I hope you're miserable.

TONY: Oh, well, it'll have its compensations.

DUCHESSE: Such as?

TONY: I shall be my own master. I was about fed up with this, I can tell you.

DUCHESSE: Yes, you can say that now.

TONY: D'you think it was all jam, never being able to call my soul my own? I was sick to death of it.

DUCHESSE: You cad!

TONY: Well, you may just as well know the truth.

DUCHESSE: D'you mean to say you never cared for me? Not even at the beginning?

> [He shrugs his shoulders, but does not answer. She speaks the next phrases in little gasps gradually weakening as her emotion overcomes her. He stands before her in sulky silence.

DUCHESSE: Tony, I've done everything in the world for you. I've been like a mother to you. How *can* you be so ungrateful. You haven't got any heart. If you had you'd have asked me to forgive you. You'd have made some attempt to . . . Don't you *want* me to forgive you?

TONY: What d'you mean by that?

DUCHESSE: If you'd only asked me, if you'd only shown you were sorry, I'd have been angry with you, I wouldn't have spoken to you for a week, but I'd have forgiven you—I'd have forgiven you, Tony. But you never gave me a chance. It's cruel of you, cruel!

TONY: Well, anyhow, it's too late now.

DUCHESSE: Do you want it to be too late?

TONY: It's no good grousing about the past. The thing's over now.

DUCHESSE: Aren't you sorry?

TONY: I don't know. I suppose I am in a way. I don't want to make you unhappy.

DUCHESSE: If you wanted to be unfaithful to me, why didn't you prevent me from finding out? You didn't even trouble to take a little precaution.

TONY: I was a damned fool, I know that.

DUCHESSE: Are you in love with that woman?

TONY: No.

DUCHESSE: Then why did you? Oh, Tony, how could you?

TONY: If one felt about things at night as one does next morning, life would be a dashed sight easier.

DUCHESSE: If I said to you, Let's let bygones be bygones and start afresh, what would you say, Tony?

[*She looks away. He rests his eyes on her reflectively.*

TONY: We've made a break now. We'd better leave it at that. I shall go out to the colonies.

DUCHESSE: Tony, you don't mean that seriously. You could never stand it. You know, you're not strong. You'll only die.

TONY: Oh, well, one can only die once.

DUCHESSE: I'm sorry for all I said just now, Tony. I didn't mean it.

TONY: It doesn't matter.

DUCHESSE: I can't live without you, Tony.

TONY: I've made up my mind. It's no good talking.

DUCHESSE: I'm sorry I was horrid to you, Tony. I'll never be again. Won't you forget it? Oh, Tony, won't you forgive me? I'll do anything in the world for you if only you won't leave me.

TONY: It's a rotten position I'm in. I must think of the future.

DUCHESSE: Oh, but Tony, I'll make it all right for you.

TONY: It's very kind of you, but it's not good enough. Let's part good friends, Minnie. If I've got to walk to the station, it's about time I was starting. [*He holds out his hand to her.*]

DUCHESSE: D'you mean to say it's good-bye? Good-bye for ever? Oh, how can you be so cruel!

TONY: When one's made up one's mind to do a thing, it's best to do it at once.

DUCHESSE: Oh, I can't bear it. I can't bear it. [*She begins to cry.*] Oh, what a fool I was! I ought to have pretended not to see anything. I wish I'd never known. Then you wouldn't have thought of leaving me.

TONY: Come, my dear, pull yourself together. You'll get over it.

DUCHESSE: [*Desperately.*] Tony, if you want to marry me—I'm willing to marry you. [*A pause.*

TONY: I should be just as dependent on you. D'you think it would be jolly for me having to come to you for every five pounds I wanted?

DUCHESSE: I'll settle something on you so that you'll be independent. A thousand a year. Will that do?

TONY: You are a good sort, Minnie. [*He goes over and sits down beside her.*]

DUCHESSE: You will be kind to me, won't you?

TONY: Rather! And look here, you needn't give me that two-seater. I shall be able to drive the Rolls-Royce.

DUCHESSE: You didn't want to go to the colonies, did you?

TONY: Not much.

DUCHESSE: Oh, Tony, I do love you so.

TONY: That's right.

DUCHESSE: We won't stay another minute in this house. Ring the bell, will you? You'll come with me in the luggage cart?

TONY: [*Touching the bell.*] I much prefer that to walking.

DUCHESSE: It's monstrous that there shouldn't be a motor to take luggage to the station. It's a most uncomfortable house to stay in.

TONY: Oh, beastly. D'you know that I didn't have a bath-room attached to my bedroom?   [POLE *comes in.*

DUCHESSE: Is the luggage cart ready, Pole?

POLE: I'll enquire, your grace.

DUCHESSE: My maid is to follow in the morning with the luggage. Mr. Paxton will come with me. [*To* TONY.] What about your things?

TONY: Oh, they'll be all right. I brought my man with me.

POLE: Her ladyship is just coming downstairs, your grace.

DUCHESSE: Oh, is she? Thank you, that'll do, Pole.

POLE: Very good, your grace.

> [*He goes out. As soon as he closes the door behind him the* DUCHESSE *springs to her feet.*

DUCHESSE: I won't see her. Tony, see if Thornton is on the terrace.

TONY: All right. [*He goes to the French window.*] Yes. I'll call him, shall I? Clay, come here a minute, will you?

> [*He goes out.* THORNTON CLAY *comes in, followed immediately by the* PRINCESS *and* FLEMING.

DUCHESSE: Thornton, I'm told Pearl is coming downstairs.

CLAY: At last.

DUCHESSE: I won't see her. Nothing will induce me to see her.

PRINCESS: My dear, what is to be done? We can't make her remain upstairs in her own house.

DUCHESSE: No, but Thornton can speak to her. She's evidently ashamed of herself. I only ask one thing, that she should keep out of the way till I'm gone.

CLAY: I'll do my best.

DUCHESSE: I'm going to walk up and down till the luggage cart is ready. I haven't taken my exercise to-day.

[*She goes out.*

CLAY: If Pearl is in a temper that's not a very pleasant message to give her.

PRINCESS: You won't find her in a temper. If she's dreadfully upset, tell her what Minnie says gently.

FLEMING: Here is Bessie. [*She comes in.*] It appears that Pearl is just coming downstairs.

BESSIE: Is she?

PRINCESS: Have you seen her this morning, Bessie?

BESSIE: No. She sent her maid to ask me to go to her, but I had a headache and couldn't.

[*They look at her curiously. She is inclined to be abrupt and silent. It may be imagined that she has made up her mind to some course, but what that is the others cannot tell.* FLEMING *goes over and sits beside her.*

FLEMING: I'm thinking of going back to America next Saturday, Bessie.

BESSIE: Dear Fleming, I shall be sorry to lose you.

FLEMING: I expect you'll be too busy to think about me. You'll have to see all kinds of people, and then there's your trousseau to get.

BESSIE: I wish you could come over to Paris with me, Princess, and help me with it.

PRINCESS: I? [*She gets an inkling of what* BESSIE *means.*] Of course, if I could be of any help to you, dear child. . . . [*She takes* BESSIE'S *hand and gives her a fond smile.* BESSIE

turns away to hide a tear that for a moment obscures her eyes.]
Perhaps it's a very good idea. We must talk about it.

[PEARL *comes in. She is perfectly cool and collected.
radiant in a wonderful, audacious gown; she is looking
her best and knows it. There is nothing in her manner to
indicate the smallest recollection of the episode that took
place on the preceding evening.*

PEARL: [*Brightly.*] Good-morning.

CLAY: Good-afternoon.

PEARL: I knew everyone would abuse me for coming down
so late. It was such a lovely day I thought it was a pity to
get up.

CLAY: Don't be paradoxical, Pearl, it's too hot.

PEARL: The sun streamed into my room, and I said, It's a sin
not to get up on a morning like this. And the more I said
I ought to get up, the more delightful I found it to lie in
bed. How is your head, Bessie?

BESSIE: Oh, it's better, thank you.

PEARL: I was sorry to hear you weren't feeling up to the
mark.

BESSIE: I didn't sleep very well.

PEARL: What have you done with your young man?

BESSIE: Harry? He's writing letters.

PEARL: Spreading the glad tidings, I suppose. You ought
to write to his mother, Bessie. It would be a graceful
attention. A charming, frank little letter, the sort of
thing one would expect an *ingénue* to write. Straight
from the heart.

CLAY: I'm sure you'd love to write it yourself, Pearl.

PEARL: And we must think about sending an announcement
to the Morning Post.

FLEMING: You think of everything, Pearl.

PEARL: I take my duties as Bessie's chaperon very seriously.

I've already got a brilliant idea for the gown I'm going to wear at the wedding.

FLEMING: Gee!

PEARL: My dear Fleming, don't say Gee, it's so American. Say By Jove.

FLEMING: I couldn't without laughing.

PEARL: Laffing. Why can't you say laughing?

FLEMING: I don't want to.

PEARL: How obstinate you are. Of course, now that Bessie is going to marry an Englishman she'll have to take lessons. I know an excellent woman. She's taught all the American peeresses.

FLEMING: You surprise me.

PEARL: She's got a wonderful method. She makes you read aloud. And she has long lists of words that you have to repeat twenty times a day—half instead of haf, and barth instead of bath, and carnt instead of can't.

FLEMING: By Jove instead of Gee?

PEARL: Peeresses don't say By Jove, Fleming. She teaches them to say Good heavens instead of Mercy.

FLEMING: Does she make money by it?

PEARL: Pots. She's a lovely woman. Eleo Dorset had an accent that you could cut with a knife when she first came over, and in three months she hadn't got any more than I have.

BESSIE: [*Getting up. To* FLEMING.] D'you think it's too hot for a turn in the garden?

FLEMING: Why, no.

BESSIE: Shall we go then?   [*They go out together*

PEARL: What's the matter with Bessie? She must have swallowed a poker last night. No wonder she couldn't sleep. It's enough to give anyone indigestion.

CLAY You know that Minnie is going this afternoon, Pearl?

PEARL: Yes, so I heard. It's such a bore there are no cars to take her to the station. She'll have to go in the luggage cart.

CLAY: She doesn't wish to see you.

PEARL: Oh, but I wish to see her.

CLAY: I daresay.

PEARL: I must see her.

CLAY: She asked me to tell you that she only wished you to do one thing, and that is to keep out of the way till she's gone.

PEARL: Then you can go and tell her that unless she sees me she shan't have the luggage cart.

CLAY: Pearl!

PEARL: That's my ultimatum.

CLAY: Can you see me taking a message like that to the Duchesse?

PEARL: It's four miles to the station, and there's not a scrap of shade all the way.

CLAY: After all, it's not a very unreasonable request she's making.

PEARL: If she wants the luggage cart she must come and say good-bye to me like a lady.

CLAY: [To the PRINCESS.] What am I to do? We used up all the sal volatile last night.

PRINCESS: I'll tell her if you like. D'you really insist on seeing her, Pearl?

PEARL: Yes, it's very important. [The PRINCESS goes out. PEARL watches her go with a smile.] I'm afraid Flora is shocked. She shouldn't know such people.

CLAY: Really, Pearl, your behaviour is monstrous.

PEARL: Never mind about my behaviour. Tell me how luncheon went off.

CLAY: My dear, it was like a gathering of relations who hate one another, after the funeral of a rich aunt who's left all her money to charity.

PEARL: It must have been priceless. I'd have given anything to be there.

CLAY: Why weren't you?

PEARL: Oh, I knew there'd be scenes, and I'm never at my best in a scene before luncheon. One of the things I've learnt from the war is that a general should choose his own time for a battle.

CLAY: Minnie moved heaven and earth to get away this morning.

PEARL: I knew she couldn't. I knew none of them could go till the afternoon.

CLAY: The train service is atrocious.

PEARL: George says that is one of the advantages of the place. It keeps it rural. There's one at nine and another at half-past four. I knew that not even the most violent disturbances would get people up at eight who never by any chance have breakfast till ten. As soon as I awoke I took the necessary steps.

CLAY: [*Interrupting.*] You slept?

PEARL: Oh yes, I slept beautifully. There's nothing like a little excitement to give me a good night.

CLAY: Well, you certainly had some excitement. I've rarely witnessed such a terrific scene.

PEARL: I sent out to the garage and gave instructions that the old Rolls-Royce was to be taken down at once and the other was to go to London.

CLAY: What for?

PEARL: Never mind. You'll know presently. Then I did a little telephoning.

CLAY: Why were you so anxious to prevent anybody from leaving the house?

PEARL: I couldn't have persuaded myself that my party was a success if half my guests had left me on Sunday morning. I thought they might change their minds by the afternoon.

CLAY: If that's your only reason, I don't think it's a very good one.

PEARL: It isn't. I will be frank with you, Thornton. I can imagine that a very amusing story might be made out of this episode. I never mind scandal, but I don't expose myself to ridicule if I can help it.

CLAY: My dear Pearl, surely you can trust the discretion of your guests. Who do you think will give it away?

PEARL: You.

CLAY: I? My dear Pearl, I give you my word of honour . . .

PEARL: [*Calmly.*] My dear Thornton, I don't care two-pence about your word of honour. You're a professional entertainer, and you'll sacrifice everything to a good story. Why, don't you remember that killing story about your father's death? You dined out a whole season on it.

CLAY: Well, it was a perfectly killing story. No one would have enjoyed it more than my poor old father.

PEARL: I'm not going to risk anything, Thornton. I think it's much better there should be no story to tell.

CLAY: No one can move the clock backwards, Pearl. I couldn't help thinking at luncheon that there were the elements of a very good story indeed.

PEARL: And you'll tell it, Thornton. Then I shall say: My dear, does it sound probable? They all stayed quite happily till Monday morning; Sturrey and the Arlingtons dined on the Sunday night, and we had a very merry evening. Besides, I was lunching with Minnie only two days afterwards. And I shall say: Poor Thornton, he *is* such a liar, isn't he?

CLAY: I confess that if you are reconciled with Minnie it will take a great deal of the point away from my story. What about Arthur Fenwick?

PEARL: He's a sensualist, and the sensual are always sentimental.

CLAY: He scared me dreadfully at luncheon. He was eating a dressed crab, and his face grew every minute more purple. I was expecting him to have an apoplectic fit.

PEARL: It's not an unpleasant death, you know, Thornton, to have a stroke while you're eating your favourite dish.

CLAY: You know, there are no excuses for you, Pearl.

PEARL: Human nature excuses so much, Thornton.

CLAY: You really might have left Tony alone. This habit you have of snitching has got you into trouble before.

PEARL: People are so selfish. It just happens that I find no man so desirable as one that a friend of mine is in love with. I make allowances for the idiosyncrasies of my friends. Why shouldn't they make allowances for mine?

[*The* DUCHESSE *comes in, erect and haughty,* with *the air of Boadicea facing the Roman legions.* PEARL *turns to her with an ingratiating smile.*

PEARL: Ah, Minnie.

DUCHESSE: I'm told the only way I can leave this house is by submitting to the odious necessity of seeing you.

PEARL: I wish you wouldn't go, Minnie. Lord Sturrey is coming over to dinner to-night, and so are the Arlingtons. I always take a lot of trouble to get the right people together, and I hate it when anybody fails me at the last minute.

DUCHESSE: D'you think anything would have induced me to stay so long if there'd been any possibility of getting away?

PEARL: It wouldn't have been nice to go without saying good-bye to me.

DUCHESSE: Don't talk nonsense, Pearl.

PEARL: D'you know that you behaved very badly last night, and I ought to be extremely angry with you?

DUCHESSE: I? Thornton, the woman's as mad as a hatter.

PEARL: You really oughtn't to have made a scene before Harry Bleane. And, you know, to tell Arthur wasn't playing the game. If you wanted to tell anyone, why didn't you tell George?

DUCHESSE: In the first place, he wasn't here. He never is.

PEARL: I know. He says that now society has taken to coming down to the country for week-ends he prefers London.

DUCHESSE: I'll never forgive you. Never. Never. Never. You'd got Arthur Fenwick. Why weren't you satisfied with him? If you wanted to have an affair with anyone, why didn't you take Thornton? He's almost the only one of your friends with whom you haven't. The omission is becoming almost marked.

PEARL: Thornton never makes love to me except when other people are looking. He can be very passionate in the front seat of my box at the opera.

CLAY: This conversation is growing excessively personal. I'll leave you.   [He goes out.

PEARL: I'm sorry I had to insist on your seeing me, but I had something quite important to say to you.

DUCHESSE: Before you go any further, Pearl, I wish to tell you that I'm going to marry Tony.

PEARL: [Aghast.] Minnie! Oh, my dear, you're not doing it to spite me? You know, honestly, he doesn't interest me in the slightest. Oh, Minnie, do think carefully.

DUCHESSE: It's the only way I can keep him.

PEARL: D'you think you'll be happy?

DUCHESSE: What should you care if I'm happy?

PEARL: Of course I care. D'you think it's wise? You're giving yourself into his hands. Oh, my dear, how can you risk it?

DUCHESSE: He said he was going out to the colonies. I love him. . . . I believe you're really distressed. How strange you are, Pearl! Perhaps it's the best thing for me. He may settle down. I was very lonely sometimes, you know. Sometimes, when I had the blues, I almost wished I'd never left home.

PEARL: And I've been moving heaven and earth to get him a job. I've been on the telephone this morning to all the Cabinet Ministers I know, and at last I've done it. That's what I wanted to tell you. I thought you'd be so pleased. I suppose now he won't want it.

DUCHESSE: Oh, I'm sure he will. He's very proud, you know. That's one of the things I liked in him. He had to be dependent on me, and that's partly why he always wanted to marry me.

PEARL: Of course, you'll keep your title.

DUCHESSE: Oh yes, I shall do that.

PEARL: [Going towards her as if to kiss her.] Well, darling, you have my very, very best wishes.

DUCHESSE: [Drawing back.] I'm not going to forgive you, Pearl.

PEARL: But you've forgiven Tony.

DUCHESSE: I don't blame him. He was led away.

PEARL: Come, Minnie, don't be spiteful. You might let bygones be bygones.

DUCHESSE: Nothing will induce me to stay in this house another night.

PEARL: It's a very slow train, and you'll have to go without your tea.

DUCHESSE: I don't care.

PEARL: You won't arrive in London till half-past eight, and you'll have to dine in a restaurant.

DUCHESSE: I don't care.

PEARL: You'll be grubby and hot. Tony will be hungry and out of temper. And you'll look your age.

DUCHESSE: You promised me the luggage cart.

PEARL: [*With a sigh.*] You shall have it; but you'll have to sit on the floor, because it hasn't got any seats.

DUCHESSE: Pearl, it's not going to break down on the way to the station?

PEARL: Oh, no. How can you suspect me of playing a trick like that on you? . . . [*With a tinge of regret.*] It never occurred to me.

[THORNTON CLAY *comes in.*

CLAY: Pearl, I thought you'd like to know that Fenwick is coming to say good-bye to you.

DUCHESSE: I'll go and tell Tony about the job you've got him. By the way, what is it?

PEARL: Oh, it's something in the Education Office.

DUCHESSE: How very nice. What do they do there?

PEARL: Nothing. But it'll keep him busy from ten to four.

[*The* DUCHESSE *goes out.*]

PEARL: She's going to marry him.

CLAY: I know.

PEARL: I'm a wonderful matchmaker. First Bessie and Harry Bleane, and now Minnie and Tony Paxton. I shall have to find someone for you, Thornton.

CLAY: How on earth did you manage to appease her?

PEARL: I reasoned with her. After all, she should be glad the boy has sown his wild oats before he marries. And besides, if he were her husband, of course she wouldn't expect fidelity from him; it seems unnatural to expect it when he isn't.

CLAY: But she's going all the same.

PEARL: I've got a quarter of an hour yet. Give me your handkerchief, will you?

CLAY: [*Handing it to her.*] You're not going to burst into tears?

PEARL: [*She rubs her cheeks violently.*] I thought I ought to look a little wan and pale when Arthur comes in.

CLAY: You'll never love me, Pearl. You tell me all your secrets.

PEARL: Shall I tell you what to do about it? Take the advice I give to Americans who come over to London and want to see the Tower: say you've been, and don't go.

CLAY: D'you think you can bring Arthur round?

PEARL: I'm sure I could if he loved me.

CLAY: My dear, he dotes on you.

PEARL: Don't be a fool, Thornton. He loves his love for me. That's quite a different thing. I've only got one chance. He sees himself as the man of iron. I'm going to play the dear little thing racket.

CLAY: You're a most unscrupulous woman, Pearl.

PEARL: Not more than most. Please go. I think he ought to find me alone.

> [CLAY *goes out.* PEARL *seats herself in a pensive attitude and looks down at the carpet; in her hand she holds dejectedly an open volume of poetry. Presently* ARTHUR FENWICK *comes in. She pretends not to see him. He is the strong man, battered but not beaten, struggling with the emotion which he tries to master.*

FENWICK: Pearl!

PEARL: [*With a jump.*] Oh, how you startled me. I didn't hear you come in.

FENWICK: I daresay you're surprised to see me. I thought it was necessary that we should have a short conversation before I left this house.

PEARL: [*Looking away.*] I'm glad to see you once more.

FENWICK: You understand that everything is over between us.

PEARL: If you've made up your mind, there's nothing for me to say. I know that nothing can move you when you've once done that.

FENWICK: [*Drawing himself up a little.*] No. That has always been part of my power.

PEARL: I wouldn't have you otherwise.

FENWICK: I don't want to part from you in anger, Pearl. Last night I could have thrashed you within an inch of your life.

PEARL: Why didn't you? D'you think I'd have minded that from the man I loved?

FENWICK: You know I could never hit a woman.

PEARL: I thought of you all through the long hours of the night, Arthur.

FENWICK: I never slept a wink.

PEARL: One would never think it. You must be made of iron.

FENWICK: I think I am sometimes.

PEARL: Am I very pale!

FENWICK: A little.

PEARL: I feel a perfect wreck.

FENWICK: You must go and lie down. It's no good making yourself ill.

PEARL: Oh, don't bother about me, Arthur.

FENWICK: I've bothered about you so long. It's difficult for me to get out of the habit all at once.

PEARL: Every word you say stabs me to the heart.

FENWICK: I'll get done quickly with what I had to tell you and then go. It's merely this. Of course, I shall continue the allowance I've always made you.

PEARL: Oh, I couldn't take it. I couldn't take it.

FENWICK: You must be reasonable, Pearl. This is a matter of business.

PEARL: It's a question I refuse to discuss. Nothing would have induced me to accept your help if I hadn't loved you. Now that there can be nothing more between us— no, no, the thought outrages me.

FENWICK: I was afraid that you'd take up that attitude. Remember that you've only got eight thousand a year of your own. You can't live on that.

PEARL: I can starve.

FENWICK: I must insist, Pearl, for my own sake. You've adopted a style of living which you would never have done if you hadn't had me at the back of you. I'm morally responsible, and I must meet my obligations.

PEARL: We can only be friends in future, Arthur.

FENWICK: I haven't often asked you to do anything for me, Pearl.

PEARL: I shall return your presents. Let me give you my pearl necklace at once.

FENWICK: Girlie, you wouldn't do that.

PEARL: [*Pretending to try and take the necklace off.*] I can't undo the clasp. Please help me.

> [*She goes up to him and turns her back so that he may get at it.*

FENWICK: I won't. I won't.

PEARL: I'll tear it off my neck.

FENWICK: Pearl, you break my heart. Do you care for me so little that you can't bear to wear the trifling presents I gave you.

PEARL: If you talk to me like that I shall cry. Don't you see that I'm trying to keep my self-control?

FENWICK: This is dreadful. This is even more painful than I anticipated.

PEARL: You see, strength is easy to you. I'm weak. That's why I put myself in your hands. I felt your power instinctively.

FENWICK: I know, I know, and it was because I felt you needed me that I loved you. I wanted to shelter you from the storms and buffets of the world.

PEARL: Why didn't you save me from myself, Arthur?

FENWICK: When I look at your poor, pale little face I wonder what you'll do without me, girlie.

PEARL: [*Her voice breaking.*] It'll be very hard. I've grown so used to depending on you. Whenever anything has gone wrong, I've come to you and you've put it right. I was beginning to think there was nothing you couldn't do.

FENWICK: I've always welcomed obstacles. I like something to surmount. It excites me.

PEARL: You seemed to take all my strength from me. I felt strangely weak beside you.

FENWICK: It wasn't necessary that we should both be strong. I loved you because you were weak. I liked you to come to me in all your troubles. It made me feel so good to be able to put everything right for you.

PEARL: You've always been able to do the impossible.

FENWICK: [*Impressively.*] I have never found anything impossible.

PEARL: [*Deeply moved.*] Except to forgive.

FENWICK: Ah, I see you know me. I never forget. I never forgive.

PEARL: I suppose that's why people feel there's something strangely Napoleonic about you.

FENWICK: Maybe. And yet—though you're only a woman, you've broken me, Pearl, you've broken me.

PEARL: Oh no, don't say that. I couldn't bear that. I want you to go on being strong and ruthless.

FENWICK: Something has gone out of my life for ever. I almost think you've broken my heart. I was so proud of you. I took so much pleasure in your success. Why, whenever I saw your name in the society columns of the papers it used to give me a thrill of satisfaction. What's going to become of you now, girlie? What's going to become of you now?

PEARL: I don't know; I don't care.

FENWICK: This fellow, does he care for you? Will he make you happy?

PEARL: Tony? He's going to marry the Duchess. [FENWICK *represses a start*.] I shall never see him again.

FENWICK: Then if I leave you, you'll have nobody but your husband.

PEARL: Nobody.

FENWICK: You'll be terribly lonely, girlie.

PEARL: You will think of me sometimes, Arthur, won't you?

FENWICK: I shall never forget you, girlie. I shall never forget how you used to leave your fine house in Mayfair and come and lunch with me down town.

PEARL: You used to give me such delicious things to eat.

FENWICK: It was a treat to see you in your beautiful clothes sharing a steak with me and a bottle of beer. I can order a steak, Pearl, can't I?

PEARL: And d'you remember those delicious little onions that we used to have? [*She seems to taste them.*] M . . . M . . . M . . . It makes my mouth water to think of them.

FENWICK: There are few women who enjoy food as much as you do, Pearl.

PEARL: D'you know, next time you dined with me, I'd made up my mind to give you an entirely English dinner. Scotch broth, herrings, mixed grill, saddle of lamb, and then enormous marrow bones.

> [FENWICK *can hardly bear the thought, his face grows red, his eyes bulge, and he gasps.*]

FENWICK: Oh, girlie! [*With utter abandonment.*] Let's have that dinner. [*He seizes her in his arms and kisses her.*] I can't leave you. You need me too much.

PEARL: Arthur, Arthur, can you forgive me?

FENWICK: To err is human, to forgive divine.

PEARL: Oh, how like you that is!

FENWICK: If you must deceive me, don't let me ever find out. I love you too much.

PEARL: I won't, Arthur, I promise you I won't.

FENWICK: Come and sit on the sofa and let me look at you. I seem to see you for the first time.

PEARL: You know, you wouldn't have liked the walk to the station. It's four miles in the sun. You're a vain old thing, and your boots are always a little too small for you.

> [BESSIE *comes in. She stops as she sees* PEARL *and* FENWICK *sitting hand in hand.*]

PEARL: Are you going out, Bessie?

BESSIE: As soon as Harry has finished his letters, we're going for a walk.

PEARL: [*To* FENWICK.] You mustn't squeeze my hand in Bessie's presence, Arthur.

FENWICK: You're a very lucky girl, Bessie, to have a sister like Pearl. She's the most wonderful woman in the world.

PEARL: You're talking nonsense, Arthur. Go and put some flannels on. It makes me quite hot to look at you in that suit. We'll try and get up a little tennis after tea.

FENWICK: Now, you mustn't tire yourself, Pearl. Remember those white cheeks of yours.

PEARL: [*With a charming look at him.*] Oh, I shall soon get my colour back now.

> [*She gives him her hand to kiss and he goes out. Pearl takes a little mirror out of her bag and looks at herself reflectively.*

PEARL: Men are very trivial, foolish creatures. They have kind hearts. But their heads. Oh dear, oh dear, it's lamentable. And they're so vain, poor dears, they're so vain.

BESSIE: Pearl, to-morrow, when we go back to London, I'm going away.

PEARL: Are you? Where?

BESSIE: The Princess is going to take me over to Paris for a few days.

PEARL: Oh, is that all? Don't stay away too long. You ought to be in London just at present.

BESSIE: On my return I'm proposing to stay with the Princess.

PEARL: [*Calmly.*] Nonsense.

BESSIE: I wasn't asking your permission, Pearl. I was telling you my plans.

PEARL: [*Looks at her for a moment reflectively.*] Are you going to make me a scene, too? I've already gone through two this afternoon. I'm rather tired of them.

BESSIE: Please don't be alarmed. I've got nothing more to say.

> [*She makes as though to leave the room.*

PEARL: Don't be a little fool, Bessie. You've been staying with me all the season. I can't allow you to leave my

house and go and live with Flora. We don't want to
go out of our way to make people gossip.

BESSIE: Please don't argue with me, Pearl. It's not my
business to reproach you for anything you do. But it
isn't my business, either, to stand by and watch.

PEARL: You're no longer a child, Bessie.

BESSIE: I've been blind and foolish. Because I was happy
and having a good time, I never stopped to ask for
explanations of this, that and the other. I never thought.
. . . The life was so gay and brilliant—it never struck
me that underneath it all—— Oh, Pearl, don't make me
say what I have in my heart, but let me go quietly.

PEARL: Bessie, dear, you must be reasonable. Think what
people would say if you suddenly left my house. They'd
ask all sorts of questions, and heaven knows what
explanations they'd invent. People aren't charitable, you
know. I don't want to be hard on you, but I can't afford
to let you do a thing like that.

BESSIE: Now that I know what I do, I should never respect
myself again if I stayed.

PEARL: I don't know how you can be so unkind.

BESSIE: I don't want to be that, Pearl. But it's stronger
than I am. I must go.

PEARL: [*With emotion.*] I'm so fond of you, Bessie. You
don't know how much I want you with me. After all,
I've seen so little of you these last few years. It's been
such a comfort to me to have you. You were so pretty
and young and sweet, it was like a ray of April sunshine
in the house.

BESSIE: I'm afraid you think women are as trivial, foolish
creatures as men, Pearl.

> [PEARL *looks up and sees that* BESSIE *is not in the least
> taken in by the pathetic attitude.*

PEARL: [*Icily.*] Take care you don't go too far, Bessie.

BESSIE: There's no need for us to quarrel. I've made up my mind, and there's the end of it.

PEARL: Flora's a fool. I shall tell her that I won't have her take you away from me. You'll stay with me until you're married.

BESSIE: D'you want me to tell you that I can hardly bear to speak to you? You fill me with shame and disgust. I want never to see you again.

PEARL: Really, you drive me beyond endurance. I think I must be the most patient woman in the world to put up with all I've had to put up with to-day. After all, what have I done? I was a little silly and incautious. By the fuss you all make one would think no one had ever been incautious and silly before. Besides, it hasn't got anything to do with you. Why don't you mind your own business?

BESSIE: [*Bitterly.*] You talk as though your relations with Arthur Fenwick were perfectly natural.

PEARL: Good heavens, you're not going to pretend you didn't know about Arthur. After all, I'm no worse than anybody else. Why, one of the reasons we Americans like London is that we can live our own lives and people accept things philosophically. Eleo Gloster, Sadie Twickenham, Maimie Hartlepool—you don't imagine they're faithful to their husbands? They didn't marry them for that.

BESSIE: Oh, Pearl, how can you? How **can** you? Haven't you any sense of decency at all? When I came in just now and saw you sitting on the sofa with that gross, vulgar, sensual old man—oh! [*She makes a gesture of disgust.*] You can't love him. I could have understood if . . . but—oh, it's so disgraceful, it's so hideous. What can you see in him? He's nothing but rich. . . . [*She pauses, and her face changes as a thought comes to her, and coming horrifies her.*] It's not because he's rich? Pearl! Oh!

PEARL: Really, Bessie, you're very silly, and I'm tired of talking to you.

BESSIE: Pearl, it's not that. Answer me. Answer me.

PEARL: [*Roughly.*] Mind your own business.

BESSIE: He was right, then, last night, when he called you that. He was so right that you didn't even notice it. A few hours later you're sitting hand in hand with him. A slut. That's what he called you. A slut. A slut.

PEARL: How dare you! Hold your tongue. How dare you!

BESSIE: A kept woman. That's what you are.

PEARL: [*Recovering herself.*] I'm a fool to lose my temper with you.

BESSIE: Why should you? I'm saying nothing but the truth.

PEARL: You're a silly little person, Bessie. If Arthur helps me a little, that's his affair, and mine. He's got more money than he knows what to do with, and it amuses him to see me spend it. I could have twenty thousand a year from him if I chose.

BESSIE: Haven't you got money of your own?

PEARL: You know exactly what I've got. Eight thousand a year. D'you think I could have got the position I have on that? You're not under the impression all the world comes to my house because of my charm, are you? I'm not. You don't think the English want us here? You don't think they like us marrying their men? Good heavens, when you've known England as long as I have you'll realise that in their hearts they still look upon us as savages and Red Indians. We have to force ourselves upon them. They come to me because I amuse them. Very early in my career I discovered that the English can never resist getting something for nothing. If a dancer is the rage, they'll see her at my house. If a fiddler is in vogue, they'll hear him at my concert.

I give them balls. I give them dinners. I've made myself the fashion, I've got power, I've got influence. But everything I've got—my success, my reputation, my notoriety—I've bought it, bought it, bought it.

BESSIE: How humiliating!

PEARL: And, finally, I've bought you a husband.

BESSIE: That's not true. He loves me.

PEARL: D'you think he'd have loved you if I hadn't shown you to him in these surroundings, if I hadn't dazzled him by the brilliant people among whom he found you. You don't know what love is made of. D'you think it's nothing that he should hear a Prime Minister pay you compliments. Of course I bought him.

BESSIE: [*Aghast.*] It's horrible.

PEARL: You know the truth now. It'll be very useful to you in your married life. Run away and take your little walk with Harry Bleane. I'm going to arrange my face.

> [*She goes out.* BESSIE *is left ashamed and stunned.* BLEANE *comes in.*]

BLEANE: I'm afraid I've kept you waiting. I'm so sorry.

BESSIE: [*Dully.*] It doesn't matter at all.

BLEANE: Where shall we go? You know the way about these parts, and I don't.

BESSIE: Harry, I want you to release me. I can't marry you.

BLEANE: [*Aghast.*] Why?

BESSIE: I want to go back to America. I'm frightened.

BLEANE: Of me?

BESSIE: Oh no, I know that you're a dear, good creature; I'm frightened of what I may become.

BLEANE: But I love you, Bessie.

BESSIE: Then that's all the more reason for me to go. I must tell you frankly. I'm not in love with you, I only like you. I would never have dreamt of marrying you, if you hadn't been who you are. I wanted to have a title. That's why Pearl married her husband, and that's why the Duchess married. Let me go, Harry.

BLEANE: I knew you didn't love me, but I thought you might come to in time. I thought if I tried I could make you love me.

BESSIE: You didn't know that I was nothing but a self-seeking, heartless snob.

BLEANE: I don't care what you say of yourself, I know that you can be nothing but what is true and charming.

BESSIE: After what you've seen last night? After what you know of this house? Aren't you disgusted with all of us?

BLEANE: You can't think I could class you with the Duchesse and . . . [He stops.]

BESSIE: Pearl at my age was no different from what I am. It's the life.

BLEANE: But perhaps you won't want to lead it. The set you've been living in here isn't the only set in England. It makes a stir because it's in the public eye. Its doings are announced in the papers. But it isn't a very good set, and there are plenty of people who don't very much admire it.

BESSIE: You must let me try and say what I have in my heart. And be patient with me. You think I can make myself at home in your life. I've had a hint of it now and then. I've seen a glimpse of it through Pearl's laughter and the Duchesse's sneers. It's a life of dignity, of responsibilities, and of public duty.

BLEANE: [With a rueful smile.] You make it very strenuous.

BESSIE: It comes naturally to the English girls of your class. They've known it all their lives, and they've been brought up to lead it. But we haven't. To us it's just tedious, and its dignity is irksome. We're bored, and we fall back on the only thing that offers, pleasure. You've spoken to me about your house. It means everything to you because it's associated with your childhood and all your people before you. It could only mean something to me if I loved you. And I don't.

BLEANE: You've made me so wretched. I don't know what to say to you.

BESSIE: If I make you wretched now, it's so that we may both be saved a great deal of unhappiness later on. I'm glad I don't care for you, for it would make it so much harder for me to go. And I've got to go. I can't marry you. I want to go home. If I marry ever I want to marry in my own country. That is my place.

BLEANE: Don't you think you could wait a little before you decide finally?

BESSIE: Don't put difficulties in my way. Don't you see that we're not strong enough for the life over here? It goes to our head; we lose our bearings; we put away our own code, and we can't adopt the code of the country we come to. We drift. There's nothing for us to do but amuse ourselves, and we fall to pieces. But in America we're safe. And perhaps America wants us. When we come over here we're like soldiers deserting our country in time of war. Oh, I'm homesick for America. I didn't know how much it meant to me till now. Let me go back, Harry.

BLEANE: If you don't want to marry me, of course, I'm not going to try and make you.

BESSIE: Don't be angry, and be my friend always.

BLEANE: Always.

BESSIE: After all, three months ago you didn't know me. In three months more you will have forgotten me. Then marry some English girl, who can live your life and share your thoughts. And be happy.

[PEARL *comes in. She has rouged her cheeks, and has once more the healthy colour which is usual with her. She is evidently jubilant.*

PEARL: The car has just come back from London. [*She goes to the french window and calls.*] Minnie!

BESSIE: I shall tell Pearl to-morrow.

BLEANE: I won't post my letters then. I'll go **and** get them out of the box.

BESSIE: Forgive me.

[*He goes out. The* DUCHESSE *and* CLAY *appear at the window.*

DUCHESSE: Did you call me?

PEARL: The car has just come back from London, so it can take you to the station.

DUCHESSE: That's a mercy. I didn't at all like the idea of going to the station in the luggage cart. Where is Flora? I must say good-bye to her.

PEARL: Oh, there's plenty of time now. The car will run you down in ten minutes.

[TONY *comes in, then the* PRINCESS *and* FLEMING.

DUCHESSE: Tony, the car has returned, and is going to take us to the station.

TONY: Thank God for that! I should have looked a perfect fool in that luggage cart.

CLAY: But what on earth did you send the car to London for, anyway?

PEARL: In one minute you'll see.

[ARTHUR FENWICK *comes in. He has changed into flannels.*

FENWICK: Who is that gentleman that's just arrived, Pearl?

PEARL: The man of mystery.

[*The* BUTLER *comes in, followed by* ERNEST, *and after announcing him goes out.*

POLE: Mr. Ernest.

DUCHESSE: Ernest!

CLAY: Ernest?

> [*He is a little dark man, with large eyes, and long hair neatly plastered down. He is dressed like a tailor's dummy, in black coat, white gloves, silk hat, patent leather boots. He is a dancing master, and overwhelmingly gentlemanly. He speaks in mincing tones.*

ERNEST: Dear Lady Grayston.

PEARL: [*Shaking hands with him.*] I'm so glad you were able to come. [*To the others.*] You were talking about Ernest last night, and I thought we would have nothing to do this evening and he would cheer and comfort us. I sent the car up to London with orders to bring him back dead or alive.

ERNEST: My dear Lady Grayston, I'm sure I'll get into no end of trouble. I had all sorts of calls to pay this afternoon, and I was dining out, and I'd promised to go to a little hop that the dear Duchess of Gloster was giving. But I felt I couldn't refuse *you.* You've always been such a good friend to me, dear Lady Grayston. You must excuse me coming in my town clothes, but your chauffeur said there wasn't a moment to lose, so I came just as I am.

PEARL: But you look a perfect picture.

ERNEST: Oh, don't say that, dear Lady Grayston; I know this isn't the sort of thing one ought to wear in the country.

PEARL: You remember the Duchesse de Surennes?

ERNEST: Oh, of course I remember the Duchesse.

DUCHESSE: Dear Ernest!

ERNEST: Dear Duchesse!

DUCHESSE: I thought I was never going to see **you** again, Ernest.

ERNEST: Oh, don't say that, it sounds too sad.

PEARL: It's such a pity you must go, Minnie. Ernest could have shown you all sorts of new steps.

ERNEST: Oh, dear Duchesse, you're not going the very moment I come down? That is unkind of you.

DUCHESSE: [*With an effort.*] I must go. I must go.

ERNEST: Have you been practising that little step I showed you the other day? My dear friend, the Marchioness of Twickenham—not the *old* one, you know, the *new* one— is beginning to do it so well.

DUCHESSE: [*Struggling with herself.*] Have we time, Pearl? I should like Ernest to dance just one two-step with me.

PEARL: Of course there's time. Thornton, set the gramophone.

[THORNTON CLAY *at once starts it, and the notes of the two-step tinkle out.*

DUCHESSE: You don't mind, Ernest, do you?

ERNEST: I love dancing with you, Duchesse.

[*They take up their positions.*

DUCHESSE: Just one moment. It always makes me so nervous to dance with you, Ernest.

ERNEST: Oh, now, don't be silly, dear Duchesse.

[*They begin to dance.*

ERNEST: Now hold your shoulders like a lady. Arch your back, my dear, arch your back. Don't look like a sack of potatoes. If you put your foot there, I shall kick it.

DUCHESSE: Oh, Ernest, don't be cross with me.

ERNEST: I shall be cross with you, Duchesse. You don't pay any attention to what I say. You must give your mind to it.

DUCHESSE: I do! I do!

ERNEST: And don't dance like an old fish-wife. Put some vim into it. That's what I always say about these modern dances: you want two things, vim and nous.

DUCHESSE: [*Plaintively.*] Ernest!

ERNEST: Now don't cry. I'm saying all this for your good, you know. What's wrong with you is that you've got no passion.

DUCHESSE: Oh, Ernest, how can you say such a thing. I've always looked upon myself as a very passionate woman.

ERNEST: I don't know anything about that, dear Duchesse, but you don't get it into your dancing. That's what I said the other day to the dear Marchioness of Twickenham—not the *new* one, you know, the *old* one—You must put passion into it, I said. That's what these modern dances want—passion, passion.

DUCHESSE: I see exactly what you mean, Ernest.

ERNEST: And you must dance with your eyes as well, you know. You must look as if you had a knife in your garter, and as if you'd kill me if I looked at another woman. Don't you see how I'm looking, I'm looking as though I meant, Curse her! how I love her. There!

[*The music stops and they separate.*

DUCHESSE: I have improved, Ernest, haven't I?

ERNEST: Yes, you've improved, dear Duchesse, but you want more practice.

PEARL: Minnie, why on earth don't you stay, and Ernest will give you a real lesson this evening.

ERNEST: That's what you want, Duchess.

[*The* DUCHESSE *wrestles with her soul.*

DUCHESSE: Tony, d'you think we can stop?

TONY: I didn't want to go away. It's rotten going up to town this evening. What on earth are we going to do with ourselves when we get there?

DUCHESSE: Very well, Pearl, if it'll please **you**, we'll stop.

PEARL: That is nice of you, Minnie.

DUCHESSE: You're very naughty sometimes, Pearl, but you have a good heart, and I can't help being fond of you.

PEARL: [*With outstretched arms.*] Minnie!

DUCHESSE: Pearl!

[*They clasp one another and affectionately embrace.*

ERNEST: What an exquisite spectacle—two ladies of title kissing one another.

BESSIE: [*To* FLEMING.] They're not worth making a fuss about. I'm sailing for America next Saturday!

THE END

THE UNATTAINABLE

A FARCE
in Three Acts

CHARACTERS

CAROLINE ASHLEY
ISABELLA TRENCH
MAUDE FULTON
COOPER
ROBERT OLDHAM
REX CUNNINGHAM
DR. CORNISH

The action takes place during the morning and afternoon of one day in the drawing-room of Caroline's house in Regent's Park.

THE UNATTAINABLE

THE FIRST ACT

SCENE: *The drawing-room of* CAROLINE'S *house in* Regent's *Park.*
It is spacious and airy. It is furnished in a pleasantly fantastic
manner by a woman who desires to be in the latest mode, but
who tempers it with her own good taste. The influence of
futurism is apparent in the carpet, the cushions, the coverings
of sofas and chairs; but there is nothing so outrageous as to
make the room merely a curiosity. Here and there large jars
of flowers contrast the sobriety of nature with the extravagance
of human imagination.

It is early summer and late in the morning.

COOPER, *a trim parlourmaid, ushers in* MRS. TRENCH.
ISABELLA TRENCH *is a woman of thirty-five, fair, plump,*
pretty still, well dressed and debonair. She has an attractive
softness and a great gift of sympathy. Her heart melts to
every unhappiness, and people in distress go to her in-
stinctively.

COOPER: I'll tell Mrs. Ashley you're here, madam.

ISABELLA: She's not down yet?

COOPER: No, madam, she's only just had her bath.

ISABELLA: Do ask her if I can come up. I want to see her
at once.

COOPER: Very good, madam.

ISABELLA: Tell her I'm frightfully excited.

COOPER: Very good, madam.

ISABELLA: [*With a smile.*] Of course you know, Cooper?

COOPER: Oh, yes, madam; it was cook saw it first. She

always likes to have a look at The Times before it goes upstairs.

ISABELLA: Was Mrs. Ashley surprised.

COOPER: Well, madam, she never said a word. She just kept staring at the announcement. As I said to cook, I really thought her eyes would pop out of her head.

ISABELLA: I must see her at once, Cooper.

COOPER: I'll go and tell her, madam. [*As she is going the telephone bell rings.* COOPER *answers it.*] Yes—who is it, please? No, miss, this is Mrs. Ashley's maid speaking. [*To* ISABELLA.] It's Miss Fulton, madam.

ISABELLA: Oh, let me speak to her. I think I know what she wants. Go and tell Mrs. Ashley I'm here.

COOPER: Very good, madam.

[*Exit.* ISABELLA *sits down and takes the receiver.*

ISABELLA: Maude, Maude! It's Isabella Trench speaking. I rang you up this morning, and they said you hadn't come up from the country. I have not seen Caroline yet. I know no more than you do, darling. I think it must be true. After all, it's in The Times. Why don't you come round? I'm sure Caroline will want to see you. Yes, that's it. You'll find me here. Good-bye.

[*She puts down the receiver.* COOPER *ushers in* REX CUNNINGHAM. *He is a nice-looking young man with dark eyes, and dark hair brushed back over his head and plastered down. He achieves a romantic look, notwithstanding his motor-coat and the cap that he carries in his hand.*

COOPER: Mr. Cunningham.

[REX *hesitates a moment as he sees a stranger in the room, then recognizes* ISABELLA *and comes forward cordially.* ISABELLA *greets him without warmth.*

REX: How do you do?

COOPER: Mrs. Ashley will be down directly, madam.

ISABELLA: Very well.

[*Exit* COOPER.

REX: [*Looking at his wrist watch.*] She promised she'd be ready on the minute.

ISABELLA: What for?

REX: I've got a new two-seater. I'm going to take her for a turn round Richmond Park.

ISABELLA: When did you make that arrangement?

REX: Last night.

[*She looks at him for a moment puzzled.*

ISABELLA: Haven't you heard the news?

REX: What news?

ISABELLA: Why, there's an announcement in The Times this morning of Stephen Ashley's death.

REX: My hat! . . . Ought one to condole with Caroline or congratulate her?

ISABELLA: I didn't know you called her Caroline.

REX: Didn't you?

ISABELLA: She hasn't seen her husband for over ten years. One can hardly expect her to be very much upset. Still, I don't think she'll want to go for a run in your two-seater.

REX: Why not?

ISABELLA: She'll have other things to do.

REX: Was her husband an awful brute?

ISABELLA: I don't know anything about him. Caroline never discusses her relations with him. I don't believe there's one of her friends who's ever seen him even.

REX: I asked her once if he was cruel to her. She said no, he had adenoids.

ISABELLA: You seem to be on very intimate terms with Caroline.

REX: Do you disapprove?

ISABELLA: Very much.

REX: What shall we do about it?

ISABELLA: D'you know that Robert Oldham and Caroline have been madly in love with one another for the last ten years? It has given me a new faith in human nature to watch their charming affection for one another. They've waited all this time, and now at last Caroline is free. I'm so glad to think they have nothing to reproach themselves with. It's the happy ending to a fairy story.

REX: [*Dejectedly.*] I suppose you think the only thing I can do is to take myself off.

ISABELLA: Robert may be here any minute.

REX: I was looking forward enormously to our drive.

ISABELLA: Are you in love with Caroline?

REX: Desperately.

ISABELLA: [*Putting her hand on his arm.*] I'm so sorry. You must try and get over it.

REX: I shall never do that.

ISABELLA: But you knew about Robert.

REX: He's forty-five if he's a day. No man can be seriously in love at that age.

ISABELLA: Caroline oughtn't to have let you come here. She must have known that you cared for her.

REX: She told me she was in love with Robert Oldham.

ISABELLA: [*More and more sympathetic.*] Are you awfully unhappy?

REX: Awfully. Do you think there's no chance for me at all?

ISABELLA: It would be cruel to hold out any hopes to you. None—none whatever.

REX: [Sombrely.] My hat!

ISABELLA: Now you must go.

REX: All right. If you think I'd better. You've been awfully kind to me.

ISABELLA: I've got such a soft heart and you've touched it.

REX: May I call you Isabella?

ISABELLA: I'd like you to.

> [*She gives him her hand. He raises it to his lips and kisses it.*

ISABELLA: I'm such a sentimentalist. Love always moves me.

REX: Good-bye.

> [*Exit.* ISABELLA *wipes the tiny tears that glisten in the corner of her eyes.* CAROLINE *comes in. She is a very attractive woman of thirty-five, tall, slim, with humorous eyes and a charming smile. She is dressed for motoring.*

ISABELLA: Caroline!

CAROLINE: Have I kept you waiting?

ISABELLA: Why didn't you let me come up? I wanted to see you so badly.

CAROLINE: I don't let even my dearest friend see me till I've done my hair.

ISABELLA: I suppose you don't like your forehead?

CAROLINE: Not much. By the way, where is Rex? I saw his car from my window.

ISABELLA: I thought you wouldn't want to see him this morning. I sent him away.

CAROLINE: Why on earth did you do that?

ISABELLA: My dear, do you know he's in love with **you**?

CAROLINE: I should be a perfect fool if I didn't.

ISABELLA: He hasn't told you so?

CAROLINE: I'm beginning to think it's his only topic of conversation.

ISABELLA: My dear, how can you be so flippant?

CAROLINE: D'you think I ought to take him seriously?

ISABELLA: [*Not without acidity.*] Of course, he's very young, I don't suppose he means half he says.

CAROLINE: [*Chaffing her.*] Even if he means a quarter it's a good deal.

ISABELLA: D'you think he wants to marry you?

CAROLINE: I don't know. I'm sure he wants to elope with me.

ISABELLA: You're too exasperating, Caroline. But I didn't come here to talk about Rex.

CAROLINE: D'you call him Rex?

ISABELLA: He asked me to just now.

CAROLINE: [*Smiling.*] Oh!

ISABELLA: Now, Caroline, be serious. *Is it true?* When I read the births, deaths, and marriages in The Times this morning, and suddenly saw your name, I could hardly believe my eyes.

CAROLINE: Neither could I. "On the 29th ult., at the Edward and Alexandra Hospital, Nairobi, Stephen, only son of the late Algernon Ashley of Bleane Woods, Faversham, aged 41. By Cable."

ISABELLA: It must be true.

CAROLINE: Of course, it's very circumstantial, but Stephen had a peculiar sense of humour. He's been reported dead two or three times. It's true, it's never got so far as the obituary column of The Times before.

ISABELLA: Can't you make certain?

CAROLINE: I telephoned to my solicitors and they've cabled to Nairobi. Somehow I think it is true this time.

ISABELLA: Shall you go into mourning?

CAROLINE: I don't see why I should.

ISABELLA: I wouldn't unless you think it'll become you.

CAROLINE: After all, I haven't seen or heard of my husband for more than ten years. It would be hypocrisy to pretend that I regret his death.

ISABELLA: I never knew exactly why you separated from him.

CAROLINE: Oh, he had adenoids.

ISABELLA: [*Smiling.*] You are the most reserved person I ever met.

CAROLINE: I managed not to discuss his failings while he was alive. I think I may just as well hold my tongue about them now he's dead.

ISABELLA: Ah, well, whatever you suffered it's all over now. You've only got happiness to look forward to. Oh, my dear, marry Robert quickly. Don't let there be any delays. Heaven knows you've waited long enough.

CAROLINE: Ten years.

ISABELLA: Aren't you glad now that you have nothing to reproach yourselves with? I know, I'm very glad for you.

CAROLINE: There was never any possibility of anything else. Of course, we might have bolted but Robert has practised too long in the Divorce Court to fancy the rôle of co-respondent. Besides, he had nothing but his practice to live upon. And we were too fond of one another to risk the infinite tediousness of an affair.

ISABELLA: Everyone must admire your strength.

CAROLINE: It didn't require strength, only common sense.

ISABELLA: Have you heard from him this morning?

CAROLINE: No, I knew he had to be in chambers early.

ISABELLA: He's certain to come round presently.

CAROLINE: I shouldn't think so. He's in a case that's first on the list.

ISABELLA: Aren't you excited? I wonder how you can bear your impatience.

CAROLINE: I can hardly expect Robert to throw up a case to come and propose to me, can I?

> [COOPER *enters to announce* MAUDE FULTON. *She is a smartly-dressed spinster not far off forty, with bright eyes and a vivacious manner. She has a sharp tongue. She is sentimental when other people are concerned, but exceedingly practical in her own affairs.*

COOPER: Miss Fulton.

[*Exit.*

MAUDE: Oh, my dear, I've had a success. I've been followed in the street.

CAROLINE: [*Amused, greeting her.*] Maude!

MAUDE: I was rushing along here, when suddenly I realized that a man was following me. Well, I wanted to make sure, so I crossed to the other side of the street, and he crossed too. I slackened down. . . . I was simply running along, I was so anxious to see you and dear Robert—and *he* slackened down.

ISABELLA: Weren't you frightened?

MAUDE: Frightened? Of course not. I'm constantly being followed in the street. I like it. It gives an amusement to the dullest walk. Of course, it never goes any further.

CAROLINE: Do you say that with relief or with regret?

MAUDE: Oh, my dear, I should never have a moment to myself if I listened to all the men who want to make love to me. Of course, I cannot make out what it is they see in me. I know I'm not beautiful, but there's evidently something about me that they can't resist.

CAROLINE: [*Chaffing her.*] I expect it is that you throw yourself at their heads. I never knew a man yet who could resist that.

MAUDE: Oh, my dear, I quite forgot. My best congratulations.

CAROLINE: On the death of my husband?

MAUDE: And on your engagement to Robert Oldham.

CAROLINE: It's very kind of you, but I'm not engaged to Robert Oldham.

MAUDE: Oh, nonsense; that follows automatically on the death of your husband, like putting a penny in the slot and getting a piece of chocolate out. I suppose he's running along to Somerset House now to get a special licence.

CAROLINE: My dear, don't be ridiculous. He hasn't asked me to marry him.

ISABELLA: But he's going to.

CAROLINE: [*Thoughtfully.*] I suppose he is.

MAUDE: What on earth d'you mean, Caroline? You know he is.

CAROLINE: [*With exasperation.*] Yes, of course I do. But don't badger me. You talk as if we had to marry if we liked it or not. I'm not going to force the man to marry me.

MAUDE: Oh, my dear, don't talk such nonsense. He's been passionately in love with you for years.

CAROLINE: For years!

ISABELLA: And you've been just as much in love with him, Caroline.

CAROLINE: I know I have.

MAUDE: You've both been looking forward to this moment even since you met one another?

CAROLINE: And now it's come.

ISABELLA: What a funny thing to say, Caroline.

CAROLINE: It's the obvious thing to say, isn't it? I'm getting into training for married life.

ISABELLA: How strange you are this morning. I expected to
find you, oh, I scarcely know—tremulous, crying a
little, perhaps. . . .

CAROLINE: [*With a smile.*] I suppose you were prepared to
mingle your tears with mine.

ISABELLA: Happy tears. I certainly didn't expect to find
you . . .

CAROLINE: What?

MAUDE: In a beastly temper, my dear.

ISABELLA: Be nice to Robert when he comes, Caroline.
Think how he must be hating that stupid case which
is keeping him away. Don't you know what his thoughts
are? I do. He's counting the minutes—why, I can
almost hear the beating of his heart.

CAROLINE: What nonsense you talk, Isabella.

ISABELLA: Can't you see him, when he gets here at last,
ringing the bell? And the time seems interminable
till Cooper opens the door. And then he'll run up the
stairs four at a time.

CAROLINE: It's just like a penny novelette, isn't it? But he
won't, because it would make him out of breath.

ISABELLA: As if he'll think of that, you foolish creature.
He'll just take you in his arms and say: At last, at last—
I see it all.

MAUDE: I'd love to be here. I adore romance.

CAROLINE: I shall be greatly obliged if you'll both of you
go away before he comes.

ISABELLA: Of course, darling. There are moments when one
has a right to be rid of prying eyes.

MAUDE: When did he say he was coming?

CAROLINE: He hasn't said. I've not heard from him this
morning.

MAUDE: D'you mean to say he didn't telephone? I wonder
why not.

CAROLINE: Perhaps he hadn't time to look at the paper. He may not know.

MAUDE: Oh, nonsense.

ISABELLA: I think it's very natural he shouldn't have telephoned. After all, Stephen Ashley *was* your husband. Robert is a man of the greatest delicacy. It may easily have occured to him that just at that moment you might have certain memories that you preferred to be left alone with.

CAROLINE: How long do you give his delicacy?

MAUDE: Till the court rises, personally.

ISABELLA: [*Smiling.*] I believe you're just as impatient as I know he is.

CAROLINE: My dear, when you've been staying at the seaside, haven't you sometimes gone down to the beach meaning to have a bathe, and when you got there found the sea look very chilly? You try not to notice it. You go into your bathing machine, and it's grey and comfortless. But you take off your clothes and put on your bathing dress, and then you open the door. You see in front of you a narrow bit of sea. And it's cold and yellow and dreary and wet. And your heart sinks.

MAUDE: The only thing then is not to think about it, but to jump in quickly.

CAROLINE: I'm wondering if that is what Robert is saying to himself just now.

ISABELLA: What on earth makes you think that?

CAROLINE: It's a very good plan to ascribe your own feelings to other people.

MAUDE: My dear, you don't mean to say you're frightened?

CAROLINE: [*Desperately.*] Panic-stricken.

ISABELLA: How foolish you are, Caroline! You don't mean to say you have any doubt about Robert's devotion?

MAUDE: Oh, is *that* what's troubling you?

ISABELLA: Why, everyone knows he adores you. Don't you know how he speaks about you to your friends? I remember, last New Year's Eve when we were having supper together at the Savoy, I said to him: Doesn't it make you rather melancholy to think that another year is gone? No, he said, every New Year that comes brings me nearer to marrying Caroline.

CAROLINE: He's a dear old thing. Of course, I know he loves me.

MAUDE: We have inspired love, you and I, Caroline.

CAROLINE: But your adorers don't put a pistol to your head and say: Marry me.

MAUDE: No, but they frequently put one to their own and say they'll shoot themselves if I don't.

CAROLINE: You're still a spinster, Maude, how do you meet the situation?

MAUDE: I tell them the truth. After mature consideration I have come to the conclusion that one husband is not enough for one woman.

CAROLINE: Good heavens, I found one much more than I wanted.

MAUDE: That doesn't prove that you might not have found three more satisfactory.

ISABELLA: Three!

MAUDE: That is my ideal. I would live two days a week with each and have my Sundays to myself.

> [*The telephone bell rings.*

ISABELLA: That is Robert.

CAROLINE: It can't be. He must be in court just now.

> [*She goes towards the telephone. It keeps on ringing.*

ISABELLA: I have a presentiment. I'm convinced it's Robert.

> [*Just as* CAROLINE *is about to take the receiver she hesitates; she is very nervous.*

CAROLINE: Answer for me, Maude, in case . . .

MAUDE: Very well.

> [*She takes up the receiver and listens.*

CAROLINE: I hate telephones. I wish I'd never had one put in.

MAUDE: Who is that? No. This is Miss Fulton speaking, but I'll call Mrs. Ashley—yes, I'll hold on.

CAROLINE: Maude, who is it?

MAUDE: [*Significantly.*] Mr. Oldham's clerk.

CAROLINE: [*Agitated.*] Maude, say I can't speak to anybody. Say I'm out. Say you don't know when I'll be in.

MAUDE: [*Into the receiver.*] Is that you, Robert? This is Maud Fulton. Caroline is here. Yes, she'll be delighted to see you.

CAROLINE: Maude, I'm out. I'm out, I tell you. Say you've made a mistake. Maude, you cat!

MAUDE: [*Taking no notice.*] Yes, you'd better come round at once. Of course Caroline's disengaged; she's been expecting you.

CAROLINE: [*Aghast.*] Maude!

MAUDE: Good-bye. [*She puts down the receiver.*] That settles that.

CAROLINE: Maude, I'll never forgive you. It's monstrous. You had no right to say all that. I'll never speak to you again as long as I live. You said I'd been expecting him.

MAUDE: Well, haven't you? And what's more, he knows you've been expecting him. After all these years it really is not worth while for you to play hide-and-seek with one another.

CAROLINE: It's so humiliating. You've told him almost in so many words that I'm sitting here waiting for him to come and make me a proposal of marriage.

MAUDE: So you are.

CAROLINE: Has the possibility occurred to you that I may refuse him?

MAUDE: [*Decidedly.*] No.

CAROLINE: Why not?

MAUDE: You've let him wait for you year after year. He's given you the best of his life. He's sacrificed everything in the hope of marrying you some day. Now you must marry him if you want to or not.

ISABELLA: But you do want to, Caroline?

CAROLINE: [*Hesitatingly.*] I thought so yesterday.

ISABELLA: You know he dotes on you. You'll never find anyone who will love you so faithfully.

CAROLINE: It's loving that's the important thing, not being loved.

MAUDE: But you love him, Caroline. Don't be so silly. All your friends have known for ten years that you loved him. You're not like me. You're one of those constant women. You've never bothered your head about another man since first you made Robert's acquaintance.

ISABELLA: Your feelings can't have changed from one day to another.

CAROLINE: I suppose they can't.

ISABELLA: You *must* accept him, Caroline.

CAROLINE: Yes, I know. [*With a smile.*] Don't be afraid. I'm going to. . . . But don't be harsh with me. It can't be very strange that I'm a little nervous. In fact, I distinctly feel my heart beating in my boots.

ISABELLA: Never mind that. The shyness you're feeling gives you a sort of tremulous charm which, I promise you, is very effective.

CAROLINE: I must go and put on some other things. It's only fair to Robert to set out the object he's going to purchase to the best advantage.

ISABELLA: No matter what you wear he'll think you ravishing.

CAROLINE: Dear Robert. I know. But for all that I will not be proposed to in a motor-coat.

ISABELLA: You're going to make him very happy.

CAROLINE: I think I am. I was very foolish just now. I'm beginning to feel more at ease. After all, it is a great pleasure to know that after all his kindness to me, all his unselfish devotion, I have it in my power at last to give him his heart's desire.

[*Exit.*

MAUDE: That's that.

ISABELLA: Poor Caroline!

MAUDE: Now, will you tell me what is the matter with her.

ISABELLA: [*With a shrug of shoulders.*] Hope deferred. When you've wanted something very badly and it comes at last, it is somehow a little frightening.

MAUDE: You're sure there isn't another man somewhere lurking in the background!

ISABELLA: Oh, quite. Rex Cunningham was here this morning, but she didn't see him. I sent him away.

MAUDE: Very wise of you.

ISABELLA: I felt sorry for him. He's desperately in love with her. But I'm sure she isn't even interested in him. She's only known him three months.

MAUDE: A man you've known three months always has an advantage over a man you've known ten years.

ISABELLA: Now I know why you never married, Maude.

MAUDE: Why?

ISABELLA: Because nobody asked you.

MAUDE: How did you guess?

ISABELLA: Because you have common sense. Men like it in a wife, but not in a girl.

MAUDE: I'm very glad you sent Rex away. When next he comes he'll find everything settled.

> [*Enter* COOPER, *followed by* REX.

COOPER: Mr. Cunningham.

> [*Exit* COOPER. *The two ladies are taken aback by his unexpected appearance. He is not a little surprised to find* ISABELLA *still there.*

REX: Oh, I was expecting to find Caroline. [*Shaking hands with* MISS FULTON.] How do you do?

MAUDE: [*Promptly.*] She'll be down in one moment. You must stay.

REX: I was going to.

ISABELLA: I thought you were going for a drive?

REX: Alone? I just tootled round the Park, and then I made up my mind that I must see Caroline.

MAUDE: I quite understand. It's nice of you to want to be the first.

REX: [*Not comprehending.*] I beg your pardon?

MAUDE: [*Sweetly.*] To congratulate her on her engagement.

REX: [*With consternation.*] What?

MAUDE: You don't mean to say you didn't know? She's to be married to Robert Oldham almost directly. I think it's so charming that these two dear people should come together after all these years. And you know, they're madly in love with one another.

REX: But they weren't engaged a quarter of an hour ago.

MAUDE: Oh, that's nothing. I've been frequently engaged and broken it off again within twelve minutes.

REX: Of course, that's quite comprehensible.

MAUDE: Do you think so? It isn't true.

REX: It might be. Anyhow, I'm going to wait till I see Caroline.

MAUDE: Why?

REX: Because I'm going to propose to her, if you want to know. [*To* ISABELLA.] I ought never to have let you chivvy me away. It's impossible that she should marry Robert Oldham. It'll break my heart. If you have any kindness you won't try and prevent me from seeing her. I must see her.

MAUDE: Of course, you must see her. You'll hardly recognize her. She looks ten years younger. She's simply radiant. I've never seen anyone look so happy. How she adores that man! [REX *gives a gasp.*] They're going to be married by special licence. They've already made up their minds to go to Venice for their honeymoon. Robert had to go away for a few minutes; she could hardly bear to let him out of her sight.

REX: [*Sinking down crushed.*] My hat! I shall never get over this.

ISABELLA: [*Going up to him.*] My poor boy! Rex! Rex!

REX: It's just like my luck. That's the sort of thing that always happens to me.

MAUDE: I never loved a young gazelle but it was sure to die.

ISABELLA: Maude! [*To* REX *compassionately.*] It breaks my heart to see you so wretched.

REX: Nobody ever cares for me.

ISABELLA: Don't say that. It sounds so hopeless.

REX: [*Getting up.*] I'd better go. There's nothing for me to do here now.

ISABELLA: [*Taking his hand.*] Where are you going?

REX: I don't know, I don't care.

ISABELLA: I can't bear to see you like this. . . . Won't you come and dine with me to-night?

REX: You'll find me very dull.

ISABELLA: Oh, no, I shan't.

REX: [*Still holding her hand.*] Very well. You are good to me

ISABELLA: Good-bye.

REX: You have an extraordinary gift of sympathy. There's something about the blueness of your eyes that seems to console one.

ISABELLA: Dear Rex.

[*He goes out with a bow to* MAUDE.

MAUDE: Well, my dear, you're wasting no time.

ISABELLA: [*Indignantly.*] Maude! The poor boy was absolutely broken up. It made my heart bleed. I couldn't let him go without a word of comfort.

MAUDE: H'm! Why did you ask him to dinner?

ISABELLA: I thought he'd like to talk to me about Caroline. I couldn't bear to think of him passing the whole evening by himself. He would have been too wretched.

MAUDE: Oh, well, with a husband safely tucked away in India you can afford to be a sympathetic friend.

ISABELLA: What things you said to him! It simply made my hair stand on end.

MAUDE: Don't you think it was much the best thing to do? Caroline is in a funny mood. There's something pathetic and rather charming about that young man. I don't deny it for a minute. I've got a heart just as much as you have, my dear. There's no knowing what Caroline might have done in a moment of emotion. It was much better to face him with the accomplished fact.

ISABELLA: You're a wonderful liar, Maude.

MAUDE: Don't be idiotic, my dear. To lie well is one of the privileges of our sex. I don't lie any better than you do. Besides, were they lies? I was only anticipating. In half an hour all I said will be true.

ISABELLA: I don't say you weren't justified.

MAUDE: And what is half an hour? Just think how time changes from one place to another. Why, Caroline's engagement is already ancient history in Petrograd.

ISABELLA: Yes, if you look at it like that it's a white lie at the utmost.

MAUDE: Oh, my dear, not even that. Hardly more than a fib.

> [COOPER *comes in followed by* ROBERT OLDHAM. ROBERT *is a tall handsome man of five-and-forty, well-preserved, but inclined to stoutness; he is well dressed, well cared for, and evidently desirous to hold on to a semblance of youth.*

COOPER: Mr. Oldham.

> [*Exit.*

MAUDE: [*Enthusiastically.*] Robert!

ISABELLA: [*Sympathetically.*] Dear Robert.

> [ROBERT *is a little taken aback at the warmth of his greeting, but he braces himself and advances into the room.*

ROBERT: You welcome me as though I'd had a narrow shave of being run over by a motor-bus.

ISABELLA: We're very glad to see you.

MAUDE: We've been waiting for you all the morning.

ROBERT: Oh! [*With an effort at alacrity.*] I wish I'd known.

> [*Shakes hands with* MAUDE.] How do you do?

MAUDE: I *must* kiss you.

ROBERT: Must you?

MAUDE: [*Drawing back coyly.*] Don't you want me to?

ROBERT: Of course I do. I'd like it.

> [*He offers her his cheek and she kisses him.*

MAUDE: Now don't pretend you're as cool as a cucumber. Men are so silly. They're so afraid of their emotions. Of course, you're all in a flutter. Let me feel your pulse.

ROBERT: I shall not. You're very familiar with me, Maude; I don't like it.

MAUDE: Dear Robert.

F

ROBERT: [*To* ISABELLA, *taking her hand.*] And how are you, dear lady?

> [*She leaves her hand in his. It must be a habit of hers.*

ISABELLA: [*A little tremulously.*] I hardly know what to say to you. Oh, Robert, I'm so happy in your happiness. Isn't it wonderful? After all these years—it's so stupid of me, I almost feel as if I could cry.

ROBERT: You have a wonderful heart, Isabella.

ISABELLA: You know I'm not clever. . . . I can't express myself, but believe me, I feel all that you could wish me to feel.

ROBERT: You may kiss me if you wish to.

ISABELLA: [*Laughing.*] I don't.

ROBERT: A rebuff.

MAUDE: But how on earth have you managed to get here?

ROBERT: By the drastic method of taking a taxi.

MAUDE: Don't be exasperating. We were under the impression you had a case this morning.

ROBERT: Who is we?

MAUDE: Caroline, Isabella, and myself.

ROBERT: I see. No; a case which was expected to finish yesterday has turned out rather a long one. I dare say we shan't come on to-day at all.

MAUDE: [*Promptly.*] Then why didn't you come earlier?

ROBERT: It's only midday. I know that Caroline is not an early riser.

MAUDE: You might have telephoned.

ROBERT: I had some papers to read. Business before pleasure, you know. . . . Have you been discussing my silence?

ISABELLA: [*Smiling.*] I think I was right after all. I put it down to delicacy. Any nice man would realize that just at that moment a woman must prefer to be alone with her recollections.

MAUDE: Anyhow, the important thing is that you're here now. And if I know you at all you've got a ring in your pocket.

[ROBERT *gives a slight start.*

ISABELLA: Oh, Robert, do show it me! I'd love to see it.

ROBERT: But I haven't got a ring. I went straight to chambers this morning and then I came straight here. It never occurred to me.

MAUDE: You stupid man! Caroline would have been so pleased.

ISABELLA: And touched. But never mind; when she sees you she'll think of nothing but that she's free and you're here. And for ever and ever you'll be here. Oh, Robert, be kind to her! Remember all she's gone through. You can never do too much for her.

ROBERT: I know.

MAUDE: Have you made up your mind where you're going to spend your honeymoon?

ROBERT: My dear Maude, it's only a couple of hours ago that I saw the sad news of Stephen Ashley's death.

MAUDE: Sad, do you call them?

ROBERT: For him, I mean. Of course, not for me. I don't suppose there's anybody who isn't cared for by someone or other. I expect somebody is regretting him.

MAUDE: I very much doubt it. I think we may safely look upon his death as a happy release.

ROBERT: I don't know why you say that. You know nothing about him except that he had adenoids.

ISABELLA: It's so splendid of Caroline never to have said a single word against him.

ROBERT: Oh, splendid. But, after all, a man may have

adenoids and yet be possessed of all kinds of—admirable qualities.

MAUDE: You're not going to stand up for him. If Caroline refused to say anything against him, it's certainly not because there was nothing to say.

ROBERT: Of course not.

MAUDE: It almost sounded as if you were taking his part.

ROBERT: Good heavens, don't be so literal. I was making a general observation. That's why conversation is impossible with women. They *will* find a personal application in a general statement. Besides, a man with my particular experience knows that a person may have all manner of virtues and yet be insupportable to live with.

ISABELLA: Fortunately that isn't the case with Caroline.

ROBERT: Oh, no; Caroline is wonderful. Who should know it better than I?

MAUDE: Personally, I recommend you to go to Venice.

ROBERT: [*As though he were just on the verge of starting.*] Now?

MAUDE: For your honeymoon I mean.

ROBERT: Oh, I beg your pardon; I'd forgotten for the moment. Can you quite see us gushing up and down the Grand Canal? I fancy we've known one another a little too long for Venice.

MAUDE: Oh, but marriage makes such a difference. You'll have to make one another's acquaintance all over again.

ROBERT: [*Not without anxiety.*] D'you think it'll change Caroline much? I don't know that I should wish that exactly. You see I'm used to this Caroline.

MAUDE: She'll be just the same, only more so.

ROBERT: That is reassuring, but rather vague. My idea would be rather to make a tour of the capitals of Europe.

MAUDE: But you'd spend all your time in railway stations.

ROBERT: I know. That is precisely where a man shows his superiority to a woman. She is flustered and nervous. She's certain they'll miss the train. But he is calm. He sees to the luggage nonchalantly. He has the tickets safe. He keeps an eagle eye on the umbrellas. This is a man—every inch of him, she says; I am but a poor weak woman. Believe me, those are very good lines on which to start married life. I think the capitals of Europe.

ISABELLA: My own impression is that Caroline will want to go to some quiet little place by the seaside.

ROBERT: I don't look my best in bathing costume.

ISABELLA: She'll want to be alone with you surely.

ROBERT: I won't bathe. Nothing will induce me to bathe. I hate cold water. I was only thinking this morning how I hated the sea.

MAUDE: [*Surprised.*] This morning. Why?

ROBERT: I don't know. It just occurred to me. Haven't you made up your mind sometimes in a weak moment to go and have a bathe? You go down to the beach and the sea looks icy. You try not to notice it. You go into your bathing machine, and it's cold and smelly. But you take off your clothes and put on your bathing costume, and then you open the door and you see in front of you a narrow bit of sea. And you wish you were dead.

> [*During this speech* MAUDE *and* ISABELLA *have first pricked up their ears, then stared at him, and, finally, they turn and look at one another with amazement.* CAROLINE *comes in. She is now charmingly gowned.*

ROBERT: How do you do?

CAROLINE: How d'you do?

MAUDE: You absurd things.

CAROLINE: [*Sharply.*] Don't be ridiculous, Maude.

ISABELLA: We really ought to be going, dear.

CAROLINE: Oh, aren't you going to stay to luncheon?

ISABELLA: [*Obviously inventing.*] I'm lunching out. So are you, Maude, aren't you?

MAUDE: Yes.

CAROLINE: Oh, well, it's early yet. Don't go.

MAUDE: I'm so sorry, but I must go and be tried on. It's such a bore.

ISABELLA: You might drop me, perhaps; I have an appointment with my dentist. Good-bye, darling.

CAROLINE: Good-bye. It's been so nice to see you.

[*They kiss one another.*

ISABELLA: Good-bye.

MAUDE: [*To* ROBERT.] Dear Robert, we leave her in your care.

ISABELLA: Dear, dear Robert.

[*They go out.*

ROBERT: That's how elephants must behave when they're being tactful.

CAROLINE: How is it you're here so early? I wasn't expecting you till after the courts rose.

ROBERT: Oh . . . I managed to get away. Maude said you were expecting me.

CAROLINE: Yes, I was expecting you to tea. Don't you remember, you said yesterday you'd look in.

ROBERT: I suppose I couldn't have a whisky and soda?

CAROLINE: Yes, of course I'll ring. [*She touches the bell.*]

ROBERT: I've got to be back in chambers by one.

CAROLINE: You must keep your eye on the time. You mustn't be late.

ROBERT: [*Making conversation.*] What a nice woman Isabella is. Pity she doesn't get on with her husband.

CAROLINE: Oh, but she does, only she gets on better with him when he's in India and she's in England. They're devoted to one another from a distance.

ROBERT: There's something curiously feminine and sympathetic about her. She's not clever, but she's extraordinarily restful. I can imagine a man being extremely attached to Isabella.

CAROLINE: She's still quite pretty.

ROBERT: But, of course, one doesn't know what she'd be like to live with always. That's so different, isn't it?

CAROLINE: [*With conviction.*] Oh, absolutely. [COOPER *comes in.*] Bring up the whisky and soda, Cooper, and a glass.

COOPER: Very good, madam.

[*Exit* COOPER.

ROBERT: It reminds me of the case I'm in just now. Did you ever meet the Petersens?

CAROLINE: I don't think so.

ROBERT: Quite a nice woman. She was a Mrs. Macdougal. I've known Petersen for twenty years. I'd never have thought him capable of things like that.

CAROLINE: What did he do?

ROBERT: Oh, well, he'd been devoted to Mrs. Macdougal for years. It was an old-standing affair. Everybody accepted it. One always asked them to dinner together. At last they persuaded Macdougal to let himself be divorced. I'm acting for Mrs. Petersen now.

CAROLINE: I must be very stupid, but where does Mrs. Petersen come? You've not mentioned her before.

ROBERT: Mrs. Petersen was Mrs. Macdougal; you see, they got the divorce from Macdougal, then they married, and now they're divorcing.

CAROLINE: Oh, I see. Of course. Very natural. How long have they been married?

ROBERT: Eighteen months. And now they can't stand the sight of one another. She says he's dull when he's sober and brutal when he's drunk.

CAROLINE: Ah! And what does he say?

ROBERT: He marvels at his self-control. He can't imagine why he never killed her.

> [*A short silence.* COOPER *comes in with the whisky. She goes out.* ROBERT *helps himself.*

ROBERT: I did a very unprofessional thing. I had a chat with Petersen in the club the other night. I told him I couldn't discuss the matter, but he insisted on telling me that he had no ill-feeling towards me because I was appearing for his wife. He said he only had himself to blame.

CAROLINE: That was nice of him.

ROBERT: Oh, he didn't mean it like that. He meant he ought to have known better than to marry her. He said if a woman couldn't get on with one husband you might bet your boots she wouldn't get on with another. [*There is a momentary silence.*] Very nice whisky this is of yours, Caroline.

CAROLINE: You ought to like it. You chose it.

> [*He takes out a cigarette and lights it elaborately, pretending he is quite at ease.*

ROBERT: So your husband has died at last, Caroline.

CAROLINE: Yes.

ROBERT: I suppose you don't know what he died of?

CAROLINE: No, I have no idea.

ROBERT: Fever, I suppose. A man has to have a very fine physique to stand those climates indefinitely.

CAROLINE: Stephen had a very fine physique.

ROBERT: I suppose it was a great surprise to you when you read the announcement in this morning's Times?

CAROLINE: Yes, it was.

ROBERT: After all, death, even that of a person who was indifferent to you, is always a shock.

CAROLINE: Yes, when a man is dead you seem only to remember his good qualities.

ROBERT: It must be over ten years since you've seen him. I remember, when first I met you, you'd only been separated about three months. You haven't changed a bit in these ten years, Caroline.

CAROLINE: I'm afraid that's only your fancy. You've seen me almost every day since then, and you naturally wouldn't notice any difference in me.

ROBERT: That's true. In a way it's been a wonderful ten years, Caroline. We've found constant amusement in one another's society. You've been a great help to me. You've seen me rise from a struggling junior to a pretty good position. I don't see why I shouldn't be a judge before I die.

CAROLINE: We've had some very good times together, haven't we?

ROBERT: Wonderful!

CAROLINE: You've been a dear, Robert. You've always been so kind and patient.

ROBERT: It certainly hasn't been hard to be either.

CAROLINE: And you've got certain points that are strangely endearing. You never forget the little anniversaries that men find a bore to remember, but that women think so much of. You never fail to send me a little present on my birthday. Why, you even remember the day we first met and send me flowers. Ten times you've done that, Robert.

ROBERT: By George, if this had only happened ten years ago. What a difference if would have made to us. We should be quite an old married couple by now, Caroline.

CAROLINE: Do you wish it had?

ROBERT: What a question! Why, every day for ten years I've read the obituary column of The Times for that notice. It added a savour to breakfast.

CAROLINE: And now at last it's come.

ROBERT: I realize that I've lost for ever the little thrill of excitement that I always had when I took up the paper. I've often wished that your name began with a V or a W instead of an A, so that I might be able to prolong the agony a little as I read deliberately down the column.

CAROLINE: There's always something a little melancholy in getting what one wants.

ROBERT: Do you know, Caroline, I've never even seen a photograph of your husband.

CAROLINE: I'm afraid I haven't one. When we separated I destroyed everything that could possibly remind me of him.

ROBERT: I know. I shall never even know what that man looked like, and yet he has influenced my life more than anyone else in the world. What sort of a man was he, Caroline?

CAROLINE: An ordinary sort of man.

ROBERT: It's rather queer if you come to think of it. If he hadn't lived I should have had an entirely different life; if he'd died years ago I should be another man from what I am now. Just by existing, a thousand miles away, obscurely, he's made me what I am.

CAROLINE: Then we have at least something to be grateful to him for.

ROBERT: Caroline, what a charming thing to say!

CAROLINE: I never thought of it before, but I suppose I, too, have been influenced by Stephen, even though I never set eyes on him. I shouldn't be what I am either but for him.

ROBERT: Life is a strange business, Caroline.

CAROLINE: I'm beginning to think so.

[*A short silence.*

ROBERT: Well, I expect you've got a lot of things to do. I mustn't keep you.

CAROLINE: And you have an appointment, haven't you? You mustn't be late for that.

ROBERT: Oh, I've got my eye on the time.

CAROLINE: Yes, I imagined you had.

ROBERT: I thought I'd like to have a little chat with you at once.

CAROLINE: It was kind of you to come, it's been pleasant to see you.

ROBERT: I'll look in again about tea-time, may I?

CAROLINE: Oh, yes, that'll be nice. I dare say I can get one or two people so that we can have a rubber of bridge before dinner.

ROBERT: That always rests me after I've been in court. Well, good-bye, Caroline, God bless you.

CAROLINE: Good-bye. I hope you win your case.

ROBERT: Thanks.

[*He goes to the door and opens it. She steps towards the bell to ring. At the door he hesitates. She looks at him and pauses. He half shuts the door and meditates. She withdraws her hand from the bell. He opens the door again, and she stretches out her hand once more. He braces himself for the ordeal, shuts the door quickly and comes back into the room. She turns away from the bell.*

ROBERT: [*With assumed cheerfulness.*] I was almost forgetting the purpose of my visit.

CAROLINE: Oh! Didn't you come just to pass the time of day?

ROBERT: Well, not exactly, I think I'll just have a little drop more whisky if you don't mind. I can't imagine why my throat is so dry this morning.

CAROLINE: I dare say there's a touch of east in the wind.

ROBERT: [*Pouring out the whisky.*] Well, Caroline, what shall we do about it?

CAROLINE: About what?

ROBERT: [*Very busy with the siphon.*] When would you like us to be married?

CAROLINE: Well, I haven't thought about the matter.

ROBERT: We arranged that we would be as soon as your husband died.

CAROLINE: Yes, I know.

ROBERT: [*With assumed facetiousness.*] It only remains for you to name the day.

CAROLINE: I'm not going to name one.

ROBERT: My dear Caroline, you must. That is by old established custom the privilege of your sex.

CAROLINE: What day would you suggest?

ROBERT: Obstinate woman! I suppose you'll want some time to get a trousseau. And then banns take three weeks, don't they? I couldn't get away till the end of term, anyhow. What about the beginning of the Long Vacation?

CAROLINE: I'm not going to marry you, Robert.

ROBERT: Caroline!

CAROLINE: I've thought it over very carefully and I've completely made up my mind.

ROBERT: Do you mean to tell me that nothing I can say will induce you to change it?

CAROLINE: [*With a twinkle in her eyes.*] No.

ROBERT: This is an awful shock to me, Caroline. This is an awful blow. I've been living in hopes of this moment for years, and now . . . now . . . you could knock me down with a feather.

CAROLINE: [*With her tongue in her cheek.*] I'm sorry to cause you pain, Robert, but, believe me, I am acting for the best.

ROBERT: Do you mean to say that you absolutely refuse to marry me?

CAROLINE: Absolutely.

ROBERT: [*A little uneasily.*] Caroline, has anything in my behaviour led you to imagine that my heart wasn't set on marrying you? Would your answer have been different if I had expressed myself differently? Women are very strange. Haven't I been ardent enough? You must remember that I'm a shy man. This is an occasion when one may reasonably feel a certain embarrassment. I'm no longer in my first youth, Caroline. I should have felt ridiculous if I'd thrown myself on one knee and all that sort of thing. I have had no wide and varied experience in making proposals of marriages.

CAROLINE: Really. In that case I can only congratulate you. You made this one as though to the manner born. You were as cool as though you were ordering a dozen oysters and a pint of champagne.

ROBERT: I didn't feel it, Caroline. I was shaking in every limb.

CAROLINE: After all, you came to the point at once. I've known men with whom it required months of patience on the part of the object of their affections to bring them to it.

ROBERT: Then I cannot understand why you refused me.

CAROLINE: My dear Robert, we've been very happy in one another's company for ten years. We've been joined together by a very charming sentiment. Don't you think it would be a pity to expose it to the wear and tear of domestic life?

ROBERT: You're a wonderful woman, Caroline.

CAROLINE: Oh, it *had* occurred to you.

ROBERT: It hadn't exactly occurred to me, but it had crossed my mind. After all, one has to look at these things from a rational point of view. We're very well as we are.

CAROLINE: It seems a pity to make a change.

ROBERT: Not a pity, Caroline; a risk.

CAROLINE: Then you agree that I was wise to refuse you?

ROBERT: From your point of view, Caroline, I dare say there's a great deal to be said in favour of your decision. I, of course, could only have gained by the change.

CAROLINE: It's nice of you to say so. But are you sure that you're not a little relieved that I refused you?

ROBERT: I? My dear Caroline, can't you see I'm overwhelmed with disappointment?

CAROLINE: It's not visible to the naked eye, Robert.

ROBERT: You forget I have great power of self-control.

CAROLINE: I shouldn't be hurt if you confessed that at the bottom of your heart you were feeling as though you'd deliberately put your head in a noose, and then by a merciful interposition of Providence . . .

ROBERT: [*Interrupting.*] Caroline, I have been wanting to marry you for years. And now that the opportunity at last occurs you refuse me. Well, I accept your reasons. I bow to the inevitable. I know you too well to try to make you change your mind, but don't think because I take it like this that my heart isn't . . .

CAROLINE: Seared.

ROBERT: Are you laughing at me, Caroline?

> [*He looks at her. She begins to chuckle. For a moment he assumes a pose of indignation. She tries to restrain her laughter, but finds it impossible; he is gained by it, and begins to laugh also. Then they both roar till the tears run down their cheeks.*

ROBERT: Caroline, you're adorable.

CAROLINE: You humbug, Robert.

ROBERT: My dear, I had to do it. And I've done it, mind you, I've done it.

CAROLINE: Yes, you've done it. And now we'll forget all about it.

ROBERT: You know, I was terrified, Caroline.

CAROLINE: Poor dear, I know. Your heart was in your boots, wasn't it?

ROBERT: You don't bear me a grudge?

CAROLINE: Of course not.

ROBERT: You're wonderful, Caroline. Upon my soul, I could almost marry you.

CAROLINE: Dearest, I could very nearly consent to be your wife.

END OF THE FIRST ACT

THE SECOND ACT

The scene is the same.
It is a little after four o'clock in the afternoon of the same day.
CAROLINE *is standing by the window looking out.* COOPER
comes in.

COOPER: Mrs. Gilliatt has rung up to say she hopes you
haven't forgotten you're going to tea with her at
Rumplemeyer's, madam.

CAROLINE: I haven't forgotten, Cooper. But I haven't the
least intention of going.

COOPER: I said I'd give you the message, ma'am; but I said
I didn't think you were feeling very well.

CAROLINE: It hadn't occurred to me, but I don't think I *am*
feeling very well. I wish it would rain. It's so exasperating when the weather doesn't fit in with one's
moods.

COOPER: Shall I ring up Mrs. Gilliatt and say you're sorry
you can't come to tea, ma'am?

CAROLINE: Yes; I think I'll lie down. The more I think of
it the more I think I'm not very well.

[*She lies down on the sofa.*

COOPER: When one's feeling like what you are, ma'am, it
always makes one feel better not to feel very well.

CAROLINE: [*Smiling.*] That's rather confused, Cooper; but I
believe it's quite true. Put a lot of cushions behind me.
[*This* COOPER *does.*] Thank you. Now put the cigarettes
where I can reach them.

COOPER: [*Fetching them.*] Yes, madam.

CAROLINE: There are two books over there. Let me have

them, will you? Thank you. And give me the picture papers. There!

COOPER: Shall I cover up your feet, ma'am?

CAROLINE: You might put that Spanish shawl over them, Cooper. It's always satisfactory to look nice even if there's no one to see you.

[COOPER *carries out* CAROLINE's *various directions.*

COOPER: There, ma'am. Is there anything else?

CAROLINE: No. I feel better already. I'm not at home to anybody, and I won't speak to anyone on the telephone.

COOPER: Very good, ma'am.

CAROLINE: I'm extremely pleased with my own society, Cooper. It's very nice to be alone when one wants to. I like to think it's my own house and nobody can cross my threshold without permission. It's really very pleasant to be one's own mistress.

COOPER: Some people like a man about the house, ma'am, and some people don't.

CAROLINE: I don't.

COOPER: Ah, well, ma'am, you're one of the lucky ones; you can please yourself.

CAROLINE: Cooper, what *do* you mean? You're not dissatisfied with your young man?

COOPER: No, ma'am, not exactly that. But I don't know as I'd marry him if I 'ad anything better to look forward to.

CAROLINE: But you're not obliged to marry him, Cooper.

COOPER: Him or somebody else. It's not very satisfactory being in service all your life. And it isn't so easy for a parlourmaid to find places when she's getting on a bit.

CAROLINE: Tell me, Cooper, how did he propose?

COOPER: Well, ma'am, I don't know as he exactly proposed at all. You see, it was like this. I'd been walking out with him for something like two years, and he never said anything that you could take hold of, so to speak, so at last I said to him: Well, what about it? What about what? he said. You know what I mean, I said. I do not, he said. Well, do you mean it or do you not? I said. Is it a riddle? he said. No, I said, but I've been walking out with you for two years, and I just want to know if anything's to come of it or not. Oh, he said. I don't mind one way or the other, I said; but I'm not going to waste my time till doomsday, and I just want to know, that's all. Well, he said, what do you propose? Well, I said, what about August Bank Holiday? Make it Christmas, he said; I get a rise then. All right, I said, as long as I know where I am I don't mind waiting, but I like to know where I am.

CAROLINE: It wasn't very romantic, Cooper.

COOPER: Well, ma'am, my belief is that men don't want to marry. It's not in their nature. You 'ave to give them a little push or you'll never bring them to it.

CAROLINE: And supposing they regret it afterwards, Cooper?

COOPER: Oh, well, ma'am, it's too late then. And you know, ma'am, they generally try to make the best of it when they know they can't help themselves.

CAROLINE: And let us look on the bright side of things, Cooper; they're often not unhappy, poor brutes.

COOPER: Oh, no, ma'am, I think they're much happier; but sometimes they won't realize it, so to speak.

CAROLINE: That's human nature, Cooper. You won't forget to telephone to Mrs. Gilliatt.

COOPER: [*Going.*] No, ma'am, I'll ring her up at once.

CAROLINE: Oh, and Cooper, you might ring up Dr. Cornish and ask him if he can come round.

COOPER: I thought you were feeling better, ma'am?

CAROLINE: I am, but I think it would comfort me to see a doctor. To be able to talk about oneself without fear of interruption is cheap at half a guinea.

COOPER: Very good, ma'am.

> [*Exit.* CAROLINE *settles herself more comfortably than ever on the sofa; she takes one of the illustrated papers and begins to look at it. The door is quietly opened, and* MAUDE FULTON *puts a roguish head round the corner.*

MAUDE: May I come in?

CAROLINE: Good heavens, how you startled me!

MAUDE: Say I may come in, Caroline.

CAROLINE: No, you may not come in.

MAUDE: [*Edging herself in.*] Don't be brutal, Caroline.

CAROLINE: I think I've got scarlet fever.

MAUDE: [*Opening the door a little more.*] I've had it.

CAROLINE: On the other hand, it may be small-pox.

MAUDE: [*Coming right in.*] I'm constantly being vaccinated.

CAROLINE: I'm not at home, Maude.

MAUDE: I know, but I felt sure you'd see me. Cooper didn't want to let me come up.

CAROLINE: Servants are not what they were. She should only have let you force your way over her inanimate corpse.

MAUDE: Darling, surely a corpse couldn't be anything else but inanimate.

CAROLINE: Just as an intruder couldn't be anything else but intolerable.

MAUDE: Now that you've had the last word, offer me a cup of tea and tell me all about it.

CAROLINE: I shall *not*, Maude.

MAUDE: Now don't be ridiculous, Caroline. I felt I *must* see you. You can't expect me to be entirely devoid of curiosity.

CAROLINE: After knowing you for twenty years? No, my dear, I don't. But, on the other hand, you can't expect me to be such a fool as to gratify it.

MAUDE: I naturally wanted to be the first to congratulate you. [*Insinuatingly*.] Caroline, tell me now how he did it.

CAROLINE: D'you think it's fair to a man to tell a third party what romantic madness seized his tongue at such a moment?

MAUDE: [*Eagerly*.] Oh, my dear, go on. I'm thrilled to the core.

CAROLINE: [*She looks at her with an ironical smile*.] I was standing in the middle of the room, Maude, and he came up to me, and fell on one knee.

MAUDE: Yes, Sir Walter Raleigh.

CAROLINE: He took my hand. I turned a little away.

MAUDE: Yes, yes.

CAROLINE: At last, he said, at last! Oh, I have waited for this moment for a hundred years. I know I am utterly unworthy of you, but I adore the very ground you tread on. You are my ideal of woman. Oh, Caroline, Caroline, will you be mine? Clarence, I said. . . .

MAUDE: Robert, you mean, surely.

CAROLINE: [*Bursting into laughter*.] You fool, Maude. Can you see Robert making such a perfect ass of himself?

MAUDE: Really, Caroline, you are exasperating.

CAROLINE: Shall I tell you the honest truth?

MAUDE: [*Acidly*.] If you can.

CAROLINE: He fiddled about with a siphon, and said: Well, when would you like to be married?

MAUDE: Oh, I prefer the other way; but after all it comes to the same in the end. Darling, I congratulate you with all my heart.

CAROLINE: On getting an offer at my time of life? Thank you very much.

MAUDE: Don't be so silly. On your engagement.

CAROLINE: But I'm not engaged.

MAUDE: What *are* you talking about?

CAROLINE: I refused him.

MAUDE: Good heavens! Why?

CAROLINE: I thought I should be happier if I remained as I was.

MAUDE: Caroline, how cruel of you! How abominably selfish! But what did Robert say?

CAROLINE: He was almost too much surprised for words.

MAUDE: Wasn't he overwhelmed?

CAROLINE: I could see it was a disappointment, but he did all he could not to make it more difficult for me.

MAUDE: I can hardly believe my ears. What are you going to do, then?

CAROLINE: I'm going to remain a widow. And to make it quite clear, I shall go into mourning. Crêpe and weeds and all the trappings of woe. [MAUDE *meditates for a moment, while* CAROLINE *watches her, wondering whether she accepts her account of the incident.*] D'you think they'll suit me?

MAUDE. [*Tartly.*] If they don't, I think you can be trusted not to wear them long.

CAROLINE: I don't see why you should be cross with me.

MAUDE: I'm disappointed in you, Caroline, and I'm very, very, very sorry for Robert.

CAROLINE: Marry him, then.

MAUDE: I'm not a marrying woman.

CAROLINE: Neither am I. Sisters in adversity.

MAUDE: Of course, he'll ask you again.

CAROLINE: He's not such a fool.

MAUDE: What do you mean by that?

CAROLINE: [*Seeing that she has nearly given herself away.*] He knows he can go on asking me till he's blue in the face and I shall say no.

MAUDE: Then there's nothing more to be said.

CAROLINE: Nothing.

> [COOPER *comes in to announce* DR. CORNISH. *This is a very stout, red-faced, jovial gentleman, with an optimistic view of life.*

COOPER: Dr. Cornish.

CAROLINE: How do you do? Cooper, did you send that message?

COOPER: Yes, ma'am. Mrs. Gilliatt said she'd just heard the dreadful news, and it must be a terrible shock and she quite understood; you had her sincerest sympathy, and she hoped you wouldn't forget that you were playing bridge with her to-morrow afternoon.

CAROLINE: Thank you.

> [*Exit* COOPER.

CAROLINE: [*Turning to* DR. CORNISH.] Now I can attend to you.

DR. CORNISH: That's what I've come to do to you.

CAROLINE: You know Miss Fulton?

DR. CORNISH: [*Shaking hands with her.*] A homeopath, I believe.

MAUDE: Oh, no, I've given that up. But I've got a wonderful bone-setter that I go to now.

DR. CORNISH: Dear me, have you been breaking your bones?

MAUDE: No, but I might.

DR. CORNISH: I can recommend a very competent motor-omnibus if you are looking for something to run over you.

CAROLINE: Now, Maude, Dr. Cornish has come to see me professionally. You've stayed quite long enough.

MAUDE: Are you ill, darling?

CAROLINE: I shall know that when Dr. Cornish has examined me.

MAUDE: I thought you weren't looking quite up to the mark. Of course I'll go.

CAROLINE: And don't come back till you're sent for.

MAUDE: Dear Caroline. It's lucky I know she's devoted to me, or I might take offence at some of the things she says to me. Good-bye, Dr. Cornish.

DR. CORNISH: [*Shaking hands with her.*] Does the bone-setter make love to you?

MAUDE: Not more than most men.

[*Exit.*

DR. CORNISH: Now, dear lady, what is the matter with you?

CAROLINE: Ill-temper.

DR. CORNISH: An ailment very distressing to ladies' maids, I've always understood. I noticed you were suffering from it.

CAROLINE: I didn't send for you so that you might have the pleasure of making yourself disagreeable and earning half a guinea into the bargain.

DR. CORNISH: It does seem unfair, doesn't it? Let me feel your pulse.

CAROLINE: [*As he takes her wrist.*] There's nothing wrong with my body. It's my mind.

DR. CORNISH: What is amiss with that?

CAROLINE: Well, for one thing I don't know it.

DR. CORNISH: The British Empire is governed exclusively by gentlemen who suffer from the same complaint. You mustn't let that worry you.

CAROLINE: I'm vexed and bored.

DR. CORNISH: Has this got anything to do with the announcement I read in this morning's paper? I can well understand that the loss of a husband might cause any woman a momentary vexation.

CAROLINE: No, I don't think it's that. I've just redecorated my dining-room, and I don't think it's quite a success. And, you know, these new fashions don't suit me. I'm not pleased with any of the clothes I bought this spring. I dare say I'm a little run down and want a change of air.

DR. CORNISH: Quite so. Quite so. Now tell me the truth.

CAROLINE: But I'm telling you the truth.

DR. CORNISH: Yes, I know; but the true truth. Women make such distinction between the two.

CAROLINE: [*Smiling.*] You must have a very large practice, Dr. Cornish.

DR. CORNISH: I get along. Now come, dear lady.

CAROLINE: I sent for you because I wanted to tell you the truth. I've known you so long, and I can trust you. You know, I'm devoted to Robert Oldham. I've wanted to marry him ever since we first met. And now that the opportunity has come, I don't want to.

DR. CORNISH: I see.

CAROLINE: Of course, nobody knows. Robert thinks I'm dying to marry him. And all my friends. You see, it was an understood thing that we should marry as soon as I was free. He's waited for me all these years.

DR. CORNISH: It's awkward, isn't it? I can see that Robert Oldham will think you a little unreasonable. He's no longer a young man.

CAROLINE: That is what I said to myself. I thought the matter over from every standpoint. I remembered Robert's infinite patience, his devotion and self-sacrifice, and I made up my mind that it was my duty to marry him.

DR. CORNISH: It's hard to speak of duty in these matters; but if you ask my opinion, in this particular case I think you're right.

CAROLINE: He came here this morning. I discovered that he didn't want to marry me in the least.

DR. CORNISH: Well, that simplifies matters.

CAROLINE: It does nothing of the kind. I was prepared to sacrifice myself. I'd made up my mind to an act of renunciation. I'd promised myself that he should never, never know the truth. You don't think it's pleasant to realize suddenly that you're not wanted, and you can keep your self-sacrifice. It's enough to make any woman feel not very well.

DR. CORNISH: Now, don't work yourself up into a scene dear lady.

CAROLINE: Why not?

DR. CORNISH: I've seen so many. I assure you they have no effect on me at all.

CAROLINE: In that case it isn't worth while, is it? But it is vexatious, Dr. Cornish, isn't it?

DR. CORNISH: Very.

CAROLINE: Upon my word I could almost wish my husband were alive again. [*No sooner are the words out of her mouth than the telephone bell rings.*] Good heavens, how it startled me! I told Cooper I wouldn't speak to anyone. Oh, I know what it is. It's my solicitor. They've had the answer to my cable. [*She takes up the receiver and listens.*] Yes. Lester and Lester? I was expecting you to ring me up. Yes, I'll hold on. [*To* DR. CORNISH.] They're putting me through to Sir Henry. Oh, the suspense! You know, I've had two or three false alarms of Stephen's death before. Oh, if he's only alive this time it'll make such a difference. It'll put an end to all my difficulties. [*Speaking into the receiver.*] Yes. Sir

Henry? You haven't had an answer to your cable?
Then . . . Oh! [*To* Dr. Cornish.] He's seen Stephen's
solicitor. [*Listening.*] I see. Thank you very much. It
was kind of you to ring me up. Good-bye.

[*She puts down the receiver.*

Dr. Cornish: Well?

Caroline: Stephen's solicitor has had a further cable from
Nairobi. It appears my husband died in the hospital
there four days ago of cirrhosis of the liver. Is that the
sort of disease he would die from?

Dr. Cornish: You must know that better than I. I never
knew him.

Caroline: Could brandy bring it on?

Dr. Cornish: Nothing better.

Caroline: Then that settles it. There can be no more doubt.
I'm free.

Dr. Cornish: Don't say it so despondently. It's a condition
that most married people aspire to.

Caroline: Doesn't it strike you that there's something dis-
tressingly obvious in being a widow? I can quite understand why a more delicate civilization than ours ordered
the immolation of widows on their husband's pyre.

Dr. Cornish: My dear lady, you take too gloomy a view of
the situation. From the days of the ancients a certain
gaiety has been ascribed to the condition which you
now adorn.

Caroline: I refuse to be gay. My husband spited me for ten
years by living, now he spites me more than ever before
by dying.

Dr. Cornish: D'you know what's the matter with you?

Caroline: If you say appendicitis I'll kill you.

Dr. Cornish: I wish I could, for that is an ailment which
can be cured by a trifling operation. But there's no
escape from the malady I have in mind. There's no cure.

There are no palliatives even. The most eminent physician in the world can do no more than offer sympathy and consolation.

CAROLINE: My dear Dr. Cornish, you freeze the very marrow in my bones. Tell me what it is quickly. I will brace myself to bear the worst.

DR. CORNISH: Middle age.

CAROLINE: Say that again.

DR. CORNISH: Middle age.

CAROLINE: Impossible! Oh, impossible!

DR. CORNISH: Let me suggest one or two symptoms to you. Haven't you noticed lately how young the policemen are about the streets? Why, they're mere boys. But when you were a girl, don't you remember, they were middle-aged men.

CAROLINE: Now that you come to speak of it I *have* noticed that the policemen are very young nowadays.

DR. CORNISH: And when you're in a house party, haven't you noticed that some of the young people are really very rowdy? It's lucky they keep more or less to themselves because their conversation really is very tedious.

CAROLINE: But it *is* very tedious.

DR. CORNISH: It's just the same as it was fifteen years ago, and you didn't find it so then.

CAROLINE: You're beginning to frighten me.

DR. CORNISH: You're devoted to dancing, aren't you?

CAROLINE: [*Brightly*.] Passionately. That, at all events, hasn't left me.

DR. CORNISH: But don't you find by about one in the morning you're rather tired and quite ready to go home?

CAROLINE: I naturally don't want to be a wreck next day.

DR. CORNISH: Were you a wreck next day fifteen years ago?

CAROLINE: I used to be able to sleep till twelve o'clock next morning.

DR. CORNISH: And now you can't? I know. At whatever time you go to bed you awake about eight, don't you? One does, you know, as one grows older.

CAROLINE: I'm beginning to feel a hundred.

DR. CORNISH: You mustn't take it too hardly. Things haven't gone very far yet.

CAROLINE: [*Ironically.*] Thank you so much.

DR. CORNISH: Perhaps you've noticed one white hair on your head, and you've said to your friends: I'm sure I shall be prematurely grey.

CAROLINE: Are you enjoying this, Dr. Cornish?

DR. CORNISH: It's not so tragic as you think.

CAROLINE: Middle age?

DR. CORNISH: It's true there are no remedies. Rouge, dye, powder and pencil are not even palliatives; they merely emphasize the obvious.

CAROLINE: You have nothing to recommend but resignation?

DR. CORNISH: I can offer comfort.

CAROLINE: [*Shaking her head.*] No.

DR. CORNISH: Dear lady, it's the happy time of a man's life. You have learnt your limitations. They are like a pack of cards, with which the skilful conjuror can do a hundred tricks. Passion no longer holds you enslaved. You go your way and attach no more importance to the opinion of your fellows than is seemly. You are sound in wind and limb and you are free. Good heavens, when I was young I did things I didn't want to because other people did. Now I do what I like. I wear the clothes I fancy, and don't ask myself if they're the fashion. When I'm tired I go to bed. When I'm bored I betake myself to my own counsel. Believe me, middle age is very pleasant. A book, a glass of wine, and

Amaryllis sporting in the shade, while I—bask in the sun.

CAROLINE: Is it because I'm middle-aged that Robert no longer wants to marry me?

DR. CORNISH: Not at all. I was explaining why you no longer wanted to marry him.

CAROLINE: [*Taking a little mirror out of her bag and looking at herself in it.*] I see myself no different from what I was yesterday or ten years ago.

DR. CORNISH: You're a very charming and a very fascinating woman.

CAROLINE: I was never beautiful. At my best I was no more than pretty, but I've been quite content with that. People have found me amusing.

DR. CORNISH: None more than I.

CAROLINE: I've never lacked admiration. . . . It's been the breath of my nostrils, Dr. Cornish. If all that is to go, what is there left? Charity and good works? You talk like a man. You talk like a fool. You don't know what middle age is to a woman. It's very hard. It gives me such a pain in my heart. [*She begins to cry a little.* DR. CORNISH *watches her with not unkindly amusement.*] You're not going to charge me for this, are you? That would be more than I could bear.

DR. CORNISH: On the contrary, I'm going to charge you double. A doctor is only supposed to give drugs, but I've given you common sense. [CAROLINE *gives a little cry.*] What is the matter?

CAROLINE: May your hair fall out in bushels, and all your teeth rattle from your palsied gums. May your joints ache with rheumatism and your toes tingle with gout. May you wheeze and snore like an overfed pug, and blow like a ridiculous grampus.

DR. CORNISH: Mercy!

CAROLINE: What a fool I am to let myself be harassed by you. We're nothing in ourselves. We're what other people think we are. I've just thought of Rex.

DR. CORNISH: Who the dickens is Rex?

CAROLINE: Rex is passion and youth and love. To him, at all events, I'm young and charming. He loves me.

DR. CORNISH: Ho, ho!

CAROLINE: [*Going to the telephone.*] Mayfair 2315. Rex? D'you know who it is? [*She makes her voice as seductive as she knows how.*] What are you doing? Idle creature. Under the circumstances . . . Under what circumstances? Would you like to come and dine with me to-night? [*Her face changes.*] Engaged? You've never been engaged before when I've asked you. Can't you break the engagement? Oh, of course, if there's any difficulty you mustn't think of it. Anyhow, come round and see me now; we'll drink a dish of tea together. Very well. [*She puts down the receiver.*] He's coming at once.

DR. CORNISH: What are you going to do?

CAROLINE: I? Oh, I'm going to tell him that I've refused Robert.

DR. CORNISH: And then?

CAROLINE: [*Smiling.*] Then we'll see.

> [*She draws a long, triumphant breath. It is obvious that she expects the young man then to fling his passionate heart at her feet.*]

DR. CORNISH: My advice to you is to marry Robert Oldham.

CAROLINE: He doesn't want to marry me.

DR. CORNISH: Nag him a little.

CAROLINE: Why should I marry him? He's not young. I don't believe we're suited to one another.

DR. CORNISH: You try. You'll find you'll jog along quite comfortably.

CAROLINE: Good heavens, I don't want to jog along. I want poetry, passion, romance.

DR. CORNISH: [*Soothingly.*] Yes. I think I'll write you a little prescription. I dare say a gentle sedative will do you no harm.

CAROLINE: [*As he prepares to sit down.*] You can write as many prescriptions as you like, but if you think I'm going to take your beastly medicine you're very much mistaken.

DR. CORNISH: [*Writing.*] Human emotion is a queer business. Has it ever struck you that with a few grains of one drug you can make the timid heroic, and with a few grams of another the romantic, matter-of-fact. You can make the *femme incomprise* satisfied with her lot and the adventurer content to stick to his desk. You have read that the history of the world would have been different if Cleopatra's nose had been longer. My dear, I have no doubt that if Cleopatra had been treated with valerian and massage she would never have made such a fool of herself at the Battle of Actium, and I'm convinced that with the administration of a certain amount of strychnine and iron I could have persuaded Antony that it wasn't worth while to lose an empire for her sake. Take this three times a day after meals. You'll find it'll do you a lot of good.

CAROLINE: I don't want to be done good to.

[COOPER *comes in.*

COOPER: Mrs. Trench has called, ma'am.

CAROLINE: I'm not at home, Cooper.

COOPER: I said you were not at home, ma'am; but Mrs. Trench says you telephoned for her to come at once.

CAROLINE: I? I did no such thing.

COOPER: What shall I say, ma'am?

CAROLINE: I suppose she must come up.

COOPER: Very good, ma'am.

[*Exit.*

DR. CORNISH: Well, good-bye, dear lady.

CAROLINE: I'm twenty-five, Dr. Cornish. Romance is on the way to my door in a two-seater.

DR. CORNISH: Send it away, and let common sense come trundling along in a four-wheeler.

CAROLINE: Never. Good-bye.

[DR. CORNISH *goes out. In a moment* ISABELLA *comes in with* MAUDE FULTON.

CAROLINE: I'm delighted to see you, Isabella; but I can't make out what you mean by saying I telephoned.

MAUDE: *I* telephoned.

CAROLINE: You!

MAUDE: I think it's absurd that you should refuse Robert Oldham. I sent for Isabella so that we might talk it over.

CAROLINE: May I ask what business it is of Isabella's?

ISABELLA: My dear, when your friends see you about to make a terrible mistake, they wouldn't be friends if they didn't do everything they could to save you from it.

CAROLINE: I take it that you've talked the matter out downstairs.

MAUDE: I put the case before Isabella as I saw it.

ISABELLA: I can hardly believe it even now. It's the most astounding thing I've ever heard in my life.

CAROLINE: I hope you've had a pleasant chat. Now I will ask you both to go away. I'm going to lie down.

MAUDE: [*Sitting down firmly.*] No, Caroline, we will not go till you've heard what we have to say.

ISABELLA: There must be some misunderstanding. It only requires a little good-will and everything can be put right.

CAROLINE: Robert and I understand one another only too well.

ISABELLA: I wonder if you haven't known him so long that you've ceased to realize what a very attractive man he is.

CAROLINE: [*A little surprised.*] Do you find him so?

ISABELLA: He's one of the most charming men I've ever met.

CAROLINE: Oh!

ISABELLA: He's very handsome. He has charming eyes.

CAROLINE: Ah! That's just what he says about you.

ISABELLA: [*Pleased.*] Really? Do tell me what he says.

CAROLINE: What a pity you can't marry him yourself, Isabella!

ISABELLA: Oh, I! He's never had eyes for anybody when you've been there.

CAROLINE: Not till to-day. But then I'm not always there, am I?

ISABELLA: What do you mean, Caroline? You're speaking quite acidly.

CAROLINE: Oh, nothing.

MAUDE: All that is neither here nor there. You can't afford to refuse Robert. You've been a good deal talked about in connection with Robert Oldham; but your friends have been exceedingly sympathetic owing to the peculiar circumstances. But honestly you owe it to them just as much as to yourself to marry the man as soon as you can.

CAROLINE: I'm going to marry to please myself, not to please my friends.

MAUDE: Besides, it's high time you settled down.

CAROLINE: Upon my word, I don't know why.

MAUDE: You're no chicken, Caroline.

CAROLINE: At all events, I'm younger than you, darling.

MAUDE: A widow is as old as her possible husband, a spinster is as young as her latest young man.

CAROLINE: Then if I choose a husband at all I'll choose one younger than Robert.

ISABELLA: My dear, he's a perfect age. Everyone knows that young men think of nothing but themselves. It's the man of forty-five who makes much of you.

MAUDE: Dear Caroline, I think the time has arrived to be frank.

CAROLINE: Good heavens, haven't you been frank hitherto?

MAUDE: I've been doing my best to spare your feelings.

CAROLINE: I hadn't noticed it.

MAUDE: I'm afraid I shall have to make myself a little unpleasant.

CAROLINE: For my good or for your own satisfaction?

MAUDE: By a merciful interposition of providence in these matters one can generally combine the two. I feel it my duty to tell you the whole truth.

CAROLINE: Will it take very long?

MAUDE: Why?

CAROLINE: Only that I'm expecting Rex in a minute or two, and I'm afraid I must ask you to leave me when he comes.

MAUDE: That's a very strange request.

CAROLINE: He has asked to see me alone.

MAUDE: What does he want?

CAROLINE: I'm sure I don't know. I'm filled with curiosity.

MAUDE: I won't conceal from you that I'm surprised, Caroline.

CAROLINE: Are you?

MAUDE: Yes, you see, I told him you were engaged to Robert Oldham.

CAROLINE: [*Indignantly.*] You didn't. How dare you! Really, Maude, you take too much upon yourself. It's monstrous. I will not let you interfere with my affairs in this way. It's too monstrous.

MAUDE: Well, I thought you would be. And what's more, you ought to be.

CAROLINE: I'll never forgive you. How dare you? How dare you?

ISABELLA: [*At the window.*] Here he is.

CAROLINE: Rex?

ISABELLA: He's just driven up.

MAUDE: I'm not going, Caroline. We must thrash this matter out thoroughly. While Rex is here Isabella and I will have a cup of tea in your boudoir.

CAROLINE: [*Ironically.*] Make yourselves at home, won't you?

MAUDE: Come, Isabella.

CAROLINE: [*Furiously.*] If you'd like an egg to your tea, mind you order it.

> [*The two ladies go out.* CAROLINE *hurriedly looks at herself in the glass, arranges her hair a little, powders her nose, and settles herself down in a becoming attitude with a book. She is careful to arrange her skirt so that it shall make a graceful line.* COOPER *shows in* REX CUNNINGHAM.

COOPER: Mr. Cunningham.

[*Exit.*

CAROLINE: [*Very affably.*] How nice of you to come.

REX: I thought I was never going to see you again.

CAROLINE: Good heavens, why?

REX: [*With a shrug of the shoulders.*] Let me congratulate you on your engagement.

CAROLINE: D'you mean that my engagement entails the breaking of our friendship?

REX: Don't you know how I've felt for you ever since I knew you? D'you think I have no heart?

CAROLINE: No, I don't think that. You are romance, youth, passion.

REX: I could bear to think of you as the wife of a man I'd never seen. He was far away, and I knew you didn't care for him. But now it's quite different.

CAROLINE: You've known always that I was deeply attached to Robert.

REX: If you knew how I've suffered.

CAROLINE: Don't, Rex, you break my heart.

REX: And I shall go on suffering. I know myself. I know what tortures I'm capable of. I've got that nature. But what must be, must be. The only thing is, I beseech you not to ask me to go on seeing you.

CAROLINE: But I'm very fond of you.

REX: You say that because you have a kind heart. You'll be happy with the man you love. I shall only be in the way. Say good-bye to me and let me go. I'm seeing you now for the last time. I shall never get over it. My life is blighted. But at all events let me spare you the sight of my torment. Let me suffer in silence and in solitude.

CAROLINE: What would you say if I told you that I'd refused to marry Robert Oldham?

REX: You? But Miss Fulton told me you were engaged.

CAROLINE: She was mistaken.

REX: [*Looking at her blankly.*] My hat!

CAROLINE: [*A little surprised.*] Aren't you pleased?

REX Why did you refuse him?

CAROLINE: I suppose because I didn't love him enough.

REX: Are you quite sure you're wise?

CAROLINE: I beg your pardon? I didn't expect you to ask me that question!

REX: I'm thinking of your happiness.

CAROLINE: It may be that my happiness lies elsewhere.

REX: [*Not without embarrassment.*] After all, you've known Robert Oldham a great many years, haven't you?

CAROLINE: Not so many as all that.

REX: He's a very good chap. None better. He's by way of being distinguished too. I always feel rather insignificant beside him.

CAROLINE: One might almost think you wanted me to marry him.

REX: It would break my heart. You know that.

CAROLINE: But——

REX: Looking at it entirely from your point of view I can't help seeing it would be the best thing.

CAROLINE: It's nice of you to be so anxious for my welfare.

REX: That has been my first thought ever since I first saw you.

CAROLINE: It's rare to find such unselfishness in a man.

REX: I'm so accustomed to being absolutely wretched.

CAROLINE: [*With a flash of insight.*] Are you sure you don't rather like it?

REX: I? Do you know how many sleepless nights I've spent on your account?

CAROLINE: And I felt so sorry for you, poor dear. Tell me, has nobody ever been in love with you?

REX: I suppose so. But, I don't know why, it's always bored me stiff.

CAROLINE: I'm beginning to see daylight. You thrive on hopeless passion, my poor friend.

REX: I don't know what you mean. If you think that I haven't been perfectly sincere in all I've said to you——

CAROLINE: [*Interrupting.*] Oh, I'm sure you have. But hasn't my greatest attraction been that I didn't return your love?

REX: I never expected to hear *you* say such things to me, Caroline.

CAROLINE: My dear, I don't blame you. We're as we're made. You are the unhappy lover. I was a donkey not to see it before.

REX: You make me feel an awful fool, Caroline.

CAROLINE: Don't grudge me that little bit of satisfaction. By the way, where are you dining to-night?

REX: Isabella asked me to eat a chop with her.

CAROLINE: It crossed my mind that it might be she. Dear Isabella. You'll like her so much as you get to know her more. She has a husband in India and she'll never do anything to cause him any real uneasiness; but she has a very tender heart and an unlimited amount of sympathy.

REX: Caroline, you don't think for a moment——?

CAROLINE: No, but I recommend it. You see, now I've discovered that nothing can distress you more than to have your passion returned, I'm afraid I shan't succeed in being as sympathetic as you have the right to expect.

REX: You're unjust to me, Caroline. It's not my fault if I'm only really happy when I'm utterly miserable.

CAROLINE: I'm so glad I'm not. But it takes all sorts to make a world.

REX: And you know, they never give me a chance. They're quite impossible.

CAROLINE: Who?

REX: Women.

CAROLINE: They will fall on your neck, I suppose. They're affectionate creatures.

REX: They're always wanting to sacrifice themselves.

CAROLINE: I nearly did myself, Rex.

REX: They're so selfish. They never will let a man be self-sacrificing and all that sort of thing. Why shouldn't a man be an object of pity? I want to deny myself, I want to stand aside, I *can* suffer in silence. I'm made like that.

CAROLINE: Not quite in silence, Rex. But I'm keeping you, and I'm sure you have a hundred things to do. Goodbye.

REX: No one will ever understand me. Good-bye. [*He goes to the door, opens it, and pauses a moment.*] And you know, Caroline, a woman *is* more desirable when she's unattainable.

[*Exit.*

CAROLINE: [*A sudden light dawning upon her.*] A true word! [*Pause.*] My hat!

[MAUDE FULTON *and* ISABELLA TRENCH *come in.*

MAUDE: We heard him go.

CAROLINE: Heavens, I'd forgotten all about you. [*To* ISABELLA.] Well, my dear, you've not been wasting your time with Rex, have you? *He* thinks you have charming blue eyes too.

ISABELLA: Caroline, what do you mean?

CAROLINE: It appears he's dining with you to-night.

ISABELLA: I merely asked him because he seemed unhappy.

CAROLINE: Unhappy? Why, he enjoys being unhappy. I give him to you, Isabella, since you want him.

ISABELLA: [*Outraged.*] Oh!

CAROLINE: You'll just suit him. You'll listen to all his protestations of affection, and you'll weep little salt tears of sympathy when he tells you he adores you. And you'll give him to understand that your husband doesn't appreciate you. And you'll be dreadfully sorry for him. And I can trust you not to go an inch further than is quite safe. You mustn't do that because it'll put him out dreadfully. The last thing he wants is to have his feelings reciprocated.

ISABELLA: [*Beginning to cry.*] I never thought you'd say such things to me.

MAUDE: Caroline, you've asked him to marry you and he's refused.

CAROLINE: Oh, I haven't. Really that's too much. I've never been so insulted. [*She begins to cry also.*] Oh, I hate you, Maude, I hate you!

MAUDE: Caroline!

CAROLINE: You're a spiteful, envious cat.

MAUDE: You've got no right to say such things to me. I've only aimed at your good.

> [*She begins to cry. They all three sob angrily for a minute, then all three take their bags and pull out their mirrors.*

ISABELLA: Oh, my dear, what a fright I look.

CAROLINE: Good heavens! I look a perfect sight.

MAUDE: Crying doesn't suit me one bit.

> [*These three speeches are said together, then all three take their puffs and powder their noses. While they are busily engaged* COOPER *comes in.*

COOPER: Mr. Oldham has called, ma'am.

CAROLINE: Not at home.

COOPER: He said he'd come by appointment, ma'am.

MAUDE: That's quite right. Show him up, Cooper.

COOPER: Very good, miss.

> [*Exit.*

CAROLINE: What d'you mean, Maude?

MAUDE: I sent for him.

CAROLINE: Abominable woman! I'm speechless! Maude, you abominable woman!

MAUDE: I don't care if you're angry. The matter can't be left like this, and something's got to be done.

CAROLINE: [*Making for the door.*] I won't see him.

MAUDE: But he's here now.

CAROLINE: Get rid of him, then. You think he's charming, Isabella, take him too.

ISABELLA: He'll never go without seeing you.

CAROLINE: Then I'll tell you why I refused him—because he didn't want to marry me. I saw his heart sink as the words were wrung out of him by his sense of decency. He asked me only because he felt he must.

MAUDE: Oh, what nonsense! I oughtn't to have left you alone. You're a pair of children. I dare say he was a little nervous, and I'm sure you were.

CAROLINE: There's no doubt that he was. If you'd seen the amount of whisky he took! Dutch courage to propose to me! Are you going to ask him now to marry me out of pity! I dare say he's already got a ticket for the South Sea Islands in his pocket.

ISABELLA: Everyone knows that Robert has worshipped the ground you trod on for ten years. It's incredible that now, when he can at last achieve his greatest wish, he shouldn't want to.

CAROLINE: You idiot, Isabella, don't you know that the only thing men want is the unattainable?

MAUDE: I suppose you're quite sure that he did propose?

CAROLINE: You may be quite certain that I wouldn't have let him out of the room before he did. I have my self-respect to think of.

MAUDE: Perhaps you didn't make yourself alluring enough.

CAROLINE: I made myself as alluring as I knew how.

MAUDE: You should have waited till the evening. A good dinner and a bottle of champagne have a wonderful effect on the masculine heart.

ISABELLA: And no woman is so attractive that she's not improved by shaded lights and an evening frock.

CAROLINE: I didn't want him to come this morning. You did it. I knew very well that no man feels like marriage before luncheon.

MAUDE: I thought Robert was an exceptional man.

CAROLINE: No man's an exceptional man. You must know that by now.

ISABELLA: What is he doing all this time?

CAROLINE: Making up his mind to face the music. I won't come out of my room till he's gone.

> [*She flings out of the room. The two ladies are left astounded.*

MAUDE: Well!

ISABELLA: Dear Caroline is rather hard sometimes. She should show more tenderness.

> [COOPER *ushers in* ROBERT OLDHAM *and then goes out.*

COOPER: Mr. Oldham.

ROBERT: I just asked Cooper to give me a drink. Is Caroline not here? Good afternoon. [*Silence.*] Is anything the matter? When I came out of court my clerk gave me a message that I was to come at once on a matter of the greatest importance.

MAUDE: I sent the message. I'm not pleased with you, Robert.

ROBERT: How changeable you are. It's only a few hours ago since you insisted on kissing me.

MAUDE: This is no time for flippancy.

ROBERT: My dear Maude, if conscience took a human shape, I am convinced she would take yours. Believe me, nothing is further from me than flippancy.

MAUDE: Then your conscience *is* troubling you.

ROBERT: I never said so. It's perfectly at ease.

MAUDE: In that case your remark was senseless.

ROBERT: [*Desperately.*] Oh, heavens! I was only trying to be funny.

MAUDE: I should have thought you knew enough about cross-examination to realize that it was an extremely damaging admission.

ROBERT: Good God, woman, don't bully me. What is the matter?

MAUDE: [*Impressively.*] What have you done to Caroline?

ROBERT: I? I don't understand what you mean?

MAUDE: When we came here, Isabella and I, to congratulate her, we found Caroline in a state of complete collapse. Isn't that so, Isabella?

ISABELLA: [*A little doubtfully.*] Yes, Maude.

MAUDE: She was crying her eyes out. Her maid told us that she'd had one fainting fit after another. The *sal volatile* bottle was empty. Isn't that so, Isabella?

ISABELLA: [*Very uncomfortably.*] Yes, Maude.

MAUDE: We had to send for the doctor. He says her condition is most alarming, and it'll be a miracle if she escapes brain fever.

ROBERT: Good God!

MAUDE: I repeat, what have you done to Caroline?

ROBERT: Nothing. I asked her to marry me.

MAUDE: Ah! That confirms Caroline's statement, Isabella. And she refused. Weren't you a little surprised?

ROBERT: My dear Maude, surprised isn't the word. I was staggered. I'm reeling under the blow still.

MAUDE: It must have seemed incomprehensible.

ROBERT: Imagine. For ten years I've longed for the moment when I might be able to ask her to be my wife. It has been my dearest hope. There was nothing in the world I wanted more. She shatters all my expectations at a blow. At the moment it seems to me that I have nothing left to live for. I suppose I shall get over it in time, but . . .

MAUDE: Why don't you ask her again?

ROBERT: She made me understand that her decision was quite irrevocable. And, after all, my pride is deeply hurt. I cannot expose myself a second time to so monstrous a humiliation.

MAUDE: Fiddle!

ROBERT: Really, Maude, I think you might show me some sympathy in the bitterest disappointment of my life.

MAUDE: My dear friend, Caroline refused you because you showed her very plainly that you didn't want to marry her.

ROBERT: Oh, what nonsense! Everyone knows I wanted to marry her.

MAUDE: You asked her as though it was a duty you owed her. A woman of spirit would naturally refuse. I would have refused you myself.

ROBERT: Isabella, everyone knows Maude is a terrible liar. Tell me, is there a word of truth in what she says?

ISABELLA: Perhaps you didn't quite realize that a woman doesn't like these things arranged in too matter-of-fact a way. You should have made love to her. I'm sure you do it very well.

ROBERT: [Sitting down beside her.] What makes you think that?

ISABELLA: That is the sort of thing that every woman knows.

ROBERT: What intuition you have, Isabella.

ISABELLA: [Putting her hand on his.] I know you love her, Robert.

ROBERT: [Taking her hand.] I'm devoted to her.

ISABELLA: Let a charming story have a charming end.

ROBERT: I wonder if she really cares for me, Isabella.

ISABELLA: Oh, how can you doubt it? Women are faithful creatures, Robert.

ROBERT: Fidelity is not the characteristic which I have found most conspicuous in them in my practice at the Bar.

ISABELLA: D'you know that Caroline is jealous of you?

ROBERT: Oh, come; what makes you think that?

ISABELLA: She's furious with me. Of course, I know she's not quite herself to-day, but she's been unkind to me. It appears that you told her I had charming blue eyes.

ROBERT: So you have.

ISABELLA: You ought to have said it to me. I should have understood. I'm afraid she took it amiss.

ROBERT: You would understand anything.

ISABELLA: I suppose I have a natural gift of sympathy. Of course, Caroline is charming, but she *is* a little lacking in tenderness sometimes, don't you think so?

ROBERT: That is your most exquisite trait.

MAUDE: Really, Isabella, I don't know what you think you're doing.

ISABELLA: [*With some asperity.*] My dear, I wish you'd let me do things in my own way.

MAUDE: I can't see that anything you've said for the last five minutes will make it any clearer to Robert that it is his duty to marry Caroline.

ROBERT: Duty! Stern daughter of the voice of God.

MAUDE: You've compromised her. You've got her talked about. There's only one course open to you. You owe it to yourself and you owe it to her. And you owe it to us.

ROBERT: Oh, really. Do you think so?

MAUDE: We can't be deprived now of the satisfaction of seeing you both happy. You've behaved like a gentleman hitherto; I recommend you to play the rôle with elegance to the end.

ROBERT: [*He thinks it over for a moment. He makes up his mind.*] I'll see Caroline.

MAUDE: We will leave you. Come, Isabella. We have done our duty, and the saints in heaven can do no more.

ISABELLA: Good-bye.

> [*He opens the door for them and they go out. He rings the bell. He walks up and down moodily once or twice, but then braces himself; he is an Englishman, and fears no foe.* COOPER *comes in.*]

ROBERT: Will you ask Mrs. Ashley if I could see her for a few minutes?

COOPER: Mrs. Ashley is engaged, sir.

ROBERT: I'll wait till she is free.

COOPER: Very good, sir. [*Exit* COOPER. *In a moment she comes in again.*] Mrs. Ashley is ill, sir, and unable to see anyone.

ROBERT: I'll wait till she's well.

COOPER: Very good, sir. [*She goes out and in a moment more comes back.*] Mrs. Ashley is dead, sir.

ROBERT: I'll wait till she comes to life. This is the day of judgment, and the last trump is sounding loud and long.

COOPER: Very good, sir.

> [*Exit.   This brings* CAROLINE.

CAROLINE: Have they gone?

ROBERT: Thank God!

CAROLINE: [*Calling.*] Cooper.

COOPER: [*Coming in.*] Yes, ma'am?

CAROLINE: Put the chain on the door and don't let anyone in, or I'll give you your notice.

COOPER: Very good, ma'am.

> [*Exit.

CAROLINE: Your message was so pathetic that I had to come, Robert.

ROBERT: Look here, Caroline, you behaved very badly in putting all the blame on me. You didn't so very much want to marry me, did you?

CAROLINE: [*Smiling.*] Not so very much.

ROBERT: Then what's all this nonsense about floods of tears and fainting fits?

CAROLINE: Who told you that?

ROBERT: Maude. She said you were in a state of collapse, and would only escape brain fever by a miracle.

CAROLINE: [*Chuckling.*] You didn't believe it?

ROBERT: No. But I thought you might be up to some monkey trick.

CAROLINE: I bore the blasting of all my hopes with complete fortitude, Robert.

ROBERT: Well, now look here, Caroline, it's no good kicking against the pricks. We've got to marry.

CAROLINE: [*Energetically.*] I'm hanged if we do.

ROBERT: You know, this is only the beginning. We shall be left no peace. Sooner or later we shall be driven to it. We may just as well resign ourselves and bow to the inevitable.

CAROLINE: If I marry it'll be because I want to, not to please my friends.

ROBERT: My dear, I have a large experience of the reasons for which two people marry. They marry from pique, or loneliness, or fear, for money, position, or boredom; because they can't get out of it, or because their friends think it'll be a good thing, because no one has ever asked them before, or because they're afraid of being left on the shelf; but the one reason which infallibly leads to disaster is when they marry because they want to.

CAROLINE: You're only saying that to reassure me.

ROBERT: D'you think Maude and Isabella will give up the struggle? Never. They'll be joined by all your friends, who'll think it very funny that you don't marry, and by all mine, who'll think there's a discreditable reason on my side, by your uncles and aunts, by my nephews and nieces. My dear girl, we haven't a chance.

CAROLINE: I will fight to the last cartridge, Robert.

ROBERT: After all, I dare say we'll jog along well enough.

CAROLINE: [*Vehemently.*] Jog along! jog along! jog along! I don't want to jog along.

ROBERT: You know I'm devoted to you, Caroline.

CAROLINE: I'm devoted to you, Robert.

ROBERT: But I don't mind telling you now that at the first moment the thought of marriage frightened me out of my wits. It meant changing all my habits and forming new ones. It meant giving up my freedom. . . . You don't mind my saying this, do you?

CAROLINE: My dear, I didn't feel very differently myself.

ROBERT: It's not that I want to be a gay dog, but I want to be able to be a gay dog if I want to.

CAROLINE: I know. Don't you know how you feel when you've been a long journey, and your train steams in at night to some strange city that you've never been in before. All the lights are twinkling. And a wonderful excitement seizes you, and you think any adventure may happen to you. It never does, but it always may. Oh, Robert, if you were sitting on the seat opposite me I'd know it never could.

ROBERT: It's no good, Caroline; we're the heroes of romance, you and I. We've got to satisfy the human craving for a happy ending.

CAROLINE: I wish to heaven my husband had never died.

ROBERT: You know, Caroline, perhaps we shall feel quite differently about it when we *are* married.

CAROLINE: What makes you think that?

ROBERT: I knew a man in South Africa who was engaged to a girl in England, and he wasn't able to send for her till they'd been engaged for seven years. He went to meet her at Durban, but just as the boat was coming in his courage failed him, and he turned and ran. She chased him to Cape Town. He fled to Johannesburg. She chased him to Port Elizabeth. He fled to Lorenzo-Marquez. My dear, she chased him up and down the Continent of Africa, and at last she cornered him. She married him out of hand, and ever since he's been the happiest man alive.

CAROLINE: I'm not thinking of you, Robert, I'm thinking entirely of myself.

ROBERT: My dear, in another hour Maude will be on your doorstep.

CAROLINE: The chain is up.

ROBERT: She'll bring a camp-stool and sandwiches.

CAROLINE: Robert, this is intolerable? Is there nothing you can do?

ROBERT: Good heavens, what can I do? I'm a desperate man.

CAROLINE: I don't like to ask you to commit suicide.

ROBERT: That's lucky, because I have no intention of doing so.

CAROLINE: I suppose you wouldn't marry Maude?

ROBERT: No. Certainly not!

CAROLINE: Is there nothing you'll do for me?

ROBERT: I'll marry you.

CAROLINE: Pooh, you're doing that for yourself, not for me.

ROBERT: It's no good quarrelling. We shall have plenty of time for that when we're married.

CAROLINE: D'you know, we've never quarrelled once in all the time we've known one another.

ROBERT: That augurs well for the future, at all events.

CAROLINE: Robert, I don't want to marry you.

ROBERT: Come, my dear, just a little courage. I wouldn't press you if I saw a way out, but there isn't one.

CAROLINE: Are you sure?

ROBERT: Positive. It's the only way.

CAROLINE: It's a far, far better thing that I do than I have ever done before, Robert.

ROBERT: Then it's settled?

CAROLINE: [*With a sigh.*] It's settled.

ROBERT: We'd better get it over quickly, Caroline.

CAROLINE: I suppose nothing is gained by delaying.

ROBERT: It's lucky I didn't resign from those clubs as I talked of doing.

CAROLINE: Why?

ROBERT: Well, it was a mere extravagance, I never went near them; but I shall want them when I am married.

CAROLINE: I thought it was chiefly bachelors who used clubs.

ROBERT: Oh, no; bachelors don't mind staying at home.

CAROLINE: This will make a great change in your life, Robert.

ROBERT: I've always been very domestic. I dare say it'll do me good to be shaken up a bit.

CAROLINE: You spent practically all your evenings here. I'm sure it won't hurt you to see a little more of other people.

ROBERT: We were getting into a groove, Caroline. I dare say it wanted something like this to stir us up. I look forward to the future with considerable pleasure.

CAROLINE: The past was very pleasant, Robert. A *tête-à-tête* will never be the same thing again.

ROBERT: You're thinking of the little suppers we used to have at the Savoy after the play. They were jolly, weren't they?

CAROLINE: And you know, Robert, I never lost the little thrill it gave me to come and dine with you in your house. They were harmless little dinners enough, but there was always a sense of adventure when I took off my cloak in your hall.

ROBERT: By the way, what are you going to do about getting rid of your house?

CAROLINE: [*Astounded.*] I'm not going to get rid of my house.

ROBERT: My dear, we don't want two.

CAROLINE: Of course not. I naturally supposed you'd sell yours.

ROBERT: Why? I've had my house for twenty years. I'm very much attached to it. You've only got a lease.

CAROLINE: That's got nothing to do with it. I've just had it redecorated. I've spent a fortune on my bathroom.

ROBERT: You're not going to ask me to have my bath in a futurist bathroom. I never feel my best before breakfast as it is.

CAROLINE: I'm sorry you don't like my bathroom. But that's a matter of taste.

ROBERT: Personally, I don't see what anyone can want more than plain white tiles. It's clean, sanitary and cheerful.

CAROLINE: [*Beginning to be vexed.*] Oh, of course you always think your own things are better than anybody else's. Your bathroom is just like a tube station. I really can't see myself having my bath in it. I should be afraid all the time that a young man was going to pop in and say: Next station—Marble Arch!

ROBERT: My dear child, you must be sensible. It's perfectly obvious that my house is a much nicer one than yours.

CAROLINE: [*Sharply.*] I don't agree with you at all.

ROBERT: [*Impatiently.*] Of course, if you won't listen to reason, there's nothing more to be said.

CAROLINE: I tell you frankly that nothing will induce me to leave this house.

ROBERT: Really, this is sheer obstinacy. There's no room for me here. There's not even a room that I can make into a study.

CAROLINE: Oh, yes, there is. There's that very nice little room behind the dining-room.

ROBERT: [*Indignantly.*] It looks out on a blank wall.

CAROLINE: That's just why I thought it would do so well for a study. There'll be nothing to distract your thoughts.

ROBERT: You've told me a hundred times you could do nothing with it—it was like an ice-box in winter and like a furnace in summer. Really, if you have no more affection for me than that . . .

CAROLINE: It isn't a matter of affection, it's a matter of commonsense. Your house is very nice for a bachelor . . .

ROBERT: [*Interrupting.*] Thank you.

CAROLINE: But it's quite unsuitable for a woman. There are no cupboards.

ROBERT: Now you're *making* difficulties, Caroline. Cupboards can be built.

CAROLINE: And which room have you settled for my boudoir? The coal-cellar? It's preposterous.

ROBERT: [*With temper.*] I'm not going to argue the matter, Caroline. I've made up my mind and there's an end of it.

CAROLINE: [*Quite decidedly.*] I happen to have made up my mind too.

ROBERT: When I was waiting for you just now I decided exactly how to arrange matters. You shall have the best bedroom, of course.

CAROLINE: It hasn't any sun, I know it.

ROBERT: [*With dignity.*] It is the room that my poor Aunt Charlotte died in, Caroline.

CAROLINE: That doesn't make it any pleasanter for me to live in.

ROBERT: My dear Caroline, I cannot understand your attitude.

CAROLINE: It's quite simple. I'm pleased with my house and I'm going to stick to it.

ROBERT: It's fortunate that I'm the most patient man in the world. It's obvious that a woman comes to her husband's house.

CAROLINE: I don't see why at all.

ROBERT: My dear, it's one of the best-established customs of the human race. We have Biblical authority for it. A woman is enjoined to forsake all and follow her husband.

CAROLINE: You don't know what you're talking about. Before you quote the Bible I recommend you to read it.

ROBERT: [*Fuming.*] Really, Caroline, I must protest against the tone you're taking up. *I* am discussing the matter in the most friendly spirit.

CAROLINE: [*Furious.*] Surely you're not going to accuse me of being acrimonious. You said just now we'd never quarrelled. Believe me, it isn't because you haven't given me abundant provocation.

ROBERT: I think we'll resume the conversation when you're a little calmer, Caroline. You'll only say things now which you'll regret later.

CAROLINE: Don't think for an instant you can impress me by being patronizing, Robert. I have no wish to resume the conversation. I've already said all I had to say.

ROBERT: The great thing is that we should clearly understand one another. I am prepared to gratify all your whims, however unreasonable they may be, and heaven knows, for the most part they're unreasonable enough; but this is a matter of principle. I mean to begin as I mean to go on. I wish you to put this house in the agent's hands at once.

CAROLINE: I shall do nothing of the sort.

ROBERT: Caroline, I have put my request in the most courteous and obliging way possible; but I do not expect it to be disregarded.

CAROLINE: I presume you are talking for your own entertainment; you're certainly not talking for mine.

ROBERT: Let me make myself quite clear, Caroline. I refuse to come and live in this house.

CAROLINE: That is unfortunate, because nothing will induce me to come and live in yours.

ROBERT: Perhaps you'd like to think the matter over.

CAROLINE: No, thank you. I've quite made up my mind. If you want to marry me you must come and live here.

ROBERT: I will not marry you unless you consent to live in my house.

CAROLINE: Very well. That settles it.

ROBERT: Take care, Caroline. I've proposed twice now. I shall not propose a third time.

CAROLINE: I wouldn't marry you now if you crawled on your bended knees from the Tower of London to Buckingham Palace.

ROBERT: In that case the marriage is off, Caroline.

CAROLINE: I was willing to sacrifice myself, but it's a little too much to expect that all the sacrificing should be on my side.

ROBERT: Sacrifice, you call it. I was marrying you out of pure good nature.

CAROLINE: Good heavens, what an escape I've had! I might have been chained to you for life.

ROBERT: It shows what women are. Even the ablest men are children in their hands. I've known you ten years, Caroline, and this is the first time you've shown yourself in your true colours.

CAROLINE: I've always known that you were selfish, vain and dyspeptic; but I shut my eyes to it. I've been punished. I didn't like you the first time I saw you. It's always a mistake not to trust to first impressions.

ROBERT: In that case, I'm surprised that you threw yourself at my head in the way you did.

CAROLINE: Thank heaven, my eyes are opened at last! And as to throwing myself at your head, I would never have looked at you if you hadn't pestered me with your attentions.

ROBERT: [Ironically.] I suppose you were sorry for me?

CAROLINE: No, but I knew you were *safe*. And I can't imagine anything more ridiculous in a man than that.

ROBERT: [Boiling.] Oh! oh! I will never speak to you again, Caroline.

CAROLINE: You don't think I wish to continue our acquaintance, do you?

ROBERT: Have you anything more to say to me?

CAROLINE: Only this. Perhaps you'd like to meditate over it. If you were the only man in the world I wouldn't marry you.

ROBERT: Caroline, I can truthfully say that if I had to choose between the altar and the scaffold I would undoubtedly choose the scaffold. Good-bye.

CAROLINE: Good riddance! [He is going to the door. Suddenly the telephone bell rings. They both give a gasp. They look at one another in dismay. The bell rings firmly.] It's Maude.

ROBERT: Good God! I'd forgotten about her.

CAROLINE: What shall I do?

ROBERT: I'm off, Caroline.

CAROLINE: You coward! You can't leave me like that.

ROBERT: Well, you'd better answer it.

CAROLINE: You answer it, Robert. You're a man.

ROBERT: I daren't, Caroline.

> [*Meanwhile the bell rings persistently, angrily.*

CAROLINE: For goodness' sake, stop it ringing!

ROBERT: It'll never stop till you answer.

CAROLINE: I wish to heaven I'd never had the telephone put in.

ROBERT: I always disliked Maude.

CAROLINE: She's a detestable woman!

ROBERT: I can't imagine why you ever put up with her.

CAROLINE: I hate her, I hate her! [*Desperately.*] For goodness' sake, stop that ringing!

ROBERT: Take the receiver off.

CAROLINE: You take it off, Robert.

ROBERT: Caroline.

CAROLINE: Oh, Robert, if you've ever loved me.

ROBERT: I'll do it.

> [*He creeps towards the table as though it were a beast that might bite; he stalks it carefully, stealthily, then with a sudden bound leaps on to the telephone and snatches the receiver off.* CAROLINE *gives a shriek. He bounds back and they are close together. She clings to him. They tremble with fear.*

ROBERT: I've done it.

CAROLINE: Don't leave me, Robert.

ROBERT: No, I won't leave you.

CAROLINE: Oh, Robert, I shall never forget this.

ROBERT: She thinks we're listening. She's talking at her end now. I expect she's getting angry. She's making a scene.

CAROLINE: Oh, Robert, I wonder what she's saying.

ROBERT: Can't you guess?

CAROLINE: Thank God, the chain is on the door! She'll be round in ten minutes.

[*They look at one another in dismay.*

ROBERT: It's no good, Caroline. We've got to get married.

CAROLINE: I know. But what is to be done? You must think of some way out, Robert.

ROBERT: There's only one. We must give up both houses and take a new one.

CAROLINE: But I like my house, Robert.

ROBERT: I like mine.

CAROLINE: It'll be a wrench for both of us. That's some comfort.

ROBERT: Our first sacrifice on the altar of connubial bliss.

CAROLINE: You'll let me decorate the new house, Robert.

ROBERT: All except the bathroom. Give me that as a wedding-present.

CAROLINE: I tell you what, we'll each have a bathroom. You can have yours like a tube station.

ROBERT: And you shall have one like an attack of gastritis.

CAROLINE: [*With a sigh.*] If it's got to be done it had better be done at once. I'll ring up the house agent.

[*She takes up the telephone-book and looks out an address.*

ROBERT: Shall we be married by special licence?

CAROLINE: I haven't an idea.

ROBERT: I think I'll just go round to the club. Petersen is sure to be there, and he's had a lot of experience in these matters. There's no reason why I shouldn't ask him that.

CAROLINE: Oh, how did the divorce go?

ROBERT: First rate. I think it'll last for four or five days. Neither of them will have a shred of reputation by the time it's over.

CAROLINE: [*At the telephone.*] Mayfair 148. Are you Messrs. Gaskell and Birch? I want to let my house. . . . I can't say it all on the telephone. Will you send somebody round. No. At once. Where? Oh, Mrs. Ashley, Curzon Terrace, Regent's Park.

[She puts down the receiver.

ROBERT: Is there anything more you want to say to me? I'll be back presently to tell you what I've found out.

CAROLINE: Before dinner?

ROBERT: Oh, yes. By the way, about dinner. Don't you think we need cheering up a bit? I'm afraid it would be rather dull dining by ourselves.

CAROLINE: I think it would rather.

ROBERT: Why don't you ask Isabella?

CAROLINE: Rex Cunningham is dining with her. I might ask him too, and we can play bridge.

ROBERT: Oh, yes; that'll be jolly. [CAROLINE *takes out her patience cards.*] What are you going to do now?

CAROLINE: Oh, I'll have a game of patience.

ROBERT: Yes, do. It'll rest you.

[He goes towards the door.

CAROLINE: Robert.

ROBERT: Yes?

CAROLINE: It's emeralds I like, you know.

ROBERT: I'm glad you reminded me.

[*He goes out. She begins to put out her patience cards.*

END OF THE SECOND ACT

THE THIRD ACT

SCENE: *The same. It is ten minutes later.*

[CAROLINE *is finishing her game of patience.* COOPER *shows in* DR. CORNISH.

COOPER: Dr. Cornish.

[*Exit.*

CAROLINE: This is a joyful surprise. I've torn up your prescription.

DR. CORNISH: How on earth do you expect a doctor to make a living if you won't take medicine! You'll remain perfectly well.

CAROLINE: You didn't talk like that just now.

DR. CORNISH: That was a visit. This is a call.

CAROLINE: I hesitate to ask his reason.

DR. CORNISH: You need not. I was just going to tell you. I'm devoured with curiosity.

CAROLINE: That isn't one of the failings that middle-age eradicates?

DR. CORNISH: Tell me, which has won, romance or common-sense? Are you going to marry Robert Oldham or Rex Cunningham?

CAROLINE: My dear doctor, Rex Cunningham is a mere boy.

DR. CORNISH: Oh, I've known those marriages turn out very well. My last cook married the lad who came in to do the boots and knives, and they're very happy. At least I haven't heard anything to the contrary.

CAROLINE: I wonder how she worked it.

DR. CORNISH: The policy of nag, I believe.

CAROLINE: I've promised to marry Robert Oldham.

DR. CORNISH: Then it only remains for me to congratulate you.

CAROLINE: One comfort is that my friends will have to give me wedding-presents. I get back on them that way, don't I?

DR. CORNISH: I'm sure you'll be very happy.

CAROLINE: [*Tartly.*] I'm sure I shall be nothing of the sort.

DR. CORNISH: Don't jump down my throat.

CAROLINE: You know I'm very fond of Robert. I don't want to lose him.

DR. CORNISH: Is that inevitable?

CAROLINE: Haven't you noticed that other people's bread-and-butter is always much nicer than your own? Robert is like that. He always prefers somebody else's fireside. If I marry him, where is he going to spend his evenings?

DR. CORNISH: I only see one way out of it. You must marry somebody else.

CAROLINE: I believe it's the only way I can keep Robert. It's very hard if you come to think of it.

DR. CORNISH: Especially on the innocent victim.

CAROLINE: Whom d'you think I'd better marry?

DR. CORNISH: Let us examine your circle of friends and see who would meet your requirements.

CAROLINE: [*With a twinkle in her eye.*] I don't think it ought to be anyone too young.

DR. CORNISH: No, a man of a certain age.

CAROLINE: I rather like grey hair, don't you?

DR. CORNISH: A professional man, of course.

CAROLINE: Oh, yes, I'd like him to have interests in common with Robert.

DR. CORNISH: He oughtn't to be a barrister. It would be such a bore for you if they talked shop together.

CAROLINE: I don't see why he shouldn't be a doctor.

DR. CORNISH: Yes, I don't think that's a bad idea. And of course if he had a pretty large practice it would keep him busy, wouldn't it?

CAROLINE: Yes. Now, there's only one thing more. I think he ought to be a great friend of Roberts.

DR. CORNISH: Obviously that would make matters much simpler. Now, let us think. I wonder who there is.

CAROLINE: Don't bother, Dr. Cornish. I've already made up my mind.

DR. CORNISH: God bless my soul, you're very quick.

CAROLINE: *You* are going to marry me.

DR. CORNISH: [*With great decision.*] No, I'm not.

CAROLINE: Now, my dear friend, don't be unreasonable. You meet the requirements in a manner that I can only describe as miraculous.

DR. CORNISH: My dear lady, let us put things in their places. I am your medical attendant, not an aspirant to your hand.

CAROLINE: Oh, but you said just now that this was a call and not a visit.

DR. CORNISH: We can easily settle that. I will charge you half a guinea, and that makes it a visit.

CAROLINE: I thought you were a man of the world.

DR. CORNISH: If that means getting out of an awkward predicament gracefully, I flatter myself I am.

CAROLINE: No, it doesn't. It means accepting the inevitable with elegance.

DR. CORNISH: The inevitable is only what a fool has not the wit to avoid.

CAROLINE: Believe me, when a woman really makes up her mind to marry a man nothing on God's earth can save him.

DR. CORNISH: No one is more conscious than I of your advantages. I am sure any man would be lucky to get you, but you know I'm very modest. I don't deserve so much happiness.

CAROLINE: Your diffidence gives you a new charm in my eyes. It shall be the object of my life to prove you mistaken.

DR. CORNISH: I have too much affection for you to consent for an instant to your wasting your efforts on so unworthy an object.

CAROLINE: Ah, then you have an affection for me.

DR. CORNISH: A purely medical affection, if I may so put it.

CAROLINE: Good heavens, it sounds like mumps.

DR. CORNISH: You know, you should have had that prescription made up. I told you you needed soothing.

CAROLINE: I find *you* soothing. That's one of the reasons why I consent to marry you.

DR. CORNISH: Don't let us lose sight of the point that I haven't asked you.

CAROLINE: Well, do.

DR. CORNISH: You might accept me.

CAROLINE: I undoubtedly should.

DR. CORNISH: Then I don't think I'll risk it.

CAROLINE: You'd better. It will only be embarrassing for both of us if I have to make the proposal.

DR. CORNISH: I can always say no.

CAROLINE: Oh, but I wouldn't take a refusal.

DR. CORNISH: You're a perfect monster of determination.

CAROLINE: When I think of Robert's great affection for me, I'm prepared for anything.

DR. CORNISH: I don't wish to seem brutal, but I really must tell you that in my heart of hearts I am completely indifferent to Robert's affection for you.

CAROLINE: I thought he was a great friend of yours.

DR. CORNISH: He is.

CAROLINE: Then you must want to make him happy. I'm sure he'd like you to be my husband.

DR. CORNISH: You're putting me in a very embarrassing position.

CAROLINE: I wonder if you know how very pleasant it is to be married.

DR. CORNISH: I'm sure it's delightful for those who like it.

CAROLINE: There are a hundred ways in which a woman can make a man comfortable.

DR. CORNISH: There are a thousand and one in which she can do the reverse.

CAROLINE: I always think there's something rather cold and cheerless about a house that lacks a woman's touch.

DR. CORNISH: How true! I feel quite sure that if you put that before Robert as persuasively as you have before me he will realize how very lucky he is to be going to marry you.

CAROLINE: Pray, don't be flippant. *You* are going to marry me.

DR. CORNISH: No.

CAROLINE: Yes.

DR. CORNISH: [*With a smile.*] After all, you can't force me.

CAROLINE: I can make life intolerable to you unless you do.

DR. CORNISH: You're a very dangerous woman.

CAROLINE: But you're a very brave man.

DR. CORNISH: I can't help thinking that Robert would look upon it as a very unfriendly action on my part.

CAROLINE: Only for a moment. He'd soon realize that we'd only had his happiness in view.

DR. CORNISH: If you find a husband so essential, why were you so careless as to lose your last?

CAROLINE: I never knew what a useful article it was about a house.

DR. CORNISH: It doesn't inspire confidence, you know.

CAROLINE: I'll be more careful with you.

DR. CORNISH: [*With a chuckle.*] It would be an awful sell for him, wouldn't it?

CAROLINE: Can't you see his face when you tell him?

DR. CORNISH: [*Considering her.*] Of course, you're a very charming woman.

CAROLINE: People have thought so.

DR. CORNISH: [*Impulsively.*] I think Robert's a fool. He should never have hesitated.

CAROLINE: He shouldn't have, should he?

DR. CORNISH: It would serve him jolly well right if someone stepped over his head and seized the opportunity that he hadn't the courage to take.

CAROLINE: I'd rather you spoke of me as a prize than as an opportunity. That suggests a remnant at a sale.

[*He gives her a long look. There is a twinkle in his eye.*]

DR. CORNISH: Caroline, will you be my wife?

CAROLINE: I? [*For a moment she is surprised, but she quickly recovers herself.*] I hardly know what to say to you. This is so unexpected. It never entered my head that you— that you cared for me. [*She takes the plunge with determination.*] Yes, I will be your wife.

DR. CORNISH: I've always thought it would be very nice to have someone on whom I could experiment with new medicines when they're put on the market.

CAROLINE: [*Somewhat taken aback.*] Oh! How have you managed up till now?

DR. CORNISH: [*Blandly.*] I've generally tried them on the maids, but they have no interest in science; they will give me their notice. But, of course, you couldn't do that, could you?

CAROLINE: I haven't got a very great interest in science myself.

DR. CORNISH: Oh, but it'll come. I'm sure you won't hesitate at a trifling inconvenience when you realize how much it means to me.

CAROLINE: [*Pursing her lips.*] If there are any other duties which you expect of me, I hope you'll tell me at once.

DR. CORNISH: I don't know that there are. Of course, you'll have to lead a very retired life. People don't much like meeting their doctor's wife; they're always afraid she knows too much about their insides. In fact, the most desirable thing is that she should be a confirmed invalid.

CAROLINE: I imagine that would follow almost automatically on a course of medicines whose properties you were entirely unfamiliar with.

DR. CORNISH: That is one of those admirable contrivances which confirm one in the belief that the world is not a matter of pure chance.

CAROLINE: [*Shaking off the doubts which his remarks have suggested.*] Oh, well, I don't care. When I think of the faces they'll all make when you tell them the news, everything is worth while.

DR. CORNISH: I see the joke from your point of view much more than from mine.

CAROLINE: Isabella will think it very touching and she'll probably kiss you.

DR. CORNISH: She's a very pretty young woman.

CAROLINE: Maude will think I've behaved abominably, and she'll tell me so with gusto. But Robert—I wonder what Robert will look like. I'm going to telephone to Isabella. [*She touches the bell.*] They've spent a happy day here to please themselves. Now it's my turn.

DR. CORNISH: Are you expecting Robert?

H

CAROLINE: Yes. Dear Robert. He went to buy me a ring. [COOPER *comes in.*] Cooper, ring up Mrs. Trench and ask her to come round at once. I have something very important to tell her.

COOPER: Very good, ma'am.

Exit.

CAROLINE: Now listen. Maude, if I know her, is on her way to this house. I'm only surprised that she hasn't come already. Robert can't be long. Then there's Isabella. You mustn't say a word till they're all here. Then——

DR. CORNISH: Yes, what then?

CAROLINE: Then you'll stand here and you'll get into an appropriate attitude. You'll try and look merry and bright, won't you?

DR. CORNISH: Oh, d'you think so? I should have thought an air of stern resolution would be more to the point.

CAROLINE: Remember that you've loved me in secret for seven years.

DR. CORNISH: It's the seven which seems to me a little difficult to indicate on my face.

CAROLINE: Then you'll say to them: My dear friends, I have a communication to impart which will be in the nature of a surprise to all of you. Caroline has consented to be my wife. And then we'll see what happens.

DR. CORNISH: I see.

CAROLINE: What d'you think will happen?

[*Enter* COOPER, *followed by* MISS FULTON.

COOPER: Miss Fulton.

[*Exit.*

MAUDE: Well, Caroline. Oh, how do you do again, Dr. Cornish? [*To* CAROLINE.] Is anything the matter with you?

CAROLINE: [*Mysteriously.*] No. Dr. Cornish hasn't come to see me about my health.

DR. CORNISH: No.

MAUDE: Where is Robert?

CAROLINE: He's gone out.

MAUDE: You haven't sent him away?

CAROLINE: He did what you wished, Maude.

MAUDE: [*With triumph.*] Ah. I knew it only needed a little firmness and everything could be put right.

CAROLINE: Maude, something has happened which puts an entirely different complexion on things.

MAUDE: [*Suddenly suspicious.*] What on earth do you mean? Dr. Cornish!

DR. CORNISH: All in good time, my dear lady.

MAUDE: Isn't everything all right?

CAROLINE: It depends on what you mean by all right.

MAUDE: My dear . . .

CAROLINE: You must wait till Robert comes. It's only fair that nobody should know before he does. [*To* DR. CORNISH.] Don't you agree with me?

DR. CORNISH: Perfectly.

MAUDE: By the way, have you had an answer to the telegram you sent to Nairobi?

CAROLINE: No, I haven't yet.

> [COOPER *comes in to announce* ROBERT OLDHAM *and then goes out.*

COOPER: Mr. Oldham!

CAROLINE: [*Cordially.*] Ah, Robert, I've been wondering what had happened to you.

ROBERT: Good God, there's Maude.

CAROLINE: And Dr. Cornish.

ROBERT: Hulloa! I've not seen you for a long time. What d'you think of the news?

CAROLINE: Dr. Cornish has some news, too, Robert.

MAUDE: If I am not told it soon I shall have an attack of hysterics.

ROBERT: I've seen Petersen, Caroline.

CAROLINE: You shall tell me what he said later.

ROBERT: You're very strange, Caroline.

CAROLINE: You must have a moment's patience.

MAUDE: Why?

CAROLINE: I want Isabella to be here. She takes such an interest in me I feel that she, too, should know something that makes so great a difference to my future.

ROBERT: [*Somewhat irritably.*] I don't understand. I hate mysteries.

DR. CORNISH: I have something to tell you which is very important, but Mrs. Ashley does not wish me to break it to you till all her friends are gathered round her.

CAROLINE: Exactly.

MAUDE: I like mysteries, but I hate suspense.

ROBERT: Oh, Cornish, has Caroline told you what we've decided on?

DR. CORNISH: She's told me that you wish to marry her.

ROBERT: You know I've been devoted to her for years.

CAROLINE: We need not go into that now, Robert.

MAUDE: I'm beginning to grow very uneasy.

[*Enter* COOPER.

COOPER: Mrs. Trench and Mr. Cunningham.

[*They enter.*

CAROLINE: At last.

ISABELLA: What is the matter, Caroline? Fortunately Rex was at my door. He was just going to take me for a drive in the Park.

CAROLINE: His two-seater is so useful, isn't it?

ISABELLA: So I made him bring me here at once. Has anything happened? Your message has made me dreadfully anxious.

REX: We're both dreadfully anxious, Caroline.

CAROLINE: What is it, Cooper?

COOPER: There's a gentleman called. He says he has an appointment with you, ma'am.

CAROLINE: [*Taking the card.*] Gaskell and Birch. Oh, I know; they're the house agents.

ROBERT: Of course. You rang them up just before I left you. Cooper can take him round the house.

CAROLINE: Thank the gentleman for coming, Cooper, and say I'm sorry to have troubled him. I shan't be wanting to let my house just yet after all.

ROBERT: [*Astounded.*] Caroline!

CAROLINE: That's all, Cooper.

COOPER: Very good, ma'am.

[*Exit.*

ROBERT: What is the meaning of this? You agreed that you would get rid of your house. If you've changed your mind, Caroline . . .

CAROLINE: Wait one moment, Robert. Now, dear Doctor, I think the time has arrived. Will you tell them—everything?

DR. CORNISH: [*Stepping forward.*] Yes. My dear friends, I have a communication to impart which will be in the nature of a surprise to all of you.

ISABELLA: I can simply hear my heart beating.

DR. CORNISH: [*Looking steadily at* CAROLINE.] Stephen Ashley walked out of this room exactly five minutes ago.

ALL: What?

[*No one is more taken aback than* CAROLINE. DR. CORNISH *watches her with extreme, but inward, entertainment.*

DR. CORNISH: I have seen him with my own eyes. He's no more dead than I am.

REX: My hat!

ISABELLA: I don't understand. Caroline!

CAROLINE: No one can be more flabbergasted than I.

DR. CORNISH: It's not the first time his death has been announced. When I came in and found him I was hardly surprised.

CAROLINE: I don't know if I'm standing on my head or on my heels.

DR. CORNISH: He can very easily live for twenty years.

CAROLINE: D'you think he will?

DR. CORNISH: If proper care is taken of him.

MAUDE: My poor Caroline, what a disappointment for you.

DR. CORNISH: You must all of you be very gentle with Caroline. [*To* CAROLINE.] I can only offer you my sincerest sympathy.

CAROLINE: You're not going?

DR. CORNISH: [*With a smile.*] I'm going to leave you to deal with the situation as best you can.

CAROLINE: [*Under her breath.*] You brute!

DR. CORNISH: If a man of the world is one who can get out of an awkward predicament gracefully. . . . Good-bye.

[*He goes out quickly.*

ISABELLA: You're bearing it magnificently.

CAROLINE: [*Trying not to laugh.*] D'you think so? It's been an awful strain. I've just about reached the end of my strength. I think I'm going to faint.

ISABELLA: Robert, open the window. You look a perfect wreck.

CAROLINE: [*Beginning to giggle.*] No, I'm going to have a nerve storm.

MAUDE: Don't let yourself go, Caroline. Don't let yourself go.

CAROLINE: [*Gurgling.*] I can't help it.

[*She starts laughing. Her laughter grows louder and louder.
They all press round her.*

ALL: Caroline, Caroline.

CAROLINE: It was such a shock!

ISABELLA: Where are my smelling salts?

MAUDE: How stupid of me!

[*The two ladies hurriedly take salts from their bags and put
them under* CAROLINE'S *nose while she helplessly
laughs and laughs.*

MAUDE: Here are some. Slap her hands.

[*The two men take her hands and slap the palms.*

ROBERT: Stop it, Caroline, stop it!

ISABELLA: Let's send for the doctor.

MAUDE: What's the good of a doctor? I know **exactly** what
to do. Slap her feet.

CAROLINE: I won't have my feet slapped.

MAUDE: Don't pay any attention to what she says.

[*While the men continue slapping her hands the ladies slap
her feet.* CAROLINE *laughs uproariously. At last she
is exhausted.*

CAROLINE: Oh, dear!

MAUDE: Now she's getting better. I knew the best thing
was to slap her feet. If that doesn't stop it, then the
thing is to wrap her in a rug and roll her up and down the
floor.

CAROLINE: Maude, you cat! Oh, I'm beginning to feel
better.

ROBERT: After all, one can't be surprised, can one?

MAUDE: Good heavens, if my husband suddenly appeared
like that I should fall down in a fit.

REX: I didn't know you had a husband.

MAUDE: I haven't. That's why it would be such a terrible
shock.

ISABELLA: Now you must tell us everything, Caroline.

CAROLINE: There's nothing to tell.

MAUDE: Nonsense. How did he come in?

CAROLINE: On his feet.

MAUDE: Don't be silly. What did he do? What did he say? What is he up to? Where is he going?

CAROLINE: Oh!

> [*This is a long-drawn sound as she realizes what she is in for and what she must invent.*

ROBERT: Don't worry her. Hasn't she been through enough already, poor child?

CAROLINE: How good you are to me, Robert!

MAUDE: It can't hurt you just to give us the bare facts, Caroline.

CAROLINE: Sit down, then, and I will tell you all.

> [*They seat themselves on chairs, two on each side of her, eager for a full account.*

ROBERT: Now don't excite yourself, Caroline. I beseech you to be calm.

MAUDE: Hold your tongue, Robert.

CAROLINE: Well, I was sitting down quite calmly playing a game of patience. Robert had just left me.

ROBERT: On what an errand!

MAUDE: I know. You had arranged to be married. I saw it at once in Robert's look. My poor Robert!

ROBERT: [*Simply.*] I had told Caroline I couldn't live without her. She promised to be mine.

CAROLINE: He went out to buy a ring. I was wondering if it would be a cabochon.

ROBERT: [*Gloomily.*] Would you like to see?

> [*He takes out of his pocket a large emerald ring.*

CAROLINE: Oh, Robert, what a beauty! It looks frightfully expensive.

ROBERT: Oh, a mere song. I wonder if they'll take it back.

CAROLINE: Don't bother about that, Robert. I will keep it as a memento of our short engagement.

             [ROBERT's *face falls.*

ISABELLA: What a charming idea, Caroline!

ROBERT: [*With a hollow laugh.*] There's no one like Caroline to have charming ideas like that.

MAUDE: Go on, Caroline.

CAROLINE: I only wanted a seven to get my patience out. I drew a ten of clubs, a three of spades. I don't believe I shall get it, I said. Suddenly Cooper opened the door and said a gentleman wanted to see me.

ALL: Yes, yes!

             [*They draw their chairs a little closer.*

CAROLINE: I thought it was the house agent.

ROBERT: Of course. You rang him up just before I left.

CAROLINE: Oh, Robert, I want to tell you that I thought it over. It seemed cruel to make you sell your dear little house. After all, a woman should cleave to her husband. I had made up my mind to get rid of this one, and come and live in yours.

ROBERT: Caroline, were you ready to do that for me?

THE OTHERS: Go on, Caroline.

CAROLINE: I didn't hesitate. I said to Cooper: Show the gentleman up. I went on with my patience. Ah, I said, there's the seven at last! I raised my eyes, and there was my husband standing before me.

ALL: Oh! . . .

CAROLINE: [*Dramatically.*] You, I said. Yes, he said. Not dead? I said. No, he said.

MAUDE: It's the most exciting thing I've ever heard in my life.

ISABELLA: What did you do then?

CAROLINE: [*Deliberately.*] I asked him to sit down.

ROBERT: That was splendid. You always had presence of mind, Caroline. I like that. You asked him to sit down.

CAROLINE: I wanted to gain time. I was all in a flutter.

MAUDE: Of course, I think it was monstrous of him to come here at all.

CAROLINE: He did it in kindness, Maude. He saw the notice in The Times this morning, and he thought I might be anxious about him. He said he felt the only thing to do was to come here himself and tell me the announcement was premature.

ISABELLA: But, then, what is the explanation of it?

CAROLINE: The explanation? I'm just coming to that.

ROBERT: Really the papers ought to be more careful!

MAUDE: Go on, Caroline; we're simply hanging on your words.

CAROLINE: I'm not sure, but I think I'm going to have another nerve storm.

MAUDE: Get the hearthrug, Rex. That'll just do to roll her up in.

CAROLINE: No, don't bother. I think it's going off. The explanation is perfectly simple. Just give me a moment to collect my thoughts. You know. I'm quite dazed after all I've gone through to-day.

ISABELLA: Take your time, dearest.

CAROLINE: Well, I may as well confess to you now that poor Stephen has always been very wild. It appears that he was in with a man called Brown, and they'd been connected in some deal or other which I'm afraid was dreadfully shady. Of course, I didn't ask for details. It's all rather vague in my mind.

ROBERT: That's only natural.

MAUDE: Oh, be quiet, Robert.

CAROLINE: They had a row, and Brown bolted with all Stephen's belongings, his papers, his kit, everything. Then I don't know exactly what happened. Brown seems to have been taken suddenly ill. When he was brought to the hospital he was unconscious. They found Stephen's papers on him and naturally concluded he was Stephen.

MAUDE: I see it all. It's a thing that might happen to anybody.

CAROLINE: [*Eagerly.*] Yes, isn't it? Stephen saw the announcement in this morning's Times. He grasped the whole situation. I don't think he's sorry the authorities in East Africa should believe him dead. He's made up his mind to go to Texas. Stephen Ashley is dead to everyone but me.

MAUDE: At all events, you've seen him for the last time, Caroline. That's something to be thankful for.

CAROLINE: I suppose so.

ROBERT: What do you mean by that? Aren't you sure of it?

CAROLINE: There's one other thing I must tell you. I hardly know how to say it. He still loves me.

REX: Caroline.

CAROLINE: He asked me to go to Texas.

ALL: You!

CAROLINE: He's going to start a new life. He said I should give him confidence in himself. He implored me to go with him.

ROBERT: But of course you refused, Caroline?

CAROLINE: I was obliged to refuse. Then he said that I would be an inspiration to him. He would do everything in the world to make amends for the past. He would make himself a new man, and then he would come back for me.

ISABELLA: It's really very beautiful.

ROBERT: And where do I come in?

CAROLINE: I can never marry you, Robert.

ROBERT: Caroline, you fill me with anguish. . . . I must be alone for a moment. I don't want to be unmanly.

> [*He gets up and walks slowly to the window. He stands there struggling with his emotions.* REX *is sunk in blank wretchedness.*

MAUDE: Well, Isabella, we did all *we* could. We at all events have nothing to reproach ourselves with.

ISABELLA: Poor Robert. My heart bleeds for him. There's something singularly awe-inspiring in the sight of a strong man wrestling with his emotion.

MAUDE: It's not often that I confess myself beaten, but this time I really am at a loss. Good-bye, Caroline. I'll ring up this evening to see how you are.

CAROLINE: Good-bye, dearest. I can never thank you enough for all you've done for me to-day.

> [*They kiss, and* MISS FULTON *goes out.*

ISABELLA: I must leave you too, Caroline, but I'd just like to say a word or two to Robert before I go. It's just at these times that a man values a woman's sympathy.

CAROLINE: Oh, do, Isabella. I know what a heart you have. [ISABELLA *goes up to* ROBERT *and puts her hand gently on his arm. He heaves a sigh and gently pats her hand. She looks up at him softly. They step out on to the balcony.* CAROLINE *and* REX *have watched the little comedy.*] At it again. Dear Isabella, she's so sympathetic.

REX: [*Gloomily.*] If there's anyone in want of sympathy now it's me.

CAROLINE: Is anything the matter?

REX: Can *you* ask me that? Oh, Caroline, everything is the matter. I love you.

CAROLINE: Oh, you mustn't say that to me now, Rex—so loud.

REX: This changes everything.

CAROLINE: I suppose it does. I never thought of it.

REX: You never thought of me at all. Oh, Caroline, you must be quite heartless. Has anyone ever loved you as unselfishly as I have?

CAROLINE: Now that I have one man with a marriage certificate in his hand, so to speak, and another with a special licence in his pocket, it does make a difference, doesn't it?

REX: My position is absolutely intolerable.

CAROLINE: [*With a sigh of self-satisfaction.*] I am the un-attainable.

REX: [*Absorbed in himself.*] Oh, how I'm going to suffer. I'm going to endure absolute agonies.

CAROLINE: [*In exactly the same condition.*] I am young. I am beautiful. I am desired.

REX: You're not paying any attention to me. I adore you, Caroline.

CAROLINE: [*Looking away modestly.*] I can never love you, Rex.

REX: Are you quite, quite sure of that, Caroline?

CAROLINE: Quite, quite.

REX: [*With a sigh of satisfaction.*] My heart's never been so broken as this time. It'll take me all my life to piece it together again. You do believe in my love now, don't you?

CAROLINE: Oh, yes. A woman has such quick intuition. I know that you love me.

REX: I shall pass sleepless night after sleepless night.

CAROLINE: I can hardly bear to think of it.

REX: And there's nothing you can do, is there?

CAROLINE: Nothing.

REX: [*With immense enjoyment.*] I'm simply going to have a rotten time.

CAROLINE: It's wonderful to be capable of such love.

REX: Yes, I'm like that. I never knew anyone who could suffer as I can.

CAROLINE: It's only those who can who are worthy of a great love.

REX: Do you think it would be unmanly of me to cry?

CAROLINE: I shouldn't like you to do it here.

REX: Oh, no. I'll keep a stiff upper lip as long as I'm with you. But to-morrow morning I shouldn't wonder at all if my pillow was sopping.

CAROLINE: Have you a waterproof sheet?

REX: Yes. I never travel without one.

CAROLINE: [*Giving him her hand.*] I wish you could marry some nice pure young English girl.

REX: With a bit of money? I can never forget you, Caroline. Why are you giving me your hand?

CAROLINE: [*With emotion.*] I thought you were going away.

REX: I can't leave you like this. We must talk this over thoroughly. I've got masses of things I want to say to you.

CAROLINE: Not now, Rex. I'm shattered by all this emotion.

REX: Well, when can I see you again?

CAROLINE: I'm afraid I'm dreadfully full up this week.

REX: Caroline, have pity on me.

CAROLINE: Of course, if you hadn't been engaged to-night you might have come and dined here.

REX: But I'm not engaged to-night.

CAROLINE: I thought you were dining with Isabella.

REX: I can dine with Isabella any night.

CAROLINE: Won't she be hurt if you throw her over?

REX: To tell you the truth, Caroline, I don't think I'm going to get on with Isabella.

CAROLINE: D'you find her too . . . too melting?

REX: My dear Caroline, she's like butter on a hot day. No, no, too many tears have been wept on that bosom; I'm not going to bedew it with mine.

CAROLINE: In that case dinner at eight sharp.

REX: I'll come, Caroline . . . if nothing unfortunate has happened to me before then.

CAROLINE: Oh, be careful, I've got quite a nice little dinner.

REX: [Gloomily.] What have you got?

CAROLINE: I've got some fresh caviare. It's just arrived from Russia.

REX: I could eat nothing. In happier moments I don't deny that I like caviare.

CAROLINE: And I've got a little turtle soup.

REX: I might try to swallow a little turtle soup.

CAROLINE: [Softly.] Don't let anything happen before dinner.

REX: I suppose you haven't got grilled salmon?

CAROLINE: No, turbot.

REX: [Desperately.] Everything goes against me.

CAROLINE: On the other hand, I've got some dear little baby chickens just out of their shells. It seems almost unkind to eat them when so young.

REX: I dare say they've been saved a lot of unhappiness.

CAROLINE: And then nothing but a strawberry ice.

REX: I shouldn't wonder if I could eat the ice.

CAROLINE: Then you'll come?

REX: [With a deep sigh.] If it'll give you any pleasure. A dinner-jacket or a white tie?

CAROLINE: A dinner-jacket.

REX: All right. Good-bye. I . . . I can't say good-bye to the others. I'm in such a fearful state of agitation.

> [*Exit.* ISABELLA *hears the door close and comes back into the room.*

ISABELLA: Has Rex gone? He was going to drive me home.

CAROLINE: How stupid of him! I suppose he forgot.

ISABELLA: I'll get a taxi. I want to leave you alone with Robert. He's dreadfully upset, Caroline.

CAROLINE: Is he?

ISABELLA: I've been trying to console him a little.

CAROLINE: Yes, I saw you.

ISABELLA: Be very gentle with him, Caroline. Be tender.

CAROLINE: I shall never find the exquisite things to say to him that you would, Isabella.

ISABELLA: He says I have a wonderful gift of sympathy.

CAROLINE: [*With a sigh.*] I wonder if you'd come and dine with me to-night?

ISABELLA: I'm afraid I've asked Rex.

CAROLINE: I'm sure he doesn't need you half as much as I do.

ISABELLA: Oh, if you need me, Caroline, of course I'll come. Somehow I felt you'd want me to-night. We'll have a good cry together, darling.

CAROLINE: Oh, that will be nice.

ISABELLA: Good-bye till then, dearest; I suppose I'd better put on a tea-gown.

CAROLINE: Oh, yes, that'll be very suitable. Dinner at eight sharp.

ISABELLA: Only an egg for me, Caroline.

> [*She goes out.* ROBERT *hears her last word as he comes into the room.*

ROBERT: When is she going to eat an egg?

CAROLINE: For dinner.

ROBERT: How disgusting! Where?

CAROLINE: Here.

ROBERT: You don't mean to say you've invited her to dinner?

CAROLINE: Yes.

ROBERT: Why on earth have you done that?

CAROLINE: You asked me to.

ROBERT: I never did anything of the sort. Really, Caroline, you are too inconsiderate.

CAROLINE: I thought you wanted to play bridge afterwards.

ROBERT: Bridge! You might have known that this evening of all others I'd want to be alone with you. Upon my word, it's too callous!

CAROLINE: Oh, Robert!

ROBERT: I'm staggering under the bitterest disappointment of my life. I'm utterly miserable. The only thing that consoled me was the thought of having a quiet evening alone with you so that we could have a good talk. And you bring that cackling woman along.

CAROLINE: I thought you were so fond of her.

ROBERT: You know perfectly well that for ten years I've been supremely indifferent to every woman in the world but you.

CAROLINE: [*She begins to understand.*] Oh! [*With a smile.*] It's very nice of you to say so, dear Robert.

ROBERT: Caroline, I don't know how I'm going to bear it. I feel as if the earth were tottering under my feet.

CAROLINE: You must have patience, Robert.

ROBERT: Patience! I've had patience for ten years. And now just when the reward was put into my hands it's snatched away.

CAROLINE: You know, I expected you to be rather relieved at hearing that my husband was alive.

ROBERT: I? My dear Caroline, have you gone out of your mind?

CAROLINE: You weren't so very anxious to marry me this morning.

ROBERT: Nonsense, Caroline. You know very well that I've always been anxious to marry you.

CAROLINE: You dissembled with some skill, Robert.

ROBERT: I will be perfectly frank with you, Caroline. At the first moment I was a little startled. It meant beginning a new life and the change of all my habits. But that was only a natural hesitation. When you accepted me I *knew* I'd achieved the dearest wish of my heart. Caroline, I've never wanted to marry you as much as I do now.

CAROLINE: Don't you think I'm a little old to marry?

ROBERT: You?

CAROLINE: It has occurred to me sometimes that I'm not quite so young as I was. A spiteful person might say I was almost middle-aged!

ROBERT: What nonsense! Why, you haven't reached your prime yet.

CAROLINE: Are you sure you see no change in me?

ROBERT: None. This morning I thought perhaps you were almost looking your age. But now, I don't know what's happened to you, you look radiant. You've not been making up, have you?

CAROLINE: Oh, no, I never do that.

ROBERT: You look eighteen. You're ravishing. If I hadn't been madly in love with you for ten years I should fall in love with you this afternoon.

CAROLINE: It makes me feel so happy to hear you say that.

ROBERT: Oh, it's cruel that this man should come back just when we'd fixed everything up. I want to be married to you, Caroline. Why shouldn't we take the matter in our own hands and force the wretched fellow to divorce you?

CAROLINE: We've discussed that so often and we've decided it was impossible. We're slaves of our past, our circumstances, and our surroundings. It can't be done, Robert.

ROBERT: D'you mean to say we must go on like this?

CAROLINE: Are you sure we're not happier as we are? We can keep our ideals in one another. Who knows what painful surprises marriage might bring us? You might find me flirtatious and exacting. I might discover you were selfish and comfort-loving.

ROBERT: Hang it all, Caroline, I'm not selfish. I have a passion for self-sacrifice.

CAROLINE: Nothing is so pleasant as to think of the sacrifices that one will never have to make.

ROBERT: Caroline, you don't know how I love you.

CAROLINE: Our love has lasted very long, Robert. Don't you think a closer connection might give it all sorts of little rubs and wrenches till there was nothing of it left? One may reasonably ask one thing of life, that it shouldn't tear rents in the illusions it creates. Illusion may be the foundation of all our happiness, but even if it is illusion let us keep it.

ROBERT: You may talk, but that man can't live for ever.

CAROLINE: He has a wonderful physique.

ROBERT: Next time he dies, I shall seize you by the hair of your head and drag you to the altar.

CAROLINE: He'll see us both out. I'm conscious that he lives now with a new and different life. It may be that he's necessary for our happiness. So, I cannot fade and you will ever love. My husband has been found. [*With immense decision.*] And now, Robert, he will never die.

ROBERT: Caroline, I adore you.

[*He clasps her in his arms.*

THE END

HOME AND BEAUTY

A FARCE
in Three Acts

CHARACTERS

WILLIAM, a hero
FREDERICK, another
VICTORIA, a dear little thing
MR. LEICESTER PATON, a wangler
MR. A. B. RAHAM, a solicitor
MISS MONTMORENCY, a maiden lady
MRS. SHUTTLEWORTH, a mother-in-law
MISS DENNIS, a manicurist
MRS. POGSON, a respectable woman
TAYLOR, a parlourmaid
NANNIE, a nurse
CLARENCE, a boy

The action of the play takes place at Victoria's house in Westminster towards the end of November, 1918.

HOME AND BEAUTY

THE FIRST ACT

The scene is VICTORIA'S *bedroom. It is the kind of bedroom which is only used to sleep in; and but for the bed, with its hangings and its beautiful coverlet, and the great lacquer dressing-table, crowded with the necessary aids to feminine beauty, might just as well be a sitting-room. There are graceful pieces of furniture here and there, attractive pictures on the walls, flowers: it is all very comfortable, luxurious and modish. In the fire-place a bright fire is burning.*

VICTORIA, *a pretty little thing in a lovely "confection," which is partly tea-gown and partly dressing-gown, is lying on a sofa having her hands manicured.* MISS DENNIS, *the manicurist, is a neat, trim person of twenty-five. She has a slight cockney accent.*

MISS DENNIS: [*Evidently ending a long story.*] And so at last I said to him: Oh, very well, 'ave it your own way.

VICTORIA: One has to in the end, you know.

MISS DENNIS: He'd asked me five times, and I really got tired of saying no. And then, you see, in my business you get to know all the ins and outs of married life, and my impression is that, in the long run, it don't really matter very much who you marry.

VICTORIA: Oh, I do so agree with you there. It all depends on yourself. When my first husband was killed, poor darling, I went all to pieces. My bust simply went to nothing. I couldn't wear a low dress for months.

MISS DENNIS: How dreadful.

229

VICTORIA: I simply adored him. But you know, I'm just as fond of my second husband.

MISS DENNIS: You must have one of those loving natures.

VICTORIA: Of course, I should never survive it if anything happened to my present husband, but if anything did —touch wood—you know, I couldn't help myself, I'd just have to marry again, and I know I'd love my third husband just as much as I loved the other two.

MISS DENNIS: [*Sighing.*] Love is a wonderful thing.

VICTORIA: Oh, wonderful. Of course, I'd wait the year. I waited the year when my first was killed.

MISS DENNIS: Oh yes, I think one always ought to wait the year.

VICTORIA: I noticed you had an engagement ring on the moment you came in.

MISS DENNIS: I didn't really ought to wear it during business hours, but I like to feel it's there.

VICTORIA: I know the feeling so well. You turn it round under your glove, and you say to yourself: Well, that's settled. Is he nice-looking?

MISS DENNIS: Well, he's not what you might call exactly handsome, but he's got a nice face.

VICTORIA: Both my husbands have been very handsome men. You know, people say it doesn't matter what a man looks like, but that's all nonsense. There's nothing shows a woman off like a good-looking man.

MISS DENNIS: He's very fair.

VICTORIA: Of course, it's all a matter of taste, but I don't think I should like that myself. They always say fair men are deceitful. Both my husbands were dark, and they both had the D.S.O.

MISS DENNIS: That's funny, isn't it?

VICTORIA: I flatter myself there are not many women who've been married to two D.S.O.'s. I think I've done my bit.

MISS DENNIS: I should just think you had. If it's not asking too much, I should like to know which of them you liked best.

VICTORIA: Well, you know, I really can't say.

MISS DENNIS: Of course, I haven't had the experience, but I should have thought you'd prefer the one who wasn't there. That almost seems like human nature, doesn't it?

VICTORIA: The fact is, all men have their faults. They're selfish, brutal and inconsiderate. They don't understand how much everything costs. They can't *see* things, poor dears; they're cat-witted. Of course, Freddie's very unreasonable sometimes, but then so was Bill. And he adores me. He can hardly bear me out of his sight. They both adored me.

MISS DENNIS: That makes up for a great deal, I must say.

VICTORIA: I can't understand the women who complain that they're misunderstood. I don't want to be understood. I want to be loved.

[TAYLOR *opens the door and introduces* MRS. SHUTTLE-WORTH. *This is* VICTORIA'S *mother, an elderly, grey-haired lady in black.*

TAYLOR: Mrs. Shuttleworth.

[*Exit.*

VICTORIA: [*Gushing.*] Darling Mother.

MRS. SHUTTLEWORTH: My precious child.

VICTORIA: This is Miss Dennis. It's the only moment in the day she was able to give me.

MRS. SHUTTLEWORTH: [*Graciously.*] How do you do?

VICTORIA: You don't mind coming up all these stairs, do you, darling? You see, we have to be dreadfully economical with our coal. We tried to wangle more, but we couldn't manage it.

Mrs. Shuttleworth: Oh, I know. The coal controller was positively rude to me. Red tape, you know.

Victoria: They say we can only have two fires. Of course, we have to have one in the nursery, and I must have one in my bedroom. So I have to see people in here.

Mrs. Shuttleworth: And how are the precious darlings?

Victoria: Fred's got a slight cold, and Nannie thought he'd better stay in bed, but Baby's splendid. Nannie will bring him in presently.

Miss Dennis: Are they both boys, Mrs. Lowndes?

Victoria: Yes. But I'm going to have a girl next time.

Mrs. Shuttleworth: Fred will be two next month, Victoria.

Victoria: I know. I'm beginning to feel so old. Poor lamb, he wasn't born till three months after his father was killed.

Miss Dennis: How very sad. You don't like the nails too red, do you?

Victoria: Not too red.

Mrs. Shuttleworth: She looked too sweet in mourning. I wish you could have seen her, Miss Dennis.

Victoria: Mother, how can you say anything so heartless? Of course, black does suit me. There's no denying that.

Mrs. Shuttleworth: I insisted on her going to Mathilde. Mourning *must* be well made, or else it looks nothing at all.

Miss Dennis: Did you say your little boy's name was Fred? After his father, I suppose?

Victoria: Oh no, my first husband was called William. He particularly wanted the baby to be called Frederick after Major Lowndes. You see, Major Lowndes had been my husband's best man, and they'd always been such great friends.

Miss Dennis: Oh, I see.

VICTORIA: Then, when I married Major Lowndes, and my second baby was born, we thought it would be nice to give it my first husband's name, and so we called it William.

MRS. SHUTTLEWORTH: I was against it myself. I thought it would always remind the dear child of what she'd lost.

VICTORIA: Oh, but, Mother darling, I don't feel a bit like that about Bill. I shall never forget him. [*To* MISS DENNIS, *pointing to a double photograph frame.*] You see, I have their photographs side by side.

MISS DENNIS: Some men wouldn't like that very much.

VICTORIA: Freddie has me now. He can't grudge it if I give a passing thought to that poor dead hero who's lying in a nameless grave in France.

MRS. SHUTTLEWORTH: Don't upset yourself, darling. You know how bad it is for your skin. She has such a soft heart, poor dear.

VICTORIA: Of course, now the war's over, it's different, but when Freddie was at the front I always thought it must be a consolation to him to think that if anything happened to him and I married again I should always keep a little corner in my heart for him.

MISS DENNIS: There, I think that's all for to-day, Mrs. Lowndes. Would you like me to come again on Friday?

> [*She proceeds to put away the various utensils she has been using.*

VICTORIA: [*Looking at her nails.*] Please. You do them beautifully. There's something very satisfactory in a well-manicured hand. It gives you a sense of assurance, doesn't it? If I were a man I would never want to hold a hand that wasn't nicely manicured.

MISS DENNIS: The gentleman I'm going to marry said to me that the first thing that attracted him was the way my nails were polished.

VICTORIA: One never knows what'll take a man's fancy.

MRS. SHUTTLEWORTH: Personally, I am a firm believer in first impressions. And that is why I say to all the girls I know: Whenever you are being shown into a drawing-room bite both your lips hard, give them a good lick, put your head in the air, and then sail in. There's nothing men like more than a red moist mouth. I'm an old woman now, but I never go into a room without doing it.

MISS DENNIS: Fancy, now, I never thought of that. I must try it and see.

MRS. SHUTTLEWORTH: It may make all the difference to your life.

VICTORIA: Miss Dennis is engaged to be married, Mother.

MRS. SHUTTLEWORTH: Ah, my dear, don't make the common mistake of thinking that because you've got one man safe you need not make yourself attractive to others.

VICTORIA: On Friday next, then, Miss Dennis.

MISS DENNIS: Very well, Mrs. Lowndes. Is there anything you're wanting just at the moment?

VICTORIA: Nothing, thanks.

MISS DENNIS: I've got a new skin food that they've just sent me over from Paris. I would like you to give it a trial. I think it's just the thing for your complexion.

VICTORIA: I'm afraid to try anything I don't know. I've got such a delicate skin.

MISS DENNIS: It's been specially prepared for skins like yours, Mrs. Lowndes. The ordinary skin food is well enough for the ordinary skin, but a really beautiful skin like yours wants something very extra-special in the way of food.

VICTORIA: I expect it's frightfully expensive, and you know, they say we must economize. I suppose somebody's got to pay for the war.

Miss Dennis: I'll make special terms for you, Mrs. Lowndes. I'll only charge you fifty-nine and six for a three-guinea pot. It's a large pot, as large as that. [*She measures with her fingers a pot about three inches high.*] I promise you it's not an extravagance. A good skin food is an investment.

Victoria: Oh well, bring it with you next time you come.

Miss Dennis: I'm sure you won't regret it. Good afternoon, Mrs. Lowndes. [*To* Mrs. Shuttleworth.] Good afternoon.

> [*She goes out.*

Mrs. Shuttleworth: I dare say she's right. They pick up a lot of experience, those women. I always say the same thing to girls: Look after your skin, and your bills will look after themselves.

Victoria: She was telling me that the Johnston Blakes are going to divorce.

Mrs. Shuttleworth: [*Without concern.*] Really. Why?

Victoria: He's been fighting for the last four years. He says he wants a little peace now.

Mrs. Shuttleworth: I'm afraid many of these men who've been away so long will have got out of the habit of being married. I dare say it was a mercy that poor Bill was killed.

Victoria: Mother darling, how can you say anything so dreadful?

Mrs. Shuttleworth: Well, I must say I was thankful when Freddie got a job at the War Office. The difference between men and women is that men are not naturally addicted to matrimony. With patience, firmness, and occasional rewards you can train them to it just as you can train a dog to walk on its hind legs. But a dog would rather walk on all fours and a man would rather be free. Marriage is a habit.

Victoria: And a very good one, Mother.

Mrs. Shuttleworth: Of course. But the unfortunate thing about this world is that good habits are so much easier to get out of than bad ones.

Victoria. Well, one thing I do know, and that is that Freddie simply adores being married to me.

Mrs. Shuttleworth: In your place, I should have married Leicester Paton.

Victoria: Good heavens, why?

Mrs. Shuttleworth: Have you never noticed that he wears spats? Men who wear spats always make the best husbands.

Victoria: It probably only means that he has cold feet. I expect he wears bedsocks, and I should hate that.

Mrs. Shuttleworth: Nonsense. It means that he has a neat and orderly mind. He likes things just so. Everything in its place and at the proper season. In fact, a creature of habit. I am convinced that after six months of marriage Leicester Paton would forget that he'd ever been a bachelor.

Victoria: I was a soldier's widow. I don't think it would have been very patriotic to marry a civilian.

Mrs. Shuttleworth: You girls all talked as though the war would last for ever. Heroism is all very well, but at a party it's not nearly so useful as a faculty for small talk.

[Taylor *comes in.*

Taylor: Mr. Leicester Paton has called, madam. I said I didn't know if you could see him.

Victoria: Talk of the devil. Oh yes, bring him up here.

Taylor: Very good, madam.

[*Exit.*

Mrs. Shuttleworth: I didn't know you were seeing anything of him, Victoria.

VICTORIA: [*With some archness.*] He's been rather attentive lately.

MRS. SHUTTLEWORTH: I knew I was right. I felt sure you attracted him.

VICTORIA: Oh, darling, you know I can never think of anyone but Freddie, but of course it's useful to have someone to run errands for one. And he can wangle almost anything one wants.

MRS. SHUTTLEWORTH: Butter?

VICTORIA: Everything, my dear, butter, sugar, whisky.

MRS. SHUTTLEWORTH: Bite your lips, darling, and give them a good lick. [VICTORIA *carries out the suggestion.*] You missed the chance of your life.

VICTORIA: After all, he never asked me.

MRS. SHUTTLEWORTH: Don't be silly, Victoria, you should have made him.

VICTORIA: You know that I adored Freddie. Besides, ration books hadn't come in then.

MRS. SHUTTLEWORTH: By the way, where is Freddie?

VICTORIA: Oh, my dear, I'm perfectly furious with him. He promised to take me out to luncheon, and he never turned up. He never telephoned or anything; not a word. I think it's too bad of him. He may be dead for all I know.

MRS. SHUTTLEWORTH: Optimist.

> [TAYLOR *ushers in* MR. LEICESTER PATON, *and then goes out. He is a small, fat man, very well pleased with the world and with himself, beautifully dressed and obviously prosperous. You could tell at a mile that he had so much money that he did not know what to do with it. He is affable, gallant and easy.*

TAYLOR: Mr. Leicester Paton.

VICTORIA: I hope you don't mind being dragged up all these stairs. We have to be so dreadfully economical

1

with our coal. I can only afford to have a fire in my bedroom.

PATON: [*Shaking hands with her.*] You're not going to tell me that you have any trouble about getting coal. Why on earth didn't you let me know? [*Shaking hands with* MRS. SHUTTLEWORTH.] How do you do?

VICTORIA: You don't mean to say you could get me some?

PATON: It's quite out of the question that a pretty woman shouldn't have everything she wants.

VICTORIA: I told Freddie that I felt sure he could wangle it somehow. What's the use of being at the War Office if you can't have some sort of a pull?

PATON: Leave it to me. I'll see what I can do for you.

VICTORIA: You're a perfect marvel.

PATON: Now that these men are coming back from the front no one would look at us poor devils who stayed at home if we didn't at least make ourselves useful.

VICTORIA: You only stayed at home because it was your duty.

PATON: I attested, you know; I didn't wait to be called up. But the Government said to me: You're a shipbuilder: go on building ships. So I built them ships.

MRS. SHUTTLEWORTH: I think it was very noble of you.

PATON: And then they bring in a tax on excess profits. As I said to the Prime Minister myself: It's trying one's patriotism rather high. It really is.

MRS. SHUTTLEWORTH: A little bird has whispered to me that the Government intends to show its appreciation of your great services in the next Honours List.

PATON: Oh, one doesn't ask for that. One's glad to have been able to do one's bit.

VICTORIA: How true that is. That's just what I feel.

MRS. SHUTTLEWORTH: Victoria has worked like a dog, you know. It's a marvel to me how her health has stood it.

VICTORIA: I don't know how many committees I've been on. I've sold at twenty-three bazaars.

PATON: There's nothing that takes it out of one so much.

VICTORIA: At the beginning of the war I worked in a canteen, but I had to give that up, because I could never go out to lunch anywhere. I thought at one time of working in a hospital, but you know all the red tape there is in those places—they said I had no training.

MRS. SHUTTLEWORTH: I'm sure you'd have made a wonderful nurse.

VICTORIA: I didn't propose to be the ordinary sort of nurse at all. I was quite content to leave that to those unfortunate females who make their living by it. But it doesn't want any particular training to be nice to those poor, dear, wounded boys, to shake out their pillows and take them flowers, and read to them. It only wants sympathy.

PATON: I don't know anyone who has more.

VICTORIA: [*With a flash of her eyes.*] With people I like.

MRS. SHUTTLEWORTH: Have you stopped your teas, darling?

VICTORIA: Oh, yes, after the Armistice.

PATON: You used to give teas to wounded soldiers?

VICTORIA: Yes, Tommies, you know. I think it's so important to cultivate the personal relation. I used to invite a dozen every Thursday. At first I had them in the drawing-room, but it made them shy, poor dears, so I thought it would be nicer for them if they had it in the servants' hall. I'm the only woman I know who never had the smallest trouble with her maids.

MRS. SHUTTLEWORTH: Darling, I think I'll go upstairs and see how my dear little grandson is. I do hope it's not influenza.

VICTORIA: Yes, do, Mother. He'll be thrilled to see you.

[MRS. SHUTTLEWORTH *goes out.* LEICESTER PATON, *rising as she does, when he sits down again takes a place on the sofa beside* VICTORIA.

PATON: Is anything the matter with your little boy?

VICTORIA: Poor darling, he's got a cold.

PATON: I'm so sorry.

VICTORIA: I dare say it's nothing, but you know what a mother is: she can't help feeling anxious.

PATON: You're a wonderful mother.

VICTORIA: I adore my children.

PATON: [*Going on with his sentence.*] And a perfect wife.

VICTORIA: D'you think so?

PATON: Doesn't your husband?

VICTORIA: Oh, he's only my husband. His opinion doesn't count.

PATON: Does he know what a lucky man he is?

VICTORIA: If he does he's quite convinced that he deserves to be.

PATON: I envy him.

VICTORIA: [*Flashing a glance at him.*] You don't think I'm quite detestable, then?

PATON: Shall I tell you what I think of you?

VICTORIA: No, don't, you'll only exaggerate. You know, there are only two qualities that I flatter myself on: I'm not vain and I am unselfish.

[FREDERICK *comes in. He is a tall, soldierly fellow in uniform, with red tabs and a number of ribbons on his tunic. He nods to* LEICESTER PATON *and shakes hands with him.*

VICTORIA: Freddie, where *have* you been all this time?

FREDERICK: I've been at the club.

VICTORIA: But you promised to take me out to luncheon.

FREDERICK: Did I? I forgot all about it. I'm so sorry.

VICTORIA : Forgot? I suppose something more amusing turned up.

FREDERICK: Well, I only said I'd come if I wasn't too busy.

VICTORIA: Were you busy?

FREDERICK: I was.

VICTORIA: Bill was never too busy to give me luncheon when I wanted it.

FREDERICK: Fancy that.

PATON: I think I'll be getting along. Now the war's over you fellows can take things easily. My work goes on just the same.

FREDERICK: That's a new car you've got, isn't it?

PATON: I have to get about somehow, you know.

FREDERICK: So do I, but being only a soldier I manage to do it on my flat feet.

PATON: [*Shaking hands with* VICTORIA.] Good-bye.

VICTORIA: Good-bye. So nice of you to come and see me.

[LEICESTER PATON *goes out.*

VICTORIA: I should be glad to know why you threw me over like that.

FREDERICK: Are you obliged to receive visitors in your bedroom?

VICTORIA: You don't mean to say you're jealous, darling? I thought you seemed grumpy. Is he put out? Let him come and give his little wife a nice kiss.

FREDERICK: [*Irritably.*] I'm not in the least jealous.

VICTORIA: You silly old thing. You know it's the only room in the house that's got a fire.

FREDERICK: Why the dickens don't you have one in the drawing-room?

VICTORIA: My poor lamb, have you forgotten that there's

been a war and there happens to be a shortage of coal? I will tell you exactly why we don't have a fire in the drawing-room. Patriotism.

FREDERICK: Patriotism be hanged. The place is like an ice-house.

VICTORIA: Darling, don't be unreasonable. After spending two winters in the trenches I shouldn't have thought you'd be such a slave to your comfort. I know you don't mean it when you say patriotism be hanged, but you shouldn't say things like that even in jest.

FREDERICK: I'm dashed if I can see why it would be less patriotic to have a fire in the drawing-room where we could all benefit by it, rather than here where it's no good to anyone but you.

VICTORIA: [Opening her eyes very wide.] Darling, you're not going to ask me to do without a fire in my bedroom? How can you be so selfish? Heaven knows, I don't want to boast about anything I've done, but after having slaved my life out for four years I do think I deserve a little consideration.

FREDERICK: How's the kid?

VICTORIA: And it's not as if I grudged you the use of my room. You can come and sit here as much as you like. Besides, a man has his club. He can always go there if he wants to.

FREDERICK: I apologize. You're quite right. You're always right.

VICTORIA: I thought you wanted me to be happy.

FREDERICK: I do, darling.

VICTORIA: Before we were married, you said you'd make that the chief aim of your life.

FREDERICK: [Smiling.] I can't imagine that a sensible man could want a better one.

VICTORIA Confess that you've been a perfect pig.

FREDERICK: A brute beast, darling.

VICTORIA: [*Mollified.*] D'you know that I asked you to give me a kiss just now? It's not a request that I'm in the habit of having ignored.

FREDERICK: I trust it's not one that you're in the habit of making to all and sundry.

[*He kisses her.*

VICTORIA: Now tell me why you forgot to take me out to luncheon to-day.

FREDERICK: I didn't forget. I was prevented. I . . , I haven't had any luncheon myself. I'll just ring and ask the cook to send me up something.

VICTORIA: My poor lamb, the cook left this morning.

FREDERICK: Again?

VICTORIA: How d'you mean again? This is the first time she's left.

FREDERICK: Hang it all, she's only been here a week.

VICTORIA: You needn't get cross about it. It's much more annoying for me than for you.

FREDERICK: [*Irritably.*] I don't know why on earth you can't keep your servants.

VICTORIA: No one can keep servants nowadays.

FREDERICK: Other people do.

VICTORIA: Please don't speak to me like that, Freddie. I'm not used to it.

FREDERICK: I shall speak to you exactly as I choose.

VICTORIA: It's so petty to lose your temper just because you can't have something to eat. I should have thought after spending two years in the trenches you'd be accustomed to going without a meal now and then.

FREDERICK: For goodness' sake don't make a scene.

VICTORIA: It's not I who am making a scene. It's you who are making a scene.

FREDERICK: Victoria, I beg you to control yourself.

VICTORIA: I don't know how you can be so unkind to me. After all the anxiety I suffered on your account when you were in France, I do think you might have a little consideration for me.

FREDERICK: Seeing that for the last year I've had a perfectly safe, cushy job at the War Office, I think you might by now have recovered from any anxiety you felt on my account.

VICTORIA: Must I remind you that my nerves were shattered by poor Bill's death?

FREDERICK: No, but I was confident you would.

VICTORIA: The doctor said I should need the greatest attention for several years. I don't believe I shall ever quite get over it. I should have thought even if you didn't love me any more you'd have a little human pity for me. That's all I ask, just the tolerant kindness you'd show to a dog who was fond of you. [*Working herself up into a passion.*] Heaven knows I'm not exacting. I do everything I can to make you happy. I'm patience itself. Even my worst enemy would have to admit that I'm unselfish. [*As he is about to speak.*] You weren't obliged to marry me. I didn't ask you to. You pretended you loved me. I would never have married you if it hadn't been for Bill. You were his greatest friend. You made me love you because you spoke so beautifully of him. [*He is just going to say something, but she goes on implacably.*] That's my mistake. I've loved you too much. You're not big enough to bear so great a love. Oh, what a fool I've been. I let myself be taken in by you, and I've been bitterly punished. [*Heading off the words she sees he wants to speak.*] Bill would never have treated me like that. Bill wouldn't have taken my poor, loving heart and thrown it aside like an old hat. Bill loved me. He would have always loved me. I adored that man. He waited on me hand and foot. He was the most unselfish man I ever knew. He was a hero. He's the only man I ever really cared for. I was mad ever to think of marrying you, mad, mad, mad. I shall never be happy again. I would give anything in the world to have my dear, dear Bill back again.

FREDERICK: I'm glad you feel like that about it, because he'll be here in about three minutes.

VICTORIA: [*Brought up short.*] What? What on earth d'you mean by that?

FREDERICK: He rang me up at the club a little while ago.

VICTORIA: Freddie. What are you talking about? Are you mad?

FREDERICK: No. Nor drunk.

VICTORIA: I don't understand. Who talked to you?

FREDERICK: Bill .

VICTORIA: Bill. Bill who?

FREDERICK: Bill Cardew.

VICTORIA: But, poor darling, he's dead.

FREDERICK: He showed no sign of it on the telephone.

VICTORIA: But, Freddie . . . Freddie. Oh, you're pulling my leg. It's too beastly of you. How can you be so heartless?

FREDERICK: Well, just wait and you'll see for yourself. [*Looking at his wrist watch.*] In about two and a half minutes now, I should think.

VICTORIA: [*Coaxing him.*] Now, Freddie, don't be vindictive. I dare say I was rather catty. I didn't mean it. You know I adore you. You can have a fire in your study, and damn the food controller. I'm sorry for all I said just now. There, now, it's all right, isn't it?

FREDERICK: Perfectly. But it's not going to prevent Bill from walking into this room in about two minutes and a quarter.

VICTORIA: I shall scream. It's not true. Oh, Freddie, if you ever loved me, say it's not true.

FREDERICK: There's no need to take my word for it.

VICTORIA: But, Freddie, darling, do be sensible. Poor Bill was killed at the Battle of Ypres. He was actually seen to fall. He was reported dead by the War Office. You know how distressed I was. I wore mourning and everything. We even had a memorial service.

FREDERICK: I know. It'll want a devil of a lot of explaining, turning up like this.

VICTORIA: I shall go stark, staring mad in a minute. How do you know it was Bill who spoke to you on the telephone?

FREDERICK: He said so.

VICTORIA: That proves nothing. Lots of people say they're the Kaiser.

FREDERICK: Yes, but they speak from a lunatic asylum. He spoke from Harwich Station.

VICTORIA: I dare say it was somebody else of the same name.

FREDERICK: That's idiotic, Victoria. I recognized his voice.

VICTORIA: What did he say exactly?

FREDERICK: Well, he said he was at Harwich Station, and would be in London at 3.13. And would I break it to you?

VICTORIA: But he must have said more than that.

FREDERICK: No, not much.

VICTORIA: For goodness' sake, tell me exactly what he said—exactly.

FREDERICK: Well, I was just coming along to take you out to luncheon, when I was told I was wanted on the telephone. A long-distance call—Harwich.

VICTORIA: I know. A seaport town.

FREDERICK: I strolled along and took up the receiver. I said: Is that you, darling?

VICTORIA: Why did you say that?

FREDERICK: That's always a good opening on the telephone. It puts the person at the other end at their ease.

VICTORIA: Idiot.

FREDERICK: Somebody said: Is that you, Freddie? I thought I recognized the voice, and I felt all funny. Yes, I said. It's me, Bill, he said, Bill Cardew.

VICTORIA: For heaven's sake be quick about it.

FREDERICK: Hulloa, I said, I thought you were dead. I thought as much, he answered. How are you? I said. A1, he said.

VICTORIA: What an idiotic conversation.

FREDERICK: Damn it all, I had to say something.

VICTORIA: You ought to have said a thousand things.

FREDERICK: We only had three minutes.

VICTORIA: Well, go on.

FREDERICK: He said: I'm just tootling up to London. I'll be up at 3.13. You might go along and break it to Victoria. Right ho, I said. He said, So-long, and I said, So-long. And we rang off.

VICTORIA: But that was before luncheon. Why didn't you come at once and tell me?

FREDERICK: To tell you the truth I was a bit shaken by then. I thought the first thing was to have a double whisky and a small soda.

VICTORIA: And what did you do then?

FREDERICK: Well, I sat down to think. I thought steadily for a couple of hours.

VICTORIA: And what have you thought?

FREDERICK: Nothing.

VICTORIA: It seems hardly worth while to have gone without your lunch.

FREDERICK: It's a devilish awkward position for me.

VICTORIA: For you? And what about me?

FREDERICK: After all, Bill was my oldest pal. He may think it rather funny that I've married his wife.

VICTORIA: Funny!

FREDERICK: On the other hand, he may not.

VICTORIA: Why didn't you tell me the moment you came in, instead of talking about heaven knows what?

FREDERICK: It wasn't a very easy thing to say. I was trying to find an opportunity to slip it in casually, don't you know.

VICTORIA: [*Furiously.*] Wasting precious time.

FREDERICK: [*Blandly.*] Darling, you surely don't think making a scene is ever waste of time.

VICTORIA: Now we haven't got a chance to decide on anything. I haven't even time to put a frock on.

FREDERICK: What the deuce do you want to put a frock on for?

VICTORIA: After all, I am his widow. I think it would be only nice of me to be wearing mourning when he comes. What did he say when you told him?

FREDERICK: When I told him what?

VICTORIA: How can you be so stupid! When **you** told **him** you and I were married.

FREDERICK: But I didn't tell him.

VICTORIA: Do you mean to say that he's coming here under the impression that I'm his wife?

FREDERICK: Why, naturally.

VICTORIA: But why on earth didn't you tell him at once? It was the only thing to do. Surely you see that.

FREDERICK: It didn't strike me at the moment. Besides, it's rather a delicate thing to say on the telephone.

VICTORIA: Well, someone must tell him.

FREDERICK: I've come to the conclusion that you're quite the best person to do that.

VICTORIA: I? I? I? Do you think I'm going to do all your dirty work?

FREDERICK: I must say, I don't think it would come well from me.

VICTORIA: I'm not going to deal my darling Bill this bitter, bitter blow.

FREDERICK: By the way, it's—it's jolly he's alive, isn't it?

VICTORIA: Ripping.

FREDERICK: I am glad, aren't you?

VICTORIA: Yes, awfully glad.

FREDERICK: Then you'll just break the news as gently as you can, Victoria.

VICTORIA: [*As if she were weighing the matter.*] I really don't think that's my province.

FREDERICK: [*Exercising all his charm.*] Darling, you've got so much tact. I never knew anyone who could deal with a delicate situation as you can. You have such a light hand. You're so sympathetic. And you've got such a wonderful tenderness.

VICTORIA: I don't think you've got hold of the right line at all. There's only one way to manage a thing like this. You just take him by the arm and say: Look here, old man, the fact is . . .

FREDERICK: [*Interrupting.*] Victoria, you don't mean to say you're willing to give up the chance of making the biggest scene you've ever made in your life?

VICTORIA: Now look here, Freddie, this is the only thing I've ever asked you to do for me in my life. You know how frail I am. I'm not feeling at all well. You're the only man I have to lean on.

FREDERICK: It's no good, Victoria. I won't.

VICTORIA: [*Furiously.*] Damn you.

FREDERICK: By George, here he is.

VICTORIA: I've not even powdered my nose. Fortunately I have no personal vanity.

> [*She begins to powder herself feverishly. The voice is heard of someone coming up the stairs:* Hulloa! Hulloa! Hulloa! *Then the door is flung open and in bursts* WILLIAM. *He is a well-set-up, jovial fellow, wearing at the moment a very shabby suit.*

WILLIAM: Here we are again.

VICTORIA: Bill!

FREDERICK: Was I right?

VICTORIA: I can hardly believe my eyes.

WILLIAM: Give me a kiss, old lady. [*He seizes her in his arms and gives her a hearty kiss. Then he turns to* FREDERICK. *They shake hands.*] Well, Freddie, old man, how's life?

FREDERICK: A1, thanks.

WILLIAM: Are you surprised to see me?

FREDERICK: A little.

VICTORIA: In fact, a good deal.

WILLIAM: I'm jolly glad to see you here, Freddie, old man. On the way up in the train I cursed myself five times for not having asked you to wait with Victoria till I rolled up. I was afraid you might have some damned feeling of delicacy.

FREDERICK: I?

WILLIAM: You see, it struck me you might think Victoria and I would want to be alone just the first moment, but I should have been as sick as a dog if I hadn't seen your ugly old face here to welcome me. By the way, you've neither of you said you were glad to see me.

VICTORIA: Of course we're glad, Bill darling.

FREDERICK: Rather.

WILLIAM: Tactful of me to get old Freddie to come round and break the news to you, I think, Victoria.

VICTORIA: Yes, darling, and exactly like you.

WILLIAM: It's just like old times to hear you call me darling every other minute.

FREDERICK: It's one of Victoria's favourite words.

WILLIAM: You know, I nearly didn't warn you. I thought it would be rather a lark to break in on you in the middle of the night.

[FREDERICK *and* VICTORIA *give a little start.*

VICTORIA: I'm just as glad you didn't do that, Bill.

WILLIAM: What a scene, my word. The sleeping beauty on her virtuous couch. Enter a man in a shocking old suit. Shrieks of the sleeping beauty. It is I, your husband. Tableau.

VICTORIA: [*To turn the conversation.*] You're quite right, it is a shocking old suit. Where did you get it?

WILLIAM: I didn't get it. I pinched it. I must say I wouldn't mind getting into some decent things.

[*He walks towards a door that leads out of* VICTORIA's *room.*

VICTORIA: [*Hastily.*] Where are you going?

WILLIAM: I was going into my dressing-room. Upon my soul, I almost forget what I've got. I had a blue serge suit that was rather dressy.

VICTORIA: I've put all your clothes away, darling.

WILLIAM: Where?

VICTORIA: In camphor. You couldn't put them on until they've been aired.

WILLIAM: Hell, said the duchess.

[Mrs. Shuttleworth *comes in.* William *is standing so that at first she does not see him.*

Mrs. Shuttleworth: I think the little lamb is going on nicely, Victoria.

Victoria: [*Swallowing.*] Mother.

William: I was just going to ask about the kid.

[Mrs. Shuttleworth *jumps out of her skin. She turns round and sees* William.

Mrs. Shuttleworth: Who is that?

William: Who the devil d'you think it is?

Mrs. Shuttleworth: The language and the voice—Bill Cardew's. Who is that?

William: [*Walking towards her.*] Well, I may be a bit thinner and it certainly is a shocking old suit.

Mrs. Shuttleworth: Don't come near me or I shall scream.

William: You can't escape me. I'm going to kiss you.

Mrs. Shuttleworth: Take him away. Don't let him come near me. Victoria, who is that man?

Frederick: Well, Mrs. Shuttleworth, it's Bill Cardew.

Mrs. Shuttleworth: But he's dead.

Frederick: He doesn't seem to know it.

Mrs. Shuttleworth: It's absurd. Will someone wake me up.

William: Shall I pinch her, and if so, where?

Mrs. Shuttleworth: It's a horrible dream. Of course he's dead. That man's an imposter.

William: Shall I show you the strawberry mark on my left shoulder?

Mrs. Shuttleworth: I tell you Bill Cardew's dead.

William: Prove it.

Mrs. Shuttleworth: [*Indignantly.*] Prove it? The War

Office announced it officially; Victoria went into mourning.

WILLIAM: Did she look nice in it?

MRS. SHUTTLEWORTH: Sweet. Perfectly sweet. I insisted on her going to Mathilde. Mourning must be well made or else it looks nothing at all. Why, we had a memorial service.

FREDERICK: Fully choral.

WILLIAM: Did you have a memorial service for me, Victoria? That was nice of you.

VICTORIA: It was very well attended.

WILLIAM: I'm glad it wasn't a frost.

FREDERICK: I say, old man, we don't want to hurry you, you know, but we're all waiting for some sort of explanation.

WILLIAM: I was coming to that. I was just giving you time to get over your first raptures at seeing me again. Have you got over them?

FREDERICK: I can only speak for myself.

WILLIAM: Well, you know, I was damned badly wounded.

FREDERICK: Yes, at Ypres. A fellow saw you fall. He said you were shot through the head. He just stopped a minute, and saw you were killed, and went on.

WILLIAM: A superficial observer. I wasn't. I was eventually picked up and taken to Germany.

VICTORIA: Why didn't you write?

WILLIAM: Well, I think I must have been rather dotty for a bit. I don't know exactly how long I was in hospital, but when I began to sit up and take nourishment I couldn't remember a damned thing. My memory had completely gone.

MRS. SHUTTLEWORTH: Strange. To my mind very strange.

WILLIAM: I think my wound must have made me a bit

irritable. When I was being taken along to a camp I had a difference of opinion with a German officer, and I laid him out. By George, they nearly shot me for that. Anyhow, they sentenced me to about a hundred and fifty years' imprisonment, and prevented me from writing, or making any sign that I was alive.

VICTORIA: But your memory came back?

WILLIAM: Yes, gradually. And, of course, I realized then that you'd think I was dead. But I had no means of letting you know.

FREDERICK: You might have wired from Rotterdam.

WILLIAM: The lines were so congested. They told me I'd arrive before my wire.

MRS. SHUTTLEWORTH: It's all quite probable.

WILLIAM: More or less, I flatter myself. But you can bet your life on one thing: I'm not dead, and, what's more, I propose to live for another forty years, if not fifty.

[TAYLOR *comes in.*

TAYLOR: If you please, ma'am, where shall I put the gentleman's things? He told me to bring them upstairs.

WILLIAM: Oh, it's only a few odds and ends for the journey that I got on my way. Put them in the dressing-room.

VICTORIA: No, leave that for the moment, Taylor. We'll decide presently.

TAYLOR: Very good, madam.

[*She goes out.*

WILLIAM: What's the matter with the dressing-room, Victoria?

VICTORIA: My poor darling, don't forget your arrival is a complete surprise. Nothing is ready.

WILLIAM: Don't let that worry you. After what I've been used to, I can pig it anywhere. [*Looking at the bed.*] By George, a spring mattress. Father will sleep without rocking to-night.

MRS. SHUTTLEWORTH: [*Firmly.*] Something's got to be done.

WILLIAM: How d'you mean?

VICTORIA: [*Hurriedly.*] We haven't got a cook.

WILLIAM: Oh, you needn't bother about that. Freddie and I will do the cooking. My speciality is a grilled steak. What can you do, Freddie?

FREDERICK: I can boil an egg.

WILLIAM: Splendid. They always say that's the one thing a chef can't do. Nothing to worry about. We'll get in some *pâté de foie gras* and a few oysters, and there you are. Now let's have a look at the kid.

MRS. SHUTTLEWORTH: He's not very well to-day. I don't think he should leave his bed.

WILLIAM: Oh, all right. I'll toddle up and see him. I haven't made his lordship's acquaintance yet. What's his name?

VICTORIA: [*Rather nervously.*] Don't you remember, just before you went away, you said you'd like him called Frederick if he was a boy.

WILLIAM: Yes, I know I did, but you said you'd see me damned. You'd quite made up your mind to call him Lancelot.

VICTORIA: When I thought you were dead I felt I must respect your wishes.

WILLIAM: It must have been a shock if it took you like that.

VICTORIA: Of course, I asked Freddie to be godfather.

WILLIAM: Has the old ruffian been a stand-by to you while I've been away?

VICTORIA: I . . . I've seen a good deal of him.

WILLIAM: I felt you were safe with him, you know. He's a brick.

FREDERICK: I say, you might spare my blushes while you're about it.

VICTORIA: He was very kind to me during my—bereavement.

WILLIAM: Dear old chap. I knew you were a tower of strength.

FREDERICK: [*Sweating freely.*] I . . . I did what I could, you know.

WILLIAM: Well, don't be so modest about it.

MRS. SHUTTLEWORTH: [*More firmly.*] I tell you something must be done.

WILLIAM: My dear Victoria, what is the matter with your mother?

FREDERICK: [*Trying to change the conversation.*] I think we might bust ourselves and have some bubbly to-night, Victoria.

WILLIAM: And damn the expense.

FREDERICK: I wonder if it's arrived yet. I told them to send a case in the day before yesterday.

WILLIAM: Have you been running the cellar? Rash to let him do that, Victoria, very rash.

VICTORIA: I know nothing about wine.

WILLIAM: Freddie knows a thing or two. I say, do you remember that last time we went on a bat together? You were blind to the world.

FREDERICK: Go to blazes! I was nothing of the sort.

WILLIAM: Pretty little thing that was. Are you as thick with her as you used to be?

[VICTORIA *draws herself up and looks daggers at* FREDERICK.

FREDERICK: [*With dignity.*] I haven't an idea who you're referring to.

WILLIAM: Oh, my dear old boy, don't put any frills on. Victoria's a married woman, and she knows what the lads of the village are when they get out. A very nice little girl indeed, Victoria. If I hadn't been a married man I'd have had a shot at cutting Freddie out.

VICTORIA: [*Icily.*] He always told me he'd never looked at a woman in his life.

WILLIAM: You shouldn't encourage the young to lie. That's what they all say. Rapid. These wretched aeroplane fellows have been turning out engine after engine, and they can't keep pace with him. Talk of a lurid past; Mrs. Shuttleworth, veil your face.

FREDERICK: My poor Bill, your memory! When you recovered it, I'm afraid you remembered all sorts of things that had never happened.

WILLIAM: Past, did I say? Unless I'm very much mistaken, his present wouldn't bear the closest inspection.

FREDERICK: By George, I've hit it. The poor fellow thinks he's being funny.

WILLIAM: [*Going on.*] I don't blame you. Make hay while the sun shines. I admire the way you can make love to three women at a time and make each one believe she's the only one you've ever really cared for.

MRS. SHUTTLEWORTH: [*With determination.*] If someone doesn't do something at once I shall do it myself.

WILLIAM: [*In a whisper to* VICTORIA, *pointing at* MRS. SHUTTLEWORTH.] Air raids?

[*At that moment a baby's wail is heard outside.*

VICTORIA: [*With agitation.*] Willie.

WILLIAM: Hulloa, what's that? Is that the kid? [*He goes swiftly to the door and opens it. The crying is heard more loudly.*] Why, it's coming upstairs. You told me the kid was in the nursery. [*Addressing the nurse.*] Bring him along and let me have a look at him.

[*A nurse, in a neat grey uniform, comes in with a baby in her arms.*

VICTORIA: [*Desperately.*] Freddie, do something, even if it's only something stupid.

FREDERICK: The only thing that occurs to me is to stand on my head.

WILLIAM: [*Jovially.*] Hulloa, hulloa, hulloa.

FREDERICK: That's not the way to talk to a baby, you owl.

WILLIAM: Not such a baby as all that. Can he speak yet, Nurse?

NURSE: Oh no, sir, not yet.

WILLIAM: Rather backward, isn't he? Not what I should have expected in a son of mine.

[*The* NURSE *gives him a look of surprise, and then with a look at* VICTORIA *assumes an appearance of extreme primness.*

NURSE: I never knew a baby talk as young as that, sir.

WILLIAM: Upon my soul, there's not much of him. Looks to me rather a stumer. I think we've been done, Victoria.

NURSE: [*Indignantly.*] Oh, I don't think you ought to say that, sir. He's a very fine boy. He weighs more than a good many do when they're six months.

WILLIAM: What's that? How old is he?

NURSE: Four months last Tuesday, sir.

WILLIAM: You've been busy in my absence, Victoria.

VICTORIA: Freddie, for goodness' sake speak. Don't stand there like a stuffed tomato.

MRS. SHUTTLEWORTH: Leave the room, Nannie.

[*The* NURSE, *pursing her lips, intrigued and perplexed, goes out.*

FREDERICK: [*Trying to take it lightly.*] The fact is, you've made rather an absurd mistake. You've been away so long that of course there's a good deal you don't know.

WILLIAM: I'm a simple creature.

FREDERICK: Well, to cut a long story short——

WILLIAM: What story?

FREDERICK: I wish you wouldn't interrupt me. I'm telling you as quickly as I can. To cut a long story short, the infant that's just gone out of the room is not your son.

WILLIAM: I had a sort of suspicion he wasn't. I tell you that frankly.

VICTORIA: Oh, the fool. The blithering nincompoop.

WILLIAM: Well, who the deuce is his father?

FREDERICK: In point of fact, I am.

WILLIAM: You? You don't mean to say you're married?

FREDERICK: Lots of people are. In fact, marriage has been quite the thing during the war.

WILLIAM: Why on earth didn't you tell me?

FREDERICK: Hang it all, man, you've been dead for the last three years. How could I?

WILLIAM: [Seizing his hand.] Well, I'm jolly glad to hear it, old chap. I knew you'd be caught one of these days. You were a wily old bird, but—ah, well, we all come to it. My very best congratulations.

FREDERICK: That's awfully good of you. I'm—er—I'm staying here, you know.

WILLIAM: Are you? That's first rate. Is your missus here too?

FREDERICK: It's rather difficult to explain.

WILLIAM: Don't tell me she's only got one eye.

FREDERICK: Can't you guess why I'm staying here?

WILLIAM: No. [He looks round the room and his eyes fall on MRS. SHUTTLEWORTH.] You don't mean to say you've married Victoria's mother?

FREDERICK: No, not exactly.

WILLIAM: What does he mean by *not exactly?* I hope you haven't been trifling with the affections of my mother-in-law.

MRS. SHUTTLEWORTH: Do I look as if I were the mother of that baby?

WILLIAM: We live in an age of progress. One should keep an open mind about things.

FREDERICK: You quite misunderstand me, Bill.

WILLIAM: Is there nothing between you and Victoria's mother?

FREDERICK: Certainly not.

WILLIAM: Well, I'm sorry. I should have liked to be your son-in-law. And you would have done the right thing by her, wouldn't you?

VICTORIA: Really, Bill, I don't think you should talk about my mother like that.

WILLIAM: If he's compromised her he ought to marry her.

VICTORIA: He hasn't compromised her and he can't marry her.

WILLIAM: I don't want to seem inquisitive, but if you didn't marry Victoria's mother, who did you marry?

FREDERICK: Damn you, I married Victoria.

END OF THE FIRST ACT

THE SECOND ACT

The drawing-room at VICTORIA'S *house. It is very bizarre.*
VICTORIA has put the decoration into the hands of an artist in
futurism, and the result is very modern, outrageous, fantastic,
but not ugly. There is no fire in the grate and all the windows are
open. FREDERICK *is sitting in a greatcoat with a rug round his*
legs, reading the paper. MRS. SHUTTLEWORTH *enters.*

MRS. SHUTTLEWORTH: I'm going now.

FREDERICK: Are you?

MRS. SHUTTLEWORTH: I'm taking my dear little grand-
children away with me.

FREDERICK: Are you?

MRS. SHUTTLEWORTH: You don't seem in a very good temper
this morning.

FREDERICK: I'm not.

MRS. SHUTTLEWORTH: Victoria will be down presently.

FREDERICK: Will she?

MRS. SHUTTLEWORTH: I should have thought you'd ask how
she was after that dreadful shock.

FREDERICK: Would you?

MRS. SHUTTLEWORTH: She's better, poor darling, but she's
terribly shaken. I put her to bed at once with hot-water
bottles.

FREDERICK: Did you?

MRS. SHUTTLEWORTH: Of course, she was totally unfit to
discuss this terrible situation yesterday.

FREDERICK: Was she?

MRS. SHUTTLEWORTH: Surely you can see that for yourself. The only thing was to keep her perfectly quiet till she'd had time to recover a little.

FREDERICK: Was it?

MRS. SHUTTLEWORTH: But this morning I have no doubt you'll find her prepared to go into the matter.

FREDERICK: Shall I?

MRS. SHUTTLEWORTH: If you have nothing else you wish to say to me I think I'll go now.

FREDERICK: Will you?

> [MRS. SHUTTLEWORTH *purses her lips very tight and goes towards the door. At that moment* TAYLOR *comes in.*

TAYLOR: Mr. Leicester Paton has called, madam. Mrs. Lowndes says, will you see him a minute. She's just getting out of her bath.

MRS. SHUTTLEWORTH: Certainly. Show him in here.

TAYLOR: Very good, madam.

> [*Exit.*

FREDERICK: I'll go.

MRS. SHUTTLEWORTH: I wonder what he wants.

FREDERICK: Perhaps he wants Victoria's permission to pay you his addresses.

> [*He goes out. In a minute* TAYLOR *announces* LEICESTER PATON *and then goes out.*

TAYLOR: Mr. Leicester Paton.

PATON: Your daughter rang me up this morning. I thought the best thing I could do was to come along at once.

MRS. SHUTTLEWORTH: That's too good of you. I'm sure if anything can be done you are the man to do it.

PATON: It's an extraordinary situation.

MRS. SHUTTLEWORTH: Of course, I think it was very inconsiderate of Bill to turn up like that.

PATON: Poor thing, she must be quite upset.

MRS. SHUTTLEWORTH: Well, I can only tell you that the shock entirely took the wave out of her hair. She only had it done yesterday, and it was as straight as a telegraph pole this morning.

PATON: You don't say so.

MRS. SHUTTLEWORTH: Here she is.

> [VICTORIA *comes in. She has her dressing-gown on and bedroom slippers. Her hair is only partly done, but she manages to look perfectly ravishing.*

VICTORIA: I didn't want to keep you waiting. I came down just as I was. You mustn't look at me.

PATON: I can't help it.

VICTORIA: What nonsense. I know I look a perfect fright, but fortunately I have no personal vanity.

PATON: [*Holding her hand.*] What a catastrophe! You must be beside yourself.

VICTORIA: [*With a charming smile.*] I knew I could rely on your sympathy.

PATON: What in heaven's name are you going to do?

VICTORIA: It's because I haven't an idea that I telephoned to you. You see, you've taught me to bring all my difficulties to you.

PATON: To whom else should you bring them? We must think. We must discuss the matter.

VICTORIA: The position is impossible.

PATON: It's wonderful that you bear it so bravely. I was expecting to find you in a state of collapse.

VICTORIA: [*With a flash of the eyes.*] With you to lean on?

PATON: I suppose you've been having the most terrible scenes.

VICTORIA: Heartrending. You see, they both adore me.

PATON: And you?

VICTORIA: I? I only want to do—my duty.

PATON: How like you! How exactly like you.

MRS. SHUTTLEWORTH: If there's nothing more I can do for you, darling I think I'll go now.

VICTORIA: Do, darling.

MRS. SHUTTLEWORTH: [*Shaking hands with* LEICESTER PATON] Be very kind to her.

PATON: I'll try.

[MRS. SHUTTLEWORTH *goes out*.

VICTORIA: [*Almost tenderly*.] It was sweet of you to come and see me at once. I was afraid you wouldn't have time.

PATON: Do you imagine I should allow anything to stand in the way when you sent for me?

VICTORIA: Oh, but you know I shouldn't like to think that you were putting yourself out on my account.

PATON: I wish I could pretend I were. As a matter of fact, I was only going down to see a place I've just bought in the country, and as I wanted to try my new Rolls I thought I'd kill two birds with one stone.

VICTORIA: I didn't know you were buying a place.

PATON: Oh, it's a very modest little affair. The park is not more than three hundred acres, and there are only twenty-eight bedrooms. But you see, I'm a bachelor. I want so little.

VICTORIA: Where is it?

PATON: It's near Newmarket.

VICTORIA: A very nice neighbourhood.

PATON: A man in my position is bound to do something for the good of the country, and it seems to me that to patronize a good old English sport, which gives employment to numbers of respectable men, is an occupation which is truly patriotic. I'm going to take up racing.

VICTORIA: I think it's splendid of you. So many men waste their money on their own selfish pleasures. It's such a relief to come across anyone who is determined to make a thoroughly good use of it. I've often wondered that you didn't go into Parliament.

PATON: For the last four years I've been too busy winning the war to bother about governing the nation.

VICTORIA: Yes, but now. They want strong men of keen intelligence and dominating personality.

PATON: It's not impossible that very soon I shall have the opportunity to show of what metal I am made. But not in the House of Commons.

VICTORIA: [*All to pieces*.] In the House of Lords?

PATON: [*Roguishly*.] Ah, you mustn't ask me to betray the confidence of the Prime Minister.

VICTORIA: You'll look sweet in scarlet and ermine.

PATON: [*Gallantly*.] But it's too bad of me to talk about my concerns when yours are so much more important.

VICTORIA: Oh, you can't think how I love to hear you talk about yourself. One feels a brain behind every word you say.

PATON: It's easy to be brilliant when one has a sympathetic listener.

VICTORIA: Of course, Bill and Freddie are dear good fellows, but their conversation is a little limited. During the war it was rather smart to talk about guns, and flying machines, and flea-bags, but now . . .

PATON: I understand you so well, dear lady.

VICTORIA: Why do you call me that?

PATON: Out of pure embarrassment. I don't know whether to call you Mrs. Cardew or Mrs. Lowndes.

VICTORIA: Why don't you split the difference and call me Victoria?

PATON: May I?

VICTORIA: [*Giving him her hand.*] It will make me feel that you are not an entire stranger to me.

PATON: [*With surprise.*] Your wedding rings? You always used to wear two.

VICTORIA: As long as I thought that poor Bill was dead I didn't want to forget him.

PATON: But why have you removed them both?

VICTORIA: I'm all at sea. I'm married to two men, and I feel as if I were married to neither.

PATON: I wish you weren't. I wish with all my heart you weren't.

VICTORIA: How emphatic you are. Why?

PATON: Can't you guess?

VICTORIA: [*Looking down.*] I must be very stupid.

PATON: Don't you know that I dote upon you? I curse my unhappy fate that I didn't meet you before you were married.

VICTORIA: Would you have asked me to marry you?

PATON: Morning, noon and night until you consented.

VICTORIA: I never want a Paris model so much as when I know it's just been sold to somebody else. I wonder if you'd want to marry me if I were free?

PATON: Yes. With all my heart.

VICTORIA: But I'm not free.

PATON: And you—if you were, would you marry me?

VICTORIA: Tell me, why do you wear spats?

PATON: I think they're so neat.

VICTORIA: Oh, not because you suffer from cold feet?

PATON: Oh no, my circulation is excellent.

VICTORIA: I don't believe you're the sort of man who'd ever take no for an answer.

PATON: You're perfectly adorable.

VICTORIA: [*With a smile, shyly.*] I wonder if you'd take me out to luncheon?

PATON: Give me the chance.

VICTORIA: I'll just dress myself. Come back in half an hour, and you'll find me ready.

PATON: Very well.

VICTORIA: Good-bye for the present.

[*They go out together.* WILLIAM'S *voice is heard outside.*

WILLIAM: Victoria. [*He comes in, but sees nobody in the room.*] Hulloa! [*Shouting.*] Freddie.

FREDERICK: [*Outside.*] Hulloa.

WILLIAM: Freddie.

[FREDERICK *comes in with his rug and his paper.*

WILLIAM: I say, I can't find my boots.

FREDERICK: Your boots? What do you want your boots for?

WILLIAM: To put them on. What else d'you think I want them for?

FREDERICK: I saw them lying about. I thought I'd better put them away in case of accidents.

WILLIAM: Silly ass. Where did you put them?

FREDERICK: I was just trying to think.

WILLIAM: You don't mean to say you don't know where they are.

FREDERICK: Of course I know where they are because I put them there, but I don't happen to remember just at the moment.

WILLIAM: Well, you hurry up and remember.

FREDERICK: Don't fuss me. I can't possibly remember if you fuss me.

WILLIAM: Try and think where you put them.

FREDERICK: [*Looking doubtfully at a vase.*] I know I didn't put them in one of the flower vases.

WILLIAM: So I should hope.

FREDERICK: They might be in the coal-scuttle.

WILLIAM: If they are I'll black your face with them.

FREDERICK: [*Looking in the scuttle, with triumph.*] I said they weren't in the coal scuttle.

WILLIAM: Fathead. I don't want to know where they're not. I want to know where they are.

FREDERICK: If I knew that I shouldn't be hunting for them.

WILLIAM: If you don't find them in two and a half seconds I'll break every bone in your body.

FREDERICK: It's no good losing your hair about it. If we can't find your boots we can't.

WILLIAM: [*Irritably.*] I say, what the devil have you got all the windows open for?

FREDERICK: I was trying to warm the room a bit. Besides, they say it's healthy.

WILLIAM: A short life and a merry one for me. I like a fug.

[*He shuts the windows.*

FREDERICK: That won't make it any warmer. I've tried that.

WILLIAM: You silly ass, why don't you light the fire?

FREDERICK: Don't be so damned unpatriotic. Victoria must have a fire in her bedroom, and we must have one in the nursery.

WILLIAM: Why?

FREDERICK: For the children's bath.

WILLIAM: [*Astonished.*] What, every day?

FREDERICK: Yes, they wash children a lot nowadays.

WILLIAM: Poor little beggars.

FREDERICK: [*Jumping up and going towards him.*] Where the devil did you get that suit?

WILLIAM: Rather saucy, I flatter myself. Victoria sent it in to me.

FREDERICK: She needn't have sent you the only new suit I've had since the war. Upon my soul, I think it's a bit thick.

WILLIAM: Well, you didn't like the suit I wore yesterday. You can't expect me to go about in fig-leaves unless you have the house properly warmed.

FREDERICK: If you'd had the decency to ask *me* you might have had this suit I've got on.

WILLIAM: Thanks, but I don't altogether like that one. It's a bit baggy at the knees for me.

FREDERICK: You're very much mistaken if you think you're going to wear all the new clothes and I'm going to wear all the old ones.

WILLIAM: If you're going to be shirty about it, where the devil did you get that pin?

FREDERICK: Oh, Victoria gave it me on my birthday.

WILLIAM: Well, it's mine. She gave it me on my birthday first. And where did you get those links?

FREDERICK: Victoria gave them to me as a Christmas present.

WILLIAM: Oh, did she? She gave them to me as a Christmas present before she gave them to you. You jolly well take them off.

FREDERICK: I'll see you blowed first. At your death you left everything to her in your will. If she chose to give them to me it's no business of yours.

WILLIAM: Well, I'm not going to argue about it, but I think it's dashed bad form to swank about in a dead man's jewellery.

FREDERICK: By the way, did you ever have a hammered gold cigarette-case?

WILLIAM: Rather. That was Victoria's wedding present to me. Did you get it too?

K

FREDERICK: Thrifty woman, Victoria.

WILLIAM: I say, unless I have a fire I shall turn into the Albert Memorial.

FREDERICK: Apply a match and see what happens.

WILLIAM: Thanks—I will.

[*He strikes a match and lights the fire. The flames leap up.*

FREDERICK: Now I'll take my coat off. Victoria will be furious.

WILLIAM: That's your look out. You'll have to take the responsibility.

FREDERICK: It's got nothing to do with me. You're the master of this house.

WILLIAM: Not at all. I am but an honoured guest.

FREDERICK: Oh no, the moment you appeared I sank into insignificance.

WILLIAM: My dear fellow, where did I sleep last night? In the spare bedroom. That proves conclusively that I am a guest and nothing more.

FREDERICK: And where the devil do you think I slept? Here.

WILLIAM: Why did you do that? You were perfectly sober when I went to bed.

FREDERICK: Victoria said I couldn't sleep in the next room to hers now you were back.

WILLIAM: Oh, well, I dare say you made yourself very comfortable on the sofa.

FREDERICK: Look at the damned thing.

WILLIAM: By the way, what's the matter with the furniture?

FREDERICK: When you were killed Victoria was naturally very much upset, so she had the drawing-room redecorated.

WILLIAM: I dare say I'm not very bright so early in the morning, but I don't quite see the connection.

FREDERICK: You see, the old room had too many painful associations. She wanted to distract her mind.

WILLIAM: Oh, I was under the impression that you'd undertaken that.

FREDERICK: [*With dignity.*] I was sympathetic. That is surely what you would have liked me to be.

WILLIAM: Of course. I'm not blaming you.

FREDERICK: If you'd seen Victoria in tears you couldn't expect a man not to try and console her.

WILLIAM: She's the only woman I ever knew who looks as pretty when she cries as when she smiles. It's a great power.

FREDERICK: I knew you'd take it like a sensible man.

WILLIAM: Quite so.

FREDERICK: When would you like me to clear out?

WILLIAM: My dear fellow, why should you wish to do that? Surely you don't for a moment imagine that I shall be in the way. I propose to make my visit quite a brief one.

FREDERICK: I'm sorry to hear that. Victoria will be disappointed. But of course that's no concern of mine. You and your wife must arrange that between you.

WILLIAM: My dear old thing, you entirely misunderstand me. I am not the man to come between husband and wife.

FREDERICK: What the devil do you mean?

WILLIAM: Well, if it comes to that, what the devil do you mean?

> [VICTORIA *comes in. She now wears a most becoming morning dress. She carries a box of chocolates.*

VICTORIA: Good-morning.

> [*She goes to* WILLIAM *and gives him her cheek to kiss.*

WILLIAM: Good-morning.

VICTORIA: Good-morning.

[*She goes up to* FREDERICK *and gives him the other cheek to kiss.*

FREDERICK: Good-morning.

VICTORIA: [*With a nod of the head towards* WILLIAM.] I went to him first because he's been away so long.

FREDERICK: Naturally. And he was your husband long before I was.

VICTORIA: I don't want either of you to be jealous of the other. I adore you both and I'm not going to show any favouritism.

FREDERICK: I don't see why he should have the spare bedroom, while I have to double up on the drawing-room sofa.

WILLIAM: I like that. What about the fatted calf?

FREDERICK: Not unless you've brought your coupons with you.

VICTORIA: [*Catching sight of the fire.*] Who lit that fire?

FREDERICK: He did.

WILLIAM: It was your match.

[VICTORIA *draws up a chair and sits down in front of the fire in such a way as to prevent any warmth from getting into the room.*

VICTORIA: [*Eating a chocolate.*] Of course you don't care if we run so short of coal that my wretched babies die of double pneumonia. It's simply criminal to have a fire here.

WILLIAM: I'm tortured by the pangs of remorse. But, need you monopolize it?

VICTORIA: If there is a fire I may as well get some benefit out of it.

FREDERICK: Are those chocolates you're eating, Victoria?

VICTORIA: Yes, Bobbie Curtis sent them to me. They're delicious.

FREDERICK: Are they?

VICTORIA: It's so hard to get good chocolates just now.

FREDERICK: I know it is. I haven't tasted one for months.

VICTORIA: [*Biting a chocolate.*] Oh, this one's soft inside. How hateful. Would either of you like it?

WILLIAM: [*Ironically.*] It seems a pity to waste it, Victoria.

VICTORIA: [*Eating it.*] I dare say you're right. One oughtn't to be too particular in war-time.

WILLIAM: Ah, I suppose that's what you thought when you married Freddie.

VICTORIA: I did that for your sake, darling. He was such a pal of yours.

FREDERICK: She was simply inconsolable when you were killed.

WILLIAM: It's lucky you were there to console her.

VICTORIA: It was Freddie who broke the news to me. He thought of the memorial service. He came to see me twice a day.

WILLIAM: And with your practical mind I suppose you thought it hardly worth his while to wear out shoe-leather when a trifling ceremony might save him the journey.

VICTORIA: Of course we waited the year. I told him he mustn't think of it till the year was up.

WILLIAM: With leather so expensive? But you always had nice feelings, Victoria.

VICTORIA: You know how helpless I am without a man. I knew you wouldn't wish me to remain a widow.

FREDERICK: I felt I was the proper person to look after her.

WILLIAM: The way you've both of you sacrificed yourselves for my sake is almost more than I can bear. I can only hope that you didn't have to force your inclinations too much?

FREDERICK: What do you mean by that?

WILLIAM: Well, since it appears you married entirely for my sake, I presume there was nothing between you but— shall we say esteem?

VICTORIA: Oh, but, Bill darling, didn't I tell you that I adored Freddie? It was his wonderful friendship for you that won my heart.

FREDERICK: She was so devoted to you, Bill, I should have been a brute not to care for her.

WILLIAM: One would almost think you fell in love with one another.

VICTORIA: Only over your dead body, darling.

FREDERICK: I should have thought you'd be rather touched by it.

WILLIAM: It gives me quite a lump in my throat.

FREDERICK: And Victoria never forgot you, old man. Did you, Victoria?

VICTORIA: Never.

FREDERICK: I know quite well that I only came second in her heart. So long as you were round and about she would never have thought of me.

WILLIAM: Oh, I don't know about that. Even the most constant woman likes a change now and then.

FREDERICK: No, no. I know Victoria's faithful heart. She can never really love any man but you. Victoria, you know how I adore you. You are the only woman in the world for me. But I realize that there is only one thing for me to do. Bill has come back. There is only one course open to me as a gentleman and a man of honour. It is a bitter, bitter sacrifice, but I am equal to it. I renounce all rights in you. I will go away, a wiser and a sadder man, and leave you to Bill. Good-bye, Victoria. Wipe your mouth and give me one more kiss before we part for ever.

VICTORIA: Oh, how beautiful of you, Freddie. What a soul you've got.

FREDERICK: Good-bye, Victoria. Forget me and live happily with a better man than I.

VICTORIA: I shall never forget you, Freddie. Good-bye. Go quickly or I shall break down.

> [WILLIAM *has planted himself firmly in front of the door.* FREDERICK *goes up to him with outstretched hand.*]

FREDERICK: Good-bye, Bill. Be kind to her. I couldn't do this for anyone but you.

WILLIAM: [*Deliberately.*] Nothing doing.

FREDERICK: I am going out of your life for ever.

WILLIAM: Not in those boots.

FREDERICK: Damn it all, what's the matter with them? They're not yours.

WILLIAM: A figure of speech, my lad.

FREDERICK: I don't think this is exactly the moment for flippancy. You get away from that door.

WILLIAM: You shall only pass over my dead body.

FREDERICK: What's the good of that? I shouldn't get the chance then.

VICTORIA: Bill, why prolong a painful scene?

WILLIAM: My dear Victoria, I am not the man to accept a sacrifice like that. No. The War Office has decided that I'm dead. You've had a memorial service. You've redecorated the drawing-room. You are happy. It would be monstrously selfish if I disturbed a state of things which is eminently satisfactory to you both. I will not come between you.

VICTORIA: Oh, Bill, how noble.

WILLIAM: Victoria, I am a gentleman and a soldier. This being that you see before you, notwithstanding the tolerable suit he wears, is a disembodied wraith. To all intents and purposes I am as dead as mutton. I will remain so.

FREDERICK: Victoria will never be happy with me now that you've come back.

WILLIAM: Not another word. She is yours.

FREDERICK: My dear Bill, you know me very little. I am lazy, selfish, bad-tempered, mean, gouty, and predisposed to cancer, tuberculosis, and diabetes.

WILLIAM: This is terrible, my poor Freddie. You must take the greatest care of your health, and dear Victoria will do her best to correct your defects of character.

FREDERICK: If you really loved her you wouldn't expose her to the certain misery that it must be to live with a man like me.

WILLIAM: Freddie, old man, I can no longer conceal from you that with a constitution ruined by dissipation in my youth and broken by the ravages of war I have not much longer to live. Besides, Victoria knows only too well that I am vindictive and overbearing, extravagant, violent and mendacious.

VICTORIA: I understand it all. You're both so noble. You're both so heroic. You're both so unselfish.

[TAYLOR *comes in.*

TAYLOR: If you please, ma'am, someone to see you from the Alexandra Employment Agency.

[*She hands her a slip of paper.*

VICTORIA: Oh, send her in at once.

TAYLOR: Very good, madam.

[*Exit.*

VICTORIA: A cook. A cook. A cook.

FREDERICK: Good business. Is she plain or good?

VICTORIA: Plain and good.

WILLIAM: How like a woman.

[TAYLOR *shows in* MRS. POGSON *and closes the door behind her.* MRS. POGSON *is large and heavy and authoritative. She is dressed like the widow of an undertaker.*

MRS. POGSON: Good-morning.

VICTORIA: Good-morning.

[MRS. POGSON *looks round her, and seeing a handy chair sits down on it.*

MRS. POGSON: I 'ave your name on the list the Alexandra gave me as requiring a cook. I don't know as I very much like this neighbourhood, but I thought I'd just pop in and see if the position looked like suiting me.

VICTORIA: [*Ingratiatingly.*] I'm sure you'd find it a very nice one.

MRS. POGSON: I couldn't stand them air-raids and I made up my mind I wouldn't come back to London not so long as the war lasted. And the streets all dark and I don't know what all. But of course I prefer London.

VICTORIA: Naturally.

MRS. POGSON: And now that the war's over if I can find anything that suits me I don't mind coming back. Why did the last cook leave you?

VICTORIA: She was going to be married.

MRS. POGSON: Ah, that's what all you ladies say. Of course, it may be so, and on the other 'and it may not.

VICTORIA: She told me she hadn't had a nicer place for the last three months.

MRS. POGSON: Now before we go any further I'd just like to know one thing. Have you got a garage?

VICTORIA: Well, we have, but there are no cars in it. We sold our car.

MRS. POGSON: Oh, well, that would be very convenient. I always bring my Ford with me.

Victoria: Yes, of course.

Mrs. Pogson: Do you keep men-servants?

Victoria: No, I'm afraid not.

Mrs. Pogson: [*Severely.*] I've always been used to men-servants.

Victoria: You see, since the war . . .

Mrs. Pogson: Oh, you don't 'ave to tell me. I know it's very difficult. And I suppose you 'aven't got a kitchen-maid either?

Victoria: One can't get one for love or money.

Mrs. Pogson: That's a thing I shall never forgive the Government for. Taking all them girls and putting them in munitions. Still, that's not your fault, I will say that. There's many cooks I know as say they *will not* go without a kitchen-maid, but I say, it's war-time and everyone ought to do his bit. If I must do without a kitchen-maid, well, I will do without a kitchen-maid.

Victoria: I think it's very patriotic of you.

Mrs. Pogson: Of course, I leave you to make any arrangements you like about lighting the kitchen fire. All I ask is that it should be alight when I come down in the morning.

Victoria: Oh! Naturally, I see your point. But I don't quite know how I should manage about that.

Mrs. Pogson: In my last position the gentleman of the house lit the fire every morning.

Victoria: Oh, I hadn't thought of that.

William: I wouldn't if I were you, Victoria.

Mrs. Pogson: A very nice gentleman he was too. Brought me up a cup of tea and a slice of thin bread and butter every day before I got up.

Victoria: I'm sure we'd do everything we could to make you comfortable.

Mrs. Pogson: What cooking would you require?

Victoria: I'm sure you'd satisfy us there. I can see at once that you're a first-rate cook.

Mrs. Pogson: I don't 'old with a lot of fancy things meself, not in war-time. I say, be thankful you get anything to eat at all.

Victoria: Of course, I know it's very difficult to have a great variety now. I'm sure you'll do the best you can. We're out for luncheon a good deal and we dine at eight.

Mrs. Pogson: Of course, you can please yourselves there, but I never do any cooking after middle-day.

Victoria: That's rather awkward.

Mrs. Pogson: If you don't think I'll suit you I needn't waste any more of my time. I've got ten to a dozen ladies that I must interview this morning.

Victoria: Oh, I wouldn't make a point of that. I dare say we can arrange our hours to suit you.

Mrs. Pogson: Well, I always serve up my dinner at one o'clock. A nice little bit of meat and a milk pudding. And should you want anything after that you can always 'ave the cold meat for your supper and any little sweet I 'appen to 'ave in the kitchen.

Victoria: I see. And what—what wages are you asking?

Mrs. Pogson: I don't know as I'm asking any wages. I'm prepared to accept a salary of two pound a week.

Victoria: That's rather more than I've been in the habit of paying.

Mrs. Pogson: If you aren't prepared to pay that there are plenty as are.

Victoria: We won't quarrel about that. I'm sure you're worth the money.

Mrs. Pogson: I don't think there are any more questions I need ask you.

VICTORIA: No, I think that's everything. When would you be able to come in?

MRS. POGSON: I'll just go and see these other ladies and see what they 'ave to offer me, and then if I come to the conclusion that you'll suit me I'll just drop you a line.

VICTORIA: I do hope you'll come here. I'm sure you'd be happy.

MRS. POGSON: That's what I always say, the great thing is to be 'appy. And I like your face. I don't mind telling you that I've taken quite a fancy to you.

VICTORIA: I'm very glad to hear it.

MRS. POGSON: There, I was just going away and I knew I 'ad one more question to ask you. My 'ead's like a perfect sieve this morning. How many are you in the family?

VICTORIA: Well, I have two children, but they give no trouble at all, and just at present they're not staying here.

MRS. POGSON: Oh, I don't mind children. I've had too many meself to do that.

VICTORIA: And then there's just me and these two gentle-men.

MRS. POGSON: I suppose you are married to one of them.

VICTORIA: I don't know what you mean by that. I'm married to both.

MRS. POGSON: Both? Legally?

VICTORIA: Of course.

MRS. POGSON: Well, I do call that going it. [*With growing indignation.*] If it 'ad been just a gentleman friend I'd 'ave 'ad nothing to say. I've lived in the very best families and I'm quite used to that. It keeps the lady quiet and good-tempered and she ain't always fussing about one thing and another. And if he lives in the 'ouse she ain't likely to keep the dinner waiting for 'alf an hour every other day. But if you're married to 'im that's quite another thing. It's not justice. If you ladies think you're going to 'ave two 'usbands while many a working woman can't even get one—well, all I say is, it's not justice. I've bin a Conservative all me life, but thank God I've got a vote now, and I tell you straight what I'm going to do, I'm going to vote Labour.

[*She flaunts out of the room and slams the door behind her.*

WILLIAM: Bang!

VICTORIA: [*Furiously.*] The position is intolerable. I must have one husband. There are all sorts of ways in which a husband is indispensable. But only one. I cannot and will not have two.

FREDERICK: I have an idea.

WILLIAM: It's sure to be a rotten one.

FREDERICK: Let's draw lots.

WILLIAM: I knew it was a rotten one.

VICTORIA: How d'you mean, Freddie?

FREDERICK: Well, we'll take two pieces of paper and make a cross on one of them. Then we'll fold them up and put them in a hat. We'll draw, and the one who draws the cross gets Victoria.

VICTORIA: [*Mollified.*] That'll be rather thrilling.

WILLIAM: I'd sooner toss for it. I'm lucky at tossing.

FREDERICK: Do you mean to say you funk it?

WILLIAM: I don't exactly funk it. It's an awful risk to take.

VICTORIA: It'll be so romantic. Get some paper, Freddie.

FREDERICK: All right.

WILLIAM: [*Worried.*] I don't like it. This isn't my lucky day. I saw the new moon through glass. I knew something was going wrong the moment I opened my egg this morning.

[FREDERICK *goes to a desk and takes out a sheet of paper which he tears in two. Then with his back turned he draws a cross.*

FREDERICK: Whoever draws the blank paper renounces all claim to Victoria. He vanishes from the scene like a puff of smoke. He will never be heard of again.

WILLIAM: I don't like it. I repeat that I only do it under protest.

VICTORIA: Now, Bill, don't be disagreeable the moment you come back.

FREDERICK: You'll have plenty of time for that during the next forty years.

VICTORIA: You seem rather above yourself, Freddie. Supposing *you* draw the blank?

FREDERICK: I saw a dappled horse this morning. What shall we put them in?

VICTORIA: The waste-paper basket is the best thing.

FREDERICK: I'll get it. Now you quite understand. One of these papers has a cross on it. I will put the two papers in the basket, and Victoria shall hold it. It is agreed that whoever draws a blank shall leave the house at once.

WILLIAM: [*Faintly.*] Yes.

FREDERICK: [*Handing her the basket.*] Here you are, Victoria.

WILLIAM: [*With agitation.*] Shake 'em well.

VICTORIA: All right. I say, isn't this thrilling?

FREDERICK: You draw first, Bill.

WILLIAM: [*Shaking like a leaf.*] No, I can't. I really can't.

FREDERICK: It's your right. You are Victoria's first husband.

VICTORIA: He's right there, Bill. You must have the first dip in the lucky bag.

WILLIAM: This is awful. I'm sweating like a pig.

VICTORIA: It's too exciting. My heart is simply going pit-a-pat. I wonder which of you will get me.

WILLIAM: [*Hesitating.*] Going over the top is nothing to it.

FREDERICK: Courage, old man, courage.

WILLIAM: It's no good, I can't. You must remember that my nerves are all to pieces after three years in a German prison.

VICTORIA: I see how much you love me, Bill.

FREDERICK: Shut your eyes, man, and make a plunge for the basket.

WILLIAM: The only thing is to get it over. I wish I'd been a better man.

> [*He draws out one of the pieces of paper and* FREDERICK *takes the other. For a moment he looks at it nervously, unable to bring himself to unfold it.* FREDERICK *opens his, gives a sudden cry, and starts back.*

FREDERICK: [*Dramatically.*] Blank. Blank. Blank.

> [WILLIAM *gives a start, and quickly unravels the paper in his hand. He stares at it in horror.*

WILLIAM: My God!

VICTORIA: Oh, my poor Freddie!

FREDERICK: [*With enormous feeling.*] Don't pity me, Victoria. I want all my courage now. I've lost you and I must bid you good-bye for ever.

VICTORIA: Oh, Freddie, this is too dreadful! You must come and see me from time to time.

FREDERICK: I couldn't. That is more than I could bear. I shall never forget you. You are the only woman I have ever loved.

> [*At these words* WILLIAM *looks up and observes him curiously.*

VICTORIA: You'll never love another, will you? I shouldn't like that.

FREDERICK: How could I love anyone after you? Why, you might as well ask a man to see when the sun has gone down.

WILLIAM: He can turn on the electric light, you know.

FREDERICK: Ah, you can jest. I am a broken-hearted and a ruined man.

WILLIAM: I was only suggesting the possibility of consolation.

VICTORIA: I don't think that's very nice of you, Bill. I thought what he said extremely poetic. Besides, I don't want him to be consoled.

FREDERICK: Give me one last kiss, Victoria.

VICTORIA: Darling!

> [*He seizes her in his arms and kisses her.*

FREDERICK: [*The hero of romance.*] Good-bye. I go into the night.

WILLIAM: Oh, aren't you going at once?

FREDERICK: I am.

WILLIAM: Well, it happens to be the middle of the day.

FREDERICK: [*With dignity.*] I was speaking in metaphor.

WILLIAM: Before you go you might just let me have a look at that other bit of paper, the one with the blank on it.

FREDERICK: [*Walking towards the door.*] Oh, don't delay me with foolish trifling.

WILLIAM: [*Intercepting him.*] I'm sorry to detain you.

FREDERICK: [*Trying to dodge round him.*] Why d'you want to see it?

WILLIAM: [*Preventing him.*] Mere curiosity.

FREDERICK: [*Trying the other side.*] Really, Bill, I don't know how you can be so heartless as to give way to curiosity when my heart is one great aching wound.

WILLIAM: I should like to have the two pieces framed, an interesting souvenir of an important occasion.

FREDERICK: Any other piece will do just as well. I threw that one in the fire.

WILLIAM: Oh no, you didn't. You put it in your pocket.

FREDERICK: I've had enough of this. Can't you see that I'm a desperate man?

WILLIAM: Not half so desperate as I am. If you don't give me that bit of paper quietly I'll take it from you.

FREDERICK: Go to blazes!

WILLIAM: Give it up.

[*He makes a dash for* FREDERICK, *who dodges; he pursues him round the room.*

VICTORIA: What's the matter? Have you both gone mad?

WILLIAM: You'll have to sooner or later.

FREDERICK: I'll see you damned first.

VICTORIA: Why don't you give it him?

FREDERICK: Not if I know it.

VICTORIA: Why not?

FREDERICK: I won't have my feelings hurt like this.

WILLIAM: I'll hurt a lot more than your feelings in a minute.

[FREDERICK *makes a sudden bolt for the door, but* WILLIAM *catches him.*

WILLIAM: Got cher. Now will you give it up?

FREDERICK: Not on your life.

WILLIAM: I'll break your bally arm if you don't.

FREDERICK: [*Writhing.*] Oh, you devil! Stop it. You're hurting me.

WILLIAM: I'm trying to.

FREDERICK: Hit him on the head with the poker, Victoria.

WILLIAM: Don't be unlady-like, Victoria.

FREDERICK: You filthy Boche. All right, here it is.

[WILLIAM *lets him go and* FREDERICK *takes the paper out of his pocket. Just as* WILLIAM *thinks he is going to give it him, he puts it in his mouth.*

WILLIAM: [*Seizing him by the throat.*] Take it out of your mouth.

[FREDERICK *takes it out and throws it on the floor.*

FREDERICK: I don't know if you call yourself a gentleman.

[WILLIAM *takes up the paper and unfolds it.*

WILLIAM: You dirty dog.

VICTORIA: What's the matter?

[*He walks over and hands it to her.*

WILLIAM: Look.

VICTORIA: Why, it's got a cross on it.

WILLIAM: [*Indignantly.*] They both had crosses on them.

VICTORIA: I don't understand.

WILLIAM: Don't you? He was making quite sure that *I* shouldn't draw a blank.

    [VICTORIA *looks at him in astonishment. There is a moment's pause.*

FREDERICK: [*Magnanimously.*] I did it for your sake, Victoria. I knew that your heart was set on Bill, only you couldn't bear to hurt my feelings, so I thought I'd make it easier for you.

VICTORIA: That was just like you, Freddie. You have a charming nature.

WILLIAM: [*Acidly.*] It almost brings tears to my eyes.

FREDERICK: I'm made that way. I can't help sacrificing myself for others.

[TAYLOR *comes in.*

TAYLOR: May I speak to you for a minute, madam.

VICTORIA: Not now. I'm busy.

TAYLOR: I'm afraid it's very urgent, madam.

VICTORIA: Oh, very well, I'll come. Don't say anything important till I come back.

    [TAYLOR *holds the door open for her, and she goes out.*

FREDERICK: How did you guess?

WILLIAM: You were so devilish calm about it.

FREDERICK: That was the calm of despair.

> [WILLIAM *is sitting on the sofa. He happens to put his hand behind him and feels something hard. With a puzzled expression he puts down his hand between the seat and the back of the sofa and draws out first one boot and then another.*

WILLIAM: My boots!

FREDERICK: I knew I'd put them somewhere.

WILLIAM: You didn't put them anywhere. You hid them, you dirty dog.

FREDERICK: It's a lie. Why the dickens should I hide your rotten old boots?

WILLIAM: You were afraid I'd do a bunk.

FREDERICK: You needn't get ratty about it. I only ascribed to you the disinterested motives that I—that I have myself. I may be wrong, but, after all, it's a noble error.

WILLIAM: One might almost think you didn't want Victoria.

> [FREDERICK *looks at him for a moment thoughtfully, then he makes up his mind to make a clean breast of it.*

FREDERICK: Bill, old chap, you know I'm not the sort of man to say a word against my wife.

WILLIAM: Nor am I the sort of man to listen to a word against mine.

FREDERICK: But, hang it all, if a fellow can't discuss his wife dispassionately with her first husband, who can he discuss her with?

WILLIAM: I can't imagine unless it's with her second.

FREDERICK: Tell me what you really think of Victoria.

WILLIAM: She's the sweetest little woman in the world.

FREDERICK: No man could want a better wife.

WILLIAM: She's pretty.

FREDERICK: Charming.

WILLIAM: Delightful.

FREDERICK: I confess that sometimes I've thought it hard that when I wanted a thing it was selfishness, and when she wanted it, it was only her due.

WILLIAM: I don't mind admitting that sometimes I used to wonder why it was only natural of me to sacrifice my inclinations, but in her the proof of a beautiful nature.

FREDERICK: It has tried me now and then that in every difference of opinion I should always be wrong and she should always be right.

WILLIAM: Sometimes I couldn't quite understand why my engagements were made to be broken, while nothing in the world must interfere with hers.

FREDERICK: I have asked myself occasionally why my time was of no importance while hers was so precious.

WILLIAM: I did sometimes wish I could call my soul my own.

FREDERICK: The fact is, I'm not worthy of her, Bill. As you so justly say, no man could want a better wife. . . .

WILLIAM: [*Interrupting.*] No, you said that.

FREDERICK: But I'm fed up. If you'd been dead I'd have seen it through like a gentleman, but you've turned up like a bad shilling. Now you take up the white man's burden.

WILLIAM: I'll see you damned first.

FREDERICK: She must have one husband.

WILLIAM: Look here, there's only one thing to do. She must choose between us.

FREDERICK: That's not giving me a chance.

WILLIAM: I don't know what you mean by that. I think it's extraordinarily magnanimous on my part.

FREDERICK: Magnanimous be hanged. I've got a charming nature and I'm extremely handsome. Victoria will naturally choose me.

WILLIAM: Heaven knows I'm not vain, but I've always been given to understand that I'm an almost perfect specimen of manly beauty. My conversation is not only amusing, but instructive.

FREDERICK: I'd rather toss for it.

WILLIAM: I'm not going to risk anything like that. I've had enough of your hanky-panky.

FREDERICK: I thought I was dealing with a gentleman.

WILLIAM: Here she comes.

     [VICTORIA *comes in. She is in a temper.*

VICTORIA: All the servants have given notice now.

FREDERICK: They haven't!

VICTORIA: I've done everything in the world for them. I've given them double wages. I've fed them on the fat of the land. I've given them my own butter and my own sugar to eat.

FREDERICK: Only because they were bad for your figure, Victoria.

VICTORIA: They didn't know that. I've given them all the evenings out that I really didn't want them. I've let them bring the whole British Army to tea here. And now they give me notice.

WILLIAM: It's a bit thick, I must say.

VICTORIA: I argued with them, I appealed to them, I practically went down on my knees to them. They wouldn't listen. They're going to walk out of the house this afternoon.

WILLIAM: Oh, well, Freddie and I will do the housework until you get some more.

VICTORIA: Do you know that it's harder to get a parlour-maid than a peerage? Why, every day at Paddington Registry Office you'll see a queue of old bachelors taking out licences to marry their cooks. It's the only way to keep them.

WILLIAM: Well, Victoria, we've decided that there's only one thing to be done. You must choose between us.

VICTORIA: How can I? I adore you both. Besides, there's so little to choose between you.

WILLIAM: Oh, I don't know about that. Freddie has a charming nature and he's extremely handsome.

FREDERICK: I wish you wouldn't say that, Bill. Heaven knows you're not vain, but I must tell you to your face that you're an almost perfect specimen of manly beauty, and your conversation is not only amusing but instructive.

VICTORIA: I don't want to hurt anybody's feelings.

FREDERICK: Before you decide, I feel it only fair to make a confession to you. I could not bear it if our future life were founded on a lie. Victoria, in my department there is a stenographer. She is of the feminine gender. She has blue eyes and little yellow curls at the nape of her neck. The rest I leave to your imagination.

VICTORIA: How abominable. And I always thought you had such a nice mind.

FREDERICK: I am unworthy of you. I know it only too, too well. You can never forgive me.

WILLIAM: Dirty dog.

VICTORIA: That certainly simplifies matters. I don't quite see myself as the third lady in the back row of a harem.

WILLIAM: You would run no risk of being that in Canada. Women are scarce in Manitoba.

VICTORIA: What *are* you talking about?

WILLIAM: I have come to the conclusion that England offers me no future now the war is over. I shall resign my commission. The empire needs workers, and I am ready to take my part in reconstruction. Make me the happiest of men, Victoria, and we'll emigrate together.

VICTORIA: To Canada?

FREDERICK: Where the sables come from.

VICTORIA: Not the best ones.

WILLIAM: I shall buy a farm. I think it would be a very good plan if you employed your leisure in learning how to cook the simple fare on which we shall live. I believe you can wash?

VICTORIA: [*With asperity.*] Lace.

WILLIAM: But I think you should also learn how to milk cows.

VICTORIA: I don't like cows.

WILLIAM: I see the idea appeals to you. It will be a wonderful life, Victoria. You'll light the fire and scrub the floors, and you'll cook the dinner and wash the clothes. You'll vote.

VICTORIA: And what shall I do in my spare moments?

WILLIAM: We will cultivate your mind by reading the *Encyclopædia Britannica* together. Take a good look at us, Victoria, and say which of us it's to be.

VICTORIA: To tell you the truth, I don't see why it should be either.

FREDERICK: Hang it all, it must be one or the other.

VICTORIA: I think no one can deny that since the day I married you I've sacrificed myself in every mortal way. I've worked myself to the bone to make you comfortable. Very few men have ever had such a wife as I've been to both of you! But one must think of oneself sometimes.

WILLIAM: How true.

VICTORIA: The war is over now, and I think I've done my bit. I've married two D.S.O.'s. Now I want to marry a Rolls-Royce.

FREDERICK: [*Astonished.*] But I thought you adored us.

VICTORIA: Well, you see, I adore you both. It's six of one

and half a dozen of the other, and the result is . . .

WILLIAM: A wash-out.

FREDERICK: Hang it all, I think it's a bit thick. Do you mean to say that you've fixed up to marry somebody else behind our back?

VICTORIA: You know I wouldn't do a thing like that, Freddie.

FREDERICK: Well, I don't tumble.

VICTORIA: My dear Freddie, have you ever studied the domestic habits of the unicorn?

FREDERICK: I am afraid my education was very much neglected.

VICTORIA: The unicorn is a shy and somewhat timid animal, and it is impossible to catch him with the snares of the hunter. But he is strangely impressionable to the charms of the fair sex. When he hears the frou-frou of a silk petticoat he forgets his native caution. In short, a pretty woman can lead him by the nose.

[TAYLOR *comes in.*

TAYLOR: Mr. Leicester Paton is downstairs in his car, madam.

VICTORIA: Is it the Rolls-Royce?

TAYLOR: I think it is, madam.

VICTORIA: [*With a smile of triumph.*] Say I'll come down at once.

TAYLOR: Very good, madam. [*Exit.*

VICTORIA: The unicorn's going to take me out to luncheon.

[*She makes a long nose at them and goes out.*

END OF THE SECOND ACT

THE THIRD ACT

The kitchen. At one end is a range, with a gas-stove; at the other end a dresser on which are plates and dishes. At the back a door leads out to the area and near it is a window, with iron bars, through which can be seen the area steps and persons ascending and descending them. In the middle of the room is a kitchen table, and here and there kitchen chairs. There is linoleum on the floor. The place is clean, sanitary, and cheerful.

WILLIAM *is sitting on one of the chairs with his feet on another, reading a thin, paper-bound novel of the sort that is published at threepence and sold by the newsagent round the corner.* FREDERICK *comes in with a scuttle full of coals.*

FREDERICK: [*Putting down the scuttle.*] I say, these coals weigh about a ton. You might carry them upstairs.

WILLIAM: [*Cheerfully.*] I might, but I'm not going to.

FREDERICK: I wouldn't ask you, only since I was wounded in the arm serving my country I haven't the strength I had once.

WILLIAM: [*Suspiciously.*] Which arm were you wounded in?

FREDERICK: [*Promptly.*] Both arms.

WILLIAM: Carry the coals on your head then. I believe that's the best way really. And they say it improves the figure.

FREDERICK: You heartless devil.

WILLIAM: I'd do it like a shot, old man, only the doctor said it was very bad for my heart to carry heavy weights.

FREDERICK: What's the matter with your heart? You said you were wounded in the head.

WILLIAM: Besides, it isn't my work. I'm doing the cooking. You really can't expect me to do housework as well.

FREDERICK: *Are* you doing the cooking? It looks to me as though you were just sitting about doing nothing. I don't see why I should have to sweat my life out.

WILLIAM: You see, you have no organization. Housework's perfectly simple, only you must have organization. I have organization. That's my secret.

FREDERICK: I was a mug to say I'd do the housework. I might have known you'd freeze on to a soft job if there was one.

WILLIAM: I naturally undertook to do what I could do best. That is one of the secrets of organization. Cooking is an art. Any fool can do housework.

FREDERICK: I'll give you a thick ear in a minute. You just try and get a shine on a pair of boots and see if it's easy.

WILLIAM: I don't believe you know how to shine a pair of boots. Did you spit on them?

FREDERICK: No, only on the silver.

WILLIAM: You just look nippy and get the table laid while I finish my book.

FREDERICK: [*Gloomily.*] Is it luncheon or dinner?

WILLIAM: I don't know yet, but we're going to have it down here because it's easier for dishing up. Organization again.

FREDERICK: What does Victoria say to that?

WILLIAM: I haven't told her yet.

FREDERICK: She's in an awful temper this morning.

WILLIAM: Why?

FREDERICK: Because the water in the bathroom wasn't hot.

WILLIAM: Wasn't it?

FREDERICK: You know very well it wasn't.

WILLIAM: I think cold baths are much better for people.

There'd be a damned sight less illness about if cold baths were compulsory.

FREDERICK: Tell that to the horse-marines. You were too lazy to get up in time. That's all there is to it.

WILLIAM: I wish you'd get on with your work instead of interrupting me all the time.

FREDERICK: You don't look as if you were so busy as all that.

WILLIAM: I want to find out if the nursery governess married the duke after all. You should read this after I've finished it.

FREDERICK: I don't have time for reading. When I take on a job I like to do it properly.

WILLIAM: I wish you wouldn't mumble.

FREDERICK: What is there for lunch? [*He goes over to the stove and takes a cover off a saucepan.*] What's this mess?

WILLIAM: Those are potatoes. You might give one of them a jab with a fork to see how they're getting on.

FREDERICK: It seems rather unfriendly, doesn't it?

WILLIAM: Oh no, they're used to it.

[FREDERICK *takes a fork and tries to transfix a potato.*

FREDERICK: Damn it all, they won't stop still. They're wriggling all over the place. Wriggle, wriggle, little tater. How I wonder who's your mater. Poetry! Come here, you little devil. Woa there.

WILLIAM: I say, don't make such a row. This is awfully exciting. He's plunged both his hands into her hair.

FREDERICK: Dirty trick, I call it.

WILLIAM: Why? She'd washed it.

FREDERICK: [*Bringing out a potato.*] Damn it all, they're not skinned.

WILLIAM: I suppose you mean peeled.

FREDERICK: If there's anything I dislike it's potatoes in their skins.

WILLIAM: It's simply waste to peel potatoes. I never peel potatoes.

FREDERICK: Is that organization?

WILLIAM: Well, if you ask me, that's just what it is.

FREDERICK: Ever since I've been at the War Office I've heard fellows talk of organization, but I never could find anyone to tell me just what it was. It's beginning to dawn on me now.

WILLIAM: [*Still reading.*] Well, what is it?

FREDERICK: I'm not going to tell you unless you listen.

WILLIAM: [*Looking up.*] He's just glued his lips to hers. Well?

FREDERICK: Organization means getting someone else to do your job for you if you can, and if you can't, letting it rip.

WILLIAM: I suppose you think you're funny.

FREDERICK: [*Putting the potato back in the saucepan.*] The steak smells as though it was almost done.

WILLIAM: Done? It's only been on about a quarter of an hour.

FREDERICK: But in a grill-room they do you steak in ten minutes.

WILLIAM: I don't care about that. You cook meat a quarter of an hour for every pound. I should have thought any fool knew that.

FREDERICK: What's that got to do with it?

WILLIAM: I bought three pounds of steak, so I'm going to cook it for three-quarters of an hour.

FREDERICK: Well, it looks to me as if it wanted eating now.

WILLIAM: That's only its cunning. It won't be ready for ages yet. I wish you'd let me get on with my story.

FREDERICK: [*Puzzled.*] But look here, if there were three steaks of a pound each you'd cook them a quarter of an hour each.

WILLIAM: Exactly. That's what I say. That comes to three-quarters of an hour.

FREDERICK: But, hang it all, it's the same quarter of an hour.

WILLIAM: You make me tired. You might just as well say that because three men can walk four miles an hour each man can walk twelve miles an hour.

FREDERICK: But that's just what I do say.

WILLIAM: Well, it's damned idiotic, that's all.

FREDERICK: No, but I mean exactly the opposite. That's what *you* say. You've got me confused now. We'll have to start all over again.

WILLIAM: I shall never finish this story if you go on like this.

FREDERICK: It's a very important matter. Let's get a pencil and a piece of paper and work it out. We must get it right.

WILLIAM: For goodness' sake go and clean knives or something, and don't bother your head about things that are no concern of yours.

FREDERICK: Who's going to eat the steak?

WILLIAM: You won't if you're not careful.

FREDERICK: If I'm careful I don't think I will.

WILLIAM: [*Beginning to grow peevish.*] Cooking has its rules like everything else, and it's just as little use arguing about them as arguing about women.

FREDERICK: Now look here, if you cut that steak into three, would there be three pounds of steak or not?

WILLIAM: Certainly not. There'd be three steaks of one pound, and that's quite another matter.

FREDERICK: But it would be the same steak.

WILLIAM: [*Emphatically.*] It wouldn't be the same steak. It would be an entirely different steak.

FREDERICK: Do you mean to tell me that if you had a steak of a hundred pounds you'd cook it for twenty-five hours?

WILLIAM: Yes, and if I had a steak a thousand pounds I'd cook it for ten days.

FREDERICK: It seems an awful waste of gas.

WILLIAM: I don't care about that, it's logic.

[*Enter* VICTORIA.

VICTORIA: I really think it's too bad of you. I've been ringing the bell for the last quarter of an hour. There are two men in the house, and you neither of you pay the least attention.

WILLIAM: We were having an argument.

FREDERICK: Let me put it before you, Victoria.

WILLIAM: It has nothing to do with Victoria. I'm the cook, and I won't have anyone come interfering in my kitchen.

FREDERICK: You must do something, Victoria. The steak will be absolutely uneatable.

VICTORIA: I don't care. I never eat steak.

WILLIAM: It's all you'll get for luncheon.

VICTORIA: I shan't be here for luncheon.

WILLIAM: Why not?

VICTORIA: Because—because Mr. Leicester Paton has made me an offer of marriage and I have accepted it.

FREDERICK: But you've got two husbands already, Victoria.

VICTORIA: I imagine you'll both be gentlemen enough to put no obstacle in the way of my getting my freedom.

[*A ring is heard*

FREDERICK: Hulloa, who's that?

VICTORIA: That is my solicitor.

FREDERICK: Your what?

VICTORIA: I told him to come at one. Go and open the door, Freddie, will you?

FREDERICK: What the dickens does he want?

VICTORIA: He's going to fix up my divorce.

FREDERICK: You're not letting the grass grow under your feet.

[*He goes out.*

WILLIAM: This is a desperate step you're taking, Victoria.

VICTORIA: I had to do something. You must see that it's quite impossible for a woman to live without servants. I had no one to do me up this morning.

WILLIAM: How on earth did you manage?

VICTORIA: I had to put on something that didn't need doing up..

WILLIAM: That seems an adequate way out of the difficulty.

VICTORIA: It so happens that the one frock that didn't need doing up was the one frock I didn't want to wear.

WILLIAM: You look ravishing in it all the same.

VICTORIA: [*Rather stiffly.*] I'd sooner you didn't pay me compliments, Bill.

WILLIAM: Why not?

VICTORIA: Well, now that I'm engaged to Leicester Paton I don't think it's very good form.

WILLIAM: Have you quite made up your mind to divorce me?

VICTORIA: Quite.

WILLIAM: In that case, I can almost look upon you as another man's wife.

VICTORIA: What do you mean by that?

WILLIAM: Only that I can make love to you without feeling a thundering ass.

VICTORIA: [*Smiling.*] I'm not going to let you make love to me.

WILLIAM: You can't prevent me from telling you that you're the loveliest thing that ever turned a poor man's head.

VICTORIA: I can close my ears.

WILLIAM: [*Taking her hands.*] Impossible, for I shall hold your hands.

VICTORIA: I shall scream.

WILLIAM: You can't, because I shall kiss your lips.

[*He does so.*

VICTORIA: Oh, Bill, what a pity it is you were ever my husband. I'm sure you'd make a charming lover.

WILLIAM: I have often thought that is the better part.

VICTORIA: Take care. They're just coming. It would never do for my solicitor to find me in my husband's arms.

WILLIAM: It would be outrageous.

[FREDERICK *ushers in the visitor.* MR. A. B. RAHAM *is a solicitor. There is nothing more to be said about him.*

VICTORIA: How do you do, Mr. Raham? Do you know my husbands?

MR. RAHAM: I'm pleased to meet you, gentlemen. I dare say it would facilitate matters if I am told which of you is which, and which is the other.

VICTORIA: This is Major Cardew, my first husband, and this is my second husband, Major Lowndes.

MR. RAHAM: Ah, that makes it quite clear. Both Majors. Interesting coincidence.

WILLIAM: I suppose that Mrs. Lowndes has put you in possession of the facts, Mr. Raham?

MR. RAHAM: I think so. We had a long talk at my office yesterday.

FREDERICK: You can quite understand that it's a position of some delicacy for Mrs. Cardew.

MR. RAHAM: [*Puzzled.*] Mrs. Cardew? Where does Mrs. Cardew come in?

FREDERICK: This is Mrs. Cardew.

MR. RAHAM: Oh, I see what you mean. That, in short, is the difficulty. Is this lady Mrs. Cardew or Mrs. Lowndes? Well, the fact is, she has decided to be neither.

VICTORIA: I've just broken it to them.

WILLIAM: You find us still staggering from the shock.

FREDERICK: Staggering.

MR. RAHAM: She has determined to divorce you both. I have told her that this is not necessary, since she is obviously the wife of only one of you.

VICTORIA: [*Argumentatively.*] In that case, what am I to the other?

MR. RAHAM: Well, Mrs. Cardew, or shall we say Lowndes? I hardly like to mention it to a lady, but if you'll excuse me saying so, you're his concubine.

WILLIAM: I rather like that, it sounds so damned Oriental.

VICTORIA: [*Indignantly.*] I never heard of such a thing.

WILLIAM: Oh, Fatima, your face is like the full moon, and your eyes are like the eyes of a young gazelle. Come, dance to me to the sound of the lute.

VICTORIA: Well, that settles it. I shall divorce them both just to prove to everyone that they're both my husbands.

FREDERICK: I think it's just as well to take no risks.

MR. RAHAM: Do I understand that you two gentlemen are agreeable?

WILLIAM: Speaking for myself, I am prepared to sacrifice my feelings, deep as they are, to the happiness of Victoria.

MR. RAHAM: Very nicely and feelingly put.

VICTORIA: He always was a gentleman.

MR. RAHAM: [*To* FREDERICK.] Now you, Major Cardew.

FREDERICK: My name is Lowndes.

MR. RAHAM: My mistake. Of course you're Major Lowndes. I made a mental note of it when we were introduced. Cardew—camel-face. Lowndes—litigation. Pelmanism, you know.

FREDERICK: I see. It doesn't seem very effective, though.

MR. RAHAM: Anyhow, that is neither here nor there. Will you give this lady the freedom she desires?

FREDERICK: I will. [*With a puzzled look.*] When did I last say those words? [*Remembering.*] Of course, the marriage service.

MR. RAHAM: Well, so far so good. I am under the impression that when it comes to the point we shall not need to take both you gentlemen into court, but I quite agree with Mrs. Lowndes-Cardew that it will save time and trouble if we get up the case against both of you in the same way. Since you will neither of you defend the case, there is no need for you to go to the expense of legal advice, so I propose to go into the whole matter with you now.

VICTORIA: You can feel quite easy about taking Mr. Raham's advice. He has arranged more divorce cases than any man in England.

MR. RAHAM: I venture to say that there are few of the best families in this country that haven't made use of my services in one way or another. Outraged husband, deceived wife, co-respondent or intervener; it's hardly likely that anyone who is anyone won't figure sooner or later in one or other of these capacities. And although it's I as says it, if he's wise he comes to me. My maxim has always been: Do it quickly; don't let's have a lot of fuss and bother. And, just to show you how my system works, there are ladies for whom I've got a divorce from three or four successive husbands, and never a word of scandal has sullied the purity of their fair name.

WILLIAM: You must be a very busy man.

MR. RAHAM: I assure you, Major, I'm one of the busiest men in London.

WILLIAM: Fortunately, some marriages are happy.

MR. RAHAM: Don't you believe it, Major Cardew. There are no happy marriages. But there are some that are tolerable.

VICTORIA: You are a pessimist, Mr. Raham. I have made both my husbands ideally happy.

MR. RAHAM: But I will come to the point. Though, perhaps, it is hardly necessary, I will point out to you gentlemen what the law of the country needs in order to free a couple who, for reasons which merely concern themselves, have decided that they prefer to part company. If a husband wishes to divorce his wife he need prove nothing but adultery, but the English law recognizes the natural polygamy of man, and when a wife desires to divorce her husband she must prove besides cruelty or desertion. Let us take these first. Do you wish the cause of offence to be cruelty *or* desertion?

VICTORIA: Personally, I should prefer desertion.

WILLIAM: Certainly. I should very much dislike to be cruel to you, Victoria.

FREDERICK: And you know I could never hurt a fly.

MR. RAHAM: Then we will settle on desertion. I think myself it is the more gentlemanly way, and besides, it is more easily proved. The procedure is excessively simple. Mrs. Cardew-Lowndes will write you a letter, which I shall dictate, asking you to return to her—the usual phrase is "to make a home for her"—and you will refuse. I propose that you should both give me your refusals now.

WILLIAM: [*Surprised.*] Before we've had the letter?

MR. RAHAM: Precisely. The letter which she will write, and which is read out in court, is so touching that on one occasion the husband, about to be divorced, was so moved that he immediately returned to his wife. She was very angry indeed, and so now I invariably get the refusal first.

WILLIAM: It's so difficult to write an answer to a letter that hasn't been written.

MR. RAHAM: To meet that difficulty I have also prepared the replies. Have you a fountain-pen?

WILLIAM: Yes.

MR. RAHAM: [*Taking a piece of paper from his pocket-book and two sheets of paper.*] If you will kindly write to my dictation, we will settle the matter at once. Here is a sheet of paper.

WILLIAM: [*Taking it.*] The address is—Hotel Majestic.

MR. RAHAM: You will see the point later. Here is a piece for you, Major.

[*He gives it to* FREDERICK.

FREDERICK: Do we both write the same letter?

MR. RAHAM: Certainly not. I have two letters that I generally make use of, and I propose that you should each of you write one of them. The note of one is sorrow rather than anger. The other is somewhat vituperative. You can decide among yourselves which of you had better write which.

VICTORIA: They both habitually swore at me, but I think Bill's language was more varied.

MR. RAHAM: That settles it. Are you ready, Major Lowndes?

FREDERICK: [*Getting to ready write.*] Fire away.

MR. RAHAM: [*Dictating.*] My dear Victoria, I have given your letter anxious consideration. If I thought there was any hope of our making a greater success of married life in

the future than we have in the past I should be the first
to suggest that we should make one more attempt.

WILLIAM: Very touching.

MR. RAHAM: [*Continuing.*] But I have regretfully come to the
conclusion that to return to you would only be to
cause a recurrence of the unhappy life from which I
know that you have suffered no less than I. I am bound
therefore definitely to refuse your request. I do not
propose under any circumstances to return to you.
Yours sincerely.—Now sign your full name.

VICTORIA: A very nice letter, Freddie. I shall always think
pleasantly of you.

FREDERICK: I have my points.

MR. RAHAM: Now, Major Cardew, are you ready?

WILLIAM: Quite.

MR. RAHAM: My dear Victoria, I am in receipt of your letter
asking me to return to you. Our life together has been
a hell upon earth, and I have long realized that our
marriage was a tragic mistake. You have sickened me
with scenes and tortured me with jealousy. If you have
tried to make me happy you have succeeded singularly
ill. I trust that I shall never see you again, and nothing
in the world will induce me ever to resume a life which
I can only describe as a miserable degradation.

WILLIAM: Thick, eh?

MR. RAHAM: Now the crowning touch. Mark the irony of
the polite ending: I beg to remain yours most sincerely.
—Now sign your name.

WILLIAM: I've signed it.

MR. RAHAM: Then that is settled. Now we only have to
go into court, apply for a decree for restitution of
conjugal rights, and six months later bring an action
for divorce.

VICTORIA: Six months later! But when shall I be free, then?

MR. RAHAM: In about a year.

VICTORIA: Oh, but that won't do at all. I must have my freedom by—well, before the racing season ends, at all events.

MR. RAHAM: As soon as that?

VICTORIA: The Derby, if possible. Certainly by the Two Thousand Guineas.

MR. RAHAM: [*Shrugging his shoulders.*] In that case the only thing is cruelty.

VICTORIA: It can't be helped. They'll have to be cruel.

FREDERICK: I don't like the idea, Victoria.

VICTORIA: Try and be a little unselfish for once, darling.

WILLIAM: I could never strike a woman.

VICTORIA: If I don't mind I don't see why you should.

MR. RAHAM: Cruelty has its advantages. If it's properly witnessed it has a convincing air which desertion never has.

VICTORIA: My mother will swear to anything.

MR. RAHAM: Servants are better. The judges are often unduly suspicious of the mother-in-law's testimony. Of course, one has to be careful. Once, I remember, on my instructions the guilty husband hit the lady I was acting for in the jaw, which unfortunately knocked out her false teeth. The gentleman she had arranged to marry happened to be present and he was so startled that he took the night train for the Continent and has never been heard of since.

WILLIAM: I'm happy to say that Victoria's teeth are all her own.

MR. RAHAM: On another occasion I recommended a gentleman to take a stick and give his wife a few strokes with it. I don't know if he got excited or what, but he gave her a regular hiding.

VICTORIA: How awful!

MR. RAHAM: It was indeed, for she threw her arms round his neck, and, saying she adored him, refused to have anything more to do with the divorce. She was going to marry a colonel in the army, and he was most offensive to me about it. I had to tell him that if he didn't leave my office I would send for the police.

VICTORIA: You're dreadfully discouraging.

MR. RAHAM: Oh, I merely tell you that to show you what may happen. But I have devised my own system and have never known it fail. I always arrange for three definite acts of cruelty. First at the dinner-table. Now, please listen to me carefully, gentlemen, and follow my instructions to the letter. When you have tasted your soup you throw down the spoon with a clatter and say: Good Lord, this soup is uneatable. Can't you get a decent cook? You, madam, will answer: I do my best, darling. Upon which you, crying with a loud voice: Take that, you damned fool, throw the plate straight at her. With a little ingenuity the lady can dodge the plate, and the only damage is done to the table-cloth.

VICTORIA: I like that.

MR. RAHAM: The second act is a little more violent. I suppose you have a revolver.

WILLIAM: At all events, I can get one.

MR. RAHAM: Having carefully removed the cartridges, you ring the bell for the servant, and just as she opens the door, you point it at the lady and say: You lying devil, I'll kill you. Then you, madam, give a loud shriek, and cry to the maid: Oh, save me, save me.

VICTORIA: I shall love doing that. So dramatic.

MR. RAHAM: I think it's effective. When the servant tells her story in court it is very seldom that an audible thrill does not pass over the audience. They describe it in the papers as: Sensation.

VICTORIA: [*Practising.*] Oh, save me. Save me.

MR. RAHAM: Now we come to physical as opposed to moral cruelty. It's as well to have two witnesses to this. The gentleman takes the lady by the throat, at the same time hissing malevolently: I'll throttle you if I swing for it, by God. It's very important to leave a bruise so that the doctor, who should be sent for immediately, can swear to it.

VICTORIA: I don't like that part so much.

MR. RAHAM: Believe me, it's no more unpleasant than having a tooth stopped. Now if one of you gentlemen would just go up to the lady we'll practise that. I set great store on this particular point, and it's important that there should be no mistake. Major Cardew, would you mind obliging?

WILLIAM: Not at all.

VICTORIA: Be careful, Bill.

WILLIAM: Do I take her with both hands or only one?

MR. RAHAM: Only one.

[WILLIAM *seizes* VICTORIA *by the throat.*

MR. RAHAM: That's right. If he doesn't press hard enough kick him on the shins.

WILLIAM: If you do, Victoria, I swear I'll kick you back.

MR. RAHAM: That's the spirit. You can't make a bruise without a little violence. Now hiss.

VICTORIA: I'm choking.

MR. RAHAM: Hiss, hiss.

WILLIAM: I'll throttle you if I swing for it, by God.

MR. RAHAM: Splendid! A real artist. You're as good as divorced already.

VICTORIA: He did say it well, didn't he? It really made my blood turn cold.

FREDERICK: Do you want me to do it too?

MR. RAHAM: Now you've seen the idea I think it'll do if you just practise it once or twice with Major Cardew.

FREDERICK: Oh, all right.

MR. RAHAM: Now we come to a point trivial enough in itself, but essential in order to satisfy the requirements of our English law. Adultery.

WILLIAM: That I think you can safely leave to us.

MR. RAHAM: By no means. I think that would be most dangerous.

WILLIAM: Hang it all, man, human nature can surely be trusted there.

MR. RAHAM: We are not dealing with human nature, we are dealing with law.

WILLIAM: Law be blowed. With the price of a supper in my pocket and an engaging manner I am prepared to supply you with all the evidence you want.

MR. RAHAM: I am shocked and horrified by your suggestion. Do you expect a man in my position to connive at immorality.

WILLIAM: Immorality. Well, there must be—shall we say a *soupçon* of it—under the painful circumstances.

MR. RAHAM: Not at all. I always arrange this part of the proceedings with the most scrupulous regard to propriety. And before we go any further I should like to inform you that unless you are prepared to put out of your mind anything that is suggestive of indecent behaviour I shall decline to have anything more to do with the case.

VICTORIA: I think you must have a nasty mind, Bill.

WILLIAM: But, my dear Victoria, I only wanted to make things easy for you. I apologize. I put myself in your hands, Mr. Raham.

MR. RAHAM: Then please listen to me. I will engage a suite

of rooms for you at the Hotel Majestic. You will remember it was from there you wrote the letter in which you declined to return to your wife. The judge never fails to remark on the coincidence. On a date to be settled hereafter you will come to my office, where you will meet a lady.

WILLIAM: Do you mean to say you provide her too?

MR. RAHAM: Certainly.

FREDERICK: What's she like?

MR. RAHAM: A most respectable person. I have employed her in these cases for many years.

WILLIAM: It sounds as though she made a business of it.

MR. RAHAM: She does.

FREDERICK: What!

MR. RAHAM: Yes, she had the idea—a most ingenious one to my mind—that in these days of specialized professions there was great need for someone to undertake the duties of intervener. That is the name by which the lady is known adultery with whom is the motive for divorce. She has been employed by the best legal firms in London, and she has figured in practically all the fashionable divorces of the last fifteen years.

WILLIAM: You amaze me.

MR. RAHAM: I have felt it my duty to give her all the work I can on account of a paralyzed father, whom she supports entirely by her exertions.

VICTORIA: Not an unpleasant existence, I should imagine.

MR. RAHAM: If you knew her you would realize that no thought of that has ever entered her mind. A most unselfish, noble-minded woman.

WILLIAM: Does she make money by it?

MR. RAHAM: Sufficient for her simple needs. She only charges twenty guineas for her services.

WILLIAM: I'm sure I could get it done for less.

MR. RAHAM: Not by a woman of any refinement.

WILLIAM: Well, well, with most of us it's only once in a lifetime.

MR. RAHAM: I will proceed. You will fetch this lady at my office, and you will drive with her to the Hotel Majestic, where you will register as Major and Mrs. Cardew. You will be shown into the suite of rooms which I shall engage for you, and supper will be served in the sitting-room. You will partake of this, and you will drink champagne.

WILLIAM: I should like to choose the brand myself.

MR. RAHAM: [*Magnanimously.*] I have no objection to that.

WILLIAM: Thanks.

MR. RAHAM: Then you will play cards. Miss Montmorency is a wonderful card-player. She not only has an unparalleled knowledge of all games for two, but she can do a great number of tricks. In this way you will find the night pass without tediousness, and in the morning you will ring for breakfast.

FREDERICK: I'm not sure if I should have much appetite for it.

MR. RAHAM: I never mind my clients having brandy and soda instead. It looks well in the waiter's evidence. And after having paid your bill, you will take Miss Montmorency in a taxi-cab and deposit her at my office.

WILLIAM: It sounds a devil of a beano.

FREDERICK: I should like to see her first.

MR. RAHAM: That is perfectly easy. I know that ladies in these cases often like to see the intervener themselves. Ladies are sometimes very suspicious, and even though they're getting rid of their husbands, they don't want them to—well, run any risks; and so I took the liberty of bringing Miss Montmorency with me. She is waiting in the taxi at the door, and if you like I will go and fetch her.

FREDERICK: A1. I'll go along and bring her down.

VICTORIA: Is she the sort of person I should like to meet, Mr. Raham?

MR. RAHAM: Oh, a perfect lady. She comes from one of the best families in Shropshire.

VICTORIA: Do fetch her, Freddie. Now I come to think of it, I should like to see her. Men are so weak, and I shall be easier in my mind if I can be sure that these poor boys won't be led astray.

[FREDERICK *goes out*.

WILLIAM: Do you mean to say that with this evidence you will be able to get a divorce?

MR. RAHAM: Not a doubt of it. I've got hundreds.

WILLIAM: I am only a soldier, and I dare say you will not be surprised if I am mentally deficient.

MR. RAHAM: Not at all. Not at all.

WILLIAM: Why on earth does such a state of things exist?

MR. RAHAM: Ah, that is a question which at one time I often asked myself. I confess it seemed to me that when two married persons agreed to separate it was nobody's business but their own. I think if they announced their determination before a justice of the peace, and were given six months to think the matter over, so that they might be certain they knew their minds, the marriage might then be dissolved without further trouble. Many lies would never be told, much dirty linen would never be washed in public, and the sanctity of the marriage tie would be strengthened rather than lessened if the world were spared the spectacle of the sordid aspect the state which is called blessed too often wears. There would be a notable saving of time, money and decency. But at last I hit upon the explanation.

WILLIAM: What is it, then?

MR. RAHAM: If the law were always wise and reasonable it would be obeyed so easily that to obey the law would become an instinct. Now, it is not for the good of the community that the people should be too law-abiding. So our ancestors in the wisdom of their hearts devised certain laws which were vexatious or absurd, so that men should break them and therefore be led insensibly to break others.

WILLIAM: But why is it not for the good of the community that the people should be too law-abiding?

MR. RAHAM: My dear sir, how else would the lawyers earn their living?

WILLIAM: I had forgotten. I see your point.

MR. RAHAM: I hope I have convinced you.

WILLIAM: Completely.

> [*At this moment* FREDERICK *comes in. He is pale and dishevelled. He staggers into the room like a man who has been exposed to a tremendous shock.*

FREDERICK: [*Gasping.*] Brandy! Brandy!

WILLIAM: What's the matter?

FREDERICK: Brandy!

> [*He fills almost half a glass with brandy and tosses it off. A voice is heard outside the door.*

MISS MONTMORENCY: Is this the way?

MR. RAHAM: Come straight in, Miss Montmorency.

> [*She enters. She is a spinster of uncertain age. She might be fifty-five. She looks rather like a hard-boiled egg, but there is in her gestures a languid grace. She speaks with a slight drawl, pronouncing her words with refinement, and her manner is a mixture of affability and condescension. She might be a governess in a very good family in the suburbs. Her respectability is portentous.*

MISS MONTMORENCY: But this is the kitchen.

> [WILLIAM *takes a long look at her, then gets up and goes to the brandy. His hand shakes so violently that the neck of the bottle rattles against the glass. He takes a long drink.*

VICTORIA: I'm afraid it's the only room in the house that's habitable at the moment.

MISS MONTMORENCY: To the practised observer the signs of domestic infelicity jump to the eye, as the French say.

MR. RAHAM: Miss Montmorency—Mrs. Frederick Lowndes.

MISS MONTMORENCY: [*Graciously.*] I'm charmed to make your acquaintance. The injured wife, I presume?

VICTORIA: Er—yes.

MISS MONTMORENCY: So sad. So sad. I'm afraid the war is responsible for the rupture of many happy marriages. I'm booked up for weeks ahead. So sad. So sad.

VICTORIA: Do sit down, won't you.

MISS MONTMORENCY: Thank you. Do you mind if I get out my note-book? I like to get everything perfectly clear, and my memory isn't what it was.

VICTORIA: Of course.

MISS MONTMORENCY: And now, which of these gentlemen is the erring husband?

VICTORIA: Well, they both are.

MISS MONTMORENCY: Oh, really. And which are you going to marry after you've got your divorce.

VICTORIA: Neither.

MISS MONTMORENCY: This is a very peculiar case, Mr. Raham. When I saw these two gentlemen I naturally concluded that one of them was the husband Mrs. Frederick Lowndes was discarding and the other the husband she was acquiring. The eternal triangle, you know.

WILLIAM: In this case the triangle is four-sided.

MISS MONTMORENCY: Oh, how very peculiar.

MR. RAHAM: We see a lot of strange things in our business, Miss Montmorency.

MISS MONTMORENCY: To whom do you say it, as the French say.

VICTORIA: I don't want you to think that I've been at all light or careless, but the fact is, through no fault of my own, they're both my husbands.

MISS MONTMORENCY: [*Taking it as a matter of course.*] Oh, really. How very interesting. And which are you divorcing?

VICTORIA: I'm divorcing them both.

MISS MONTMORENCY: Oh, I see. Very sad. Very sad.

WILLIAM: We're taking as cheerful a view of it as we can.

MISS MONTMORENCY: Ah, yes, that's what I say to my clients. Courage. Courage.

FREDERICK: [*With a start.*] When?

VICTORIA: Be quiet, Freddie.

MISS MONTMORENCY: I think I ought to tell you at once that I shouldn't like to misconduct myself—I use the technical expression—with both these gentlemen.

MR. RAHAM: Oh, Miss Montmorency, a woman of your experience isn't going to strain at a gnat.

MISS MONTMORENCY: No, but I shouldn't like to swallow a camel.

MR. RAHAM: We shall be generous, Miss Montmorency.

MISS MONTMORENCY: I have to think of my self-respect. One gentleman is business, but two would be debauchery.

MR. RAHAM: Mrs. Lowndes is anxious to put this matter through as quickly as possible.

MISS MONTMORENCY: I dare say my friend Mrs. Onslow Jervis would oblige if I asked her as a personal favour.

VICTORIA: Are you sure she can be trusted?

MISS MONTMORENCY: Oh, she's a perfect lady and most respectable. She's the widow of a clergyman, and she has two sons in the army. They've done so well in the war.

MR. RAHAM: Unless we can get Miss Montmorency to reconsider her decision I'm afraid we shall have to put up with Mrs. Onslow Jervis.

MISS MONTMORENCY: I am adamant, Mr. Raham. Adamant.

FREDERICK: I'm all for Mrs. Onslow Jervis personally.

MISS MONTMORENCY: Then you fall to me, Major . . . I didn't catch your name.

WILLIAM: Cardew.

MISS MONTMORENCY: I hope you play cards.

WILLIAM: Sometimes.

MISS MONTMORENCY: I'm a great card-player. Piquet, écarté, cribbage, double dummy, baccarat, bezique, I don't mind what I play. It's such a relief to find a gentleman who's fond of cards.

WILLIAM: Otherwise I daresay the night seems rather long.

MISS MONTMORENCY: Oh, not to me, you know. I'm such a student of human nature. But my gentlemen begin to grow a little restless when I've talked to them for six or seven hours.

WILLIAM: I can hardly believe it.

MISS MONTMORENCY: One gentleman actually said he wanted to go to bed, but, of course, I told him that would never do.

VICTORIA: Forgive my asking—you know what men are— do they never attempt to take any liberties with you?

MISS MONTMORENCY: Oh no. If you're a lady you can always keep a man in his place. And Mr. Raham only takes the very best sort of divorces. The only unpleasantness I've ever had was with a gentleman sent to me by a firm of solicitors in a cathedral city. I took a dislike to him the first moment I saw him, and when he refused to drink anything at supper but ginger-beer I was on my guard. A cold sensualist, I said to myself.

VICTORIA: Oh, I know so well what you mean.

MISS MONTMORENCY: He had no sooner finished his second bottle of ginger-beer than, without any warning at all, he said: I am going to kiss you. You could have heard a pin drop. I pretended to think he was joking, so I said: We have met for business rather than pleasure. And what d'you think he answered? He said: This is one of the rare occasions on which one can combine the two. I didn't lose my presence of mind. I expostulated with him. I told him I was a woman and defenceless, and he said: That's just it. Not a gentleman, of course, not in the best sense of the word. I appealed to his better nature. But all in vain. I didn't know what to do, when suddenly I had an inspiration. I rushed to the door and called in the detective who was watching us. He protected me.

MR. RAHAM: It was risky, Miss Montmorency. The judge might have said there was collusion.

MISS MONTMORENCY: Necessity knows no law, Mr. Raham, as those dreadful Germans say, and I was terribly frightened.

WILLIAM: I can assure you, Miss Montmorency, that you need have no fear that I shall take advantage of your delicate position.

MISS MONTMORENCY: Of course, you will divest yourself of none of your raiment.

WILLIAM: On the contrary, I propose to put on an extra suit of clothes.

MISS MONTMORENCY: Oh, Mr. Raham, please don't forget that I only drink Pommery. In the Twickenham divorce they sent up Pol Roger, and Pol Roger always gives me indigestion. Fortunately the dear Marquis, who suffers from dyspepsia, had some pepsin tabloids with him or I don't know what I should have done.

MR. RAHAM: I'll make a note of it at once.

MISS MONTMORENCY: 1906. [*To* WILLIAM.] I'm sure we shall have a delightful night. I can see that we have much in common.

WILLIAM: It's too good of you to say so.

MISS MONTMORENCY: [*To* FREDERICK.] And I know you'll like Mrs. Onslow Jervis. A perfect lady. She has such charm of manner. So much ease. You can see that she did a lot of entertaining when her husband was Vicar of Clacton. They have a very nice class of people at Clacton.

FREDERICK: I shall be charmed to meet her.

MISS MONTMORENCY: You will take care not to be at all risqué, as the French say, in your conversation, won't you? Of course, she's a woman of the world, but as the widow of the Vicar of Clacton she feels it only due to herself to be a little particular.

FREDERICK: I promise you I'll be very careful.

MISS MONTMORENCY: I don't know what Mr. Raham would say to our sharing a suite. We could play bridge. She's a very fine bridge-player, and we only play threepence a hundred, because in her position she can hardly gamble, can she?

MR. RAHAM: I always like to oblige you, Miss Montmorency, but I hardly think that arrangement would do. You know how fussy the judges are. We might hit upon one of them who saw nothing in it.

MISS MONTMORENCY: I know. They're tiresome, silly creatures.

MR. RAHAM: Why, the other day I came across one who wouldn't believe the worst had happened when a man and a woman, not related in any way, mind you, were proved to have been alone in a room together for three-quarters of an hour.

MISS MONTMORENCY: Oh, well, let us take no risks. Business is business. It must be you and me alone then, Major Cardew. You will let me know in good time when you fix the fatal night. I'm very much booked up just now.

MR. RAHAM: Of course, we will do everything to suit your convenience, Miss Montmorency. And now, Mrs. Lowndes, since we have settled everything, I think Miss Montmorency and I will go.

VICTORIA: I can't think of anything else.

MISS MONTMORENCY: Excuse my taking the liberty, Mrs. Frederick Lowndes, but after your great trouble is over should you be wanting any face massage, may I give you my card. ?

VICTORIA: Oh, do you do face massage?

MISS MONTMORENCY: Only for ladies who are personally recommended to me. Here is my card.

VICTORIA: [*Looking at it.*] Esmeralda.

MISS MONTMORENCY: Yes, it's a pretty name, isn't it? I also make the Esmeralda cream. The Marchioness of Twickenham's face was simply ravaged when she was divorcing the Marquis, and, believe me, after a course of twelve treatments you wouldn't have known her.

VICTORIA: Of course, all this sort of thing is a great nervous shock.

MISS MONTMORENCY: Oh, I know. And there's nothing like face massage for soothing the nerves.

VICTORIA: I'll certainly keep your card.

MISS MONTMORENCY: Good-bye, then. [*To* WILLIAM.] I'm not going to say good-bye to you, but au revoir.

WILLIAM: Believe me, I look forward to our next meeting.

MR. RAHAM: Good morning, Mrs. Lowndes. Good

morning. [*Moving towards the door that leads into the area.*]
Shall we go out this way?

MISS MONTMORENCY: [*Just a little taken aback.*] The area
steps? Oh, very well. It's so quaint and old-fashioned.
I always think a lady if she is a lady can do anything.

> [*She gives a gracious bow and goes out, followed by*
> MR. RAHAM.

WILLIAM: This is a bit of all right that you've let us in for,
Victoria.

VICTORIA: Well, darling, it's the only thing I've ever asked
you to do for me in all my life, so you needn't complain.

WILLIAM: I will bear it like a martyr.

VICTORIA: Now, the only thing left is for me to bid you
good-bye.

FREDERICK: Already?

VICTORIA: You must understand that under the circumstances it wouldn't be quite nice for me to stay here.
Besides, without servants, it's beastly uncomfortable.

WILLIAM: Won't you even stay to luncheon?

VICTORIA: I don't think I will, thanks. I think I shall get
a better one at mother's.

FREDERICK: Oh, are you going there?

VICTORIA: Where else do you expect a woman to go in a
crisis like this?

WILLIAM: I should think the steak was about done, Freddie.

FREDERICK: Oh, I'd give it another hour or two to make
sure.

VICTORIA: Of course, I realize that it's a painful moment
for both of you, but as you say, we shan't make it any
easier by dragging it out.

WILLIAM: True.

VICTORIA: Good-bye, Bill. I forgive you everything, and
I hope we shall always be good friends.

WILLIAM: Good-bye, Victoria. I hope this will not be by any means your last marriage.

VICTORIA: When everything is settled you must come and dine with us. I'm sure you'll find that Leicester has the best wines and cigars that money can buy.

[She turns to him an indifferent cheek.

WILLIAM: [*Kissing it.*] Good-bye.

VICTORIA: And now, Freddie, it's your turn. Now that there's nothing more between us you might give me back that pin I gave you.

FREDERICK: [*Taking it out of his tie.*] Here you are.

VICTORIA: And there was a cigarette-case.

FREDERICK: [*Giving it her.*] Take it.

VICTORIA: They say jewellery has gone up tremendously in value since the war. I shall give Leicester a cigarette-case as a wedding present.

WILLIAM: You always do, Victoria.

VICTORIA: Men like it. Good-bye, Freddie dear. I shall always have a pleasant recollection of you.

[She turns the other cheek to him.

FREDERICK: Good-bye, Victoria.

WILLIAM: Would you like a taxi?

VICTORIA: No, thanks. I think the exercise will do me good

[She goes out, and is seen tripping up the area steps.

FREDERICK: A wonderful woman.

WILLIAM: I shall never regret having married her. Now let's have lunch.

FREDERICK: I wish I looked forward to it as much as you do.

WILLIAM: Dear old man, has this affecting scene taken away your appetite?

FREDERICK: It's not the appetite I'm doubtful about. It's the steak.

WILLIAM: Oh, don't you worry yourself about that. I'll just dish up. [*He goes over to the stove and tries to get the steak out of the frying-pan.*] Come out, you great fat devil. It won't come out.

FREDERICK: That's your trouble.

WILLIAM. [*Bringing the frying-pan to the table.*] Oh, well, we can eat it just as well out of the frying-pan. Shall I carve it?

FREDERICK: [*Sitting down.*] Please.

> [WILLIAM *takes a knife and starts to cut the steak. It won't cut. He applies force. The steak resists stealthily. A little surprised,* WILLIAM *puts somewhat more strength into it. He makes no impression. He begins to grow vexed. He starts to struggle. He sets his teeth. It is all in vain. The sweat pours from his brow.* FREDERICK *watches him in gloomy silence. At last in a passion* WILLIAM *throws down the knife.*

WILLIAM: [*Furiously.*] Why don't you say something, you fool?

FREDERICK: [*Gently.*] Shall I go and fetch my little hatchet?

WILLIAM: [*Attacking the steak again angrily with the knife.*] I know my theory's right. If you cook a pound of meat a quarter of an hour you must cook three pounds of meat three quarters of an hour.

> [*A boy, carrying a large, square, covered basket, is seen coming down the area steps. He knocks at the door.*

FREDERICK: Hulloa, who's this? [*He goes to the door and opens.*] What can I do for you, my son?

CLARENCE: Does Mrs. Frederick Lowndes live here?

FREDERICK: In a manner of speaking.

CLARENCE: [*Coming in.*] From the Ritz Hotel.

FREDERICK: What's that? Walk right in, my boy. Put it on the table.

WILLIAM: [*Looking at the label.*] With Mr. Leicester Paton's compliments.

FREDERICK: It's luncheon.

CLARENCE: I was told to give the basket to the lady personally.

FREDERICK: That's all right, my boy.

CLARENCE: If the lady's not here I'm to take it back again.

WILLIAM: [*Promptly.*] She's just coming downstairs. [*He goes to the door and calls.*] Victoria, my darling, that kind Mr. Leicester Paton has sent you a little light refreshment from the Ritz.

FREDERICK: There's half-a-crown for you, my lad. Now, you hop it quick.

CLARENCE: Thank you, sir.

                                    [*He goes out.*

FREDERICK: Now you can eat the steak if you like. I'm going to eat Victoria's luncheon.

WILLIAM: It's a damned unscrupulous thing to do. I'll join you.

          [*They hurriedly begin to unpack the basket.*

FREDERICK: [*Taking off a cover.*] What's here? Chicken *en casserole?*

WILLIAM: That's all right. Here, give me that bottle and see me open it.

     [*He takes out a bottle of champagne and proceeds to open it.*

FREDERICK: *Pâté de foie gras.* Good. Caviare? No. Smoked salmon. Stout fellow, Mr. Leicester Paton.

WILLIAM: Don't stand there staring at it. Get it out.

FREDERICK: This is a regular beano.

WILLIAM: I'm beginning to think the wangler won the war after all.

FREDERICK: *Mousse au jambon.* He's got some idea of Victoria's appetite.

WILLIAM: My dear fellow, love is always blind.

FREDERICK: Thank God for it, that's all I say. How's that cork going?

WILLIAM: Half a mo. It's just coming.

FREDERICK: This is what I call a nice little snack. Dear Victoria, she was a good sort.

WILLIAM: In her way.

FREDERICK: But give me *pâté de foie gras.*

WILLIAM: [*Getting the bottle opened.*] Pop. Hand over your glass.

FREDERICK: Here you are. I'm as hungry as a trooper.

WILLIAM: Before we start, I want you to drink a toast.

FREDERICK: I'll drink anything.

WILLIAM: [*Holding up his glass.*] Victoria's third husband.

FREDERICK: God help him!

WILLIAM: And for us—liberty.

> [*As they drain their glasses the curtain falls quickly*

THE END

THE CIRCLE

A COMEDY
in Three Acts

CHARACTERS

CLIVE CHAMPION-CHENEY
ARNOLD CHAMPION-CHENEY, M.P.
LORD PORTEOUS
EDWARD LUTON
LADY CATHERINE CHAMPION-CHENEY
ELIZABETH
MRS. SHENSTONE
A FOOTMAN AND A BUTLER

The action takes place at Aston-Adey, Arnold Champion-Cheney's house in Dorset.

THE CIRCLE

THE FIRST ACT

The Scene is a stately drawing-room at Aston-Adey, with fine pictures on the walls and Georgian furniture. Aston-Adey has been described, with many illustrations, in Country Life. *It is not a house, but a place. Its owner takes a great pride in it, and there is nothing in the room which is not of the period. Through the French windows at the back can be seen the beautiful gardens which are one of the features.*

It is a fine summer morning.

ARNOLD *comes in. He is a man of about thirty-five, tall and good-looking, fair, with a clean-cut, sensitive face. He has a look that is intellectual, but somewhat bloodless. He is very well dressed.*

ARNOLD: [*Calling.*] Elizabeth! [*He goes to the window and calls again.*] Elizabeth! [*He rings the bell. While he is waiting he gives a look round the room. He slightly alters the position of one of the chairs. He takes an ornament from the chimney-piece and blows the dust from it.*]

> [*A* FOOTMAN *comes in.*

Oh, George! See if you can find Mrs. Cheney, and ask her if she'd be good enough to come here.

FOOTMAN: Very good, sir.

> [*The* FOOTMAN *turns to go.*

ARNOLD: Who is supposed to look after this room?

FOOTMAN: I don't know, sir.

ARNOLD: I wish when they dust they'd take care to replace the things exactly as they were before.

FOOTMAN: Yes, sir.

ARNOLD: [*Dismissing him.*] All right.

> [*The* FOOTMAN *goes out. He goes again to the window and calls.*

ARNOLD: Elizabeth! [*He sees* MRS. SHENSTONE.] Oh, Anna, do you know where Elizabeth is?

> [MRS. SHENSTONE *comes in from the garden. She is a woman of forty, pleasant and of elegant appearance.*

ANNA: Isn't she playing tennis?

ARNOLD: No, I've been down to the tennis court. Something very tiresome has happened.

ANNA: Oh?

ARNOLD: I wonder where the deuce she is.

ANNA: When do you expect Lord Porteous and Lady Kitty?

ARNOLD: They're motoring down in time for luncheon.

ANNA: Are you sure you want me to be here? It's not too late yet, you know. I can have my things packed and catch a train for somewhere or other.

ARNOLD: No, of course we want you. It'll make it so much easier if there are people here. It was exceedingly kind of you to come.

ANNA: Oh, nonsense!

ARNOLD: And I think it was a good thing to have Teddie Luton down.

ANNA: He is so breezy, isn't he?

ARNOLD: Yes, that's his great asset. I don't know that he's very intelligent, but, you know, there are occasions when you want a bull in a china shop. I sent one of the servants to find Elizabeth.

ANNA: I daresay she's putting on her shoes. She and Teddie were going to have a single.

ARNOLD: It can't take all this time to change one's shoes.

ANNA: [*With a smile.*] One can't change one's shoes without powdering one's nose, you know.

> [ELIZABETH *comes in. She is a very pretty creature in the early twenties. She wears a light summer frock.*

ARNOLD: My dear, I've been hunting for you everywhere. What *have* you been doing?

ELIZABETH: Nothing! I've been standing on my head.

ARNOLD: My father's here.

ELIZABETH: [*Startled.*] Where?

ARNOLD: At the cottage. He arrived last night.

ELIZABETH: Damn!

ARNOLD: [*Good-humouredly.*] I wish you wouldn't say that, Elizabeth.

ELIZABETH: If you're not going to say Damn when a thing's damnable, when are you going to say Damn?

ARNOLD: I should have thought you could say, Oh, bother! or something like that.

ELIZABETH: But that wouldn't express my sentiments. Besides, at that speech day when you were giving away the prizes you said there were no synonyms in the English language.

ANNA: [*Smiling.*] Oh, Elizabeth! It's very unfair to expect a politician to live in private up to the statements he makes in public.

ARNOLD: I'm always willing to stand by anything I've said. There *are* no synonyms in the English language.

ELIZABETH: In that case I shall be regretfully forced to continue to say Damn whenever I feel like it.

> [EDWARD LUTON *shows himself at the window. He is an attractive youth in flannels.*

TEDDIE: I say, what about this tennis?

ELIZABETH: Come in. We're having a scene.

TEDDIE: [*Entering.*] How splendid! What about?

ELIZABETH: The English language.

TEDDIE: Don't tell me you've been splitting your infinitives.

ARNOLD: [*With the shadow of a frown.*] I wish you'd be serious, Elizabeth. The situation is none too pleasant.

ANNA: I think Teddie and I had better make ourselves scarce.

ELIZABETH: Nonsense! You're both in it. If there's going to be any unpleasantness we want your moral support. That's why we asked you to come.

TEDDIE: And I thought I'd been asked for my blue eyes.

ELIZABETH: Vain beast! And they happen to be brown.

TEDDIE: Is anything up?

ELIZABETH: Arnold's father arrived last night.

TEDDIE: Did he, by Jove! I thought he was in Paris.

ARNOLD: So did we all. He told me he'd be there for the next month.

ANNA: Have you seen him?

ARNOLD: No! He rang me up. It's a mercy he had a telephone put in the cottage. It would have been a pretty kettle of fish if he'd just walked in.

ELIZABETH: Did you tell him Lady Catherine was coming?

ARNOLD: Of course not. I was flabbergasted to know he was here. And then I thought we'd better talk it over first.

ELIZABETH: Is he coming along here?

ARNOLD: Yes. He suggested it, and I couldn't think of any excuse to prevent him.

TEDDIE: Couldn't you put the other people off?

ARNOLD: They're coming by car. They may be here any minute. It's too late to do that.

ELIZABETH: Besides, it would be beastly.

ARNOLD: I knew it was silly to have them here. Elizabeth insisted.

ELIZABETH: After all, she *is* your mother, Arnold.

ARNOLD: That meant precious little to her when she—went away. You can't imagine it means very much to me now.

ELIZABETH: It's thirty years ago. It seems so absurd to bear malice after all that time.

ARNOLD: I don't bear malice, but the fact remains that she did me the most irreparable harm. I can find no excuse for her.

ELIZABETH: Have you ever tried to?

ARNOLD: My dear Elizabeth, it's no good going over all that again. The facts are lamentably simple. She had a husband who adored her, a wonderful position, all the money she could want, and a child of five. And she ran away with a married man.

ELIZABETH: Lady Porteous is not a very attractive woman, Arnold. [*To* ANNA.] Do you know her?

ANNA: [*Smiling.*] Forbidding is the word, I think.

ARNOLD: If you're going to make little jokes about it, I have nothing more to say.

ANNA: I'm sorry, Arnold.

ELIZABETH: Perhaps your mother couldn't help herself—if she was in love?

ARNOLD: And had no sense of honour, duty, or decency? Oh, yes, under those circumstances you can explain a great deal.

ELIZABETH: That's not a very pretty way to speak of your mother.

ARNOLD: I can't look on her as my mother.

ELIZABETH: What you can't get over is that she didn't think of you. Some of us are more mother and some of us more woman. It gives me a little thrill when I think that

M

she loved that man so much. She sacrificed her name, her position and her child to him.

ARNOLD: You really can't expect the said child to have any great affection for the mother who treated him like that.

ELIZABETH: No, I don't think I do. But I think it's a pity after all these years that you shouldn't be friends.

ARNOLD: I wonder if you realise what it was to grow up under the shadow of that horrible scandal. Everywhere, at school, and at Oxford, and afterwards in London, I was always the son of Lady Kitty Cheney. Oh, it was cruel, cruel!

ELIZABETH: Yes, I know, Arnold. It was beastly for you.

ARNOLD: It would have been bad enough if it had been an ordinary case, but the position of the people made it ten times worse. My father was in the House then, and Porteous—he hadn't succeeded to the title—was in the House too; he was Under-Secretary for Foreign Affairs, and he was very much in the public eye.

ANNA: My father always used to say he was the ablest man in the party. Every one was expecting him to be Prime Minister.

ARNOLD: You can imagine what a boon it was to the British public. They hadn't had such a treat for a generation. The most popular song of the day was about my mother. Did you ever hear it? "Naughty Lady Kitty. Thought it such a pity . . ."

ELIZABETH: [*Interrupting.*] Oh, Arnold, don't!

ARNOLD: And then they never let people forget them. If they'd lived quietly in Florence and not made a fuss the scandal would have died down. But those constant actions between Lord and Lady Porteous kept on reminding everyone.

TEDDIE: What were they having actions about?

ARNOLD: Of course my father divorced his wife, but Lady

Porteous refused to divorce Porteous. He tried to force her by refusing to support her and turning her out of her house, and heaven knows what. They were constantly wrangling in the law courts.

ANNA: I think it was monstrous of Lady Porteous.

ARNOLD: She knew he wanted to marry my mother, and she hated my mother. You can't blame her.

ANNA: It must have been very difficult for them.

ARNOLD: That's why they've lived in Florence. Porteous has money. They found people there who were willing to accept the situation.

ELIZABETH: This is the first time they've ever come to England.

ARNOLD: My father will have to be told, Elizabeth.

ELIZABETH: Yes.

ANNA: [To ELIZABETH.] Has he ever spoken to you about Lady Kitty?

ELIZABETH: Never.

ARNOLD: I don't think her name has passed his lips since she ran away from this house thirty years ago.

TEDDIE: Oh, they lived here?

ARNOLD: Naturally. There was a house-party, and one evening neither Porteous not my mother came down to dinner. The rest of them waited. They couldn't make it out. My father sent up to my mother's room, and a note was found on the pin-cushion.

ELIZABETH: [With a faint smile.] That's what they did in the Dark Ages.

ARNOLD: I think he took a dislike to this house from that horrible night. He never lived here again, and when I married he handed the place over to me. He just has a cottage now on the estate that he comes to when he feels inclined.

ELIZABETH: It's been very nice for us.

ARNOLD: I owe everything to my father. I don't think he'll ever forgive me for asking these people to come here.

ELIZABETH: I'm going to take all the blame on myself, Arnold.

ARNOLD: [*Irritably.*] The situation was embarrassing enough anyhow. I don't know how I ought to treat them.

ELIZABETH: Don't you think that'll settle itself when you see them.

ARNOLD: After all, they're my guests. I shall try and behave like a gentleman.

ELIZABETH: I wouldn't. We haven't got central heating.

ARNOLD: [*Taking no notice.*] Will she expect me to kiss her?

ELIZABETH: [*With a smile.*] Surely.

ARNOLD: It always makes me uncomfortable when people are effusive.

ANNA: But I can't understand why you never saw her before.

ARNOLD: I believe she tried to see me when I was little, but my father thought it better she shouldn't.

ANNA: Yes, but when you were grown up?

ARNOLD: She was always in Italy. I never went to Italy.

ELIZABETH: It seems to me so pathetic that if you saw one another in the street you wouldn't recognise each other.

ARNOLD: Is it my fault?

ELIZABETH: You've promised to be very gentle with her and very kind.

ARNOLD: The mistake was asking Porteous to come too. It looks as though we condoned the whole thing. And how am I to treat him? Am I to shake him by the hand and slap him on the back? He absolutely ruined my father's life.

ELIZABETH: [*Smiling.*] How much would you give for a nice motor accident that prevented them from coming?

ARNOLD: I let you persuade me against my better judgment, and I've regretted it ever since.

ELIZABETH: [*Good-humouredly.*] I think it's very lucky that Anna and Teddie are here. I don't foresee a very successful party.

ARNOLD: I'm going to do my best. I gave you my promise and I shall keep it. But I can't answer for my father.

ANNA: Here is your father.

[MR. CHAMPION-CHENEY *shows himself at one of the french windows.*]

C.-C.: May I come in through the window, or shall I have myself announced by a supercilious flunkey?

ELIZABETH: Come in. We've been expecting you.

C.-C.: Impatiently, I hope, my dear child.

[MR. CHAMPION-CHENEY *is a tall man in the early sixties, spare, with a fine head of grey hair and an intelligent, somewhat ascetic face. He is very carefully dressed. He is a man who makes the most of himself. He bears his years jauntily. He kisses* ELIZABETH *and then holds out his hand to* ARNOLD.]

ELIZABETH: We thought you'd be in Paris for another month.

C.-C.: How are you, Arnold? I always reserve to myself the privilege of changing my mind. It's the only one elderly gentlemen share with pretty women.

ELIZABETH: You know Anna.

C.-C.: [*Shaking hands with her.*] Of course I do. How very nice to see you here. Are you staying long?

ANNA: As long as I'm welcome.

ELIZABETH: And this is Mr. Luton.

C.-C.: How do you do? Do you play bridge?

LUTON: I do.

C.-C.: Capital. Do you declare without top honours?

LUTON: Never.

C.-C.: Of such is the kingdom of heaven. I see that **you** are a good young man.

LUTON: But, like the good in general, I am poor.

C.-C.: Never mind; if your principles are right, you can play ten shillings a hundred without danger. I never play less, and I never play more.

ARNOLD: And you—are you going to stay long, father?

C.-C.: To luncheon, if you'll have me.

[ARNOLD *gives* ELIZABETH *a harassed look.*

ELIZABETH: That'll be jolly.

ARNOLD: I didn't mean that. Of course you're going to stay for luncheon. I meant, how long are you going to stay down here?

C.-C.: A week.

[*There is a moment's pause. Everyone but* CHAMPION-CHENEY *is slightly embarrassed.*

TEDDIE: I think we'd better chuck our tennis.

ELIZABETH: Yes. I want my father-in-law to tell me what they're wearing in Paris this week.

TEDDIE: I'll go and put the rackets away.

[TEDDIE *goes out.*

ARNOLD: It's nearly one o'clock, Elizabeth.

ELIZABETH: I didn't know it was so late.

ANNA: [*To* ARNOLD.] I wonder if I can persuade you to take a turn in the garden before luncheon.

ARNOLD: [*Jumping at the idea.*] I'd love it.

[ANNA *goes out of the window, and as he follows her he stops irresolutely.*

I want you to look at this chair I've just got. I think it's rather good.

C.-C.: Charming.

ARNOLD: About 1750, I should say. Good design, isn't it? It hasn't been restored or anything.

C.-C.: Very pretty.

ARNOLD: I think it was a good buy, don't you?

C.-C.: Oh, my dear boy, you know I'm entirely ignorant about these things.

ARNOLD: It's exactly my period . . . I shall see you at luncheon, then.

                    [*He follows* ANNA *through the window.*

C.-C.: Who is that young man?

ELIZABETH: Mr. Luton. He's only just been demobilised. He's the manager of a rubber estate in the F.M.S.

C.-C.: And what are the F.M.S. when they're at home?

ELIZABETH: The Federated Malay States. He joined up at the beginning of the war. He's just going back there.

C.-C.: And why have we been left alone in this very marked manner?

ELIZABETH: Have we? I didn't notice it.

C.-C.: I suppose it's difficult for the young to realise that one may be old without being a fool.

ELIZABETH: I never thought you that. Everyone knows you're very intelligent.

C.-C.: They certainly ought to by now. I've told them often enough. Are you a little nervous?

ELIZABETH: Let me feel my pulse. [*She puts her finger on her wrist.*] It's perfectly regular.

C.-C.: When I suggested staying to luncheon Arnold looked exactly like a dose of castor oil.

ELIZABETH: I wish you'd sit down.

C.-C.: Will it make it easier for you? [*He takes a chair.*] You have evidently something very disagreeable to say to me.

ELIZABETH: You won't be cross with me?

C.-C.: How old are you?

ELIZABETH: Twenty-five.

C.-C.: I'm never cross with a woman under thirty.

ELIZABETH: Oh, then, I've got ten years.

C.-C.: Mathematics?

ELIZABETH: No. Paint.

C.-C.: Well?

ELIZABETH: [*Reflectively.*] I think it would be easier if I sat on your knees.

C.-C.: That is a pleasing taste of yours, but you must take care not to put on weight.

[*She sits down on his knees.*

ELIZABETH: Am I boney?

C.-C.: On the contrary. . . . I'm listening.

ELIZABETH: Lady Catherine's coming here.

C.-C.: Who's Lady Catherine?

ELIZABETH: Your—Arnold's mother.

C.-C.: Is she?

[*He withdraws himself a little and* ELIZABETH *gets up.*

ELIZABETH: You mustn't blame Arnold. It's my fault. I insisted. He was against it. I nagged him till he gave way. And then I wrote and asked her to come.

C.-C.: I didn't know you knew her.

ELIZABETH: I don't. But I heard she was in London. She's staying at Claridge's. It seemed so heartless not to take the smallest notice of her.

C.-C.: When is she coming?

ELIZABETH: We're expecting her in time for luncheon.

C.-C.: As soon as that? I understand the embarrassment.

ELIZABETH: You see, we never expected you to be here. You said you'd be in Paris for another month.

C.-C.: My dear child, this is your house. There's no reason why you shouldn't ask whom you please to stay with you.

ELIZABETH: After all, whatever her faults, she's Arnold's mother. It seemed so unnatural that they should never see one another. My heart ached for that poor lonely woman.

C.-C.: I never heard that she was lonely, and she certainly isn't poor.

ELIZABETH: And there's something else. I couldn't ask her by herself. It would have been so—so insulting. I asked Lord Porteous, too.

C.-C.: I see.

ELIZABETH: I daresay you'd rather not meet them.

C.-C.: I daresay they'd rather not meet me. I shall get a capital luncheon at the cottage. I've noticed you always get the best food if you come in unexpectedly and have the same as they're having in the servants' hall.

ELIZABETH: No one's ever talked to me about Lady Kitty. It's always been a subject that everyone has avoided. I've never even seen a photograph of her.

C.-C.: The house was full of them when she left. I think I told the butler to throw them in the dust-bin. She was very much photographed.

ELIZABETH: Won't you tell me what she was like?

C.-C.: She was very like you, Elizabeth, only she had dark hair instead of red.

ELIZABETH: Poor dear! It must be quite white now.

C.-C.: I daresay. She was a pretty little thing.

ELIZABETH: But she was one of the great beauties of her day. They say she was lovely.

C.-C.: She had the most adorable little nose, like yours. . . .

ELIZABETH: D'you like my nose?

C.-C.: And she was very dainty, with a beautiful little figure; very light on her feet. She was like a *marquise* in an old French comedy. Yes, she was lovely.

ELIZABETH: And I'm sure she's lovely still.

C.-C.: She's no chicken, you know.

ELIZABETH: You can't expect me to look at it as you and Arnold do. When you've loved as she's loved you may grow old, but you grow old beautifully.

C.-C.: You're very romantic.

ELIZABETH: If everyone hadn't made such a mystery of it I daresay I shouldn't feel as I do. I know she did a great wrong to you and a great wrong to Arnold. I'm willing to acknowledge that.

C.-C.: I'm sure it's very kind of you.

ELIZABETH: But she loved and she dared. Romance is such an illusive thing. You read of it in books, but it's seldom you see it face to face. I can't help it if it thrills me.

C.-C.: I am painfully aware that the husband in these cases is not a romantic object.

ELIZABETH: She had the world at her feet. You were rich. She was a figure in society. And she gave up everything for love.

C.-C.: [*Dryly.*] I'm beginning to suspect it wasn't only for her sake and for Arnold's that you asked her to come here.

ELIZABETH: I seem to know her already. I think her face is a little sad, for a love like that doesn't leave you gay, it leaves you grave, but I think her pale face is unlined. It's like a child's.

C.-C.: My dear, how you let your imagination run away with you!

ELIZABETH: I imagine her slight and frail.

C.-C.: Frail, certainly.

ELIZABETH: With beautiful thin hands and white hair. I've pictured her so often in that Renaissance palace that they live in, with old masters on the walls and lovely carved things all round, sitting in a black silk dress with old lace round her neck and old-fashioned diamonds. You see, I never knew my mother; she died when I was a baby. You can't confide in aunts with huge families of their own. I want Arnold's mother to be a mother to me. I've got so much to say to her.

C.-C.: Are you happy with Arnold?

ELIZABETH: Why shouldn't I be?

C.-C.: Why haven't you got any babies?

ELIZABETH: Give us a little time. We've only been married three years.

C.-C.: I wonder what Hughie is like now?

ELIZABETH: Lord Porteous?

C.-C.: He wore his clothes better than any man in London. You know he'd have been Prime Minister if he'd remained in politics.

ELIZABETH: What was he like then?

C.-C.: He was a nice-looking fellow. Fine horseman. I suppose there was something very fascinating about him. Yellow hair and blue eyes, you know. He had a very good figure. I liked him. I was his parliamentary secretary. He was Arnold's godfather.

ELIZABETH: I know.

C.-C.: I wonder if he ever regrets.

ELIZABETH: I wouldn't.

C.-C.: Well, I must be strolling back to my cottage.

ELIZABETH: You're not angry with me?

C.-C.: Not a bit.

> [*She puts up her face for him to kiss. He kisses her on both cheeks and then goes out. In a moment* TEDDIE *is seen at the window.*

TEDDIE: I saw the old blighter go.

ELIZABETH: Come in.

TEDDIE: Everything all right?

ELIZABETH: Oh, quite, as far as he's concerned. He's going to keep out of the way.

TEDDIE: Was it beastly?

ELIZABETH: No, he made it very easy for me. He's a nice old thing.

TEDDIE: You were rather scared.

ELIZABETH: A little. I am still. I don't know why.

TEDDIE: I guessed you were. I thought I'd come and give you a little moral support. It's ripping here, isn't it?

ELIZABETH: It is rather nice.

TEDDIE: It'll be jolly to think of it when I'm back in the F.M.S.

ELIZABETH: Aren't you homesick sometimes?

TEDDIE: Oh, everyone is now and then, you know.

ELIZABETH: You could have got a job in England if you'd wanted to, couldn't you?

TEDDIE: Oh, but I love it out there. England's ripping to come back to, but I couldn't live here now. It's like a woman you're desperately in love with as long as you don't see her, but when you're with her she maddens you so that you can't bear her.

ELIZABETH: [*Smiling.*] What's wrong with England?

TEDDIE: I don't think anything's wrong with England. I expect something's wrong with me. I've been away too long.   England seems to me full of people doing things they don't want to because other people expect it of them.

ELIZABETH: Isn't that what you call a high degree of civilisation?

TEDDIE: People seem to me so insincere. When you go to parties in London they're all babbling about art, and you feel that in their hearts they don't care twopence about it. They read the books that everybody is talking about because they don't want to be out of it. In the F.M.S. we don't get very many books, and we read those we have over and over again. They mean so much to us. I don't think the people over there are half so clever as the people at home, but one gets to know them better. You see, there are so few of us that we have to make the best of one another.

ELIZABETH: I imagine that frills are not much worn in the F.M.S. It must be a comfort.

TEDDIE: It's not much good being pretentious where everyone knows exactly who you are and what your income is.

ELIZABETH: I don't think you want too much sincerity in society. It would be like an iron girder in a house of cards.

TEDDIE: And then, you know, the place is ripping. You get used to a blue sky and you miss it in England.

ELIZABETH: What do you do with yourself all the time?

TEDDIE: Oh, one works like blazes. You have to be a pretty hefty fellow to be a planter. And then there's ripping bathing. You know, it's lovely, with palm trees all along the beach. And there's shooting. And now and then we have a little dance to a gramophone.

ELIZABETH: [*Pretending to tease him.*] I think you've got a young woman out there, Teddie.

TEDDIE: [*Vehemently.*] Oh, no!

> [*She is a little taken aback by the earnestness of his dis-*
> *claimer. There is a moment's silence, then she recovers*
> *herself.*

ELIZABETH: But you'll have to marry and settle down one of these days, you know.

TEDDIE: I want to, but it's not a thing you can do lightly.

ELIZABETH: I don't know why there more than elsewhere.

TEDDIE: In England if people don't get on they go their own ways and jog along after a fashion. In a place like that you're thrown a great deal on your own resources.

ELIZABETH: Of course.

TEDDIE: Lots of girls come out because they think they're going to have a good time. But if they're empty-headed, then they're just faced with their own emptiness and they're done. If their husbands can afford it they go home and settle down as grass-widows.

ELIZABETH: I've met them. They seem to find it a very pleasant occupation.

TEDDIE: It's rotten for their husbands, though.

ELIZABETH: And if the husbands can't afford it?

TEDDIE: Oh, then they tipple.

ELIZABETH: It's not a very alluring prospect.

TEDDIE: But if the woman's the right sort she wouldn't exchange it for any life in the world. When all's said and done, it's we who've made the Empire.

ELIZABETH: What sort is the right sort?

TEDDIE: A woman of courage and endurance and sincerity. Of course, it's hopeless unless she's in love with her husband.

> [*He is looking at her earnestly and she, raising her eyes,*
> *gives him a long look. There is silence between them.*

TEDDIE: My house stands on the side of a hill, and the

coconut trees wind down to the shore. Azaleas grow in my garden, and camellias, and all sorts of ripping flowers. And in front of me is the winding coast line, and then the blue sea.

[*A pause.*

Do you know that I'm awfully in love with you?

ELIZABETH: [*Gravely.*] I wasn't quite sure. I wondered.

TEDDIE: And you?

[*She nods slowly.*

I've never kissed you.

ELIZABETH: I don't want you to.

[*They look at one another steadily. They are both grave.*
ARNOLD comes in hurriedly.

ARNOLD: They're coming, Elizabeth.

ELIZABETH: [*As though returning from a distant world.*] Who?

ARNOLD: [*Impatiently.*] My dear! My mother, of course. The car is just coming up the drive.

TEDDIE: Would you like me to clear out?

ARNOLD: No, no! For goodness' sake stay.

ELIZABETH: We'd better go and meet them, Arnold.

ARNOLD: No, no; I think they'd much better be shown in. I feel simply sick with nervousness.

[*ANNA comes in from the garden.*

ANNA: Your guests have arrived.

ELIZABETH: Yes, I know.

ARNOLD: I've given orders that luncheon should be served at once.

ELIZABETH: Why? It's not half-past one already, is it?

ARNOLD: I thought it would help. When you don't know exactly what to say you can always eat.

[*The BUTLER comes in and announces.*

BUTLER: Lady Catherine Champion-Cheney. Lord Porteous.

[LADY KITTY *comes in followed by* PORTEOUS, *and the* BUTLER *goes out.* LADY KITTY *is a gay little lady, with dyed red hair and painted cheeks. She is somewhat outrageously dressed. She never forgets that she has been a pretty woman and she still behaves as if she were twenty-five.* LORD PORTEOUS *is a very bald, elderly gentleman in loose, rather eccentric clothes. He is snappy and gruff. This is not at all the couple that* ELIZABETH *expected, and for a moment she stares at them with round, startled eyes.* LADY KITTY *goes up to her with outstretched hands.*

LADY KITTY: Elizabeth! Elizabeth! [*She kisses her effusively.*] What an adorable creature! [*Turning to* PORTEOUS.] Hughie, isn't she adorable?

PORTEOUS: [*With a grunt.*] Ugh!

[ELIZABETH, *smiling now, turns to him and gives him her hand.*

ELIZABETH: How d'you do?

PORTEOUS: Damnable road you've got down here. How d'you do, my dear? Why d'you have such damnable roads in England?

[LADY KITTY'S *eyes fall on* TEDDIE *and she goes up to him with her arms thrown back, prepared to throw them round him.*

LADY KITTY: My boy, my boy! I should have known you anywhere!

ELIZABETH: [*Hastily.*] That's Arnold.

LADY KITTY: [*Without a moment's hesitation.*] The image of his father! I should have known him anywhere! [*She throws her arms round his neck.*] My boy, my boy!

PORTEOUS: [*With a grunt.*] Ugh!

LADY KITTY: Tell me, would you have known me again? Have I changed?

ARNOLD: I was only five, you know, when—when you . . .

LADY KITTY: [*Emotionally.*] I remember as if it was yester-day. I went up into your room. [*With a sudden change of manner.*] By the way, I always thought that nurse drank. Did you ever find out if she really did?

PORTEOUS: How the devil can you expect him to know that, Kitty?

LADY KITTY: You've never had a child, Hughie; how can you tell what they know and what they don't?

ELIZABETH: [*Coming to the rescue.*] This is Arnold, Lord Porteous.

PORTEOUS: [*Shaking hands with him.*] How d'you do? I knew your father.

ARNOLD: Yes.

PORTEOUS: Alive still?

ARNOLD: Yes.

PORTEOUS: He must be getting on. Is he well?

ARNOLD: Very.

PORTEOUS: Ugh! Takes care of himself, I suppose. I'm not at all well. This damned climate doesn't agree with me.

ELIZABETH: [*To* LADY KITTY.] This is Mrs. Shenstone. And this is Mr. Luton. I hope you don't mind a very small party.

LADY KITTY: [*Shaking hands with* ANNA *and* TEDDIE.] Oh, no, I shall enjoy it. I used to give enormous parties here. Political, you know. How nice you've made this room!

ELIZABETH: Oh, that's Arnold.

ARNOLD: [*Nervously.*] D'you like this chair? I've just bought it. It's exactly my period.

PORTEOUS: [*Bluntly.*] It's a fake.

ARNOLD: [*Indignantly.*] I don't think it is for a minute.

PORTEOUS: The legs are not right.

ARNOLD: I don't know how you can say that. If there is anything right about it, it's the legs.

LADY KITTY: I'm sure they're right.

PORTEOUS: You know nothing whatever about it, Kitty.

LADY KITTY: That's what you think. *I* think it's a beautiful chair. Hepplewhite?

ARNOLD: No, Sheraton.

LADY KITTY: Oh, I know. The School for Scandal.

PORTEOUS: Sheraton, my dear. Sheraton.

LADY KITTY: Yes, that's what I say. I acted the screen scene at some amateur theatricals in Florence, and Ermete Novelli, the great Italian tragedian, told me he'd never seen a Lady Teazle like me.

PORTEOUS: Ugh!

LADY KITTY: [*To* ELIZABETH.] Do you act?

ELIZABETH: Oh, I couldn't. I should be too nervous.

LADY KITTY: I'm never nervous. I'm a born actress. Of course, if I had my time over again I'd go on the stage. You know, it's extraordinary how they keep young. Actresses, I mean. I think it's because they're always playing different parts. Hughie, do you think Arnold takes after me or after his father? Of course I think he's the very image of me. Arnold, I think I ought to tell you that I was received into the Catholic Church last winter. I'd been thinking about it for years, and last time we were at Monte Carlo I met such a nice monsignore. I told him what my difficulties were and he was too wonderful. I knew Hughie wouldn't approve, so I kept it a secret. [*To* ELIZABETH.] Are you interested in religion? I think it's too wonderful. We must have a long talk about it one of these days. [*Pointing to her frock.*] Callot?

ELIZABETH: No, Worth.

LADY KITTY: I knew it was either Worth or Callot. Of course, it's line that's the important thing. I go to Worth myself, and I always say to him, Line, my dear

Worth, line. What *is* the matter, Hughie?

PORTEOUS: These new teeth of mine are so damned uncomfortable.

LADY KITTY: Men are extraordinary. They can't stand the smallest discomfort. Why, a woman's life is uncomfortable from the moment she gets up in the morning till the moment she goes to bed at night. And d'you think it's comfortable to sleep with a mask on your face.

PORTEOUS: They don't seem to hold up properly.

LADY KITTY: Well, that's not the fault of your teeth. That's the fault of your gums.

PORTEOUS: Damned rotten dentist. That's what's the matter.

LADY KITTY: I thought he was a very nice dentist. He told me *my* teeth would last till I was fifty. He has a Chinese room. It's so interesting; while he scrapes your teeth he tells you all about the dear Empress Dowager. Are you interested in China? I think it's too wonderful. You know they've cut off their pigtails. I think it's such a pity. They were so picturesque.

[*The* BUTLER *comes in.*

BUTLER: Luncheon is served, sir.

ELIZABETH: Would you like to see your rooms?

PORTEOUS: We can see our rooms after luncheon.

LADY KITTY: I must powder my nose, Hughie.

PORTEOUS: Powder it down here.

LADY KITTY: I never saw any one so inconsiderate.

PORTEOUS: You'll keep us all waiting half an hour. I know you.

LADY KITTY: [*Fumbling in her bag.*] Oh, well, peace at any price, as Lord Beaconsfield said.

PORTEOUS: He said a lot of damned silly things, Kitty, but he never said that.

[LADY KITTY's *face changes. Perplexity is followed by dismay, and dismay by consternation.*

LADY KITTY: Oh!

ELIZABETH: What is the matter?

LADY KITTY: [*With anguish.*] My lip-stick!

ELIZABETH: Can't you find it?

LADY KITTY: I had it in the car. Hughie, you remember that I had it in the car.

PORTEOUS: I don't remember anything about it.

LADY KITTY: Don't be so stupid, Hughie. Why, when we came through the gates I said: My home, my home! and I took it out and put some on my lips.

ELIZABETH: Perhaps you dropped it in the car.

LADY KITTY: For heaven's sake send someone to look for it.

ARNOLD: I'll ring.

LADY KITTY: I'm absolutely lost without my lip-stick. Lend me yours, darling, will you?

ELIZABETH: I'm awfully sorry. I'm afraid I haven't got one.

LADY KITTY: Do you mean to say you don't use a lip-stick?

ELIZABETH: Never.

PORTEOUS: Look at her lips. What the devil d'you think she wants muck like that for?

LADY KITTY: Oh, my dear, what a mistake you make! You *must* use a lip-stick. It's so good for the lips. Men like it, you know. I couldn't *live* without a lip-stick.

[CHAMPION-CHENEY *appears at the window holding in his upstretched hand a little gold case.*

C.-C.: [*As he comes in.*] Has any one here lost a diminutive utensil containing, unless I am mistaken, a favourite preparation for the toilet?

[ARNOLD *and* ELIZABETH *are thunderstruck at his*

appearance and even TEDDIE *and* ANNA *are taken aback. But* LADY KITTY *is overjoyed.*

LADY KITTY: My lip-stick!

C.-C.: I found it in the drive and I ventured to bring it in.

LADY KITTY: It's Saint Antony. I said a little prayer to him when I was hunting in my bag.

PORTEOUS: Saint Antony be blowed! It's Clive, by God!

LADY KITTY: [*Startled, her attention suddenly turning from the lip-stick.*] Clive!

C.-C.: You didn't recognise me. It's many years since we met.

LADY KITTY: My poor Clive, your hair has gone quite white!

C.-C.: [*Holding out his hand.*] I hope you had a pleasant journey down from London.

LADY KITTY: [*Offering him her cheek.*] You may kiss me, Clive.

C.-C.: [*Kissing her.*] You Don't mind, Hughie?

PORTEOUS: [*With a grunt.*] Ugh!

C.-C.: [*Going up to him cordially.*] And how are you, my dear Hughie?

PORTEOUS: Damned rheumatic if you want to know. Filthy climate you have in this country.

C.-C.: Aren't you going to shake hands with me, Hughie?

PORTEOUS: I have no objection to shaking hands with you.

C.-C.: You've aged, my poor Hughie.

PORTEOUS: Someone was asking me how old you were the other day.

C.-C.: Were they surprised when you told them?

PORTEOUS: Surprised! They wondered you weren't dead.

[*The* BUTLER *comes in.*

BUTLER: Did you ring, sir?

ARNOLD: No. Oh, yes, I did. It doesn't matter now.

C.-C.: [*As the* BUTLER *is going.*] One moment. My dear Elizabeth, I've come to throw myself on your mercy. My servants are busy with their own affairs. There's not a thing for me to eat in my cottage.

ELIZABETH: Oh, but we shall be delighted if you'll lunch with us.

C.-C.: It either means that or my immediate death from starvation. You don't mind, Arnold?

ARNOLD: My dear father!

ELIZABETH: [*To the* BUTLER.] Mr. Cheney will lunch here.

BUTLER: Very good, ma'am.

C.-C.: [*To* LADY KITTY.] And what do you think of Arnold?

LADY KITTY: I adore him.

C.-C.: He's grown, hasn't he? But then you'd expect him to do that in thirty years.

ARNOLD: For God's sake let's go in to lunch, Elizabeth!

END OF THE FIRST ACT

THE SECOND ACT

The Scene is the same as in the preceding Act.

It is afternoon. When the curtain rises PORTEOUS *and* LADY
  KITTY, ANNA *and* TEDDIE *are playing bridge.* ELIZABETH
  and CHAMPION-CHENEY *are watching.* PORTEOUS *and* LADY
  KITTY *are partners.*

C.-C.: When will Arnold be back, Elizabeth?

ELIZABETH: Soon, I think.

C.-C.: Is he addressing a meeting?

ELIZABETH: No, it's only a conference with his agent and
  one or two constituents.

PORTEOUS: [*Irritably.*] How any one can be expected to play
  bridge when people are shouting at the top of their
  voices all round them, I for one cannot understand.

ELIZABETH: [*Smiling.*] I'm so sorry.

ANNA: I can see your hand, Lord Porteous.

PORTEOUS: It may help you.

LADY KITTY: I've told you over and over again to hold
  your cards up. It ruins one's game when one can't help
  seeing one's opponent's hand.

PORTEOUS: One isn't obliged to look.

LADY KITTY: What was Arnold's majority at the last
  election?

ELIZABETH: Seven hundred and something.

C.-C.: He'll have to fight for it if he wants to keep his seat
  next time.

PORTEOUS: Are we playing bridge, or talking politics?

LADY KITTY: I never find that conversation interferes with
  my game.

31

PORTEOUS: You certainly play no worse when you talk than when you hold your tongue.

LADY KITTY: I think that's a very offensive thing to say, Hughie. Just because I don't play the same game as you do you think I can't play.

PORTEOUS: I'm glad you acknowledge it's not the same game as I play. But why in God's name do you call it bridge?

C.-C.: I agree with Kitty. I hate people who play bridge as though they were at a funeral and knew their feet were getting wet.

PORTEOUS: Of course you take Kitty's part.

LADY KITTY: That's the least he can do.

C.-C.: I have a naturally cheerful disposition.

PORTEOUS: You've never had anything to sour it.

LADY KITTY: I don't know what you mean by that, Hughie.

PORTEOUS: [*Trying to contain himself.*] Must you trump my ace?

LADY KITTY: [*Innocently.*] Oh, was that your ace, darling?

PORTEOUS: [*Furiously.*] Yes, it was my ace.

LADY KITTY: Oh, well, it was the only trump I had. I shouldn't have made it anyway.

PORTEOUS: You needn't have told them that. Now she knows exactly what I've got.

LADY KITTY: She knew before.

PORTEOUS: How could she know?

LADY KITTY: She said she'd seen your hand.

ANNA: Oh, I didn't. I said I could see it.

LADY KITTY: Well, I naturally supposed that if she could see it she did.

PORTEOUS: Really, Kitty, you have the most extraordinary ideas.

C.-C.: Not at all. If any one is such a fool as to show me his hand, of course I look at it.

PORTEOUS: [*Fuming.*] If you study the etiquette of bridge, you'll discover that onlookers are expected not to interfere with the game.

C.-C.: My dear Hughie, this is a matter of ethics, not of bridge.

ANNA: Anyhow, I get the game. And rubber.

TEDDIE: I claim a revoke.

PORTEOUS: Who revoked?

TEDDIE: You did.

PORTEOUS: Nonsense. I've never revoked in my life.

TEDDIE: I'll show you. [*He turns over the tricks to show the faces of the cards.*] You threw away a club on the third heart trick and you had another heart.

PORTEOUS: I never had more than two hearts.

TEDDIE: Oh, yes, you had. Look here. That's the card you played on the last trick but one.

LADY KITTY: [*Delighted to catch him out.*] There's no doubt about it, Hughie. You revoked.

PORTEOUS: I tell you I did not revoke. I never revoke.

C.-C.: You did, Hughie. I wondered what on earth you were doing.

PORTEOUS: I don't know how any one can be expected not to revoke when there's this confounded chatter going on all the time.

TEDDIE: Well, that's another hundred to us.

PORTEOUS: [*To* CHAMPION-CHENEY.] I wish you wouldn't breathe down my neck. I never can play bridge when there's somebody breathing down my neck.

[*The party have risen from the bridge-table, and they scatter about the room.*

ANNA: Well, I'm going to take a book and lie down in the hammock till it's time to dress.

TEDDIE: [*Who has been adding up.*] I'll put it down in the book, shall I?

PORTEOUS: [*Who has not moved, setting out the cards for a patience.*] Yes, yes, put it down. I never revoke.

[ANNA *goes out.*

LADY KITTY: Would you like to come for a little stroll, Hughie?

PORTEOUS: What for?

LADY KITTY: Exercise.

PORTEOUS: I hate exercise.

C.-C.: [*Looking at the patience.*] The seven goes on the eight.

[PORTEOUS *takes no notice.*

LADY KITTY: The seven goes on the eight, Hughie.

PORTEOUS: I don't choose to put the seven on the eight.

C.-C.: That knave goes on the queen.

PORTEOUS: I'm not blind, thank you.

LADY KITTY: The three goes on the four.

C.-C.: All these go over.

PORTEOUS: [*Furiously.*] Am I playing this patience, or are you playing it?

LADY KITTY: But you're missing everything.

PORTEOUS: That's my business.

C.-C.: It's no good losing your temper over it, Hughie.

PORTEOUS: Go away, both of you. You irritate me.

LADY KITTY: We were only trying to help you, Hughie.

PORTEOUS: I don't want to be helped. I want to do it by myself.

LADY KITTY: I think your manners are perfectly deplorable, Hughie.

PORTEOUS: It's simply maddening when you're playing patience and people won't leave you alone.

C.-C.: We won't say another word.

PORTEOUS: That three goes. I believe it's coming out. If I'd been such a fool as to put that seven up I shouldn't have been able to bring these down.

[*He puts down several cards while they watch him silently.*

LADY KITTY: AND C.-C.: [*Together.*] The four goes on the five.

PORTEOUS: [*Throwing down the cards violently.*] Damn you! Why don't you leave me alone? It's intolerable.

C.-C.: It was coming out, my dear fellow.

PORTEOUS: I know it was coming out. Confound you!

LADY KITTY: How petty you are, Hughie!

PORTEOUS: Petty, be damned! I've told you over and over again that I will not be interfered with when I'm playing patience.

LADY KITTY: Don't talk to me like that, Hughie.

PORTEOUS: I shall talk to you as I please.

LADY KITTY: [*Beginning to cry.*] Oh, you brute! You brute!
[*She flings out of the room.*

PORTEOUS: Oh, damn! Now she's going to cry.

[*He shambles out into the garden.* CHAMPION-CHENEY, ELIZABETH *and* TEDDIE *are left alone. There is a moment's pause.* CHAMPION-CHENEY *looks from* TEDDIE *to* ELIZABETH, *with an ironical smile.*

C.-C.: Upon my soul, they might be married. They frip so much.

ELIZABETH: [*Frigidly.*] It's been nice of you to come here so often since they arrived. It's helped to make things easy.

C.-C.: Irony? It's a rhetorical form not much favoured in this blessed plot, this earth, this realm, this England.

ELIZABETH: What exactly are you getting at?

C.-C.: How slangy the young women of the present day are! I suppose the fact that Arnold is a purist leads you to the contrary extravagance.

ELIZABETH: Anyhow you know what I mean.

C.-C.: [*With a smile.*] I have a dim, groping suspicion.

ELIZABETH: You promised to keep away. Why did you come back the moment they arrived?

C.-C.: Curiosity, my dear child. A surely pardonable curiosity.

ELIZABETH: And since then you've been here all the time. You don't generally favour us with so much of your company when you're down at your cottage.

C.-C.: I've been excessively amused.

ELIZABETH: It has struck me that whenever they started fripping you took a malicious pleasure in goading them on.

C.-C.: I don't think there's much love lost between them now, do you?

[TEDDIE *is making as though to leave the room.*

ELIZABETH: Don't go, Teddie.

C.-C.: No, please don't. I'm only staying a minute. We were talking about Lady Kitty just before she arrived. [*To* ELIZABETH.] Do you remember? The pale, frail lady in black satin and old lace.

ELIZABETH: [*With a chuckle.*] You are a devil, you know.

C.-C.: Ah, well, he's always had the reputation of being a humorist and a gentleman.

ELIZABETH: Did *you* expect her to be like that, poor dear?

C.-C.: My dear child, I hadn't the vaguest idea. You were asking me the other day what she was like when she ran away. I didn't tell you half. She was so gay and so natural. Who would have thought that animation would turn into such frivolity, and that charming impulsiveness lead to such a ridiculous affectation?

ELIZABETH: It rather sets my nerves on edge to hear the way you talk of her.

C.-C.: It's the truth that sets your nerves on edge, not I.

ELIZABETH: You loved her once. Have you no feeling for her at all?

C.-C.: None. Why should I?

ELIZABETH: She's the mother of your son.

C.-C.: My dear child, you have a charming nature, as simple, frank and artless as hers was. Don't let pure humbug obscure your common sense.

ELIZABETH: We have no right to judge. She's only been here two days. We know nothing about her.

C.-C.: My dear, her soul is as thickly rouged as her face. She hasn't an emotion that's sincere. She's tinsel. You think I'm a cruel, cynical old man. Why, when I think of what she was, if I didn't laugh at what she has become I should cry.

ELIZABETH: How do you know she wouldn't be just the same now if she'd remained your wife? Do you think your influence would have had such a salutary effect on her?

C.-C.: [*Good-humouredly.*] I like you when you're bitter and rather insolent.

ELIZABETH: D'you like me enough to answer my question?

C.-C.: She was only twenty-seven when she went away. She might have become anything. She might have become the woman you expected her to be. There are very few of us who are strong enough to make circumstances serve us. We are the creatures of our environment. She's a silly worthless woman because she's led a silly worthless life.

ELIZABETH: [*Disturbed.*] You're horrible to-day.

C.-C.: I don't say it's I who could have prevented her from becoming this ridiculous caricature of a pretty woman grown old. But life could. Here she would have had the friends fit to her station, and a decent activity, and worthy interests. Ask her what her life has been all these years among divorced women and kept women and the men who consort with them. There is no more lamentable pursuit than a life of pleasure.

ELIZABETH: At all events she loved and she loved greatly. I have only pity and affection for her.

C.-C.: And if she loved what d'you think she felt when she saw that she had ruined Hughie? Look at him. He was tight last night after dinner and tight the night before.

ELIZABETH: I know.

C.-C.: And she took it as a matter of course. How long do you suppose he's been getting tight every night? Do you think he was like that thirty years ago? Can you imagine that that was a brilliant young man, whom every one expected to be Prime Minister? Look at him now. A grumpy sodden old fellow with false teeth.

ELIZABETH: You have false teeth, too.

C.-C.: Yes, but damn it all, they fit. She's ruined him and she knows she's ruined him.

ELIZABETH: [*Looking at him suspiciously.*] Why are you saying all this to me?

C.-C.: Am I hurting your feelings?

ELIZABETH: I think I've had enough for the present.

C.-C.: I'll go and have a look at the gold-fish. I want to see Arnold when he comes in. [*Politely.*] I'm afraid we've been boring Mr. Luton.

TEDDIE: Not at all.

C.-C.: When are you going back to the F.M.S.?

TEDDIE: In about a month.

C.-C.: I see.

> [*He goes out.*

ELIZABETH: I wonder what he has at the back of his head.

TEDDIE: D'you think he was talking *at* you?

ELIZABETH: He's as clever as a bagful of monkeys.

> [*There is a moment's pause.* TEDDIE *hesitates a little, and when he speaks it is in a different tone. He is grave and somewhat nervous.*

TEDDIE: It seems very difficult to get a few minutes alone with you. I wonder if you've been making it difficult?

ELIZABETH: I wanted to think.

TEDDIE: I've made up my mind to go away to-morrow.

ELIZABETH: Why?

TEDDIE: I want you altogether or not at all.

ELIZABETH: You're so arbitrary.

TEDDIE: You said you—you said you cared for me.

ELIZABETH: I do.

TEDDIE: Do you mind if we talk it over now?

ELIZABETH: No.

TEDDIE: [*Frowning.*] It makes me feel rather shy and awkward. I've repeated to myself over and over again exactly what I want to say to you, and now all I'd prepared seems rather footling.

ELIZABETH: I'm so afraid I'm going to cry.

TEDDIE: I feel it's all so tremendously serious and I think we ought to keep emotion out of it. You're rather emotional, aren't you?

ELIZABETH: [*Half smiling and half in tears.*] So are you for the matter of that.

TEDDIE: That's why I wanted to have everything I meant to say to you cut and dried. I think it would be awfully unfair if I made love to you and all that sort of thing, and you were carried away. I wrote it all down and thought I'd send it you as a letter.

ELIZABETH: Why didn't you?

TEDDIE: I got the wind up. A letter seems so—so cold. You see, I love you so awfully.

ELIZABETH: For goodness' sake don't say that.

TEDDIE: You mustn't cry. Please don't, or I shall go all to pieces.

ELIZABETH: [*Trying to smile.*] I'm sorry. It doesn't mean anything really. It's only tears running out of my eyes.

TEDDIE: Our only chance is to be awfully matter-of-fact.

> [*He stops for a moment. He finds it quite difficult to control himself. He clears his throat. He frowns with annoyance at himself.*

ELIZABETH: What's the matter?

TEDDIE: I've got a sort of lump in my throat. It is idiotic. I think I'll have a cigarette.

> [*She watches him in silence while he lights a cigarette.*

You see, I've never been in love with anyone before, not really. It's knocked me endways. I don't know how I can live without you now. . . . Does that old fool know I'm in love with you?

ELIZABETH: I think so.

TEDDIE: When he was talking about Lady Kitty smashing up Lord Porteous' career I thought there was something at the back of it.

ELIZABETH: I think he was trying to persuade me not to smash up yours.

TEDDIE: I'm sure that's very considerate of him, but I don't happen to have one to smash. I wish I had. It's the only time in my life I've wished I were a hell of a swell so that

I could chuck it all and show you how much more you are to me than anything else in the world.

ELIZABETH: [*Affectionately.*] You're a dear old thing, Teddie.

TEDDIE: You know, I don't really know how to make love, but if I did I couldn't do it now because I just want to be absolutely practical.

ELIZABETH: [*Chaffing him.*] I'm glad you don't know how to make love. It would be almost more than I could bear.

TEDDIE: You see, I'm not at all romantic and that sort of thing. I'm just a common or garden business man. All this is so dreadfully serious and I think we ought to be sensible.

ELIZABETH: [*With a break in her voice.*] You owl!

TEDDIE: No, Elizabeth, don't say things like that to me. I want you to consider all the *pros* and *cons*, and my heart's thumping against my chest, and you know I love you, I love you, I love you.

ELIZABETH: [*In a sigh of passion.*] Oh, my precious.

TEDDIE: [*Impatiently, but with himself, rather than with* ELIZABETH.] Don't be idiotic, Elizabeth. I'm not going to tell you that I can't live without you and a lot of muck like that. You know that you mean everything in the world to me. [*Almost giving it up as a bad job.*] Oh, my God!

ELIZABETH: [*Her voice faltering.*] D'you think there's anything you can say to me that I don't know already?

TEDDIE: [*Desperately.*] But I haven't said a single thing I wanted to. I'm a business man and I want to put it all in a business way, if you understand what I mean.

ELIZABETH: [*Smiling.*] I don't believe you're a very good business man.

TEDDIE: [*Sharply.*] You don't know what you're talking about. I'm a first-rate business man, but somehow this is different. [*Hopelessly.*] I don't know why it won't go right.

ELIZABETH: What are we going to do about it?

TEDDIE: You see, it's not just because you're awfully pretty that I love you. I'd love you just as much if you were old and ugly. It's you I love, not what you look like. And it's not only love; love be blowed! It's that I *like* you so tremendously. I think you're such a ripping good sort. I just want to be with you. I feel so jolly and happy just to think you're there. I'm so awfully *fond* of you.

ELIZABETH: [*Laughing through her tears.*] I don't know if this is your idea of introducing a business proposition.

TEDDIE: Damn you, you won't let me.

ELIZABETH: You said, Damn you.

TEDDIE: I meant it.

ELIZABETH: Your voice sounded as if you meant, you perfect duck.

TEDDIE: Really, Elizabeth, you're intolerable.

ELIZABETH: I'm doing nothing.

TEDDIE: Yes, you are, you're putting me off my blow. What I want to say is perfectly simple. I'm a very ordinary business man.

ELIZABETH: You've said that before.

TEDDIE: [*Angrily.*] Shut up. I haven't got a bob besides what I earn. I've got no position. I'm nothing. You're rich and you're a big pot and you've got everything that anyone can want. It's awful cheek my saying anything to you at all. But after all there's only one thing that really matters in the world, and that's love. I love you. Chuck all this, Elizabeth, and come to me.

ELIZABETH: Are you cross with me?

TEDDIE: Furious.

ELIZABETH: Darling!

TEDDIE: If you don't want me tell me so at once and let me get out quickly.

ELIZABETH: Teddie, nothing in the world matters anything to me but you. I'll go wherever you take me. I love you.

TEDDIE: [*All to pieces.*] Oh, my God!

ELIZABETH: Does it mean as much to you as that? Oh, Teddie!

TEDDIE: [*Trying to control himself.*] Don't be a fool, Elizabeth.

ELIZABETH: It's you're the fool. You're making me cry.

TEDDIE: You're so damned emotional.

ELIZABETH: Damned emotional yourself. I'm sure you're a rotten business man.

TEDDIE: I don't care what you think. You've made me so awfully happy. I say, what a lark life's going to be.

ELIZABETH: Teddie, you are an angel.

TEDDIE: Let's get out quick. It's no good wasting time. Elizabeth.

ELIZABETH: What?

TEDDIE: Nothing. I just like to say Elizabeth.

ELIZABETH: You fool.

TEDDIE: I say, can you shoot?

ELIZABETH: No.

TEDDIE: I'll teach you. You don't know how ripping it is to start out from your camp at dawn and travel through the jungle. And you're so tired at night and the sky's all starry. It's a fair treat. Of course I didn't want to say anything about all that till you'd decided. I'd made up my mind to be absolutely practical.

ELIZABETH: [*Chaffing him.*] The only practical thing you said was that love is the only thing that really matters.

TEDDIE: [*Happily.*] Pull the other leg next time, will you? I should hate to have one longer than the other.

ELIZABETH: Isn't it fun being in love with someone who's in love with you?

TEDDIE: I say, I think I'd better clear out at once, don't you? It seems rather rotten to stay on in—in this house.

ELIZABETH: You can't go to-night. There's no train.

TEDDIE: I'll go to-morrow. I'll wait in London till you're ready to join me.

ELIZABETH: I'm not going to leave a note on the pincushion like Lady Kitty, you know. I'm going to tell Arnold.

TEDDIE: Are you? Don't you think there'll be an awful bother?

ELIZABETH: I must face it. I should hate to be sly and deceitful.

TEDDIE: Well, then, let's face it together.

ELIZABETH: No, I'll talk to Arnold by myself.

TEDDIE: You won't let anyone influence you?

ELIZABETH: No.

> *He holds out his hand and she takes it. They look into one another's eyes with grave, almost solemn affection. There is the sound outside of a car driving up.*

ELIZABETH: There's the car. Arnold's come back. I must go and bathe my eyes. I don't want them to see I've been crying.

TEDDIE: All right. [*As she is going.*] Elizabeth.

ELIZABETH: [*Stopping.*] What?

TEDDIE: Bless you.

ELIZABETH: [*Affectionately.*] Idiot!

> [*She goes out of the door and* TEDDIE *through the french window into the garden. For an instant the room is empty.* ARNOLD *comes in. He sits down and takes some papers out of his dispatch-case.* LADY KITTY *enters. He gets up.*

LADY KITTY: I saw you come in. Oh, my dear, don't get up. There's no reason why you should be so dreadfully polite to me.

ARNOLD: I've just rung for a cup of tea.

LADY KITTY: Perhaps we shall have the chance of a little talk. We don't seem to have had five minutes by ourselves. I want to make your acquaintance, you know.

ARNOLD: I should like you to know that it's not by my wish that my father is here.

LADY KITTY: But I'm so interested to see him.

ARNOLD: I was afraid that you and Lord Porteous must find it embarrassing.

LADY KITTY: Oh, no. Hughie was his greatest friend. They were at Eton and Oxford together. I think your father has improved so much since I saw him last. He wasn't good-looking as a young man, but now he's quite handsome.

[*The* FOOTMAN *brings in a tray on which are tea-things.*

LADY KITTY: Shall I pour it out for you?

ARNOLD: Thank you very much.

LADY KITTY: Do you take sugar?

ARNOLD: No. I gave it up during the war.

LADY KITTY: So wise of you. It's so bad for the figure. Besides being patriotic, of course. Isn't it absurd that I should ask my son if he takes sugar or not? Life is really very quaint. Sad, of course, but oh, so quaint! Often I lie in bed at night and have a good laugh to myself as I think how quaint life is.

ARNOLD: I'm afraid I'm a very serious person.

LADY KITTY: How old are you now, Arnold?

ARNOLD: Thirty-five.

LADY KITTY: Are you really? Of course, I was a child when I married your father.

ARNOLD: Really. He always told me you were twenty-two.

LADY KITTY: Oh, what nonsense! Why, I was married out of the nursery. I put my hair up for the first time on my wedding-day.

ARNOLD: Where is Lord Porteous?

LADY KITTY: My dear, it sounds too absurd to hear you call him Lord Porteous. Why don't you call him—Uncle Hughie?

ARNOLD: He doesn't happen to be my uncle.

LADY KITTY: No, but he's your godfather. You know, I'm sure you'll like him when you know him better. I'm so hoping that you and Elizabeth will come and stay with us in Florence. I simply adore Elizabeth. She's too beautiful.

ARNOLD: Her hair is very pretty.

LADY KITTY: It's not touched up, is it?

ARNOLD: Oh, no.

LADY KITTY: I just wondered. It's rather a coincidence that her hair should be the same colour as mine. I suppose it shows that your father and you are attracted by just the same thing. So interesting, heredity, isn't it?

ARNOLD: Very.

LADY KITTY: Of course, since I joined the Catholic Church I don't believe in it any more. Darwin and all that sort of thing. Too dreadful. Wicked, you know. Besides, it's not very good form, is it?

[CHAMPION-CHENEY *comes in from the garden.*

C.-C.: Do I intrude?

LADY KITTY: Come in, Clive. Arnold and I have been having such a wonderful heart-to-heart talk.

C.-C.: Very nice.

ARNOLD: Father, I stepped in for a moment at the Harveys'

on my way back. It's simply criminal what they're doing with that house.

C.-C.: What are they doing?

ARNOLD: It's an almost perfect Georgian house and they've got a lot of dreadful Victorian furniture. I gave them my ideas on the subject, but it's quite hopeless. They said they were attached to their furniture.

C.-C.: Arnold should have been an interior decorator.

LADY KITTY: He has wonderful taste. He gets that from me.

ARNOLD: I suppose I have a certain *flair*. I have a passion for decorating houses.

LADY KITTY: You've made this one charming.

C.-C.: D'you remember, we just had chintzes and comfortable chairs when we lived here, Kitty.

LADY KITTY: Perfectly hideous, wasn't it?

C.-C.: In those days gentlemen and ladies were not expected to have taste.

ARNOLD: You know, I've been looking at this chair again. Since Lord Porteous said the legs weren't right I've been very uneasy.

LADY KITTY: He only said that because he was in a bad temper.

C.-C.: His temper seems to me very short these days, Kitty.

LADY KITTY: Oh, it is.

ARNOLD: You feel he knows what he's talking about. I gave seventy-five pounds for that chair. I'm very seldom taken in. I always think if a thing's right you feel it.

C.-C.: Well, don't let it disturb your night's rest.

ARNOLD: But, my dear father, that's just what it does. I had a most horrible dream about it last night.

LADY KITTY: Here is Hughie.

ARNOLD: I'm going to fetch a book I have on Old English

furniture. There's an illustration of a chair which is almost identical with this one.

[PORTEOUS *comes in.*

PORTEOUS: Quite a family gathering, by George!

C.-C.: I was thinking just now we'd make a very pleasing picture of a typical English home.

ARNOLD: I'll be back in five minutes. There's something I want to show you, Lord Porteous.

[*He goes out.*

C.-C.: Would you like to play piquet with me, Hughie?

PORTEOUS: Not particularly.

C.-C.: You were never much of a piquet player, were you?

PORTEOUS: My dear Clive, you people don't know what piquet is in England.

C.-C.: Let's have a game then. You may make money.

PORTEOUS: I don't want to play with you.

LADY KITTY: I don't know why not, Hughie.

PORTEOUS: Let me tell you that I don't like your manner.

C.-C.: I'm sorry for that. I'm afraid I can't offer to change it at my age.

PORTEOUS: I don't know what you want to be hanging around here for.

C.-C.: A natural attachment to my home.

PORTEOUS: If you'd had any tact you'd have kept out of the way while we were here.

C.-C.: My dear Hughie, I don't understand your attitude at all. If I'm willing to let bygones be bygones why should you object?

PORTEOUS: Damn it all, they're not bygones.

C.-C.: After all, I am the injured party.

PORTEOUS: How the devil are you the injured party?

C.-C.: Well, you did run away with my wife, didn't you?

LADY KITTY: Now, don't let's go into ancient history. I can't see why we shouldn't all be friends.

PORTEOUS: I beg you not to interfere, Kitty.

LADY KITTY: I'm very fond of Clive.

PORTEOUS: You never cared two straws for Clive. You only say that to irritate me.

LADY KITTY: Not at all. I don't see why he shouldn't come and stay with us.

C.-C.: I'd love to. I think Florence in spring-time is delightful. Have you central heating?

PORTEOUS: I never liked you, I don't like you now, and I never shall like you.

C.-C.: How very unfortunate! Because I liked you, I like you now, and I shall continue to like you.

LADY KITTY: There's something very nice about you, Clive.

PORTEOUS: If you think that, why the devil did you leave him?

LADY KITTY: Are you going to reproach me because I loved you? How utterly, utterly, utterly detestable you are!

C.-C.: Now, now, don't quarrel with one another.

LADY KITTY: It's all his fault. I'm the easiest person in the world to live with. But really he'd try the patience of a saint.

C.-C.: Come, come, don't get upset, Kitty. When two people live together there must be a certain amount of give and take.

PORTEOUS: I don't know what the devil you're talking about.

C.-C.: It hasn't escaped my observation that you are a little inclined to frip. Many couples are. I think it's a pity.

PORTEOUS: Would you have the very great kindness to mind your own business?

LADY KITTY: It is his business. He naturally wants me to be happy.

C.-C.: I have the very greatest affection for Kitty.

PORTEOUS: Then why the devil didn't you look after her properly?

C.-C.: My dear Hughie, you were my greatest friend. I trusted you. It may have been rash.

PORTEOUS: It was inexcusable.

LADY KITTY: I don't know what you mean by that, Hughie.

PORTEOUS: Don't, don't, don't try and bully me, Kitty.

LADY KITTY: Oh, I know what you mean.

PORTEOUS: Then why the devil did you say you didn't?

LADY KITTY: When I think that I sacrificed everything for that man! And for thirty years I've had to live in a filthy marble palace with no sanitary conveniences.

C.-C.: D'you mean to say you haven't got a bathroom?

LADY KITTY: I've had to wash in a tub.

C.-C.: My poor Kitty, how you've suffered!

PORTEOUS: Really, Kitty, I'm sick of hearing of the sacrifices you made. I suppose you think I sacrificed nothing. I should have been Prime Minister by now if it hadn't been for you.

LADY KITTY: Nonsense!

PORTEOUS: What do you mean by that? Every one said I should be Prime Minister. Shouldn't I have been Prime Minister, Clive?

C.-C.: It was certainly the general expectation.

PORTEOUS: I was the most promising young man of my day. I was bound to get a seat in the Cabinet at the next election.

LADY KITTY: They'd have found you out just as I've found you out. I'm sick of hearing that I ruined your career.

You never had a career to ruin. Prime Minister! You haven't the brain. You haven't the character.

C.-C.: Cheek, push, and a gift of the gab will serve very well instead, you know.

LADY KITTY: Besides, in politics it's not the men that matter. It's the women at the back of them. I could have made Clive a Cabinet Minister if I'd wanted to.

PORTEOUS: Clive?

LADY KITTY: With my beauty, my charm, my force of character, my wit, I could have done anything.

PORTEOUS: Clive was nothing but my political secretary. When I was Prime Minister I might have made him Governor of some Colony or other. Western Australia, say. Out of pure kindliness.

LADY KITTY: [*With flashing eyes.*] D'you think I would have buried myself in Western Australia? With my beauty? My charm?

PORTEOUS: Or Barbadoes, perhaps.

LADY KITTY: [*Furiously.*] Barbadoes! Barbadoes can go to —Barbadoes.

PORTEOUS: That's all you'd have got.

LADY KITTY: Nonsense! I'd have India.

PORTEOUS: I would never have given you India.

LADY KITTY: You would have given me India.

PORTEOUS: I tell you I wouldn't.

LADY KITTY: The King would have given me India. The nation would have insisted on my having India. I would have been a vice-reine or nothing.

PORTEOUS: I tell you that as long as the interests of the British Empire—Damn it all, my teeth are coming out!

[*He hurries from the room.*

LADY KITTY: It's too much. I can't bear it any more. I've

put up with him for thirty years and now I'm at the end of my tether.

C.-C.: Calm yourself, my dear Kitty.

LADY KITTY: I won't listen to a word. I've quite made up my mind. It's finished, finished, finished. [*With a change of tone.*] I was so touched when I heard that you never lived in this house again after I left it.

C.-C.: The cuckoos have always been very plentiful. Their note has a personal application which, I must say, I have found extremely offensive.

LADY KITTY: When I saw that you didn't marry again I couldn't help thinking that you still loved me.

C.-C.: I am one of the few men I know who is able to profit by experience.

LADY KITTY: In the eyes of the Church I am still your wife. The Church is so wise. It knows that in the end a woman always comes back to her first love. Clive, I am willing to return to you.

C.-C.: My dear Kitty, I couldn't take advantage of your momentary vexation with Hughie to let you take a step which I know you would bitterly regret.

LADY KITTY: You've waited for me a long time. For Arnold's sake.

C.-C.: Do you think we really need bother about Arnold? In the last thirty years he's had time to grow used to the situation.

LADY KITTY: [*With a little smile.*] I think I've sown my wild oats, Clive.

C.-C.: I haven't. I was a good young man, Kitty.

LADY KITTY: I know.

C.-C.: And I'm very glad, because it has enabled me to be a wicked old one.

LADY KITTY: I beg your pardon.

[ARNOLD *comes in with a large book in his hand.*

ARNOLD: I say, I've found the book I was hunting for. Oh, isn't Lord Porteous here?

LADY KITTY: One moment, Arnold. Your father and I are busy.

ARNOLD: I'm so sorry.

[*He goes out into the garden.*

LADY KITTY: Explain yourself, Clive.

C.-C.: When you ran away from me, Kitty, I was sore and angry and miserable. But above all I felt a fool.

LADY KITTY: Men are so vain.

C.-C.: But I was a student of history, and presently I reflected that I shared my misfortune with very nearly all the greatest men.

LADY KITTY: I'm a great reader myself. It has always struck me as peculiar.

C.-C.: The explanation is very simple. Women dislike intelligence, and when they find it in their husbands they revenge themselves on them in the only way they can, by making them—well, what you made me.

LADY KITTY: It's ingenious. It may be true.

C.-C.: I felt I had done my duty by society and I determined to devote the rest of my life to my own entertainment. The House of Commons had always bored me excessively and the scandal of our divorce gave me an opportunity to resign my seat. I have been relieved to find that the country got on perfectly well without me.

LADY KITTY: But has love never entered your life?

C.-C.: Tell me frankly, Kitty, don't you think people make a lot of unnecessary fuss about love?

LADY KITTY: It's the most wonderful thing in the world.

C.-C.: You're incorrigible. Do you really think it was worth sacrificing so much for?

LADY KITTY: My dear Clive, I don't mind telling you that if I had my time over again I should be unfaithful to you, but I should not leave you.

C.-C.: For some years I was notoriously the prey of a secret sorrow. But I found so many charming creatures who were anxious to console that in the end it grew rather fatiguing. Out of regard to my health I ceased to frequent the drawing-rooms of Mayfair.

LADY KITTY: And since then?

C.-C.: Since then I have allowed myself the luxury of assisting financially a succession of dear little things, in a somewhat humble sphere, between the ages of twenty and twenty-five.

LADY KITTY: I cannot understand the infatuation of men for young girls. I think they're so dull.

C.-C.: It's a matter of taste. I love old wine, old friends and old books, but I like young women. On their twenty-fifth birthday I give them a diamond ring and tell them they must no longer waste their youth and beauty on an old fogey like me. We have a most affecting scene, my technique on these occasions is perfect, and then I start all over again.

LADY KITTY: You're a wicked old man, Clive.

C.-C.: That's what I told you. But, by George! I'm a happy one.

LADY KITTY: There's only one course open to me now.

C.-C.: What is that!

LADY KITTY: [*With a flashing smile.*] To go and dress for dinner.

C.-C.: Capital. I will follow your example.

[*As* LADY KITTY *goes out* ELIZABETH *comes in.*

ELIZABETH: Where is Arnold?

C.-C.: He's on the terrace. I'll call him.

ELIZABETH: Don't bother.

C.-C.: I was just strolling along to my cottage to put on a dinner jacket. [*As he goes out.*] Arnold.

[*Exit* C.-C.

ARNOLD: Hulloa! [*He comes in.*] Oh, Elizabeth, I've found an illustration here of a chair which is almost identical with mine. It's dated 1750. Look!

ELIZABETH: That's very interesting.

ARNOLD: I want to show it to Porteous. [*Moving a chair which has been misplaced.*] You know, it does exasperate me the way people will not leave things alone. I no sooner put a thing in its place than somebody moves it.

ELIZABETH: It must be maddening for you.

ARNOLD: It is. You are the worst offender. I can't think why you don't take the pride that I do in the house. After all, it's one of the show places in the county.

ELIZABETH: I'm afraid you find me very unsatisfactory.

ARNOLD: [*Good-humouredly.*] I don't know about that. But my two subjects are politics and decoration. I should be a perfect fool if I didn't see that you don't care two straws about either.

ELIZABETH: We haven't very much in common, Arnold, have we?

ARNOLD: I don't think you can blame me for that.

ELIZABETH: I don't. I blame you for nothing. I have no fault to find with you.

ARNOLD: [*Surprised at her significant tone.*] Good gracious me, what's the meaning of all this?

ELIZABETH: Well, I don't think there's any object in beating about the bush. I want you to let me go.

ARNOLD: Go where?

ELIZABETH: Away. For always.

ARNOLD: My dear child, what *are* you talking about?

ELIZABETH: I want to be free.

ARNOLD: [*Amused rather than disconcerted.*] Don't be ridiculous, darling. I daresay you're run down and want a change. I'll take you over to Paris for a fortnight if you like.

ELIZABETH: I shouldn't have spoken to you if I hadn't quite made up my mind. We've been married for three years and I don't think it's been a great success. I'm frankly bored by the life you want me to lead.

ARNOLD: Well, if you'll allow me to say so, the fault is yours. We lead a very distinguished, useful life. We know a lot of extremely nice people.

ELIZABETH: I'm quite willing to allow that the fault is mine. But how does that make it any better? I'm only twenty-five. If I've made a mistake I have time to correct it.

ARNOLD: I can't bring myself to take you very seriously.

ELIZABETH: You see, I don't love you.

ARNOLD: Well, I'm awfully sorry. But you weren't obliged to marry me. You've made your bed and I'm afraid you must lie on it.

ELIZABETH: That's one of the falsest proverbs in the English language. Why should you lie on the bed you've made if you don't want to? There's always the floor.

ARNOLD: For goodness' sake don't be funny, Elizabeth.

ELIZABETH: I've quite made up my mind to leave you, Arnold.

ARNOLD: Come, come, Elizabeth, you must be sensible. You haven't any reason to leave me.

ELIZABETH: Why should you wish to keep a woman tied to you who wants to be free?

ARNOLD: I happen to be in love with you.

ELIZABETH: You might have said that before.

ARNOLD: I thought you'd take it for granted. You can't expect a man to go on making love to his wife after three years. I'm very busy. I'm awfully keen on politics and I've worked like a dog to make this house a thing of beauty. After all, a man marries to have a home, but also because he doesn't want to be bothered with sex and all that sort of thing. I fell in love with you the first time I saw you and I've been in love ever since.

ELIZABETH: I'm sorry, but if you're not in love with a man his love doesn't mean very much to you.

ARNOLD: It's so ungrateful. I've done everything in the world for you.

ELIZABETH: You've been very kind to me. But you've asked me to lead a life I don't like and that I'm not suited for. I'm awfully sorry to cause you pain, but now you must let me go.

ARNOLD: Nonsense! I'm a good deal older than you are and I think I have a little more sense. In your interest as well as in mine I'm not going to do anything of the sort.

ELIZABETH: [*With a smile.*] How can you prevent me? You can't keep me under lock and key.

ARNOLD: Please don't talk to me as if I were a foolish child. You're my wife and you're going to remain my wife.

ELIZABETH: What sort of a life do you think we should lead? Do you think there'd be any more happiness for you than for me?

ARNOLD: But what is it precisely that you suggest?

ELIZABETH: Well, I want you to let me divorce you.

ARNOLD: [*Astounded.*] Me? Thank you very much. Are you under the impression I'm going to sacrifice my career for a whim of yours?

ELIZABETH: How will it do that?

ARNOLD: My seat's wobbly enough as it is. Do you think I'd be able to hold it if I were in a divorce case? Even if it were a put-up job, as most divorces are nowadays, it would damn me.

ELIZABETH: It's rather hard on a woman to be divorced.

ARNOLD: [*With sudden suspicion.*] What do you mean by that? Are you in love with someone?

ELIZABETH: Yes.

ARNOLD: Who?

ELIZABETH: Teddie Luton.

[*He is astonished for a moment, then bursts into a laugh.*

ARNOLD: My poor child, how can you be so ridiculous? Why, he hasn't a bob. He's a perfectly commonplace young man. It's so absurd I can't even be angry with you.

ELIZABETH: I've fallen desperately in love with him, Arnold.

ARNOLD: Well, you'd better fall desperately out.

ELIZABETH: He wants to marry me.

ARNOLD: I daresay he does. He can go to hell.

ELIZABETH: It's no good talking like that.

ARNOLD: Is he your lover?

ELIZABETH: No, certainly not.

ARNOLD: It shows that he's a mean skunk to take advantage of my hospitality to make love to you.

ELIZABETH: He's never even kissed me.

ARNOLD: I'd try telling that to the horse marines if I were you.

ELIZABETH: It's because I wanted to do nothing shabby that I told you straight out how things were.

ARNOLD: How long have you been thinking of this?

ELIZABETH: I've been in love with Teddie ever since I knew him.

ARNOLD: And you never thought of me at all, I suppose.

ELIZABETH: Oh, yes, I did. I was miserable. But I can't help myself. I wish I loved you, but I don't.

ARNOLD: I recommend you to think very carefully before you do anything foolish.

ELIZABETH: I have thought very carefully.

ARNOLD: By God, I don't know why I don't give you a sound hiding. I'm not sure if that wouldn't be the best thing to bring you to your senses.

ELIZABETH: Oh, Arnold, don't take it like that.

ARNOLD: How do you expect me to take it? You come to me quite calmly and say: "I've had enough of you. We've been married three years and I think I'd like to marry somebody else now. Shall I break up your home? What a bore for you! Do you mind my divorcing you? It'll smash up your career, will it? What a pity!" Oh, no, my girl, I may be a fool, but I'm not a damned fool.

ELIZABETH: Teddie is leaving here by the first train to-morrow. I warn you that I mean to join him as soon as he can make the necessary arrangements.

ARNOLD: Where is he?

ELIZABETH: I don't know. I suppose he's in his room.

[ARNOLD *goes to the door and calls.*

ARNOLD: George!

[*For a moment he walks up and down the room impatiently.* ELIZABETH *watches him. The* FOOTMAN *comes in.*

FOOTMAN: Yes, sir.

ARNOLD: Tell Mr. Luton to come here at once.

ELIZABETH: Ask Mr. Luton if he wouldn't mind coming here for a moment.

FOOTMAN: Very good, madam.

[*Exit* FOOTMAN.

ELIZABETH: What are you going to say to him?

ARNOLD: That's my business.

ELIZABETH: I wouldn't make a scene if I were you.

ARNOLD: I'm not going to make a scene.

[*They wait in silence.*

Why did you insist on my mother coming here?

ELIZABETH: It seemed to me rather absurd to take up the attitude that I should be contaminated by her when . . .

ARNOLD: [*Interrupting.*] When you were proposing to do exactly the same thing. Well, now you've seen her what do you think of her? Do you think it's been a success? Is that the sort of woman a man would like his mother to be?

ELIZABETH: I've been ashamed. I've been so sorry. It all seemed dreadful and horrible. This morning I happened to notice a rose in the garden. It was all overblown and bedraggled. It looked like a painted old woman. And I remembered that I'd looked at it a day or two ago. It was lovely then, fresh and blooming and fragrant. It may be hideous now, but that doesn't take away from the beauty it had once. That was real.

ARNOLD: Poetry, by God! As if this were the moment for poetry!

[TEDDIE *comes in. He has changed into a dinner jacket.*

TEDDIE: [*To* ELIZABETH.] Did you want me?

ARNOLD: *I* sent for you.

TEDDIE *looks from* ARNOLD *to* ELIZABETH. *He sees that something has happened.*

When would it be convenient for you to leave this house?

TEDDIE: I was proposing to go to-morrow morning. But I can very well go at once if you like.

ARNOLD: I do like.

TEDDIE: Very well. Is there anything else you wish to say to me?

ARNOLD: Do you think it was a very honourable thing to come down here and make love to my wife?

TEDDIE: No, I don't. I haven't been very happy about it. That's why I wanted to go away.

ARNOLD: Upon my word you're cool.

TEDDIE: I'm afraid it's no good saying I'm sorry and that sort of thing. You know what the situation is.

ARNOLD: Is it true that you want to marry Elizabeth?

TEDDIE: Yes. I should like to marry her as soon as ever I can.

ARNOLD: Have you thought of me at all? Has it struck you that you're destroying my home and breaking up my happiness?

TEDDIE: I don't see how there could be much happiness for you if Elizabeth doesn't care for you.

ARNOLD: Let me tell you that I refuse to have my home broken up by a twopenny-halfpenny adventurer who takes advantage of a foolish woman. I refuse to allow myself to be divorced. I can't prevent my wife from going off with you if she's determined to make a damned fool of herself, but this I tell you: nothing will induce me to divorce her.

ELIZABETH: Arnold, that would be monstrous.

TEDDIE: We could force you.

ARNOLD: How?

TEDDIE: If we went away together openly you'd have to bring an action.

ARNOLD: Twenty-four hours after you leave this house I shall go down to Brighton with a chorus-girl. And neither you nor I will be able to get a divorce. We've had enough divorces in our family. And now get out, get out, get out!

> [TEDDIE *looks uncertainly at* ELIZABETH.

ELIZABETH: [*With a little smile.*] Don't bother about me. I shall be all right.

ARNOLD: Get out! Get out!

END OF THE SECOND ACT

THE THIRD ACT

The Scene is the same.

It is the night of the same day as that on which takes place the action of the second Act.

CHAMPION-CHENEY *and* ARNOLD, *both in dinner jackets, are discovered.* CHAMPION-CHENEY *is seated.* ARNOLD *walks restlessly up and down the room.*

C.-C.: I think, if you'll follow my advice to the letter, you'll probably work the trick.

ARNOLD: I don't like it, you know. It's against all my principles.

C.-C.: My dear Arnold, we all hope that you have before you a distinguished political career. You can't learn too soon that the most useful thing about a principle is that it can always be sacrificed to expediency.

ARNOLD: But supposing it doesn't come off? Women are incalculable.

C.-C.: Nonsense! Men are romantic. A woman will always sacrifice herself if you give her the opportunity. It is her favourite form of self-indulgence.

ARNOLD: I never know whether you're a humorist or a cynic, father.

C.-C.: I'm neither, my dear boy; I'm merely a very truthful man. But people are so unused to the truth that they're apt to mistake it for a joke or a sneer.

ARNOLD: [*Irritably.*] It seems so unfair that this should happen to me.

C.-C.: Keep your head, my boy, and do what I tell you.

> [LADY KITTY *and* ELIZABETH *come in.* LADY KITTY *is in a gorgeous evening gown.*

ELIZABETH: Where is Lord Porteous?

C.-C.: He's on the terrace. He's smoking a cigar. [*Going to window.*] Hughie!

> [PORTEOUS *comes in.*

PORTEOUS: [*With a grunt.*] Yes? Where's Mrs. Shenstone?

ELIZABETH: Oh, she had a headache. She's gone to bed.

> [*When* PORTEOUS *comes in* LADY KITTY *with a very haughty air purses her lips and takes up an illustrated paper.* PORTEOUS *gives her an irritated look, takes another illustrated paper and sits himself down at the other end of the room. They are not on speaking terms.*

C.-C.: Arnold and I have just been down to my cottage.

ELIZABETH: I wondered where you'd gone.

C.-C.: I came across an old photograph album this afternoon. I meant to bring it along before dinner, but I forgot, so we went and fetched it.

ELIZABETH: Oh, do let me see it. I love old photographs.

> [*He gives her the album, and she, sitting down, puts it on her knees and begins to turn over the pages. He stands over her.* LADY KITTY *and* PORTEOUS *take surreptitious glances at one another.*

C.-C.: I thought it might amuse you to see what pretty women looked like five-and-thirty years ago. That was the day of beautiful women.

ELIZABETH: Do you think they were more beautiful then than they are now?

C.-C.: Oh, much. Now you see lots of pretty little things, but very few beautiful women.

ELIZABETH: Aren't their clothes funny?

C.-C.: [*Pointing to a photograph.*] That's Mrs. Langtry.

ELIZABETH: She has a lovely nose.

C.-C.: She was the most wonderful thing you ever saw. Dowagers used to jump on chairs in order to get a good look at her when she came into a drawing-room. I was riding with her once, and we had to have the gates of the livery stable closed when she was getting on her horse because the crowd was so great.

ELIZABETH: And who's that?

C.-C.: Lady Lonsdale. That's Lady Dudley.

ELIZABETH: This is an actress, isn't it?

C.-C.: It is, indeed. Ellen Terry. By George, how I loved that woman!

ELIZABETH: [*With a smile.*] Dear Ellen Terry!

C.-C.: That's Bwabs. I never saw a smarter man in my life. And Oliver Montagu. Henry Manners with his eyeglass.

ELIZABETH: Nice-looking, isn't he? And this?

C.-C.: That's Mary Anderson. I wish you could have seen her in A Winter's Tale. Her beauty just took your breath away. And look! There's Lady Randolph. Bernal Osborne—the wittiest man I ever knew.

ELIZABETH: I think it's too sweet. I love their absurd bustles and those tight sleeves.

C.-C.: What figures they had! In those days a woman wasn't supposed to be as thin as a rail and as flat as a pancake.

ELIZABETH: Oh, but aren't they laced in? How could they bear it?

C.-C.: They didn't play golf then, and nonsense like that, you know. They hunted, in a tall hat and a long black habit, and they were very gracious and charitable to the poor in the village.

ELIZABETH: Did the poor like it?

C.-C.: They had a very thin time if they didn't. When they were in London they drove in the Park every afternoon, and they went to ten-course dinners, where they never

met anybody they didn't know. And they had their
box at the opera when Patti was singing or Madame
Albani.

ELIZABETH: Oh, what a lovely little thing! Who on earth
is that?

C.-C.: That?

ELIZABETH: She looks so fragile, like a piece of exquisite
china, with all those furs on and her face up against her
muff, and the snow falling.

C.-C.: Yes, there was quite a rage at that time for being
taken in an artificial snowstorm.

ELIZABETH: What a sweet smile, so roguish and frank, and
debonair! Oh, I wish I looked like that. Do tell me
who it is.

C.-C.: Don't you know?

ELIZABETH: No.

C.-C.: Why—it's Kitty.

ELIZABETH: Lady Kitty! [*To* LADY KITTY.] Oh, my dear,
do look. It's too ravishing. [*She takes the album over to
her impulsively.*] Why didn't you tell me you looked like
that? Everybody must have been in love with you.

   [LADY KITTY *takes the album and looks at it. Then
      she lets it slip from her hands and covers her face
      with her hands. She is crying.*

   [*In consternation.*] My dear, what's the matter? Oh, what
   have I done? I'm so sorry.

LADY KITTY: Don't, don't talk to me. Leave me alone.
It's stupid of me.

   [ELIZABETH *looks at her for a moment perplexed, then,
      turning round, slips her arm in* CHAMPION-CHENEY'*s
      and leads him out on to the terrace.*

ELIZABETH: [*As they are going, in a whisper.*] Did you do
that on purpose?

[PORTEOUS *gets up and goes over to* LADY KITTY. *He puts his hand on her shoulder. They remain thus for a little while.*

PORTEOUS: I'm afraid I was very rude to you before dinner, Kitty.

LADY KITTY: [*Taking his hand which is on her shoulder.*] It doesn't matter. I'm sure I was very exasperating.

PORTEOUS: I didn't mean what I said, you know.

LADY KITTY: Neither did I.

PORTEOUS: Of course I know that I'd never have been Prime Minister.

LADY KITTY: How can you talk such nonsense, Hughie? No one would have had a chance if you'd remained in politics.

PORTEOUS: I haven't the character.

LADY KITTY: You have more character than anyone I've ever met.

PORTEOUS: Besides, I don't know that I much wanted to be Prime Minister.

LADY KITTY: Oh, but I should have been so proud of you. Of course you'd have been Prime Minister.

PORTEOUS: I'd have given you India, you know. I think it would have been a very popular appointment.

LADY KITTY: I don't care twopence about India. I'd have been quite content with Western Australia.

PORTEOUS: My dear, you don't think I'd have let you bury yourself in Western Australia?

LADY KITTY: Or Barbadoes.

PORTEOUS: Never. It sounds like a cure for flat feet. I'd have kept you in London.

[*He picks up the album and is about to look at the photograph of Lady Kitty. She puts her hand over it.*

LADY KITTY: No, don't look.

[*He takes her hand away.*

PORTEOUS: Don't be so silly.

LADY KITTY: Isn't it hateful to grow old?

PORTEOUS: You know, you haven't changed much.

LADY KITTY: [*Enchanted.*] Oh, Hughie, how can you talk such nonsense?

PORTEOUS: Of course you're a little more mature, but that's all. A woman's all the better for being rather mature.

LADY KITTY: Do you really think that?

PORTEOUS: Upon my soul I do.

LADY KITTY: You're not saying it just to please me?

PORTEOUS: No, no.

LADY KITTY: Let me look at the photograph again.

[*She takes the album and looks at the photograph complacently.*

The fact is, if your bones are good, age doesn't really matter. You'll always be beautiful.

PORTEOUS: [*With a little smile, almost as if he were talking to a child.*] It was silly of you to cry.

LADY KITTY: It hasn't made my eyelashes run, has it?

PORTEOUS: Not a bit.

LADY KITTY: It's very good stuff I use now. They don't stick together either.

PORTEOUS: Look here, Kitty, how much longer do you want to stay here?

LADY KITTY: Oh, I'm quite ready to go whenever you like.

PORTEOUS: Clive gets on my nerves. I don't like the way he keeps hanging about you.

LADY KITTY: [*Surprised, rather amused, and delighted.*] Hughie, you don't mean to say you're jealous of poor Clive?

PORTEOUS: Of course I'm not jealous of him, but he does look at you in a way that I can't help thinking rather objectionable.

LADY KITTY: Hughie, you may throw me downstairs like Amy Robsart; you may drag me about the floor by the hair of my head; I don't care, you're jealous. I shall never grow old.

PORTEOUS: Damn it all, the man was your husband.

LADY KITTY: My dear Hughie, he never had your style. Why, the moment you come into a room everyone looks and says, Who the devil is that?

PORTEOUS: What? You think that, do you? Well, I daresay there's something in what you say. These damned Radicals can say what they like, but, by God, Kitty, when a man's a gentleman—well, damn it all, you know what I mean.

LADY KITTY: I think Clive has degenerated dreadfully since we left him.

PORTEOUS: What do you say to making a bee line for Italy and going to San Michele?

LADY KITTY: Oh, Hughie! It's years since we were there.

PORTEOUS: Wouldn't you like to see it again—just once more?

LADY KITTY: Do you remember the first time we went? It was the most heavenly place I'd ever seen. We'd only left England a month, and I said I'd like to spend all my life there.

PORTEOUS: Of course, I remember. And in a fortnight it was yours, lock, stock and barrel.

LADY KITTY: We were very happy there, Hughie.

PORTEOUS: Let's go back once more.

LADY KITTY: I daren't. It must be all peopled with the ghosts of our past. One should never go again to a place where one has been happy. It would break my heart.

PORTEOUS: Do you remember how we used to sit on the terrace of the old castle and look at the Adriatic? We might have been the only people in the world, you and I, Kitty.

LADY KITTY: [*Tragically.*] And we thought our love would last for ever.

[*Enter* CHAMPION-CHENEY.

PORTEOUS: Is there any chance of bridge this evening?

C.-C.: I don't think we can make up a four.

PORTEOUS: What a nuisance that boy went away like that! He wasn't a bad player.

C.-C.: Teddie Luton?

LADY KITTY: I think it was very funny his going without saying good-bye to anyone.

C.-C.: The young men of the present day are very casual.

PORTEOUS: I thought there was no train in the evening.

C.-C.: There isn't. The last train leaves at 5.45.

PORTEOUS: How did he go then?

C.-C.: He went.

PORTEOUS: Damned selfish I call it.

LADY KITTY: [*Intrigued.*] Why did he go, Clive?

[CHAMPION-CHENEY *looks at her for a moment reflectively*.

C.-C.: I have something very grave to say to you. Elizabeth wants to leave Arnold.

LADY KITTY: Clive! What on earth for?

C.-C.: She's in love with Teddie Luton. That's why he went. The men of my family are really very unfortunate.

PORTEOUS: Does she want to run away with him

LADY KITTY: [*With consternation.*] My dear, what's to be done?

C.-C.: I think you can do a great deal.

LADY KITTY: I? What?

C. C.: Tell her, tell her what it means.

> [*He looks at her fixedly. She stares at him.*

LADY KITTY: Oh, no, no!

C.-C.: She's a child. Not for Arnold's sake. For her sake. You must.

LADY KITTY: You don't know what you're asking.

C.-C.: Yes, I do.

LADY KITTY: Hughie, what shall I do?

PORTEOUS: Do what you like. I shall never blame you for anything.

> [*The* FOOTMAN *comes in with a letter on a salver. He hesitates on seeing that* ELIZABETH *is not in the room.*

C.-C.: What is it?

FOOTMAN: I was looking for Mrs. Champion-Cheney, sir.

C.-C.: She's not here. Is that a letter?

FOOTMAN: Yes, sir. It's just been sent up from The Champion Arms.

C.-C.: Leave it. I'll give it to Mrs. Cheney.

FOOTMAN: Very good, sir.

> [*He brings the tray to* CLIVE, *who takes the letter. The* FOOTMAN *goes out.*

PORTEOUS: Is The Champion Arms the local pub?

C.-C.: [*Looking at the letter.*] It's by way of being a hotel, but I never heard of anyone staying there.

LADY KITTY: If there was no train I suppose he had to go there.

C.-C.: Great minds. I wonder what he has to write about. [*He goes to the door leading on to the garden.*] Elizabeth.

ELIZABETH: [*Outside.*] Yes.

C.-C.: Here's a note for you.

> [*There is silence. They wait for* ELIZABETH *to come. She enters.*

ELIZABETH: It's lovely in the garden to-night.

C.-C.: They've just sent this up from The Champion Arms.

ELIZABETH: Thank you.

> [*Without embarrassment she opens the letter. They watch her while she reads it. It covers three pages. She puts it away in her bag.*

LADY KITTY: Hughie, I wish you'd fetch me a cloak. I'd like to take a little stroll in the garden, but after thirty years in Italy I find these English summers rather chilly.

> [*Without a word* PORTEOUS *goes out.* ELIZABETH *is lost in thought.*

I want to talk to Elizabeth, Clive.

C.-C.: I'll leave you.

> [*He goes out.*

LADY KITTY: What does he say?

ELIZABETH: Who?

LADY KITTY: Mr. Luton.

ELIZABETH: [*Gives a little start. Then she looks at* LADY KITTY.] They've told you?

LADY KITTY: Yes. And now they have I think I knew it all along.

ELIZABETH: I don't expect you to have much sympathy for me. Arnold is your son.

LADY KITTY: So pitifully little.

ELIZABETH: I'm not suited for this sort of existence. Arnold wants me to take what he calls my place in Society. Oh, I get so bored with those parties in London. All those middle-aged painted women, in beautiful clothes, lolloping round ball-rooms with rather old young men. And the endless luncheons where they gossip about so-and-so's love affairs.

LADY KITTY: Are you very much in love with Mr. Luton?

ELIZABETH: I love him with all my heart.

LADY KITTY: And he?

ELIZABETH: He's never cared for anyone but me. He never will.

LADY KITTY: Will Arnold let you divorce him?

ELIZABETH: No, he won't hear of it. He refuses even to divorce me.

LADY KITTY: Why?

ELIZABETH: He thinks a scandal will revive all the old gossip.

LADY KITTY: Oh, my poor child.

ELIZABETH: It can't be helped. I'm quite willing to accept the consequences.

LADY KITTY: You don't know what it is to have a man tied to you only by his honour. When married people don't get on they can separate, but if they're not married it's impossible. It's a tie that only death can sever.

ELIZABETH: If Teddie stopped caring for me I shouldn't want him to stay with me for five minutes.

LADY KITTY: One says that when one's sure of a man's love, but when one isn't any more—oh, it's so different. In those circumstances one's got to keep a man's love. It's the only thing one has.

ELIZABETH: I'm a human being. I can stand on my own feet.

LADY KITTY: Have you any money of your own?

ELIZABETH: None.

LADY KITTY: Then how can you stand on your own feet? You think I'm a silly, frivolous woman, but I've learnt something in a bitter school. They can make what laws they like, they can give us the suffrage, but when you come down to bedrock it's the man who pays the piper who calls the tune. Woman will only be the equal of

o

man when she earns her living in the same way that he
does.

ELIZABETH: [*Smiling.*] It sounds rather funny to hear you
talk like that.

LADY KITTY: A cook who marries a butler can snap her
fingers in his face because she can earn just as much as
he can. But a woman in your position and a woman in
mine will always be dependent on the men who keep
them.

ELIZABETH: I don't want luxury. You don't know how sick
I am of all this beautiful furniture. These over-decorated
houses are like a prison in which I can't breathe. When
I drive about in a Callot frock and a Rolls-Royce I envy
the shop-girl in a coat and skirt whom I see jumping
on the tailboard of a bus.

LADY KITTY: You mean that if need be you could earn your
own living?

ELIZABETH: Yes.

LADY KITTY: What could you be? A nurse or a typist.
It's nonsense. Luxury saps a woman's nerve. And when
she's known it once it becomes a necessity.

ELIZABETH: That depends on the woman.

LADY KITTY: When we're young we think we're different
from everyone else, but when we grow a little older we
discover we're all very much of a muchness.

ELIZABETH: You're very kind to take so much trouble
about me.

LADY KITTY: It breaks my heart to think that you're going
to make the same pitiful mistake that I made.

ELIZABETH: Oh, don't say it was that, don't, don't.

LADY KITTY: Look at me, Elizabeth, and look at Hughie.
Do you think it's been a success? If I had my time over
again do you think I'd do it again? Do you think he
would?

ELIZABETH: You see, you don't know how much I love Teddie.

LADY KITTY: And do you think I didn't love Hughie? Do you think he didn't love me?

ELIZABETH: I'm sure he did.

LADY KITTY: Oh, of course in the beginning it was heavenly. We felt so brave and adventurous and we were so much in love. The first two years were wonderful. People cut me, you know, but I didn't mind. I thought love was everything. It *is* a little uncomfortable when you come upon an old friend and go towards her eagerly, so glad to see her, and are met with an icy stare.

ELIZABETH: Do you think friends like that are worth having?

LADY KITTY: Perhaps they're not very sure of themselves. Perhaps they're honestly shocked. It's a test one had better not put one's friends to if one can help it. It's rather bitter to find how few one has.

ELIZABETH: But one has some.

LADY KITTY: Yes, they ask you to come and see them when they're quite certain no one will be there who might object to meeting you. Or else they say to you, My dear, you know I'm devoted to you, and I wouldn't mind at all, but my girl's growing up—I'm sure you understand; you won't think it unkind of me if I don't ask you to the house?

ELIZABETH: [*Smiling.*] That doesn't seem to me very serious.

LADY KITTY: At first I thought it rather a relief, because it threw Hughie and me together more. But you know, men are very funny. Even when they are in love they're not in love all day long. They want change and recreation.

ELIZABETH: I'm not inclined to blame them for that, poor dears.

LADY KITTY: Then we settled in Florence. And because we couldn't get the society we'd been used to, we became used to the society we could get. Loose women and vicious men. Snobs who liked to patronise people with a handle to their names. Vague Italian princes who were glad to borrow a few francs from Hughie and seedy countesses who liked to drive with me in the Cascine. And then Hughie began to hanker after his old life. He wanted to go big game shooting, but I dared not let him go. I was afraid he'd never come back.

ELIZABETH: But you knew he loved you.

LADY KITTY: Oh, my dear, what a blessed institution marriage is—for women, and what fools they are to meddle with it! The Church is so wise to take its stand on the indi—indi——

ELIZABETH: Solu——

LADY KITTY: Bility of marriage. Believe me, it's no joke when you have to rely only on yourself to keep a man. I could never afford to grow old. My dear, I'll tell you a secret that I've never told a living soul.

ELIZABETH: What is that?

LADY KITTY: My hair is not naturally this colour.

ELIZABETH: Really.

LADY KITTY: I touch it up. You would never have guessed, would you?

ELIZABETH: Never.

LADY KITTY: Nobody does. My dear, it's white, prematurely of course, but white. I always think it's a symbol of my life. Are you interested in symbolism? I think it's too wonderful.

ELIZABETH: I don't think I know very much about it.

LADY KITTY: However tired I've been I've had to be brilliant and gay. I've never let Hughie see the aching heart behind my smiling eyes.

ELIZABETH: [*Amused and touched.*] You poor dear.

LADY KITTY: And when I saw he was attracted by someone else the fear and the jealousy that seized me! You see, I didn't dare make a scene as I should have done if I'd been married. I had to pretend not to notice.

ELIZABETH: [*Taken aback.*] But do you mean to say he fell in love with anyone else?

LADY KITTY: Of course he did eventually.

ELIZABETH: [*Hardly knowing what to say.*] You must have been very unhappy.

LADY KITTY: Oh, I was, dreadfully. Night after night I sobbed my heart out when Hughie told me he was going to play cards at the club and I knew he was with that odious woman. Of course, it wasn't as if there weren't plenty of men who were only too anxious to console me. Men have always been attracted by me, you know.

ELIZABETH: Oh, of course, I can quite understand it.

LADY KITTY: But I had my self-respect to think of. I felt that whatever Hughie did I would do nothing that I should regret.

ELIZABETH: You must be very glad now.

LADY KITTY: Oh, yes. Notwithstanding all my temptations I've been absolutely faithful to Hughie in spirit.

ELIZABETH: I don't think I quite understand what you mean.

LADY KITTY: Well, there was a poor Italian boy, young Count Castel Giovanni, who was so desperately in love with me that his mother begged me not to be too cruel. She was afraid he'd go into a consumption. What could I do? And then, oh, years later, there was Antonio Melita. He said he'd shoot himself unless I—well, you understand I couldn't let the poor boy shoot himself.

ELIZABETH: D'you think he really would have shot himself?

LADY KITTY: Oh, one never knows, you know. Those Italians are so passionate. He was really rather a lamb. He had such beautiful eyes.

> [ELIZABETH *looks at her for a long time and a certain horror seizes her of this dissolute, painted old woman.*

ELIZABETH: [*Hoarsely.*] Oh, but I think that's—dreadful.

LADY KITTY: Are you shocked? One sacrifices one's life for love and then one finds that love doesn't last. The tragedy of love isn't death or separation. One gets over them. The tragedy of love is indifference.

> [ARNOLD *comes in.*

ARNOLD: Can I have a little talk with you, Elizabeth?

ELIZABETH: Of course.

ARNOLD: Shall we go for a stroll in the garden?

ELIZABETH: If you like.

LADY KITTY: No, stay here. I'm going out anyway.

> [*Exit* LADY KITTY.

ARNOLD: I want you to listen to me for a few minutes, Elizabeth. I was so taken aback by what you told me just now that I lost my head. I was rather absurd and I beg your pardon. I said things I regret.

ELIZABETH: Oh, don't blame yourself. I'm sorry that I should have given you occasion to say them.

ARNOLD: I want to ask you if you've quite made up your mind to go.

ELIZABETH: Quite.

ARNOLD: Just now I seem to have said all that I didn't want to say and nothing that I did. I'm stupid and tongue-tied. I never told you how deeply I loved you.

ELIZABETH: Oh, Arnold.

ARNOLD: Please let me speak now. It's so very difficult. If I seemed absorbed in politics and the house, and so on, to the exclusion of my interest in you, I'm dreadfully sorry. I suppose it was absurd of me to think you would take my great love for granted.

ELIZABETH: But, Arnold, I'm not reproaching you.

ARNOLD: I'm reproaching myself. I've been tactless and neglectful. But I do ask you to believe that it hasn't been because I didn't love you. Can you forgive me?

ELIZABETH: I don't think that there's anything to forgive.

ARNOLD: It wasn't till to-day when you talked of leaving me that I realised how desperately in love with you I was.

ELIZABETH: After three years?

ARNOLD: I'm so proud of you. I admire you so much. When I see you at a party, so fresh and lovely, and everybody wondering at you, I have a sort of little thrill because you're mine, and afterwards I shall take you home.

ELIZABETH: Oh, Arnold, you're exaggerating.

ARNOLD: I can't imagine this house without you. Life seems on a sudden all empty and meaningless. Oh, Elizabeth, don't you love me at all?

ELIZABETH: It's much better to be honest. No.

ARNOLD: Doesn't my love mean anything to you?

ELIZABETH: I'm very grateful to you. I'm sorry to cause you pain. What would be the good of my staying with you when I should be wretched all the time?

ARNOLD: Do you love that man as much as all that? Does my unhappiness mean nothing to you?

ELIZABETH: Of course it does. It breaks my heart. You see, I never knew I meant so much to you. I'm so touched. And I'm so sorry, Arnold, really sorry. But I can't help myself.

ARNOLD: Poor child, it's cruel of me to torture you.

ELIZABETH: Oh, Arnold, believe me, I have tried to make the best of it. I've tried to love you, but I can't. After all, one either loves or one doesn't. Trying is no help. And now I'm at the end of my tether. I can't help the consequences—I must do what my whole self yearns for.

ARNOLD: My poor child, I'm so afraid you'll be unhappy. I'm so afraid you'll regret.

ELIZABETH: You must leave me to my fate. I hope you'll forget me and all the unhappiness I've caused you.

ARNOLD: [*There is a pause. Arnold walks up and down the room reflectively. He stops and faces her.*] If you love this man and want to go to him I'll do nothing to prevent you. My only wish is to do what is best for you.

ELIZABETH: Arnold, that's awfully kind of you. If I'm treating you badly at least I want you to know that I'm grateful for all your kindness to me.

ARNOLD: But there's one favour I should like you to do me. Will you?

ELIZABETH: Oh, Arnold, of course I'll do anything I can.

ARNOLD: Teddie hasn't very much money. You've been used to a certain amount of luxury, and I can't bear to think that you should do without anything you've had. It would kill me to think that you were suffering any hardship or privation.

ELIZABETH: Oh, but Teddie can earn enough for our needs. After all, we don't want much money.

ARNOLD: I'm afraid my mother's life hasn't been very easy, but it's obvious that the only thing that's made it possible is that Porteous was rich. I want you to let me make you an allowance of two thousand a year.

ELIZABETH: Oh, no, I couldn't think of it. It's absurd.

ARNOLD: I beg you to accept it. You don't know what a difference it will make.

ELIZABETH: It's awfully kind of you, Arnold. It humiliates me to speak about it. Nothing would induce me to take a penny from you.

ARNOLD: Well, you can't prevent me from opening an account at my bank in your name. The money shall be paid in every quarter whether you touch it or not, and if you happen to want it, it will be there waiting for you.

ELIZABETH: You overwhelm me, Arnold. There's only one thing I want you to do for me. I should be very grateful if you would divorce me as soon as you possibly can.

ARNOLD: No, I won't do that. But I'll give you cause to divorce me.

ELIZABETH: You!

ARNOLD: Yes. But of course you'll have to be very careful for a bit. I'll put it through as quickly as possible, but I'm afraid you can't hope to be free for over six months.

ELIZABETH: But, Arnold, your seat and your political career!

ARNOLD: Oh, well, my father gave up his seat under similar circumstances. He's got along very comfortably without politics.

ELIZABETH: But they're your whole life.

ARNOLD: After all one can't have it both ways. You can't serve God and Mammon. If you want to do the decent thing you have to be prepared to suffer for it.

ELIZABETH: But I don't want you to suffer for it.

ARNOLD: At first I rather hesitated at the scandal. But I daresay that was only weakness on my part. In the circumstances I should have liked to keep out of the Divorce Court if I could.

ELIZABETH: Arnold, you're making me absolutely miserable.

ARNOLD: What you said before dinner was quite right. It's nothing for a man, but it makes so much difference to a woman. Naturally I must think of you first.

ELIZABETH: That's absurd. It's out of the question. Whatever there's to pay I must pay it.

ARNOLD: It's not very much I'm asking for, Elizabeth.

ELIZABETH: I'm taking everything from you.

ARNOLD: It's the only condition I make. My mind is absolutely made up. I will never divorce you, but I will enable you to divorce me.

ELIZABETH: Oh, Arnold, it's cruel to be so generous.

ARNOLD: It's not generous at all. It's the only way I have of showing you how deep and passionate and sincere my love is for you.

> [*There is a silence. He holds out his hand.*

Good-night. I have a great deal of work to do before I go to bed.

ELIZABETH: Good-night.

ARNOLD: Do you mind if I kiss you?

ELIZABETH: [*With agony.*] Oh, Arnold!

> [*He gravely kisses her on the forehead and then goes out.* ELIZABETH *stands lost in thought. She is shattered.* LADY KITTY *and* PORTEOUS *come in.* LADY KITTY *wears a cloak.*

LADY KITTY: You're alone, Elizabeth?

ELIZABETH: That note you asked me about, Lady Kitty, from Teddie . . .

LADY KITTY: Yes?

ELIZABETH: He wanted to have a talk with me before he went away. He's waiting for me in the summer house by the tennis court. Would Lord Porteous mind going down and asking him to come here?

PORTEOUS: Certainly. Certainly.

ELIZABETH: Forgive me for troubling you. But it's very important.

PORTEOUS: No trouble at all.

> [*He goes out.*

LADY KITTY: Hughie and I will leave you alone.

ELIZABETH: But I don't want to be left alone. I want you to stay.

LADY KITTY: What are you going to say to him?

ELIZABETH: [*Desperately.*] Please don't ask me questions. I'm so frightfully unhappy.

LADY KITTY: My poor child.

ELIZABETH: Oh, isn't life rotten? Why can't one be happy without making other people unhappy?

LADY KITTY: I wish I knew how to help you. I'm simply devoted to you. [*She hunts about in her mind for something to do or say.*] Would you like my lip-stick?

ELIZABETH: [*Smiling through her tears.*] Thanks. I never use one.

LADY KITTY: Oh, but just try. It's such a comfort when you're in trouble.

[*Enter* PORTEOUS *and* TEDDIE.

PORTEOUS: I brought him. He said he'd be damned if he'd come.

LADY KITTY: When a lady sent for him? Are these the manners of the young men of to-day?

TEDDIE: When you've been solemnly kicked out of a house once I think it seems rather pushing to come back again as though nothing had happened.

ELIZABETH: Teddie, I want you to be serious.

TEDDIE: Darling, I had such a rotten dinner at that pub. If you ask me to be serious on the top of that I shall cry.

ELIZABETH: Don't be idiotic, Teddie. [*Her voice faltering.*] I'm so utterly wretched.

[*He looks at her for a moment gravely.*

TEDDIE: What is it?

ELIZABETH: I can't come away with you, Teddie.

TEDDIE: Why not?

ELIZABETH: [*Looking away in embarrassment.*] I don't love you enough.

TEDDIE: Fiddle!

ELIZABETH: [*With a flash of anger.*] Don't say Fiddle to me.

TEDDIE: I shall say exactly what I like to you.

ELIZABETH: I won't be bullied.

TEDDIE: Now look here, Elizabeth, you know perfectly well that I'm in love with you, and I know perfectly well that you're in love with me. So what are you talking nonsense for?

ELIZABETH: [*Her voice breaking.*] I can't say it if you're cross with me.

TEDDIE: [*Smiling very tenderly.*] I'm not cross with you, silly.

ELIZABETH: It's harder still when you're being rather an owl.

TEDDIE: [*With a chuckle.*] Am I mistaken in thinking you're not very easy to please?

ELIZABETH: Oh, it's monstrous. I was all wrought up and ready to do anything, and now you've thoroughly put me out. I feel like a great big fat balloon that some one has put a long pin into. [*With a sudden look at him.*] Have you done it on purpose?

TEDDIE: Upon my soul I don't know what you're talking about.

ELIZABETH: I wonder if you're really much cleverer than I think you are.

TEDDIE: [*Taking her hands and making her sit down.*] Now tell me exactly what you want to say. By the way, do you want Lady Kitty and Lord Porteous to be here?

ELIZABETH: Yes.

LADY KITTY: Elizabeth asked us to stay.

TEDDIE: Oh, I don't mind, bless you. I only thought you might feel rather in the way.

LADY KITTY: [*Frigidly.*] A gentlewoman never feels in the way, Mr. Luton.

TEDDIE: Won't you call me Teddie? Everybody does, you know.

> [LADY KITTY *tries to give him a withering look, but she finds it very difficult to prevent herself from smiling.* TEDDIE *strokes* ELIZABETH'S *hands. She draws them away.*

ELIZABETH: No, don't do that. Teddie, it wasn't true when I said I didn't love you. Of course I love you. But Arnold loves me, too. I didn't know how much.

TEDDIE: What has he been saying to you?

ELIZABETH: He's been very good to me, and so kind. I didn't know he could be so kind. He offered to let me divorce him.

TEDDIE: That's very decent of him.

ELIZABETH: But don't you see, it ties my hands. How can I accept such a sacrifice? I should never forgive myself if I profited by his generosity.

TEDDIE: If another man and I were devilish hungry and there was only one mutton chop between us, and he said, You eat it, I wouldn't waste a lot of time arguing. I'd wolf it before he changed his mind.

ELIZABETH: Don't talk like that. It maddens me. I'm trying to do the right thing.

TEDDIE: You're not in love with Arnold; you're in love with me. It's idiotic to sacrifice your life for a slushy sentiment.

ELIZABETH: After all, I did marry him.

TEDDIE: Well, you made a mistake. A marriage without love is no marriage at all.

ELIZABETH: *I* made the mistake. Why should he suffer for it? If anyone has to suffer it's only right that I should.

TEDDIE: What sort of a life do you think it would be with him? When two people are married it's very difficult for one of them to be unhappy without making the other unhappy too.

ELIZABETH: I can't take advantage of his generosity.

TEDDIE: I daresay he'll get a lot of satisfaction out of it.

ELIZABETH: You're being beastly, Teddie. He was simply wonderful. I never knew he had it in him. He was really noble.

TEDDIE: You are talking rot, Elizabeth.

ELIZABETH: I wonder if you'd be capable of acting like that.

TEDDIE: Acting like what?

ELIZABETH: What would you do if I were married to you and came and told you I loved somebody else and wanted to leave you?

TEDDIE: You have very pretty blue eyes, Elizabeth. I'd black first one and then the other. And after that we'd see.

ELIZABETH: You damned brute!

TEDDIE: I've often thought I wasn't quite a gentleman. Had it never struck you?

[*They look at one another for a while.*

ELIZABETH: You know, you are taking an unfair advantage of me. I feel as if I came to you quite unsuspectingly and when I wasn't looking you kicked me on the shins.

TEDDIE: Don't you think we'd get on rather well together?

PORTEOUS: Elizabeth's a fool if she don't stick to her husband. It's bad enough for the man, but for the woman—it's damnable. I hold no brief for Arnold. He plays bridge like a foot. Saving your presence, Kitty, I think he's a prig.

LADY KITTY: Poor dear, his father was at his age. I daresay he'll grow out of it.

PORTEOUS: But you stick to him, Elizabeth, stick to him. Man is a gregarious animal. We're members of a herd. If we break the herd's laws we suffer for it. And we suffer damnably.

LADY KITTY: Oh, Elizabeth, my dear child, don't go. It's not worth it. It's not worth it. I tell you that, and I've sacrificed everything to love.

[*A pause.*

ELIZABETH: I'm afraid.

TEDDIE: [*In a whisper.*] Elizabeth.

ELIZABETH: I can't face it. It's asking too much of me. Let's say good-bye to one another, Teddie. It's the only thing to do. And have pity on me. I'm giving up all my hope of happiness.

[*He goes up to her and looks into her eyes.*

TEDDIE: But I wasn't offering you happiness. I don't think my sort of love tends to happiness. I'm jealous. I'm not a very easy man to get on with. I'm often out of temper and irritable. I should be fed to the teeth with you sometimes, and so would you be with me. I daresay we'd fight like cat and dog, and sometimes we'd hate each other. Often you'd be wretched and bored stiff and lonely, and often you'd be frightfully homesick, and then you'd regret all you'd lost. Stupid women would be rude to you because we'd run away together. And some of them would cut you. I don't offer you peace and quietness. I offer you unrest and anxiety. I don't offer you happiness. I offer you love.

ELIZABETH: [*Stretching out her arms.*] You hateful creature, I absolutely adore you.

[*He throws his arms round her and kisses her passionately on the lips.*]

LADY KITTY: Of course the moment he said he'd give her a black eye I knew it was finished.

PORTEOUS: [*Good-humouredly.*] You are a fool, Kitty.

LADY KITTY: I know I am, but I can't help it.

TEDDIE: Let's make a bolt for it now.

ELIZABETH: Shall we?

TEDDIE: This minute.

PORTEOUS: You're damned fools, both of you, damned fools. If you like you can have my car.

TEDDIE: That's awfully kind of you. As a matter of fact, I got it out of the garage. It's just along the drive.

PORTEOUS: [*Indignantly.*] How do you mean, you got it out of the garage?

TEDDIE: Well, I thought there'd be a lot of bother, and it seemed to me the best thing would be for Elizabeth and me not to stand upon the order of our going, you know. Do it now. An excellent motto for a business man.

PORTEOUS: Do you mean to say you were going to steal my car.

TEDDIE: Not exactly. I was only going to bolshevise it, so to speak.

PORTEOUS: I'm speechless. I'm absolutely speechless.

TEDDIE: Hang it all, I couldn't carry Elizabeth all the way to London. She's so damned plump.

ELIZABETH: You dirty dog!

PORTEOUS: [*Spluttering.*] Well, well, well! . . . [*Helplessly.*] I like him, Kitty, it's no good pretending I don't. I like him.

TEDDIE: The moon's shining, Elizabeth. We'll drive all through the night.

PORTEOUS: They'd better go to San Michele. I'll wire to have it got ready for them.

LADY KITTY: That's where we went when Hughie and I . . . [*Faltering.*] Oh, you dear things, how I envy you.

PORTEOUS: [*Mopping his eyes.*] Now don't cry, Kitty. Confound you, don't cry.

TEDDIE: Come, darling.

ELIZABETH: But I can't go like this.

TEDDIE: Nonsense! Lady Kitty will lend you her cloak. Won't you?

LADY KITTY: [*Taking it off.*] You're capable of tearing it off my back if I don't.

TEDDIE: [*Putting the cloak on* ELIZABETH.] And we'll buy you a tooth-brush in London in the morning.

LADY KITTY: She must write a note for Arnold, I'll put it on her pincushion.

TEDDIE: Pincushion be blowed. Come, darling. We'll drive through the dawn and through the sunrise.

ELIZABETH: [*Kissing* LADY KITTY *and* PORTEOUS.] Goodbye. Good-bye.

> [TEDDIE *stretches out his hand and she takes it. Hand in hand they go out into the night.*

LADY KITTY: Oh, Hughie, how it all comes back to me. Will they suffer all we suffered? And have we suffered all in vain?

PORTEOUS: My dear, I don't know that in life it matters so much what you do as what you are. No one can learn by the experience of another because no circumstances are quite the same. If we made rather a hash of things perhaps it was because we were rather trivial people. You can do anything in this world if you're prepared to take the consequences, and consequences depend on character.

[*Enter* CHAMPION-CHENEY, *rubbing his hands. He is as pleased as Punch.*

C.-C.: Well, I think I've settled the hash of that young man.

LADY KITTY: Oh?

C.-C.: You have to get up very early in the morning to get the better of your humble servant.

[*There is the sound of a car starting.*

LADY KITTY: What is that?

C.-C.: It sounds like a car. I expect it's your chauffeur taking one of the maids for a joy-ride.

PORTEOUS: Whose hash are you talking about?

C.-C.: Mr. Edward Luton's, my dear Hughie. I told Arnold exactly what to do and he's done it. What makes a prison? Why, bars and bolts. Remove them and a prisoner won't want to escape. Clever, I flatter myself.

PORTEOUS: You were always that, Clive, but at the moment you're obscure.

C.-C.: I told Arnold to go to Elizabeth and tell her she could have her freedom. I told him to sacrifice himself all along the line. I know what women are. The moment every obstacle was removed to her marriage with Teddie Luton, half the allurement was gone.

LADY KITTY: Arnold did that?

C.-C.: He followed my instructions to the letter. I've just seen him. She's shaken. I'm willing to bet five hundred pounds to a penny that she won't bolt. A downy old bird, eh? Downy's the word. Downy.

[*He begins to laugh. They laugh too. Presently they are all three in fits of laughter.*

THE END

THE CONSTANT WIFE

A COMEDY
in Three Acts

CHARACTERS

CONSTANCE
JOHN MIDDLETON, F.R.C.S.
BERNARD KERSAL
MRS. CULVER
MARIE-LOUISE
MARTHA
BARBARA
MORTIMER DURHAM
BENTLEY

The action of the play takes place in John's house in Harley Street.

THE CONSTANT WIFE

THE FIRST ACT

SCENE: CONSTANCE'S *drawing-room. It is a room furnished with singularly good taste.* CONSTANCE *has a gift for decoration and has made this room of hers both beautiful and comfortable.*

It is afternoon.

MRS. CULVER *is seated alone. She is an elderly lady with a pleasant face and she is dressed in walking costume. The door is opened and* BENTLEY *the butler introduces* MARTHA CULVER. *This is her daughter and a fine young woman.*

BENTLEY: Miss Culver.

[*He goes out.*

MARTHA: [*With astonishment.*] Mother.

MRS. CULVER: [*Very calmly.*] Yes, darling.

MARTHA: You're the last person I expected to find here. You never told me you were coming to see Constance.

MRS. CULVER: [*Good-humouredly.*] I didn't intend to till I saw in your beady eye that *you* meant to. I thought I'd just as soon be here first.

MARTHA: Bentley says she's out.

MRS. CULVER: Yes. . . . Are you going to wait?

MARTHA: Certainly.

MRS. CULVER: Then I will, too.

MARTHA: That'll be very nice.

MRS. CULVER: Your words are cordial, but your tone is slightly frigid, my dear.

MARTHA: I don't know what you mean by that, mother.

95

MRS. CULVER: My dear, we've known one another a great many years, haven't we? More than we always find it convenient to mention.

MARTHA: Not at all. I'm thirty-two. I'm not in the least ashamed of my age. Constance is thirty-six.

MRS. CULVER: And yet we still think it worth while to be a trifle disingenuous with one another. Our sex takes a natural pleasure in dissimulation.

MARTHA: I don't think anyone can accuse me of not being frank.

MRS. CULVER: Frankness of course is the pose of the moment. It is often a very effective screen for one's thoughts.

MARTHA: I think you're being faintly disagreeable to me, mother.

MRS. CULVER: I, on the other hand, think you're inclined to be decidedly foolish.

MARTHA: Because I want to tell Constance something she ought to know?

MRS. CULVER: Ah, I *was* right then. And it's to tell her that you've broken an engagement, and left three wretched people to play cut-throat.

MARTHA: It is.

MRS. CULVER: And may I ask why you think Constance ought to know?

MARTHA: Why? Why? Why? That's one of those questions that really don't need answering.

MRS. CULVER: I've always noticed that the questions that really don't need answering are the most difficult to answer.

MARTHA: It isn't at all difficult to answer. She ought to know the truth because it's the truth.

MRS. CULVER: Of course truth is an excellent thing, but before one tells it one should be quite sure that one does so for the advantage of the person who hears it rather than for one's own self-satisfaction.

MARTHA: Mother, Constance is a very unhappy person.

MRS. CULVER: Nonsense. She eats well, sleeps well, dresses well, and she's losing weight. No woman can be unhappy in those circumstances.

MARTHA: Of course if you won't understand it's no use my trying to make you. You're a darling, but you're the most unnatural mother. Your attitude simply amazes me.

[*The door opens and* BENTLEY *ushers in* MRS. FAWCETT. MRS. FAWCETT *is a trim, business-like woman of forty.*]

BENTLEY: Mrs. Fawcett.

MRS. CULVER: Oh, Barbara, how very nice to see you.

BARBARA: [*Going up to her and kissing her.*] Bentley told me you were here and Constance was out. What are you doing?

MRS. CULVER: Bickering.

BARBARA: What about?

MRS. CULVER: Constance.

MARTHA: I'm glad you've come, Barbara. . . . Did you know that John was having an affair with Marie-Louise?

BARBARA: I hate giving a straight answer to a straight question.

MARTHA: I suppose everyone knows but us. How long have you known? They say it's been going on for months. I can't think how it is we've only just heard it.

MRS. CULVER: [*Ironically.*] It speaks very well for human nature that with the masses of dear friends we have it's only to-day that one of them broke the news to us.

BARBARA: Perhaps the dear friend only heard it this morning.

MARTHA: At first I refused to believe it.

MRS. CULVER: Only quite, quite at first, darling. You surrendered to the evidence with an outraged alacrity that took my breath away.

MARTHA: Of course I put two and two together. After the first shock I understood everything. I'm only astonished that it never occurred to me before.

BARBARA: Are you very much upset, Mrs. Culver?

MRS. CULVER: Not a bit. I was brought up by a very strict mother to believe that men were naturally wicked. I am seldom surprised at what they do and never upset.

MARTHA: Mother has been simply maddening. She treats it as though it didn't matter a row of pins.

MRS. CULVER: Constance and John have been married for fifteen years. John is a very agreeable man. I've sometimes wondered whether he was any more faithful to his wife than most husbands, but as it was really no concern of mine I didn't let my mind dwell on it.

MARTHA: Is Constance your daughter or is she not your daughter?

MRS. CULVER: You certainly have a passion for straight questions, my dear. The answer is yes.

MARTHA: And are you prepared to sit there quietly and let her husband grossly deceive her with her most intimate friend?

MRS. CULVER: So long as she doesn't know I can't see that she's any the worse. Marie-Louise is a nice little thing, silly of course, but that's what men like, and if John is going to deceive Constance it's much better that it should be with someone we all know.

MARTHA: [*To* BARBARA.] Did you ever hear a respectable woman—and mother is respectable. . . .

MRS. CULVER: [*Interrupting.*] Oh, quite.

MARTHA: Talk like that?

BARBARA: You think that something ought to be done about it?

MARTHA: I am determined that something shall be done about it.

MRS. CULVER: Well, my dear, I'm determined that there's at least one thing you shan't do and that is to tell Constance.

BARBARA: [*A trifle startled.*] Is that what you want to do?

MARTHA: Somebody ought to tell her. If mother won't I must.

BARBARA: I'm extremely fond of Constance. Of course I've known what was going on for a long time and I've been dreadfully worried.

MARTHA: John has put her into an odious position. No man has the right to humiliate his wife as he has humiliated Constance. He's made her perfectly ridiculous.

MRS. CULVER: If women were ridiculous because their husbands are unfaithful to them, there would surely be a great deal more merriment in the world than there is.

BARBARA: [*Delighted to have a good gossip.*] You know they were lunching together to-day?

MARTHA: We hadn't heard that. But they were dining together the night before last.

MRS. CULVER: [*Brightly.*] We know what they had to eat for dinner. Do you know what they had to eat for luncheon?

MARTHA: Mother.

MRS. CULVER: Well, I thought she seemed rather uppish about the lunch.

MARTHA: You have no sense of decency, mother.

MRS. CULVER: Oh, my dear, don't talk to me about decency. Decency died with dear Queen Victoria.

BARBARA: [*To* MRS. CULVER.] But you can't approve of John having an open and flagrant intrigue with Constance's greatest friend.

MRS. CULVER: It may be that with advancing years my arteries have hardened. I am unable to attach any great importance to the philanderings of men. I think it's their nature. John is a very hard-working surgeon. If he likes to lunch and dine with a pretty woman now and then I don't think he's much to blame. It must be very tiresome to have three meals a day with the same woman for seven days a week. I'm a little bored myself at seeing Martha opposite me at the dinner-table. And men can't stand boredom as well as women.

MARTHA: I'm sure I'm very much obliged to you, mother.

BARBARA: [*Significantly.*] But they're not only lunching and dining together.

MRS. CULVER: You fear the worst, my dear?

BARBARA: [*With solemnity.*] I know the worst.

MRS. CULVER: I always think that's such a comfort. With closed doors and no one listening to us, so long as a man is kind and civil to his wife do you blame him very much if he strays occasionally from the narrow path of virtue?

MARTHA: Do you mean to say that you attach no importance to husbands and wives keeping their marriage vows?

MRS. CULVER: I think wives should.

BARBARA: But that's grossly unfair. Why should *they* any more than men?

MRS. CULVER: Because on the whole they like it. We ascribe a great deal of merit to ourselves because we're faithful to our husbands. I don't believe we deserve it for a minute. We're naturally faithful creatures and we're faithful because we have no particular inclination to be anything else.

BARBARA: I wonder.

MRS. CULVER: My dear, you are a widow and perfectly free. Have you really had any great desire to do anything that the world might say you shouldn't?

BARBARA: I have my business. When you work hard eight hours a day you don't much want to be bothered with love. In the evening the tired business woman wants to go to a musical comedy or play cards. She doesn't want to be worried with adoring males.

MARTHA: By the way, how is your business?

BARBARA: Growing by leaps and bounds. As a matter of fact I came here to-day to ask Constance if she would like to come in with me.

MRS. CULVER: Why should she? John earns plenty of money.

BARBARA: Well, I thought if things came to a crisis she might like to know that her independence was assured.

MRS. CULVER: Oh, you want them to come to a crisis, too?

BARBARA: No, of course I don't. But, you know, they can't go on like this. It's a miracle that Constance hasn't heard yet. She's bound to find out soon.

MRS. CULVER: I suppose it's inevitable.

MARTHA: I hope she'll find out as quickly as possible. I still think it's mother's duty to tell her.

MRS. CULVER: Which I have no intention of doing.

MARTHA: And if mother won't I think I ought.

MRS. CULVER: Which I have no intention of permitting.

MARTHA: He's humiliated her beyond endurance. Her position is intolerable. I have no words to express my opinion of Marie-Louise, and the first time I see her I shall tell her exactly what I think of her. She's a horrid, ungrateful, mean and contemptible little cat.

BARBARA: Anyhow, I think it would be a comfort to Constance to know that if anything happened she has me to turn to.

MRS. CULVER: But John would make her a handsome allowance. He's a very generous man.

MARTHA: [*Indignantly.*] Do you think Constance would accept it?

BARBARA: Martha's quite right, Mrs. Culver. No woman in those circumstances would take a penny of his money.

MRS. CULVER: That's what she'd say. But she'd take care that her lawyer made the best arrangement he could. Few men know with what ingenuity we women can combine the disinterested gesture with a practical eye for the main chance.

BARBARA: Aren't you rather cynical, Mrs. Culver?

MRS. CULVER: I hope not. But when women are alone together I don't see why they shouldn't tell the truth now and then. It's a rest from the weary round of pretending to be something that we quite well know we're not.

MARTHA: [*Stiffly.*] I'm not aware that I've ever pretended to be anything I wasn't.

MRS. CULVER: I dare say not, my dear. But I've always thought you were a little stupid. You take after your poor father. Constance and I have the brains of the family.

[CONSTANCE *comes into the room. She is a handsome woman of six and thirty. She has been out and wears a hat.*

BARBARA: [*Eagerly.*] Constance.

CONSTANCE: I'm so sorry I wasn't in. How nice of you all to wait. How are you, mother darling?

[*She kisses them one after another.*

MARTHA: What have you been doing all day, Constance?

CONSTANCE: Oh, I've been shopping with Marie-Louise. She's just coming up.

BARBARA: [*With dismay.*] Is she here?

CONSTANCE: Yes. She's telephoning.

MARTHA: [*Ironically.*] You and Marie-Louise are quite inseparable.

CONSTANCE: I like her. She amuses me.

MARTHA: Were you lunching together?

CONSTANCE: No, she was lunching with a beau.

MARTHA: [*With a glance at* MRS. CULVER.] Oh, really. [*Breezily.*] John always comes home to luncheon, doesn't he?

CONSTANCE: [*With great frankness.*] When he doesn't have to be at the hospital too early.

MARTHA: Was he lunching with you to-day?

CONSTANCE: No. He was engaged.

MARTHA: Where?

CONSTANCE: Good heavens, I don't know. When you've been married as long as I have you never ask your husband where he's going.

MARTHA: I don't know why not.

CONSTANCE: [*Smiling.*] Because he might take it into his head to ask *you*.

MRS. CULVER: And also because if you're a wise woman you have confidence in your husband.

CONSTANCE: John has never given me a moment's uneasiness yet.

MARTHA: You're lucky.

CONSTANCE: [*With her tongue in her cheek.*] Or wise.

> [MARIE-LOUISE *appears. She is a very pretty little thing, beautifully dressed, of the clinging, large-eyed type.*

MARIE-LOUISE: Oh, I didn't know there was a party.

MRS. CULVER: Martha and I are just going.

CONSTANCE: You know my mother, Marie-Louise.

MARIE-LOUISE: Of course I do.

CONSTANCE: She's a very nice mother.

MRS. CULVER: With her head screwed on the right way and very active for her years.

[MARIE-LOUISE *kisses* BARBARA *and* MARTHA.

MARIE-LOUISE: How do you do.

MARTHA: [*Looking at her dress.*] That's new, isn't it, Marie-Louise?

MARIE-LOUISE: Yes, I've never had it on before.

MARTHA: Oh, did you put it on because you were lunching with a beau?

MARIE-LOUISE: What makes you think I was lunching with a beau?

MARTHA: Constance told me so.

CONSTANCE: It was only a guess on my part. [*To* MARIE-LOUISE.] When we met I noticed that your eyes were shining and you had that pleased, young look a woman always gets when some one has been telling her she's the most adorable thing in the world.

MARTHA: Tell us who it was, Marie-Louise.

CONSTANCE: Do nothing of the kind, Marie-Louise. Keep it a secret and give us something to gossip about.

BARBARA: How is your husband, dear?

MARIE-LOUISE: Oh, he's very well. I've just been telephoning to him.

BARBARA: I never saw anyone adore his wife so obviously as he adores you.

MARIE-LOUISE: Yes, he's sweet, isn't he?

BARBARA: But doesn't it make you a little nervous sometimes? It must be nerve-racking to be obliged to live up to such profound devotion. It would be a dreadful shock if he ever found out that you were not everything he thought you.

CONSTANCE: [*Charmingly.*] But Marie-Louise is everything he thinks her.

MARIE-LOUISE: And even if I weren't I think it would require more than the evidence of his eyes to persuade him.

CONSTANCE: Listen. There's John. [*She goes to the door and calls.*] John! John!

JOHN: [*Downstairs.*] Hulloa.

CONSTANCE: Are you coming up? Marie-Louise is here.

JOHN: Yes, I'm just coming.

CONSTANCE: He's been operating all the afternoon. I expect he's tired out.

MARTHA: [*With a look at* MARIE-LOUISE.] I dare say he only had a sandwich for luncheon.

[JOHN *comes in. He is a tall, spare man of about forty.*

JOHN: Good Lord, I never saw such a lot of people. How is my mother-in-law?

MRS. CULVER: Mother-in-lawish.

JOHN: [*Kissing her—to* BARBARA.] You know, I only married Constance because her mother wouldn't have me.

MRS. CULVER: I was too young at the time to marry a boy twenty years younger than myself.

CONSTANCE: It hasn't prevented you from flirting outrageously with the creature ever since. It's lucky I'm not a jealous woman.

JOHN: What have you been doing all day, darling?

CONSTANCE: I've been shopping with Marie-Louise.

P

JOHN: [*Shaking hands with* MARIE-LOUISE.] Oh, how do you do? Did you lunch together?

MARTHA: No, she lunched with a beau.

JOHN: I wish it had been me. [*To* MARIE-LOUISE.] What have you been doing with yourself lately? We haven't seen you for ages.

MARIE-LOUISE: You're never about. Constance and I almost live in one another's pockets.

JOHN: How's that rich husband of yours?

MARIE-LOUISE: I've just been speaking to him. Isn't it a bore, he's got to go down to Birmingham for the night.

CONSTANCE: You'd better come and dine with us.

MARIE-LOUISE: Oh, it's awfully nice of you. But I'm tired out. I shall just go to bed and have an egg.

JOHN: I was just going to tell you, Constance. I shan't be in this evening. I've got an acute appendix to do.

CONSTANCE: Oh, what a nuisance.

MARTHA: You've got a wonderful profession, John. If you ever want to do anything or go anywhere you've only got to say you've got an operation and no one can prove it's a lie.

CONSTANCE: Oh, my dear, you mustn't put suspicions into my innocent head. It would never occur to John to be so deceitful. [*To* JOHN.] Would it?

JOHN: I think I'd have to go an awful long way before I managed to deceive you, darling.

CONSTANCE: [*With a little smile.*] Sometimes I think you're right.

MARIE-LOUISE: I do like to see a husband and wife so devoted to one another as you and John. You've been married fifteen years, haven't you?

JOHN: Yes. And it doesn't seem a day too much.

MARIE-LOUISE: Well, I must be running along. I'm late already. Good-bye, darling. Good-bye, Mrs. Culver.

CONSTANCE: Good-bye, darling. We've had such a nice afternoon.

MARIE-LOUISE: [*Giving her hand to* JOHN.] Good-bye.

JOHN: Oh, I'll come downstairs with you.

MARTHA: I was just going, Marie-Louise. I'll come with you.

MARIE-LOUISE: [*With presence of mind.*] John, I wonder if you'd mind looking at my knee for a minute. It's been rather painful for the last day or two.

JOHN: Of course not. Come into my consulting-room. These knee-caps are troublesome things when you once get them out of order.

MARTHA: [*Firmly.*] I'll wait for you. You won't be long, will you? We might share a taxi.

MARIE-LOUISE: I've got my car.

MARTHA: Oh, how nice! You can give me a lift then.

MARIE-LOUISE: Of course. I shall be delighted.

> [JOHN *opens the door for* MARIE-LOUISE. *She goes out and he follows her.* CONSTANCE *has watched this little scene coolly, but with an alert mind.*

MARTHA: What is the matter with her knee?

CONSTANCE: It slips.

MARTHA: What happens then?

CONSTANCE: She slips too.

MARTHA: Are you never jealous of these women who come and see John in his consulting-room?

CONSTANCE: He always has a nurse within call in case they should attempt to take liberties with him.

MARTHA: [*Amiably.*] Is the nurse there now?

CONSTANCE: And anyway I can't help thinking that the sort

of woman who wants to be made love to in a consulting-room with a lively odour of antiseptics is the sort of woman who wears horrid undies. I could never bring myself to be jealous of her.

MARTHA: Marie-Louise gave me two of her chemises to copy only the other day.

CONSTANCE: Oh, did she give you the cerise one with the Irish lace insertions? I thought that sweet. I've copied that.

BARBARA: It's true that Marie-Louise is very pretty.

CONSTANCE: Marie-Louise is a darling. But she and John have known each other far too long. John likes her of course, but he says she has no brain.

MARTHA: Men don't always say what they think.

CONSTANCE: Fortunately, or we shouldn't always know what they feel.

MARTHA: Don't you think John has any secrets from you?

CONSTANCE: I'm sure of it. But of course a good wife always pretends not to know the little things her husband wishes to keep hidden from her. That is an elementary rule in matrimonial etiquette.

MARTHA: Don't forget that men were deceivers ever.

CONSTANCE: My dear, you talk like a confirmed spinster. What woman was ever deceived that didn't want to be? Do you really think that men are mysterious? They're children. Why, my dear, John at forty isn't nearly so grown up as Helen at fourteen.

BARBARA: How is your girl, Constance?

CONSTANCE: Oh, she's very well. She loves boarding-school, you know. They're like little boys, men. Sometimes of course they're rather naughty and you have to pretend to be angry with them. They attach so much importance to such entirely unimportant things that it's really touching. And they're so helpless. Have you never nursed a man when he's ill? It wrings your heart. It's just like a dog or a horse. They haven't got the sense to come in out of the rain, poor darlings. They have all the charming qualities that accompany general incompetence. They're sweet and good and silly and tiresome and selfish. You can't help liking them, they're so ingenuous and so simple. They have no complexity or finesse. I think they're sweet, but it's absurd to take them seriously. You're a wise woman, mother. What do you think?

MRS. CULVER: I think you're not in love with your husband.

CONSTANCE: What nonsense.

[JOHN *comes in.*

JOHN: Marie-Louise is waiting for you, Martha. I've just put a little bandage round her knee.

CONSTANCE: I hope you weren't rough.

MARTHA: [*To* CONSTANCE.] Good-bye, dear. Are you coming, mother?

MRS. CULVER: Not just yet.

MARTHA: Good-bye, Barbara.

[MARTHA *and* JOHN *go out.*

BARBARA: Constance, I've got a suggestion to make to you. You know that my business has been growing by leaps and bounds and I simply cannot get along alone any more. I was wondering if you'd like to come in with me.

CONSTANCE: Oh, my dear, I'm not a business woman.

BARBARA: You've got marvellous taste and you have ideas. You could do all the decorating and I'd confine myself to buying and selling furniture.

CONSTANCE: But I've got no capital.

BARBARA: I've got all the capital I want. I must have help and I know no one more suitable than you. We'd go fifty-fifty and I think I can promise that you'd make a thousand to fifteen hundred a year.

CONSTANCE: I've been an idle woman so long. I think I'd find it dreadfully hard to work eight hours a day.

BARBARA: Won't you think it over? It's very interesting, you know. You're naturally energetic. Don't you get bored with doing nothing all the time?

CONSTANCE: I don't think John would like it. After all, it would look as though he couldn't afford to support me.

BARBARA: Oh, not nowadays, surely. There's no reason why a woman shouldn't have a career just as much as a man.

CONSTANCE: I think my career is looking after John—running a house for him, entertaining his friends and making him happy and comfortable.

BARBARA: Don't you think it rather a mistake to put all your eggs in one basket? Supposing that career failed you?

CONSTANCE: Why should it?

BARBARA: Of course I hope it won't. But men, you know, are fluctuating and various. Independence is a very good thing, and a woman who stands on her own feet financially can look upon the future with a good deal of confidence.

CONSTANCE: It's sweet of you, but so long as John and I are happy together I think I should be a fool to do anything that would vex him.

BARBARA: Of course I'm in no immediate hurry. One never knows what the future will bring forth. I want you to know that if you change your mind the job is open to you. I don't think I shall ever find any one so competent as you. You have only to say the word.

CONSTANCE: Oh, Barbara, you are kind to me. It's a splendid offer and I'm ever so grateful to you. Don't think me horrid if I say I hope I shall never need to accept it.

BARBARA: Of course not. Good-bye, darling.

CONSTANCE: Good-bye, dear.

> [*They kiss, and* BARBARA *goes out.* CONSTANCE *rings the bell.*

MRS. CULVER: Are you quite happy, dear?

CONSTANCE: Oh, quite. Don't I look it?

MRS. CULVER: I'm bound to say you do. So far as I can judge by the look of you I should say you haven't a trouble in the world.

CONSTANCE: You'd be wrong. My cook has given notice and she makes the best meringues I've ever eaten.

MRS. CULVER: I like John.

CONSTANCE: So do I. He has all the solid qualities that make a man a good husband, an agreeable temper, a sense of humour and an entire indifference to petty extravagance.

MRS. CULVER: How right you are, darling, to realise that those are the solid qualities.

CONSTANCE: It's not the seven deadly virtues that make a man a good husband, but the three hundred pleasing amiabilities.

MRS. CULVER: Of course one has to compromise in life. One has to make the best of things. One mustn't expect too much from people. If one wants to be happy in one's own way one must let others be happy in theirs. If one can't get this, that and the other the wise thing is to make up one's mind to do without it. The great thing is not to let vanity warp one's reasonable point of view.

CONSTANCE: Mother, mother, pull yourself together.

MRS. CULVER: Everybody's so clever nowadays. They see everything but the obvious. I've discovered that I only have to say it quite simply in order to be thought a most original and amusing old lady.

CONSTANCE: Spare me, darling.

MRS. CULVER: [*Affectionately.*] If at any time anything went wrong with you, you would tell your mother, wouldn't you?

CONSTANCE: Of course.

MRS. CULVER: I hate the thought that you might be unhappy and let a foolish pride prevent you from letting me console and advise you.

CONSTANCE: [*With feeling.*] It wouldn't, mother dear.

MRS. CULVER: I had rather an odd experience the other day. A little friend of mine came to see me and told me that her husband was neglecting her. I asked her why she told me and not her own mother. She said that her mother had never wanted her to marry and it would mortify her now to have to say that she had made a mistake.

CONSTANCE: Oh, well, John never neglects me, mother.

MRS. CULVER: Of course I gave her a good talking to. She didn't get much sympathy from me.

CONSTANCE: [*With a smile.*] That was very unkind, wasn't it?

MRS. CULVER: I have my own ideas about marriage. If a man neglects his wife it's her own fault, and if he's systematically unfaithful to her in nine cases out of ten she only has herself to blame.

CONSTANCE: [*Ringing the bell.*] Systematically is a grim word.

MRS. CULVER: No sensible woman attaches importance to an occasional slip. Time and chance are responsible for that.

CONSTANCE: And shall we say, masculine vanity?

MRS. CULVER: I told my little friend that if her husband was unfaithful to her it was because he found other women more attractive. Why should she be angry with him for that? Her business was to be more attractive than they.

CONSTANCE: You are not what they call a feminist, mother, are you?

MRS. CULVER: After all, what is fidelity?

CONSTANCE: Mother, do you mind if I open the window?

MRS. CULVER: It is open.

CONSTANCE: In that case do you mind if I shut it? I feel that when a woman of your age asks such a question I should make some sort of symbolic gesture.

MRS. CULVER: Don't be ridiculous. Of course I believe in fidelity for women. I suppose no one has ever questioned the desirability of that. But men are different. Women should remember that they have their homes and their name and position and their family, and they should learn to close their eyes when it's possible they may see something they are not meant to.

[*The* BUTLER *comes in.*

BENTLEY: Did you ring, Madam?

CONSTANCE: Yes. I am expecting Mr. Bernard Kersal. I'm not at home to anybody else.

BENTLEY: Very good, madam.

CONSTANCE: Is Mr. Middleton in?

BENTLEY: Yes, madam. He's in the consulting-room.

CONSTANCE: Very well.

[*The* BUTLER *goes out.*

MRS. CULVER: Is that a polite way of telling me that I had better take myself off?

CONSTANCE: Of course not. On the contrary I particularly want you to stay.

MRS. CULVER: Who is this mysterious gentleman?

CONSTANCE: Mother. Bernard.

MRS. CULVER: That says nothing to me at all. Not Saint Bernard, darling?

CONSTANCE: Pull yourself together, my pet. You must remember Bernard Kersal. He proposed to me.

MRS. CULVER: Oh, my dear, you cannot expect me to remember the names of all the young men who proposed to you.

CONSTANCE: Yes, but he proposed more than any of the others.

MRS. CULVER: Why?

CONSTANCE: I suppose because I refused him. I can't think of any other reason.

MRS. CULVER: He made no impression on me.

CONSTANCE: I don't suppose he tried to.

MRS. CULVER: What did he look like?

CONSTANCE: He was tall.

MRS. CULVER: They were all tall.

CONSTANCE: He had brown hair and brown eyes.

MRS. CULVER: They all had brown hair and brown eyes.

CONSTANCE: He danced divinely.

MRS. CULVER: They all danced divinely.

CONSTANCE: I very nearly married him, you know.

MRS. CULVER: Why didn't you?

CONSTANCE: I think he was a trifle too much inclined to lie down on the floor and let me walk over him.

MRS. CULVER: In short he had no sense of humour.

CONSTANCE: I was quite certain that he loved me, and I was never absolutely sure that John did.

MRS. CULVER: Well, you're sure now, dear, aren't you?

CONSTANCE: Oh, yes. John adores me.

MRS. CULVER: And what's this young man coming for to-day?

CONSTANCE: He's not such a very young man any more. He was twenty-nine then and so he must be nearly forty-five now.

MRS. CULVER: He isn't still in love with you?

CONSTANCE: I shouldn't think so. Do you think it possible after fifteen years? It's surely very unlikely. Don't look at me like that, mother. I don't like it.

MRS. CULVER: Don't talk stuff and nonsense to me, child. Of course you know if he's in love with you or not.

CONSTANCE: But I haven't seen him since I married John. You see he lives in Japan. He's a merchant or something in Kobe. He was here during the war on leave. But that was when I was so dreadfully ill and I didn't see him.

MRS. CULVER: Oh! Why's he here now then? Have you been corresponding with him?

CONSTANCE: No. One can't write letters to any one one never sees for fifteen years. He always sends me flowers on my birthday.

MRS. CULVER: That's rather sweet of him.

CONSTANCE: And the other day I had a letter from him saying he was in England and would like to see me. So I asked him to come to-day.

MRS. CULVER: I wondered why you were so smart.

CONSTANCE: Of course he may be terribly changed. Men go off so dreadfully, don't they? He may be bald and fat now.

MRS. CULVER: He may be married.

CONSTANCE: Oh, if he were I don't think he'd want to come and see me, would he?

MRS. CULVER: I see you're under the impression that he's still in love with you.

CONSTANCE: Oh, I'm not.

MRS. CULVER: Then why are you so nervous?

CONSTANCE: It's only natural that I shouldn't want him to think me old and haggard. He adored me, mother. I suppose he still thinks of me as I was then. It wouldn't be very nice if his face fell about a yard and a half when he came into the room.

MRS. CULVER: I think I'd much better leave you to face the ordeal alone.

CONSTANCE: Oh, no, mother, you must stay. I particularly want you. You see, he may be awful and I may wish I'd never seen him again. It'll be so much easier if you're here. I may not want to be alone with him at all.

MRS. CULVER: Oh.

CONSTANCE: [*With a twinkle in her eye.*] On the other hand I may.

MRS. CULVER: It seems to me you're putting me in a slightly embarrassing situation.

CONSTANCE: Now listen. If I think he's awful we'll just talk about the weather and the crops for a few minutes and then we'll have an ominous pause and stare at him. That always makes a man feel a perfect fool and the moment a man feels a fool he gets up and goes.

MRS. CULVER: Sometimes they don't know how to, poor dears, and the earth will never open and swallow them up.

CONSTANCE: On the other hand if I think he looks rather nice I shall just take out my handkerchief and carelessly place it on the piano.

MRS. CULVER: Why?

CONSTANCE: Darling, in order that you may rise to your aged feet and say, well, you really must be running along.

MRS. CULVER: Yes, I know that, but why should you carelessly place your handkerchief on the piano?

CONSTANCE: Because I am a creature of impulse. I shall have an impulse to place my handkerchief on the piano.

MRS. CULVER: Oh, very well. But I always mistrust impulses.

> [BENTLEY *enters and announces* BERNARD KERSAL. *He is a tall good-looking man, sunburned and of healthy appearance. He is evidently very fit and he carries his forty-five years well.*

BENTLEY: Mr. Kersal.

CONSTANCE: How do you do? Do you remember my mother?

BERNARD: [*Shaking hands with her.*] I'm sure she doesn't remember me.

> [CONSTANCE *takes a small handkerchief out of her bag.*

MRS. CULVER: That is the soft answer that turneth away wrath.

CONSTANCE: It's rather late for tea, isn't it? Would you like a drink?

> [*As she says this she goes towards the bell and places her handkerchief on the piano.*

BERNARD: No, thanks. I've just this moment had one.

CONSTANCE: To brace you for seeing me?

BERNARD: I was nervous.

CONSTANCE: Have I changed as much as you expected?

BERNARD: Oh, that's not what I was nervous about.

MRS. CULVER: Is it really fifteen years since you saw Constance?

BERNARD: Yes. I didn't see her when I was last in England. When I got demobbed I had to go out to Japan again and get my business together. I haven't had a chance to come home before.

> [CONSTANCE *has been giving her mother significant looks, but her mother does not notice them.* CONSTANCE *takes*

> *a second handkerchief out of her bag and when the
> opportunity arises places it neatly on the piano beside
> the first one.*

MRS. CULVER: And are you home for long?

BERNARD: A year.

MRS. CULVER: Have you brought your wife with you?

BERNARD: I'm not married.

MRS. CULVER: Oh, Constance said you were married to a Japanese lady.

CONSTANCE: Nonsense, mother. I never said anything of the sort.

MRS. CULVER: Oh, perhaps I was thinking of Julia Linton. She married an Egyptian pasha. I believe she's very happy. At all events he hasn't killed her yet.

BERNARD: How is your husband?

CONSTANCE: He's very well. I dare say he'll be in presently.

BERNARD: Haven't you got a little sister? I suppose she's out now?

MRS. CULVER: He means Martha. She's come out and gone in again.

CONSTANCE: She was not so very much younger than me, you know. She's thirty-two now.

> [MRS. CULVER *has taken no notice of the handkerchiefs
> and in desperation* CONSTANCE *takes a third from her
> bag and places it beside the other two.*

MRS. CULVER: Do you like the East, Mr. Kersal?

BERNARD: One has a pretty good time there, you know.

> [*Now* MRS. CULVER *catches sight of the three handker-
> chiefs and starts.*

MRS. CULVER: I wonder what the time is.

CONSTANCE: It's late, mother. Are you dining out to-night? I suppose you want to have a lie-down before you dress for dinner.

MRS. CULVER: I hope I shall see you again, Mr. Kersal.

BERNARD: Thank you very much.

> [CONSTANCE *accompanies her to the door.*]

MRS. CULVER: Good-bye, darling. [*In a whisper.*] I couldn't remember if the handkerchiefs meant go or stay.

CONSTANCE: You had only to use your eyes. You can see at a glance that he is the kind of man one would naturally want to have a heart-to-heart talk with after fifteen years.

MRS. CULVER: You only confused me by putting more and more handkerchiefs on the piano.

CONSTANCE: For goodness' sake go, mother. [*Aloud.*] Good-bye, my sweet. I'm sorry you've got to run away so soon.

MRS. CULVER: Good-bye.

> [*She goes out and* CONSTANCE *comes back into the room.*]

CONSTANCE: Did you think it very rude of us to whisper? Mother has a passion for secrets.

BERNARD: Of course not.

CONSTANCE: Now let's sit down and make ourselves comfortable. Let me look at you. You haven't changed much. You're a little thinner and perhaps a little more lined. Men are so lucky, if they have any character they grow better-looking as they grow older. Do you know I'm thirty-six now?

BERNARD: What does that matter?

CONSTANCE: Shall I tell you something? When you wrote and suggested coming here I was delighted at the thought of seeing you again and wrote at once making a date. And then I was panic-stricken. I would have given almost anything not to have sent that letter. And all to-day I've had such a horrible feeling at the pit of my stomach. Didn't you see my knees wobble when you came into the room?

BERNARD: In God's name, why?

CONSTANCE: Oh, my dear, I think you must be a little stupid. I should be a perfect fool if I didn't know that when I was a girl I was very pretty. It's rather a pang when you are forced to the conclusion that you're not quite so pretty as you were. People don't tell one. One tries to hide it from oneself. Anyhow I thought I'd rather know the worst. That's one of the reasons I asked you to come.

BERNARD: Whatever I thought you can hardly imagine that I should be deliberately rude.

CONSTANCE: Of course not. But I watched your face. I was afraid I'd see there: By God, how she's gone off.

BERNARD: And did you?

CONSTANCE: You were rather shy when you came in. You weren't thinking of me.

BERNARD: It's quite true, fifteen years ago you were a pretty girl. Now you're lovely. You're ten times more beautiful than you were then.

CONSTANCE: It's nice of you to say so.

BERNARD: Don't you believe it?

CONSTANCE: I think you do. And I confess that's sufficiently gratifying. Now tell me, why aren't you married? It's time you did, you know, or it'll be too late. You'll have a very lonely old age if you don't.

BERNARD: I never wanted to marry anyone but you.

CONSTANCE: Oh, come, you're not going to tell me that you've never been in love since you were in love with me?

BERNARD: No, I've been in love half a dozen times, but when it came to the point I found I still loved you best.

CONSTANCE: I like you for saying that. I shouldn't have believed it if you'd said you'd never loved anybody else and I should have been vexed with you for thinking me such a fool as to believe it.

BERNARD: You see, it was you I loved in the others. One because she had hair like yours and another because her smile reminded me of your smile.

CONSTANCE: I hate to think that I've made you unhappy.

BERNARD: But you haven't. I've had a very good time; I've enjoyed my work; I've made a bit of money and I've had a lot of fun. I don't blame you for having married John instead of me.

CONSTANCE: Do you remember John?

BERNARD: Of course I do. He was a very nice fellow. I dare say he's made you a better husband than I should have. I've had my ups and downs. I'm very irritable sometimes. John's been able to give you everything you wanted. You were much safer with him. By the way, I suppose I can still call you Constance.

CONSTANCE: Of course. Why not? Do you know, I think you have a very nice nature, Bernard.

BERNARD: Are you happy with John?

CONSTANCE: Oh, very. I don't say that he has never given me a moment's uneasiness. He did once, but I took hold of myself and saw that I mustn't be silly. I'm very glad I did. I think I can quite honestly say that ours has been a very happy and successful marriage.

BERNARD: I'm awfully glad to hear that. Do you think it's cheek to ask if John loves you?

CONSTANCE: I'm sure he loves me.

BERNARD: And do you love him?

CONSTANCE: Very much.

BERNARD: May I make you a short speech?

CONSTANCE: If I may interrupt at suitable moments.

BERNARD: I hope you're going to let me see a great deal of you during this year I've got at home.

CONSTANCE: I want to see a great deal of you.

BERNARD: There's just one thing I want to get off my chest and then I needn't refer to it again. I am just as madly in love with you as I was when I asked you to marry me fifteen years ago. I think I shall remain in love with you all my life. I'm too old a dog to learn new tricks. But I want you to know that you needn't have the smallest fear that I shall make a nuisance of myself. I should think it an awfully caddish thing to try to come between you and John. I suppose we all want to be happy, but I don't believe the best way of being that is to try to upset other people's happiness.

CONSTANCE: That's not such a very long speech after all. At a public dinner they would hardly even call it a few remarks.

BERNARD: All I ask for is your friendship and if in return I care to give you my love I don't see that it's any one's business but my own.

CONSTANCE: I don't think it is. I think I can be a very good friend, Bernard.

[The door opens and JOHN *comes in.*

JOHN: Oh, I'm sorry. I didn't know you were engaged.

CONSTANCE: I'm not. Come in. This is Bernard Kersal.

JOHN: How do you do?

BERNARD: I'm afraid you don't remember me.

JOHN: If you ask me point-blank I think it's safer to confess I don't.

CONSTANCE: Don't be so silly, John. He used to come to mother's.

JOHN: Before we were married, d'you mean?

CONSTANCE: Yes. You spent several week-ends with us together.

JOHN: My dear, that was fifteen years ago. I'm awfully sorry not to remember you, but I'm delighted to see you now.

CONSTANCE: He's just come back from Japan.

JOHN: Oh, well, I hope we shall see you again. I'm just going along to the club to have a rubber before dinner, darling. [*To* BERNARD.] Why don't you dine here with Constance? I've got an acute appendix and she'll be all alone, poor darling.

BERNARD: Oh, that's awfully kind of you.

CONSTANCE: It would be a friendly act. Are you free?

BERNARD: Always to do a friendly act.

CONSTANCE: Very well. I shall expect you at eight-fifteen.

END OF THE FIRST ACT

THE SECOND ACT

The Scene is the same.

A Fortnight has passed.

MARTHA *in walking costume and a hat is looking at an illustrated paper.*

BENTLEY *comes in.*

BENTLEY: Mr. Kersal is here, Miss.

MARTHA: Oh! Ask him if he won't come up.

BENTLEY: Very good, Miss. [*He goes out and in a moment comes in again to announce* BERNARD, *and then goes.*] Mr. Kersal.

MARTHA: Constance is dressing. She won't be very long.

BERNARD: Oh, I see. Well, there's no violent hurry.

MARTHA: You're taking her to Ranelagh, aren't you?

BERNARD: That was the idea. I know some of the fellows who are playing to-day.

MARTHA: Are you having a good time in London?

BERNARD: Marvellous. When a man's lived in the East as long as I have, he's apt to feel rather out of it when he comes home. But Constance and John have been ripping to me.

MARTHA: Do you like John?

BERNARD: Yes. He's been awfully kind.

MARTHA: Do you know, I remember you quite well.

BERNARD: Oh, you can't. You were a kid when I used to come down and stay with your mother.

MARTHA: I was sixteen. Do you imagine I wasn't thrilled to the marrow by Constance's young men?

BERNARD: There were a good many of them. I should have thought your marrow got callous.

MARTHA: But you were one of the serious ones. I always thought you terribly romantic.

BERNARD: I was terribly romantic. I think it's becoming in the young.

MARTHA: I don't think it's unbecoming in the not quite as young.

BERNARD: Don't think I'm romantic now. I make a considerable income and I'm putting on weight. The price of silk has ousted love's young dream in my manly bosom.

MARTHA: You're an unconscionable liar.

BERNARD: To which I can only retort that you're excessively rude.

MARTHA: You were madly in love with Constance in those days, weren't you?

BERNARD: You know, it's so long ago I forget.

MARTHA: I advised her to marry you rather than John.

BERNARD: Why?

MARTHA: Well, for one thing you lived in Japan. I would have married any one who would take me there.

BERNARD: I live there still.

MARTHA: Oh, I don't want to marry you.

BERNARD: I couldn't help suspecting that.

MARTHA: I could never really quite understand what she saw in John.

BERNARD: I suppose she loved him.

MARTHA: I wonder if she ever regrets that she married John rather than you.

BERNARD: Well, don't. She's perfectly satisfied with John and wouldn't change him for anything in the world.

MARTHA: It's exasperating, isn't it?

BERNARD: I don't think so. It must make it much more comfortable for a husband and wife to be content with one another.

MARTHA: You're in love with her still, aren't you?

BERNARD: Not a bit.

MARTHA: Upon my soul, you've got a nerve. Why, you donkey, you're giving it away all the time. Do you know what you look like when she's in the room? Have you any idea how your eyes change when they rest on her? When you speak her name it sounds as though you were kissing it.

BERNARD: I thought you were an odious child when you were sixteen, Martha, and now that you're thirty-two I think you're a horrible woman.

MARTHA: I'm not really. But I'm very fond of Constance and I'm inclined to be rather fond of you.

BERNARD: Don't you think you could show your attachment by minding your own business?

MARTHA: Why does it make you angry because I've told you that no one can see you with Constance for five minutes without knowing that you adore her?

BERNARD: My dear, I'm here for one year. I want to be happy. I don't want to give trouble or cause trouble. I value my friendship with Constance and I hate the idea that anything should interfere with it.

MARTHA: Hasn't it occurred to you that she may want more than your friendship?

BERNARD: No, it has not.

MARTHA: You need not jump down my throat.

BERNARD: Constance is perfectly happy with her husband.

You must think me a damned swine if you think I'm going to butt in and try to smash up a perfectly wonderful union.

MARTHA: But, you poor fool, don't you know that John has been notoriously unfaithful to Constance for ages?

BERNARD: I don't believe it.

MARTHA: Ask any one you like. Mother knows it. Barbara Fawcett knows it. Every one knows it but Constance.

BERNARD: That certainly isn't true. Mrs. Durham told me when I met her at dinner two or three days ago that John and Constance were the most devoted couple she'd ever known.

MARTHA: Did Marie-Louise tell you that?

BERNARD: She did.

[MARTHA *begins to laugh. She can hardly restrain herself.*

MARTHA: The nerve. Marie-Louise. Oh, my poor Bernard. Marie-Louise is John's mistress.

BERNARD: Marie-Louise is Constance's greatest friend.

MARTHA: Yes.

BERNARD: If this is a pack of lies I swear I'll damned well wring your neck.

MARTHA: All right.

BERNARD: That was a silly thing to say. I'm sorry.

MARTHA: Oh, I don't mind. I like a man to be violent. I think you're just the sort of man Constance needs.

BERNARD: What the devil do you mean by that?

MARTHA: It can't go on. Constance is being made perfectly ridiculous. Her position is monstrous. I thought she ought to be told and as every one else seemed to shirk the job I was prepared to do it myself. My mother was so disagreeable about it, I've had to promise not to say a word.

BERNARD: You're not under the delusion that I'm going to tell her?

MARTHA: No, I don't really think it would come very well from you. But things can't go on. She's bound to find out. All I want you to do is to . . . well, stand by.

BERNARD: But Marie-Louise has got a husband. What about him?

MARTHA: His only ambition in life is to make a million. He's the sort of a fool who thinks a woman loves him just because he loves her. Marie-Louise can turn him round her little finger.

BERNARD: Has Constance never suspected?

MARTHA: Never. You've only got to look at her. Really, her self-confidence sometimes is positively maddening.

BERNARD: I wonder if it wouldn't be better that she never did find out. She's so happy. She's entirely care-free. You've only got to look at that open brow and those frank, trustful eyes.

MARTHA: I thought you loved her.

BERNARD: Enough to want her happiness above all things.

MARTHA: You *are* forty-five, aren't you? I forgot that for a moment.

BERNARD: Dear Martha. You have such an attractive way of putting things.

[CONSTANCE'S *voice on the stairs is heard calling:* BENTLEY, BENTLEY.

MARTHA: Oh, there's Constance. I can't imagine where mother is. I think I'll go into the brown room and write a letter.

[BERNARD *takes no notice of what she says nor does he make any movement when she goes out. A moment later* CONSTANCE *comes in.*

CONSTANCE: Have I kept you waiting?

BERNARD: It doesn't matter.

CONSTANCE: Hulloa! What's up?

BERNARD: With me? Nothing. Why?

CONSTANCE: You look all funny. Why are your eyes suddenly opaque?

BERNARD: I didn't know they were.

CONSTANCE: Are you trying to hide something from me?

BERNARD: Of course not.

CONSTANCE: Have you had bad news from Japan?

BERNARD: No. Far from it. Silk is booming.

CONSTANCE: Then you're going to tell me that you've just got engaged to a village maiden.

BERNARD: No, I'm not.

CONSTANCE: I hate people who keep secrets from me.

BERNARD: I have no secrets from you.

CONSTANCE: Do you think I don't know your face by now?

BERNARD: You'll make me vain. I would never have ventured to think that you took the trouble to look twice at my ugly face.

CONSTANCE: [*With sudden suspicion.*] Wasn't Martha here when you came? She hasn't gone, has she?

BERNARD: She's waiting for her mother. She's gone into another room to write letters.

CONSTANCE: Did you see her?

BERNARD: [*Trying to be very casual.*] Yes. We had a little chat about the weather.

CONSTANCE: [*Immediately grasping what has happened.*] Oh—— Don't you think we ought to be starting?

BERNARD: There's plenty of time. It's no good getting there too early.

CONSTANCE: Then I'll take off my hat.

BERNARD: And it's jolly here, isn't it? I love your room.

CONSTANCE: Do you think it's a success? I did it myself. Barbara Fawcett wants me to go into the decorating business. She's in it, you know, and she's making quite a lot of money.

BERNARD: [*Smiling to hide his anxiety in asking the question.*] Aren't you happy at home?

CONSTANCE: [*Breezily.*] I don't think it necessarily means one's unhappy at home because one wants an occupation. One may very easily grow tired of going to parties all the time. But as a matter of fact I refused Barbara's offer.

BERNARD: [*Insisting.*] You are happy, aren't you?

CONSTANCE: Very.

BERNARD: You've made *me* very happy during this last fortnight. I feel as though I'd never been away. You've been awfully kind to me.

CONSTANCE: I'm very glad you think so. I don't know that I've done anything very much for you.

BERNARD: Yes, you have. You've let me see you.

CONSTANCE: I let the policeman at the corner do that, you know.

BERNARD: You mustn't think that because I take care only to talk to you of quite casual things I don't still love you with all my heart.

CONSTANCE: [*Quite coolly.*] We agreed when first you came back that your feelings were entirely your business.

BERNARD: Do you mind my loving you?

CONSTANCE: Oughtn't we all to love one another?

BERNARD: Don't tease me.

CONSTANCE: My dear, I can't help being pleased and flattered and rather touched. It is rather wonderful that any one should care for me. . . .

BERNARD: [*Interrupting.*] So much?

CONSTANCE: After so many years.

BERNARD: If any one had asked me fifteen years ago if I could love you more than I loved you then I should have said it was impossible. I love you ten times more than I ever loved you before.

CONSTANCE: [*Going on with her own speech.*] But I don't in the least want you to make love to me now.

BERNARD: I know. I'm not going to. I know you far too well.

CONSTANCE: [*Amused and a trifle taken aback.*] I don't quite know what you've been doing for the last five minutes.

BERNARD: I was merely stating a few plain facts.

CONSTANCE: Oh, I beg your pardon. I thought it was something quite different. I'm afraid you might mistake my meaning if I said I'm quite curious to see how you *do* make love.

BERNARD: [*Good-humouredly.*] I have a notion that you're laughing at me.

CONSTANCE: In the hope of teaching you to laugh at yourself.

BERNARD: I've been very good during the last fortnight, haven't I?

CONSTANCE: Yes, I kept on saying to myself: I wonder if a pat of butter really would melt in his mouth.

BERNARD: Well, for just a minute I'm going to let myself go.

CONSTANCE: I wouldn't if I were you.

BERNARD: Yes, but you're not. I want to tell you just once that I worship the ground you tread on. There's never been any one in the world for me but you.

CONSTANCE: Oh, nonsense. There have been half a dozen. We are seven.

BERNARD: They were all you. I love you with all my heart. I admire you more than any woman I've ever met. I respect you. I'm an awful fool when it comes to the point. I don't know how to say all I've got in my heart without feeling like a perfect ass. I love you. I want you to know that if ever you're in trouble I should look upon it as the greatest possible happiness to be allowed to help you.

CONSTANCE: That's very kind of you. I don't see why I should be in any trouble.

BERNARD: Always and in all circumstances you can count on me absolutely. I will do anything in the world for you. If ever you want me you have only to give me a sign. I should be proud and happy to give my life for you.

CONSTANCE: It's sweet of you to say so.

BERNARD: Don't you believe it?

CONSTANCE: [*With a charming smile.*] Yes.

BERNARD: I should like to think that it meant—oh, not very much, but just a little to you.

CONSTANCE: [*Almost shaken.*] It means a great deal. I thank you.

BERNARD: Now we won't say anything more about it.

CONSTANCE: [*Recovering her accustomed coolness.*] But why did you think it necessary to say all this just now?

BERNARD: I wanted to get it off my chest.

CONSTANCE: Oh, really.

BERNARD: You're not angry with me?

CONSTANCE: Oh, Bernard, I'm not that kind of a fool at all. . . . It's a pity that Martha doesn't marry.

BERNARD: Don't think that I'm going to marry her.

CONSTANCE: I don't. I merely thought that a husband would be a pleasant and useful occupation for her. She's quite a nice girl, you know. A liar, of course, but otherwise all right.

BERNARD: Oh?

CONSTANCE: Yes, a terrible liar, even for a woman. . . . Shall we start now? It's no good getting there when the polo is over.

BERNARD: All right. Let's start.

CONSTANCE: I'll put my hat on again. By the way, you haven't had a taxi waiting all this time, have you?

BERNARD: No, I've got a car. I thought I'd like to drive you down myself.

CONSTANCE: Open or shut?

BERNARD: Open.

CONSTANCE: Oh, my dear, then I must get another hat. A broad brim like this is such a bore in an open car.

BERNARD: Oh, I am sorry.

CONSTANCE: It doesn't matter a bit. I shall only be a minute. And why on earth shouldn't one be comfortable if one can?

[*She goes out. In a moment* BENTLEY *shows in* MARIE-LOUISE.

MARIE-LOUISE: Oh, how do you do. [*To* BENTLEY.] Will you tell Mr. Middleton at once?

BENTLEY: Yes, madam.

[*Exit* BENTLEY.

MARIE-LOUISE: [*Rather flustered.*] I particularly wanted to see John for a minute and there are patients waiting to see him, so I asked Bentley if he couldn't come here.

BERNARD: I'll take myself off.

MARIE-LOUISE: I'm awfully sorry, but it's rather urgent. John hates to be disturbed like this.

BERNARD: I'll go into the next room.

MARIE-LOUISE: Are you waiting for Constance?

BERNARD: Yes, I'm taking her to Ranelagh. She's changing her hat.

MARIE-LOUISE: I see. Bentley told me she was upstairs. Good-bye. I shall only be a minute. [BERNARD *goes into the adjoining room just as* JOHN *comes in.*] Oh, John, I'm sorry to drag you away from your patients.

JOHN: There's nothing urgent. They can wait for a few minutes. [BERNARD *has closed the door behind him, and* JOHN's *tone changes. They speak now in a low voice and quickly.*] Is anything the matter?

MARIE-LOUISE: Mortimer.

JOHN: What about Mortimer?

MARIE-LOUISE: I'm convinced he suspects.

JOHN: Why?

MARIE-LOUISE: He was so funny last night. He came into my room to say good-night to me. He sat on my bed. He was chatting nicely and he was asking what I'd been doing with myself all the evening. . . .

JOHN: Presumably you didn't tell him.

MARIE-LOUISE: No, I said I'd been dining here. And suddenly he got up and just said good-night and went out. His voice was so strange that I couldn't help looking at him. He was as red as a turkey cock.

JOHN: Is that all?

MARIE-LOUISE: He never came in to say good-morning to me before he went to the City.

JOHN: He may have been in a hurry.

MARIE-LOUISE: He's never in too much of a hurry for that.

JOHN: I think you're making a mountain of a mole heap.

MARIE-LOUISE: Don't be stupid, John. Can't you see I'm as nervous as a cat?

JOHN: I can. But I'm trying to persuade you there's nothing to be nervous about.

MARIE-LOUISE: What fools men are. They never will see

that it's the small things that matter. I tell you I'm frightened out of my wits.

JOHN: You know there's a devil of a distance between suspicion and proof.

MARIE-LOUISE: Oh, I don't think he could prove anything. But he can make himself awfully unpleasant. Supposing he put ideas in Constance's head?

JOHN: She'd never believe him.

MARIE-LOUISE: If the worst came to worst I could manage Mortimer. He's awfully in love with me. That always gives one such an advantage over a man.

JOHN: Of course you can twist Mortimer round your little finger.

MARIE-LOUISE: I should die of shame if Constance knew. After all, she's my greatest friend and I'm absolutely devoted to her.

JOHN: Constance is a peach. Of course I don't believe there's anything in this at all, but if there were, I'd be in favour of making a clean breast of it to Constance.

MARIE-LOUISE: Never!

JOHN: I expect she'd kick up a row. Any woman would. But she'd do anything in the world to help us out.

MARIE-LOUISE: A lot you know about women. She'd help you out, I dare say. But she'd stamp on me with both feet. That's only human nature.

JOHN: Not Constance's.

MARIE-LOUISE: Upon my word, it's lucky I'm fairly sure of you, John, or the way you talk of Constance would really make me jealous.

JOHN: Thank God you can smile. You're getting your nerve back.

MARIE-LOUISE: It's been a comfort to talk it over. It doesn't seem so bad now.

JOHN: I'm sure you've got nothing to be frightened about.

MARIE-LOUISE: I dare say it was only my fancy. It was a stupid risk to take all the same.

JOHN: Perhaps. Why did you look so devilish pretty?

MARIE-LOUISE: Oughtn't you to be getting back to your wretched patients?

JOHN: I suppose so. Will you stop and see Constance?

MARIE-LOUISE: I may as well. It would look rather odd if I went away without saying how d'you do to her.

JOHN: [*Going.*] I'll leave you then. And don't worry.

MARIE-LOUISE: I won't. I dare say it was only a guilty conscience. I'll go and have my hair washed.

> [*As* JOHN *is about to go,* MARTHA *comes in followed by* BERNARD.

MARTHA: [*With an almost exaggerated cordiality.*] I had no idea you were here, Marie-Louise.

MARIE-LOUISE: It's not very important.

MARTHA: I was just writing letters, waiting for mother, and Bernard's only just told me.

MARIE-LOUISE: I wanted to see John about something.

MARTHA: I hope you haven't got anything the matter with you, darling.

MARIE-LOUISE: No. Mortimer's been looking rather run-down lately and I want John to persuade him to take a holiday.

MARTHA: Oh, I should have thought he'd be more likely to take a physician's advice than a surgeon's in a thing like that.

MARIE-LOUISE: He's got a tremendous belief in John, you know.

MARTHA: In which I'm sure he's justified. John is so very reliable.

JOHN: What can I do for you, Martha? If you'd like me to cut out an appendix or a few tonsils I shall be happy to oblige you.

MARTHA: My dear John, you've only left me the barest necessities of existence as it is. I don't think I could manage with anything less than I have.

JOHN: My dear, as long as a woman has a leg to stand on she need not despair of exciting her surgeon's sympathy and interest.

[CONSTANCE *comes in with* MRS. CULVER.

MARIE-LOUISE: [*Kissing her.*] Darling.

CONSTANCE: How is your knee, still slipping?

MARIE-LOUISE: It always gives me more or less trouble, you know.

CONSTANCE: Yes, of course. I think you're very patient. In your place I should be furious with John. Of course I would never dream of consulting him if I had anything the matter with me.

MRS. CULVER: I'm sorry I've been so long, Martha. Have you been very impatient?

MARTHA: No, I've been passing the time very pleasantly.

MRS. CULVER: For others, darling, or only for yourself?

CONSTANCE: I met mother on the stairs and she came up with me while I changed my hat. Bernard is taking me down to Ranelagh.

JOHN: Oh, that'll be jolly.

BERNARD: We shall be dreadfully late.

CONSTANCE: Does it matter?

BERNARD: No.

[BENTLEY *comes in with a card on a small salve ana takes it to* CONSTANCE. *She looks at the card and hesitates.*

CONSTANCE: How very odd.

JOHN: What's the matter, Constance?

CONSTANCE: Nothing. [*For an instant she reflects.*] Is he downstairs?

BENTLEY: Yes, madam.

CONSTANCE: I don't know why he should send up a card. Show him up.

BENTLEY: Very good, madam.

[*Exit* BENTLEY.

JOHN: Who is it, Constance?

CONSTANCE: Come and sit down, Marie-Louise.

MARIE-LOUISE: I must go and so must you.

CONSTANCE: There's plenty of time. Do you like this hat?

MARIE-LOUISE: Yes. I think it's sweet.

CONSTANCE: What are *you* doing here, John? Haven't you got any patients to-day?

JOHN: Yes, there are two or three waiting. I'm just going down. As a matter of fact I thought I deserved a cigarette. [*He puts his hand to his hip pocket.*] Hang, I've mislaid my cigarette-case. You haven't seen it about, Constance?

CONSTANCE: No, I haven't.

JOHN: I looked for it everywhere this morning. I can't think where I left it. I must ring up the nursing-home and ask if I left it there.

CONSTANCE: I hope you haven't lost it.

JOHN: Oh, no. I'm sure I haven't. I've just put it somewhere.

[*The door opens and* BENTLEY *announces the visitor.*

BENTLEY: Mr. Mortimer Durham.

MARIE-LOUISE: [*Startled out of her wits.*] Oh!

CONSTANCE: [*Quickly, seizing her wrist.*] Sit still, you fool.

[MORTIMER DURHAM *comes in. He is a stoutish biggish man of about forty, with a red face and an irascible manner. At the moment he is a prey to violent emotion.* BENTLEY *goes out.*]

Hulloa, Mortimer. What are you doing in these parts at this hour? Why on earth did you send up a card?

[*He stops and looks around.*

MARIE-LOUISE: What is the matter, Mortimer?

MORTIMER: [*To* CONSTANCE, *with difficulty restraining his fury.*] I thought you might like to know that your husband is my wife's lover.

MARIE-LOUISE: Morty!

CONSTANCE: [*Keeping a firm hand on* MARIE-LOUISE *and very coolly to* MORTIMER.] Oh? What makes you think that?

MORTIMER: [*Taking a gold cigarette-case out of his pocket.*] Do you recognize this? I found it under my wife's pillow last night.

CONSTANCE: Oh, I am relieved. I couldn't make out where I'd left it. [*Taking it from him.*] Thank you so much.

MORTIMER: [*Angrily.*] It's not yours.

CONSTANCE: Indeed it is. I was sitting on Marie-Louise's bed and I must have slipped it under the pillow without thinking.

MORTIMER: It has John's initials on it.

CONSTANCE: I know. It was presented to him by a grateful patient and I thought it much too nice for him, so I just took it.

MORTIMER: What sort of fool do you take me for, Constance?

CONSTANCE: My dear Morty, why should I say it was my cigarette-case if it wasn't?

MORTIMER: They had dinner together.

CONSTANCE: My poor Morty, I know that. You were going to a City banquet or something, and Marie-Louise rang up and asked if she might come and take pot-luck with us.

MORTIMER: Do you mean to say she dined here?

CONSTANCE: Isn't that what she told you?

MORTIMER: Yes.

CONSTANCE: It's quite easy to prove. If you won't take my word for it we can ring for the butler, and you can ask him yourself. . . . Ring the bell, John, will you?

MORTIMER: [*Uneasily.*] No, don't do that. If you give me your word, of course I must take it.

CONSTANCE: That's very kind of you. I'm grateful to you for not exposing me to the humiliation of making my butler corroborate my statement.

MORTIMER: If Marie-Louise was dining here why were you sitting on her bed?

CONSTANCE: John had to go out and do an operation, and Marie-Louise wanted to show me the things she'd got from Paris, so I walked round to your house. It was a lovely night. You remember that, don't you?

MORTIMER: Damn it, I've got more important things to do than look at the night.

CONSTANCE: We tried them all on and then we were rather tired, so Marie-Louise got into bed and I sat down and we talked.

MORTIMER: If you were tired why didn't you go home and go to bed.

CONSTANCE: John had promised to come round and fetch me.

MORTIMER: And did he? At what time did he come?

JOHN: I couldn't manage it. The operation took much longer than I expected. It was one of those cases where when you once start cutting you really don't know where to stop. You know the sort of thing, don't you, Mortimer?

MORTIMER: No, I don't. How the devil should I?

CONSTANCE: All that is neither here nor there. This is a terrible accusation you've made against John and Marie-Louise and I'm very much upset. But I will remain perfectly calm till I've heard everything. Now let me have your proofs.

MORTIMER: My proofs? What d'you mean? The cigarette-case. When I found the cigarette-case I naturally put two and two together.

CONSTANCE: [*With her eyes flashing.*] I quite understand, but why did you make them five?

MORTIMER: [*Emphatically, in order not to show that he is wavering.*] It isn't possible that I should have made a mistake.

CONSTANCE: Even the richest of us may err. I remember when Mr. Pierpont Morgan died, he was found to own seven million dollars of worthless securities.

MORTIMER: [*Uneasily.*] You don't know what a shock it was, Constance. I had the most implicit confidence in Marie-Louise. I was knocked endways. I've been brooding over it ever since till I was afraid I should go mad.

CONSTANCE: And do you mean to say that you've come here and made a fearful scene just because you found my cigarette-case in Marie-Louise's room? I can't believe it. You're a man of the world and a business man. You're extremely intelligent. Surely you have something to go upon. You must be holding something back. Don't be afraid of hurting my feelings. You've said so much now that I must insist on your saying everything. I want the truth and the whole truth.

[*There is a pause.* MORTIMER *looks from* MARIE-LOUISE, *who is quietly weeping, to* CONSTANCE, *with the utmost bewilderment.*

MORTIMER: I'm afraid I've made a damned fool of myself.

CONSTANCE: I'm afraid you have.

MORTIMER: I'm awfully sorry, Constance. I beg your pardon.

CONSTANCE: Oh, don't bother about me. You've exposed me to the most bitter humiliation. You've sown seeds of distrust between me and John which can never be . . .

[*She looks for a word.*

MRS. CULVER: [*Supplying it.*] Fertilized.

CONSTANCE: [*Ignoring it.*] Uprooted. But I don't matter. It's Marie-Louise's pardon you must beg.

MORTIMER: [*Humbly.*] Marie-Louise.

MARIE-LOUISE: Don't touch me. Don't come near me.

MORTIMER: [*To* CONSTANCE, *miserably.*] You know what jealousy is.

CONSTANCE: Certainly not. I think it's a most ugly and despicable vice.

MORTIMER: [*To* MARIE-LOUISE.] Marie-Louise, I'm sorry. Won't you forgive me?

MARIE-LOUISE: You've insulted me before all my friends. You know how devotedly I love Constance. You might have accused me of having an affair with anyone else— but not John.

CONSTANCE: Not her greatest friend's husband. The milkman or the dustman if you like, but not her greatest friend's husband.

MORTIMER: I've been a perfect swine. I don't know what came over me. I really wasn't responsible for my actions.

MARIE-LOUISE: I've loved you all these years. No one has ever loved you as I've loved you. Oh, it's cruel, cruel.

MORTIMER: Come away, darling. I can't say here what I want to say.

MARIE-LOUISE: No, no, no.

CONSTANCE: [*Putting her hand on his arm, gently.*] I think you'd better leave her here for a little while, Morty. I'll talk to her when you've gone. She's naturally upset. A sensitive little thing like that.

MORTIMER: We're dining with the Vancouvers at 8.15.

CONSTANCE: For eighty-thirty. I promise I'll send her home in good time to dress.

MORTIMER: She'll give me another chance?

CONSTANCE: Yes, yes.

MORTIMER: I'd do anything in the world for her. [CONSTANCE *puts her fingers to her lips and then points significantly to the pearl chain she is wearing. For a second* MORTIMER *does not understand, but as soon as her notion dawns on him he gives a pleased nod.*] You're the cleverest woman in the world. [*As he goes out he stops and holds out his hand to* JOHN.] Will you shake hands with me, old man? I made a mistake and I'm man enough to acknowledge it.

JOHN: [*Very cordially.*] Not at all, old boy. I quite agree that it did look fishy, the cigarette-case. If I'd dreamt that Constance was going to leave an expensive thing like that lying about all over the place, I'm hanged if I'd have let her pinch it.

MORTIMER: You don't know what a weight it is off my mind. I felt a hundred when I came here, and now I feel like a two-year-old.

> [*He goes out. The moment the door is closed behind him there is a general change in every attitude. The tension disappears and there is a feeling of relief.*

JOHN: Constance, you're a brick. I shall never forget this. Never, so long as I live. And by George, what presence of mind you showed. I went hot and cold all over, and you never batted an eye-lash.

CONSTANCE: By the way, here is your cigarette-case. You'd better have a ring made and hang it on your key-chain.

JOHN: No, no. Keep it. I'm too old to take these risks.

CONSTANCE: By the way, did anyone see you go into Morty's house last night?

JOHN: No, we let ourselves in with Marie-Louise's latch key.

CONSTANCE: That's all right then. If Mortimer asks the servants they can tell him nothing. I had to take that chance.

MARIE-LOUISE: [*With a little gesture of ashamed dismay.*] Oh, Constance, what must you think of me?

CONSTANCE: I? Exactly the same as I thought before. I think you're sweet, Marie-Louise.

MARIE-LOUISE: You have every right to be angry with me.

CONSTANCE: Perhaps, but not the inclination.

MARIE-LOUISE: Oh, it's not true. I've treated you shame-fully. You've made me feel such a pig. And you had your chance to get back on me and you didn't take it. I'm so ashamed.

CONSTANCE: [*Amused.*] Because you've been having an affair with John, or because you've been found out?

MARIE-LOUISE: Oh, Constance, don't be heartless. Say anything you like, curse me, stamp on me, but don't smile at me. I'm in a terrible position.

CONSTANCE: And you want me to make a scene. I know and I sympathize. [*Very calmly.*] But the fact is that Mortimer told me nothing I didn't know before.

MARIE-LOUISE: [*Aghast.*] Do you mean to say that you've known all along?

CONSTANCE: All along, darling. I've been spending the last six months in a desperate effort to prevent my friends and relations from telling me your ghastly secret. It's been very difficult sometimes. Often mother's profound under-standing of life, Martha's passion for truth at any price, and Barbara's silent sympathy, have almost worn me down. But until to-day the t's were not definitely crossed nor the i's distinctly dotted, and I was able to ignore the facts that were staring at me—rather rudely, I must say—in the face.

MARIE-LOUISE: But why, why? It's not human. Why didn't you do anything?

CONSTANCE: That, darling, is my affair.

MARIE-LOUISE: [*Thinking she understands.*] Oh, I see.

CONSTANCE: [*Rather tartly.*] No, you don't. I have always been absolutely faithful to John. I have not winked at your intrigue in order to cover my own.

MARIE-LOUISE: [*Beginning to be a little put out.*] I almost think you've been laughing at me up your sleeve all the time.

CONSTANCE: [*Good-humouredly.*] Oh, my dear, you mustn't be offended just because I've taken away from you the satisfaction of thinking that you have been deceiving me all these months. I should hate you to think me capable of an intentional meanness.

MARIE-LOUISE: My head's going round and round.

CONSTANCE: Such a pretty head, too. Why don't you go and lie down? You want to look your best if you're dining with the Vancouvers.

MARIE-LOUISE: I wonder where Mortimer is?

CONSTANCE: You know that pearl necklace you showed me the other day and you said that Mortimer thought it cost a lot of money—well, he's gone to Cartier's to buy it for you.

MARIE-LOUISE: [*Excitedly.*] Oh, Constance, do you think he has?

CONSTANCE: I think all men are born with the knowledge that when they have wounded a woman's soul—and our souls are easily wounded—the only cure is a trifling, but expensive jewel.

MARIE-LOUISE: Do you think he'll have the sense to bring it home with him so that I can wear it to-night?

CONSTANCE: Oh, my dear, don't be such a fool as to accept it with alacrity. Remember that Mortimer has grievously insulted you, he's made the most shocking accusation that a man can make against his wife, he's trampled on your love and now he's destroyed your trust in him.

MARIE-LOUISE: Oh, how right you are, Constance.

CONSTANCE: Surely I need not tell you what to do. Refuse to speak to him, but never let him get a word of defence in edgeways. Cry enough to make him feel what a brute he is, but not enough to make your eyes swell. Say you'll leave him and run sobbing to the door, but take care to let him stop you before you open it. Repeat yourself. Say the same thing over and over again—it wears them down—and if he answers you take no notice, but just say it again. And at last when you've reduced him to desperation, when his head is aching as though it would split, when he's sweating at every pore, when he's harassed and miserable and haggard and broken—then consent as an unmerited favour, as a sign of your forgiving temper and the sweetness of your nature, to accept, no, don't consent, *deign* to accept the pearl necklace for which the wretch has just paid ten thousand pounds.

MARIE-LOUISE: [*With peculiar satisfaction.*] Twelve, darling.

CONSTANCE: And don't thank him. That wouldn't be playing the game. Let him thank *you* for the favour you do him in allowing him to make you a paltry gift. Have you got your car here?

MARIE-LOUISE: No, I was in such a state when I came I took a taxi.

CONSTANCE: John, do take Marie-Louise down and put her in a taxi.

JOHN: All right.

MARIE-LOUISE: No, not John. I couldn't. After all, I have some delicacy.

CONSTANCE: Oh, have you? Well, let Bernard go.

BERNARD: I shall be pleased.

CONSTANCE: [*To* BERNARD.] But come back, won't you?

BERNARD: Certainly.

MARIE-LOUISE: [*Kissing* CONSTANCE.] This has been a lesson to me, darling. I'm not a fool, Constance. I can learn.

CONSTANCE: At least prudence, I hope.

[MARIE-LOUISE *goes out followed by* BERNARD KERSAL.

JOHN: How did you guess that Marie-Louise had said she was dining here?

CONSTANCE: She's too crafty a woman to invent a new lie when an old one will serve.

JOHN: It would have been awkward if Mortimer had insisted on asking Bentley if it was true.

CONSTANCE: I knew he wouldn't dare. It's only if a man's a gentleman that he won't hesitate to do an ungentlemanly thing. Mortimer is on the boundary line and it makes him careful.

MARTHA: [*Significantly.*] Don't you imagine your patients are growing a trifle restless, John?

JOHN: I like to keep them waiting. They grow more and more nervous as the minutes pass and when I recommend an operation that will cost them two hundred and fifty pounds they are too shaken to protest.

MARTHA: [*Pursing her lips.*] I can't imagine you'll very much like to hear what I'm determined to say to Constance.

JOHN: It's because I shrewdly suspect that you have some very unpleasant things to say about me that I am prepared reluctantly to neglect the call of duty and listen to you with my own ears.

CONSTANCE: She's been exercising miracles of restraint for

the last three months, John. I think she has a right to let herself go now.

JOHN: If she's suffering from suppressed desires she's come to the wrong establishment. She ought to go to a psycho-analyst.

MARTHA: I've only got one thing to say, John, and I'm perfectly willing that you should hear it. [*To* CONSTANCE.] I don't know what your reasons were for shielding that abominable woman. I can only suppose you wanted to avoid more scandal than was necessary. . . .

MRS. CULVER: [*Interrupting.*] Before you go any further, my dear, you must let me put my word in. [*To* CONSTANCE.] My dear child, I beg you not to decide anything in a hurry. We must all think things over. First of all you must listen to what John has to say for himself.

MARTHA: What can he have to say for himself?

CONSTANCE: [*Ironically.*] What indeed?

JOHN: Not the right thing anyway. I've seen too much of married life. . . .

CONSTANCE: [*Interrupting, with a smile.*] Let us be just. Other people's rather than your own.

JOHN: [*Going on.*] To imagine that even the Archangel Gabriel could say the right thing.

CONSTANCE: I've no reason, however, to suppose that the Archangel Gabriel could ever find himself in such a predicament.

JOHN: I'm for it and I'm prepared to take what's coming to me.

CONSTANCE: [*To the world in general.*] No man could say handsomer than that.

JOHN: I'm expecting you to make a scene, Constance. It's your right and your privilege. I'm willing to bear it. Give me hell. I deserve it. Drag me up and down the room by the hair of the head. Kick me in the face. Stamp on me. I'll grovel. I'll eat the dust. My name is mud. Mud.

CONSTANCE: My poor John, what is there to make a scene about?

JOHN: I know how badly I've treated you. I had a wife who was good, loving and faithful, devoted to my interests, a perfect mother and an excellent housekeeper. A woman ten times too good for me. If I'd had the smallest spark of decency I couldn't have treated you like this. I haven't a word to say for myself.

MARTHA: [*Interrupting him.*] You've humiliated her to all her friends.

JOHN: I've behaved neither like a gentleman nor a sportsman.

MARTHA: Your conduct is inexcusable.

JOHN: I haven't a leg to stand on.

MARTHA: Even if you didn't love her, you might have treated her with respect.

JOHN: I've been as heartless as a crocodile and as unscrupulous as a typhoid bacillus.

CONSTANCE: Between you, of course, you're leaving me very little to say.

MARTHA: There *is* nothing to say. You're quite right. This is the sort of occasion when it's beneath a woman's dignity to make a scene. It just shows how little John knows women to think that you could demean yourself to vulgar abuse. [*To* JOHN.] I suppose you'll have the decency to put no obstacle in the way of Constance's getting her freedom.

MRS. CULVER: Oh, Constance, you're not going to divorce him?

MARTHA: Mother, you're so weak. How can she go on living with a man for whom she has no respect? What would her life be with this creature whom she can only mistrust and despise? Besides, you have to think of their child. How can Constance allow her daughter to be contaminated by the society of a person of this character?

CONSTANCE: John has always been an excellent father. Let us give the devil his due.

MRS. CULVER: Don't be too hard, darling. I can understand that at the moment you feel bitter, but it would be very sad if you let your bitterness warp your judgment.

CONSTANCE: I don't feel in the least bitter. I wish I looked as sweet as I feel.

MRS. CULVER: You can't deceive a mother, my dear. I know the angry resentment that you feel. Under the unfortunate circumstances it's only too natural.

CONSTANCE: When I look into my heart I can't find a trace of resentment, except perhaps for John's being so stupid as to let himself be found out.

JOHN: Let me say this in justification for myself, Constance. I did my little best to prevent it. Angels could do no more.

CONSTANCE: And angels presumably have not the pernicious habit of smoking straight-cut cigarettes.

JOHN: When you once get the taste for them, you prefer them to gippies.

MRS. CULVER: Don't be cynical, darling. That is the worst way to ease an aching heart. Come to your mother's arms, my dear, and let us have a good cry together. And then you'll feel better.

CONSTANCE: It's sweet of you, mother, but honestly I couldn't squeeze a tear out of my eyes if my life depended on it.

MRS. CULVER: And don't be too hard. Of course John is to blame. I admit that. He's been very, very naughty. But men are weak and women are so unscrupulous. I'm sure he's sorry for all the pain he's caused you.

MARTHA: What puzzles me is that you didn't do something the moment you discovered that John was having an affair.

CONSTANCE: To tell you the truth, I thought it no business of mine.

MARTHA: [*Indignantly.*] Aren't you his wife?

CONSTANCE: John and I are very lucky people. Our marriage has been ideal.

MARTHA: How can you say that?

CONSTANCE: For five years we adored each other. That's much longer than most people do. Our honeymoon lasted five years and then we had a most extraordinary stroke of luck: we ceased to be in love with one another simultaneously.

JOHN: I protest, Constance. I've never ceased to be absolutely devoted to you.

CONSTANCE: I never said you had, darling. I'm convinced of it. I've never ceased to be devoted to you. We've shared one another's interests, we've loved to be together, I've exulted in your success and you've trembled in my illness. We've laughed at the same jokes and sighed over the same worries. I don't know any couple that's been bound together by a more genuine affection. But honestly, for the last ten years have you been in love with me?

JOHN: You can't expect a man who's been married for fifteen years. . . .

CONSTANCE: My dear, I'm not asking for excuses. I'm only asking for a plain answer.

JOHN: In the long run I enjoy your society much more than anybody else's. There's no one I like so much as you.

You're the prettiest woman I've ever known and I shall say the same when you're a hundred.

CONSTANCE: But does your heart leap into your mouth when you hear my footstep on the stairs, and when I come into the room, is your first impulse to catch me in your manly arms? I haven't noticed it.

JOHN: I don't want to make a fool of myself.

CONSTANCE: Then I think you've answered my question. You're no more in love with me than I am with you.

JOHN: You never said a word of this before.

CONSTANCE: I think most married couples tell one another far too much. There are some things that two people may know very well, but which it's much more tactful for them to pretend they don't.

JOHN: How did you find out?

CONSTANCE: I'll tell you. One night as we were dancing together, all at once I noticed that we weren't keeping such good step as we generally did. It was because my mind was wandering. I was thinking how it would suit me to do my hair like a woman who was dancing alongside of us. Then I looked at you and I saw you were thinking what pretty legs she'd got. I suddenly realized that you weren't in love with me any more and at the same moment I realized that it was a relief, because I wasn't in love with you.

JOHN: I must say it never occurred to me for a moment.

CONSTANCE: I know. A man thinks it quite natural that he should fall out of love with a woman, but it never strikes him for a moment that a woman can do anything so unnatural as to fall out of love with him. Don't be upset at that, darling, that is one of the charming limitations of your sex.

MARTHA: Do you mean mother and me to understand that since then John has been having one affair after another and you haven't turned a hair?

CONSTANCE: Since this is the first time he's been found out. let us give him the benefit of the doubt and hope that till now he has never strayed from the strict and narrow path. You're not angry with me, John?

JOHN: No, darling, not angry. But I *am* a little taken aback. I think you've been making rather a damned fool of me. It never struck me that your feelings for me had changed so much. You can't expect me to like it.

CONSTANCE: Oh, come now, you must be reasonable. You surely wouldn't wish me to have languished for all these years in a hopeless passion for you when you had nothing to give me in return but friendship and affection. Think what a bore it is to have someone in love with you whom you're not in love with.

JOHN: I can't conceive of your ever being a bore, Constance.

CONSTANCE: [*Kissing her hand to him.*] Don't you realize that we must thank our lucky stars? We are the favoured of the gods. I shall never forget those five years of exquisite happiness you gave me when I loved you, and I shall never cease to be grateful to you, not because you loved me, but because you inspired me with love. Our love never degenerated into weariness. Because we ceased loving one another at the very same moment we never had to put up with quarrels and reproaches, recriminations and all the other paraphernalia of a passion that has ceased on one side and is still alive and eager on the other. Our love was like a cross-word puzzle in which we both hit upon the last word at the same moment. That is why our lives since have been so happy; that is why ours is a perfect marriage.

MARTHA: Do you mean to say that it meant nothing to you when you found out that John was carrying on with Marie-Louise?

CONSTANCE: Human nature is very imperfect. I'm afraid I must admit that at the first moment I was vexed. But only at the first moment. Then I reflected that it was most unreasonable to be angry with John for giving to another something that I had no use for. That would be too much like a dog in the manger. And then I was fond enough of John to be willing that he should be happy in his own way. And if he was going to indulge in an intrigue . . . isn't that the proper phrase, John?

JOHN: I have not yet made up my mind whether it really is an indulgence.

CONSTANCE: Then it was much better that the object of his affections should be so intimate a friend of mine that I could keep a maternal eye on him.

JOHN: Really, Constance.

CONSTANCE: Marie-Louise is very pretty so that my self-esteem was not offended, and so rich that it was certain John would have no reason to squander money on her to the inconvenience of myself. She's not clever enough to acquire any ascendancy over him, and so long as I kept his heart I was quite willing that she should have his senses. If you wanted to deceive me, John, I couldn't have chosen anyone with whom I would more willingly be deceived than Marie-Louise.

JOHN: I don't gather that you have been very grossly deceived, darling. You have such penetration that when you look at me I feel as though I were shivering without a stitch of clothing on.

MRS. CULVER: I don't approve of your attitude, Constance. In my day when a young wife discovered that her husband had been deceiving her, she burst into a flood of tears and went to stay with her mother for three weeks, not returning to her husband till he had been brought to a proper state of abjection and repentance.

MARTHA: Are we to undertsand, then, that you are not going to divorce John?

CONSTANCE: You know, I can never see why a woman should give up a comfortable home, a considerable part of her income and the advantage of having a man about to do all the tiresome and disagreeable things for her, because he has been unfaithful to her. She's merely cutting off her nose to spite her face.

MARTHA: I am at a loss for words. I cannot conceive how a woman of any spirit can sit down and allow her husband to make a perfect damned fool of her.

CONSTANCE: You've been very stupid, my poor John. In the ordinary affairs of life stupidity is much more tiresome than wickedness. You can mend the vicious, but what in Heaven's name are you to do with the foolish?

JOHN: I've been a fool, Constance. I know it, but I'm capable of learning by experience, so I can't be a damned fool.

CONSTANCE: You mean that in the future you'll be more careful to cover your tracks?

MRS. CULVER: Oh, no, Constance, he means that this has been a lesson to him, and that in the future you'll have no cause for complaint.

CONSTANCE: I've always been given to understand that men only abandon their vices when advancing years have made them a burden rather than a pleasure. John, I'm happy to say, is still in the flower of his age. I suppose you give yourself another fifteen years, John, don't you?

JOHN: Really, Constance, I don't know what you mean. The things you say sometimes are positively embarrassing.

CONSTANCE: I think at all events we may take it that Marie-Louise will have more than one successor.

JOHN: Constance, I give you my word of honour. . . .

CONSTANCE: [*Interrupting.*] That is the only gift you can make for which I can find no use. You see, so long as I was able to pretend a blissful ignorance of your goings-on we could all be perfectly happy. You were enjoying yourself and I received a lot of sympathy as the outraged wife. But now I do see that the position is very difficult. You have put me in a position that is neither elegant nor dignified.

JOHN: I'm awfully sorry, Constance.

MARTHA: You're going to leave him?

CONSTANCE: No, I'm not going to leave him. John, you remember that Barbara offered to take me into her business? I refused. Well, I've changed my mind and I'm going to accept.

JOHN: But why? I don't see your point.

CONSTANCE: I'm not prepared any more to be entirely dependent upon you, John.

JOHN: But, my dear, everything I earn is at your disposal. It's a pleasure for me to provide for your wants. Heaven knows, they're not very great.

CONSTANCE: I know. Come, John, I've been very reasonable, haven't I? Don't try and thwart me when I want to do something on which I've set my heart.

[*There is an instant's pause.*

JOHN: I don't understand. But if you put it like that, I haven't a word to say. Of course, you must do exactly as you wish.

CONSTANCE: That's a dear. Now go back to your patients or else I shall have to keep you as well as myself.

JOHN: Will you give me a kiss?

CONSTANCE: Why not?

JOHN: [*Kissing her.*] It's peace between us?

CONSTANCE: Peace and good-will. [JOHN *goes out.*] He is rather sweet, isn't he?

MRS. CULVER: What have you got on your mind, Constance?

CONSTANCE: I, mother? [*Teasing her.*] What do you suspect?

MRS. CULVER: I don't like the look of you.

CONSTANCE: I'm sorry for that. Most people find me far from plain.

MRS. CULVER: You've got some deviltry in mind, but for the life of me I can't guess it.

MARTHA: I can't see what you expect to get out of working with Barbara.

CONSTANCE: Between a thousand and fifteen hundred a year, I believe.

MARTHA: I wasn't thinking of the money, and you know it.

CONSTANCE: I'm tired of being the modern wife.

MARTHA: What do you mean by the modern wife?

CONSTANCE: A prostitute who doesn't deliver the goods.

MRS. CULVER: My dear, what would your father say if he heard you say such things?

CONSTANCE: Darling, need we conjecture the remarks of a gentleman who's been dead for five and twenty years? Had he any gift for repartee?

MRS. CULVER: None whatever. He was good, but he was stupid. That is why the gods loved him and he died young.

[BERNARD KERSAL *opens the door and looks in.*

BERNARD: May I come in?

CONSTANCE: Oh, there you are. I wondered what had become of you.

BERNARD: When Marie-Louise saw my car at the door she asked me to drive her. I couldn't very well refuse.

CONSTANCE: So you took her home.

BERNARD: No, she said she was in such a state she must have her hair washed. I drove her to a place in Bond Street.

CONSTANCE: And what did she say to you?

BERNARD: She said, I don't know what you must think of me.

CONSTANCE: That is what most women say to a man when his opinion doesn't matter two straws to them. And what did you answer?

BERNARD: Well, I said, I prefer not to offer an opinion on a matter which is no business of mine.

CONSTANCE: Dear Bernard, one of the things I like most in you is that you always remain so perfectly in character. If the heavens fell you would still remain the perfect English gentleman.

BERNARD: I thought it the most tactful thing to say.

CONSTANCE: Well, mother, I won't detain you any longer. I know that you and Martha have a thousand things to do.

MRS. CULVER: I'm glad you reminded me. Come, Martha. Good-bye, darling. Good-bye, Mr. Kersal.

BERNARD: Good-bye.

CONSTANCE: [*To* MARTHA.] Good-bye, dear. Thank you for all your sympathy. You've been a great help in my hour of need.

MARTHA: I don't understand and it's no good saying I do.

CONSTANCE: Bless you. [MRS. CULVER *and* MARTHA *go out.* BERNARD *closes the door after them.*] Shall we be very late?

BERNARD: So late that it doesn't matter if we're a little later. I have something important to say to you.

CONSTANCE: [*Teasing him a little.*] Important to me or important to you?

BERNARD: I can't tell you how distressed I was at that terrible scene.

CONSTANCE: Oh, didn't you think it had its lighter moments?

BERNARD: It's only this afternoon I learned the truth, and then I never imagined for a moment that you knew it, too. I can't tell you how brave I think it of you to have borne all this torture with a smiling face. If I admired you before, I admire you ten times more now.

CONSTANCE: You're very sweet, Bernard.

BERNARD: My heart bleeds when I think of what you've gone through.

CONSTANCE: It's not a very good plan to take other people's misfortunes too much to heart.

BERNARD: Hardly an hour ago I told you that if ever you wanted me I was only too anxious to do anything in the world for you. I little thought then that the time would come so soon. There's no reason now why I shouldn't tell you of the love that consumes me. Oh, Constance, come to me. You know that if things were as I thought they were between you and John nothing would have induced me to say a word. But now he has no longer any claims on you. He doesn't love you. Why should you go on wasting your life with a man who is capable of exposing you to all this humiliation? You know how long and tenderly I've loved you. You can trust yourself to me. I'll give my whole life to making you forget the anguish you've endured. Will you marry me, Constance?

CONSTANCE: My dear, John may have behaved very badly, but he's still my husband.

BERNARD: Only in name. You've done everything in your power to save a scandal and now if you ask him to let himself be divorced he's bound to consent.

CONSTANCE: Do you really think John has behaved so very badly to me?

BERNARD: [*Astonished.*] You don't mean to say that you have any doubts in your mind about his relationship with Marie-Louise?

CONSTANCE: None.

BERNARD: Then what in God's name do you mean?

CONSTANCE: My dear Bernard, have you ever considered what marriage is among well-to-do people? In the working classes a woman cooks her husband's dinner, washes for him and darns his socks. She looks after the children and makes their clothes. She gives good value for the money she costs. But what is a wife in our class? Her house is managed by servants, nurses look after her children, if she has resigned herself to having any, and as soon as they are old enough she packs them off to school. Let us face it, she is no more than the mistress of a man of whose desire she has taken advantage to insist on a legal ceremony that will prevent him from discarding her when his desire has ceased.

BERNARD: She's also his companion and his helpmate.

CONSTANCE: My dear, any sensible man would sooner play bridge at his club than with his wife, and he'd always rather play golf with a man than with a woman. A paid secretary is a far better helpmate than a loving spouse. When all is said and done, the modern wife is nothing but a parasite.

BERNARD: I don't agree with you.

CONSTANCE: You see, my poor friend, you are in love and your judgment is confused.

BERNARD: I don't understand what you mean.

CONSTANCE: John gives me board and lodging, money for my clothes and my amusements, a car to drive in and a certain position in the world. He's bound to do all that because fifteen years ago he was madly in love with me, and he undertook it; though, if you'd asked him, he would certainly have acknowledged that nothing is so fleeting as that particular form of madness called love. It was either very generous of him or very imprudent. Don't you think it would be rather shabby of me to take advantage now of his generosity or his want of foresight?

BERNARD: In what way?

CONSTANCE: He paid a very high price for something that he couldn't get cheaper. He no longer wants that. Why should I resent it? I know as well as anybody else that desire is fleeting. It comes and goes and no man can understand why. The only thing that's certain is that when it's gone it's gone forever. So long as John continues to provide for me what right have I to complain that he is unfaithful to me? He bought a toy, and if he no longer wants to play with it, why should he? He paid for it.

BERNARD: That might be all right if a man had only to think about himself. What about the woman?

CONSTANCE: I don't think you need waste too much sympathy on her. Like ninety-nine girls out of a hundred, when I married I looked upon it as the only easy, honourable and lucrative calling open to me. When the average woman who has been married for fifteen years discovers her husband's infidelity it is not her heart that is wounded but her vanity. If she had any sense, she would regard it merely as one of the necessary inconveniences of an otherwise pleasant profession.

BERNARD: Then the long and short of it is that you don't love me.

CONSTANCE: You think that my principles are all moonshine?

BERNARD: I don't think they would have much influence if you were as crazy about me as I am about you. Do you still love John?

CONSTANCE: I'm very fond of him, he makes me laugh, and we get on together like a house on fire, but I'm not in love with him.

BERNARD: And is that enough for you? Isn't the future sometimes a trifle desolate? Don't you want love?

[*A pause. She gives him a long reflective look.*

CONSTANCE: [*Charmingly.*] If I did I should come to you for it, Bernard.

BERNARD: Constance, what do you mean? Is it possible that you could ever care for me? Oh, my darling, I worship the ground you tread on.

[*He seizes her in his arms and kisses her passionately.*

CONSTANCE: [*Releasing herself.*] Oh, my dear, don't be so sudden. I should despise myself entirely if I were unfaithful to John so long as I am entirely dependent on him.

BERNARD: But if you love me?

CONSTANCE: I never said I did. But even if I did, so long as John provides me with all the necessities of existence I wouldn't be unfaithful. It all comes down to the economic situation. He has bought my fidelity and I should be worse than a harlot if I took the price he paid and did not deliver the goods.

BERNARD: Do you mean to say there's no hope for me at all?

CONSTANCE: The only hope before you at the moment is to start for Ranelagh before the game is over.

BERNARD: Do you still want to go?

CONSTANCE: Yes.

BERNARD: Very well. [*With a burst of passion.*] I love you.

CONSTANCE: Then go down and start up the car, put a spot of oil in the radiator or something, and I'll join you in a minute. I want to telephone.

BERNARD: Very well.

    [*He goes out.* CONSTANCE *takes up the telephone.*

CONSTANCE: Mayfair 2646 . . . Barbara? It's Constance. That offer you made me a fortnight ago—is it still open? Well, I want to accept it . . . No, no, nothing has happened. John is very well. He's always sweet, you know. It's only that I want to earn my own living. When can I start? The sooner the better.

END OF THE SECOND ACT

THE THIRD ACT

The scene is still the same. A year has passed. It is afternoon.

CONSTANCE *is seated at a desk writing letters. The* BUTLER *shows in* BARBARA FAWCETT *and* MARTHA.

BENTLEY: Mrs. Fawcett and Miss Culver.

CONSTANCE: Oh! Sit down, I'm just finishing a note.

BARBARA: We met on the doorstep.

MARTHA: I thought I'd just look round and see if there was anything I could do to help you before you start.

CONSTANCE: That's very nice of you, Martha. I really don't think there is. I'm packed and ready, and for once I don't believe I've forgotten one of the things I shan't want.

BARBARA: I felt I must run in to say good-bye to you.

CONSTANCE: Now, my dear, you mustn't neglect your work the moment my back is turned.

BARBARA: Well, it's partly the work that's brought me. An order has just come in for a new house and they want an Italian room.

CONSTANCE: I don't like that look in your beady eye, Barbara.

BARBARA: Well, it struck me that as you're going to Italy you might go round the shops and buy any nice pieces that you can find.

CONSTANCE: Perish the thought. I've worked like a dog for a year and last night at six o'clock I downed tools. I stripped off my grimy overalls, wrung the sweat from my honest brow and scrubbed my horny hands. You said I could take six weeks' holiday.

BARBARA: I admit that you've thoroughly earned it.

CONSTANCE: When I closed the shop-door behind me, I ceased to be a British working-man and resumed the position of a perfect English lady.

MARTHA: I never saw you in such spirits.

CONSTANCE: Something accomplished, something done. But what I was coming to was this: for the next six weeks I refuse to give a moment's thought to bath-rooms or wall-papers, kitchen sinks, scullery floors, curtains, cushions and refrigerators.

BARBARA: I wasn't asking you to. I only wanted you to get some of that painted Italian furniture and a few mirrors.

CONSTANCE: No, I've worked hard and I've enjoyed my work, and now I'm going to enjoy a perfect holiday.

BARBARA: Oh, well, have it your own way.

MARTHA: Constance dear, I think there's something you ought to know.

CONSTANCE: I should have thought you had discovered by now that I generally know the things I ought to know.

MARTHA: You'll never guess whom I saw in Bond Street this morning.

CONSTANCE: Yes, I shall. Marie-Louise.

MARTHA: Oh!

CONSTANCE: I'm sorry to disappoint you, darling. She rang me up an hour ago.

MARTHA: But I thought she wasn't coming back for another month. She was going to stay away a year.

CONSTANCE: She arrived last night and I'm expecting her every minute.

MARTHA: Here?

CONSTANCE: Yes. She said she simply must run in and see me before I left.

MARTHA: I wonder what she wants.

CONSTANCE: Perhaps to pass the time of day. I think it's rather sweet of her, considering how busy she must be on getting back after so long.

BARBARA: She's been all over the place, hasn't she?

CONSTANCE: Yes, she's been in Malaya; Mortimer has interests there, you know, and in China, and now they've just come from India.

MARTHA: I often wondered if it was at your suggestion that they set off on that long tour immediately after that unfortunate scene.

CONSTANCE: Which, you must confess, no one enjoyed more than you, darling.

BARBARA: It was certainly the most sensible thing they could do.

MARTHA: Of course you know your own business best, darling, but don't you think it's a little unfortunate that you should be going away for six weeks just as she comes back?

CONSTANCE: We working-women have to take our holidays when we can.

BARBARA: Surely John has had his lesson. He's not going to make a fool of himself a second time.

MARTHA: Do you think he has really got over his infatuation, Constance?

CONSTANCE: I don't know at all. But here he is, you'd better ask him.

[*As she says these words,* JOHN *enters.*

JOHN: Ask him what?

MARTHA: [*Not at all at a Joss.*] I was just wondering what you'd do with yourself during Constance's absence.

JOHN: I've got a lot of work, you know, and I shall go to the club a good deal.

MARTHA: It seems a pity that you weren't able to arrange things so that you and Constance should take your holidays together.

BARBARA: Don't blame me for that. I was quite willing to make my arrangements to suit Constance.

CONSTANCE: You see, I wanted to go to Italy and the only places John likes on the Continent are those in which it's only by an effort of the imagination that you can tell you're not in England.

MARTHA: What about Helen?

CONSTANCE: We've taken a house at Henley for August. John can play golf and go on the river, and I shall be able to come up to town every day to look after the business.

BARBARA: Well, dear, I'll leave you. I hope you'll have a wonderful holiday. You've deserved it. Do you know, I think I'm a very clever woman, John, to have persuaded Constance to work. She's been absolutely invaluable to me.

JOHN: I never liked the idea and I'm not going to say I did.

BARBARA: Haven't you forgiven me yet?

JOHN: She insisted on it and I had to make the best of a bad job.

BARBARA: Good-bye.

CONSTANCE: [*Kissing her.*] Good-bye, dear. Take care of yourself.

MARTHA: I'll come with you, Barbara. Mother said she'd look in for a minute to say good-bye to you.

CONSTANCE: Oh, all right. Good-bye.

> [*She kisses the two and accompanies them to the door. They go out.*

JOHN: I say, Constance, I thought you had to go now because Barbara couldn't possibly get away.

CONSTANCE: Did I say that?

JOHN: Certainly.

CONSTANCE: Oh!

JOHN: If I'd dreamt that you could just as easily take your holiday when I take mine . . .

CONSTANCE: [*Interrupting.*] Don't you think it's a mistake for husbands and wives to take their holidays together? The only reason one takes a holiday is for rest and change and recreation. Do you think a man really gets that when he goes away with his wife?

JOHN: It depends on the wife.

CONSTANCE: I know nothing more depressing than the sight of all those couples in a hotel dining-room, one little couple to one little table, sitting opposite to one another without a word to say.

JOHN: Oh, nonsense. You often see couples who are very jolly and cheerful.

CONSTANCE: Yes, I know, but look closely at the lady's wedding-ring and you'll see that it rests uneasily on the hand it adorns.

JOHN: We always get on like a house on fire and when I slipped a wedding-ring on your finger a bishop supervised the process. You're not going to tell me that I bore *you*.

CONSTANCE: On the contrary, you tickle me to death. It's that unhappy modesty of mine: I was afraid that you could have too much of my society. I thought it would refresh you if I left you to your own devices for a few weeks.

JOHN: If you go on pulling my leg so persistently I shall be permanently deformed.

CONSTANCE: Anyhow, it's too late now. My bags are packed, my farewells made, and nothing bores people so much as to see you to-morrow when they've made up their minds to get on without you for a month.

JOHN: H'm. Eyewash. . . . Look here, Constance, there's something I want to say to you.

CONSTANCE: Yes?

JOHN: Do you know that Marie-Louise has come back?

CONSTANCE: Yes. She said she'd try and look in to say how do you do before I started. It'll be nice to see her again after so long.

JOHN: I want you to do something for me, Constance.

CONSTANCE: What is it?

JOHN: Well, you've been a perfect brick to me, and hang it all, I can't take advantage of your good nature. I must do the square thing.

CONSTANCE: I'm afraid I don't quite understand.

JOHN: I haven't seen Marie-Louise since that day when Mortimer came here and made such a fool of himself. She's been away for nearly a year and taking all things into consideration I think it would be a mistake to resume the relations that we were on then.

CONSTANCE: What makes you think she wishes to?

JOHN: The fact that she rang you up the moment she arrived looks ominous to me.

CONSTANCE: Ominous? You know some women can't see a telephone without taking the receiver off and then, when the operator says, Number, please, they have to say something. I dare say ours was the first that occurred to Marie-Louise.

JOHN: It's no good blinking the fact that Marie-Louise was madly in love with me.

CONSTANCE: Well, we can neither of us blame her for that.

R

JOHN: I don't want to be unkind, but after all, circumstances have forced a break upon us and I think we had better look upon it as permanent.

CONSTANCE: Of course you must please yourself.

JOHN: I'm not thinking of myself, Constance. I'm thinking partly of course of Marie-Louise's good, but, I confess, chiefly of you. I could never look you in the face again if everything between Marie-Louise and me were not definitely finished.

CONSTANCE: I should hate you to lose so harmless and inexpensive a pleasure.

JOHN: Of course it'll be painful, but if one's made up one's mind to do a thing I think it's much better to do it quickly.

CONSTANCE: I think you're quite right. I'll tell you what I'll do, as soon as Marie-Louise comes I'll make an excuse and leave you alone with her.

JOHN: That wasn't exactly my idea.

CONSTANCE: Oh?

JOHN: It's the kind of thing that a woman can do so much better than a man. It struck me that it would come better from you than from me.

CONSTANCE: Oh, did it?

JOHN: It's a little awkward for me, but it would be quite easy for you to say—well, you know the sort of thing, that you have your self-respect to think of, and to cut a long story short, she must either give me up or you'll raise hell.

CONSTANCE: But you know what a soft heart I have. If she bursts into tears and says she can't live without you I shall feel so sorry for her that I shall say, Well, damn it all, keep him.

JOHN: You wouldn't do me a dirty trick like that, Constance.

CONSTANCE: You know that your happiness is my chief interest in life.

JOHN: [*After a moment's hesitation.*] Constance, I will be perfectly frank with you. I'm fed up with Marie-Louise.

CONSTANCE: Darling, why didn't you say that at once?

JOHN: Be a sport, Constance. You know that's not the kind of thing one can say to a woman.

CONSTANCE: I admit it's not the kind of thing she's apt to take very well.

JOHN: Women are funny. When they're tired of you they tell you so without a moment's hesitation and if you don't like it you can lump it. But if you're tired of them you're a brute and a beast and boiling oil's too good for you.

CONSTANCE: Very well, leave it to me. I'll do it.

JOHN: You're a perfect brick. But you'll let her down gently, won't you? I wouldn't hurt her feelings for the world. She's a nice little thing, Constance.

CONSTANCE: Sweet.

JOHN: And it's hard luck on her.

CONSTANCE: Rotten.

JOHN: Make her understand that I'm more sinned against than sinning. I don't want her to think too badly of me.

CONSTANCE: Of course not.

JOHN: But be quite sure it's definite.

CONSTANCE: Leave it to me.

JOHN: You're a ripper, Constance. By George, no man could want a better wife.

[*The* BUTLER *introduces* MARIE-LOUISE.

BUTLER: Mrs. Durham.

[*The two women embrace warmly.*

MARIE-LOUISE: Darling, how perfectly divine to see you again. It's too, too wonderful.

CONSTANCE: My dear, how well you're looking. Are those the new pearls?

MARIE-LOUISE: Aren't they sweet? But Mortimer bought me the most heavenly emeralds when we were in India. Oh, John, how are you?

JOHN: Oh, I'm all right, thanks.

MARIE-LOUISE: Aren't you a little fatter than when I saw you last?

JOHN: Certainly not.

MARIE-LOUISE: I've lost pounds. [*To* CONSTANCE.] I'm so glad I caught you. I should have been so disappointed to miss you. [*To* JOHN.] Where are you going?

JOHN: Nowhere. Constance is going alone.

MARIE-LOUISE: Is she? How perfectly divine. I suppose you can't get away. Are you making pots of money?

JOHN: I get along. Will you forgive me if I leave you? I've got to be off.

MARIE-LOUISE: Of course. You're always busy, aren't you?

JOHN: Good-bye.

MARIE-LOUISE: I hope we shall see something of you while Constance is away.

JOHN: Thank you very much.

MARIE-LOUISE: Mortimer's golf has improved. He'd love to play with you.

JOHN: Oh, yes, I should love it.

[*He goes out*.

MARIE-LOUISE: I did so hope to find you alone. Constance, I've got heaps and heaps to tell you. Isn't it tactful of John to leave us? First of all I want to tell you how splendidly everything has turned out. You know you were quite right. I'm so glad I took your advice and made Mortimer take me away for a year.

CONSTANCE: Mortimer is no fool.

MARIE-LOUISE: Oh, no, for a man he's really quite clever. I gave him hell, you know, for ever having suspected me, and at last he was just eating out of my hand. But I could see he wasn't quite sure of me. You know what men are—when they once get an idea in their heads it's dreadfully difficult for them to get it out again. But the journey was an inspiration; I was absolutely angelic all the time, and he made a lot of money, so everything in the garden was rosy.

CONSTANCE: I'm very glad.

MARIE-LOUISE: I owe it all to you, Constance. I made Mortimer buy you a perfectly divine star sapphire in Ceylon. I told him he owed you some sort of reparation for the insult he'd put upon you. It cost a hundred and twenty pounds, darling, and we're taking it to Cartier's to have it set.

CONSTANCE: How thrilling.

MARIE-LOUISE: You mustn't think I'm ungrateful. Now listen, Constance, I want to tell you at once that you needn't distress yourself about me and John.

CONSTANCE: I never did.

MARIE-LOUISE: I know I behaved like a little beast, but I never thought you'd find out. If I had, well, you know me well enough to be positive that nothing would have induced me to have anything to do with him.

CONSTANCE: You're very kind.

MARIE-LOUISE: I want you to do something for me, Constance. Will you?

CONSTANCE: I'm always eager to oblige a friend.

MARIE-LOUISE: Well, you know what John is. Of course he's a dear and all that kind of thing, but the thing's over and it's best that he should realize it at once.

CONSTANCE: Over?

MARIE-LOUISE: Of course I know he's head over heels in love with me still. I saw that the moment I came into the room. One can't blame him for that, can one?

CONSTANCE: Men do find you fascinating.

MARIE-LOUISE: But one has to think of oneself sometimes in this world. He must see that it could never be the same after we discovered that you knew all about it.

CONSTANCE: I kept it from you as long as I could.

MARIE-LOUISE: One couldn't help feeling then that you were rather making fools of us. It seemed to take the romance away, if you see what I mean.

CONSTANCE: Dimly.

MARIE-LOUISE: You know, I wouldn't hurt John's feelings for the world, but it's no good beating about the bush and I'm quite determined to have the thing finished and done with before you go.

CONSTANCE: This is very sudden. I'm afraid it'll be an awful shock to John.

MARIE-LOUISE: I've quite made up my mind.

CONSTANCE: There isn't much time for a very long and moving scene, but I'll see if John is in still. Could you manage it in ten minutes?

MARIE-LOUISE: Oh, but *I* can't see him. I want you to tell him.

CONSTANCE: Me!

MARIE-LOUISE: You know him so well, you know just the sort of things to say to him. It's not very nice telling a man who adores you that you don't care for him in that way any more. It's so much easier for a third party.

CONSTANCE: Do you really think so?

MARIE-LOUISE: I'm positive of it. You see, you can say that for your sake I've made up my mind that from now on we can be nothing but friends. You've been so wonder-

ful to both of us, it would be dreadful if we didn't play
the game now. Say that I shall always think of him
tenderly and that he's the only man I've ever really
loved, but that we must part.

CONSTANCE: But if he insists on seeing you?

MARIE-LOUISE: It's no good, Constance, I can't see him. I
shall only cry and get my eyes all bunged up. You will
do it for me, darling. Please.

CONSTANCE: I will.

MARIE-LOUISE: I got the most divine evening frock in pale
green satin on my way through Paris, and it would look
too sweet on you. Would you like me to give it to you?
I've only worn it once.

CONSTANCE: Now tell me the real reason why you're so
determined to get rid of John without a moment's delay.

[MARIE-LOUISE *looks at her and gives a little roguish
smile*.

MARIE-LOUISE: Swear you won't tell.

CONSTANCE: On my honour.

MARIE-LOUISE: Well, my dear, we met a perfectly divine
young man in India. He was A.D.C. to one of the
governors and he came home on the same boat with us.
He simply adores me.

CONSTANCE: And of course you adore him.

MARIE-LOUISE: My dear, I'm absolutely mad about him. I
don't know what's going to happen.

CONSTANCE: I think we can both give a pretty shrewd
guess.

MARIE-LOUISE: It's simply awful to have a temperament like
mine. Of course you can't understand, you're cold.

CONSTANCE: [*Very calmly.*] You're an immoral little beast,
Marie-Louise.

MARIE-LOUISE: Oh, I'm not. I have affairs—but I'm not
promiscuous.

CONSTANCE: I should respect you more if you were an honest prostitute. She at least does what she does to earn her bread and butter. You take everything from your husband and give him nothing that he pays for. You are no better than a vulgar cheat.

MARIE-LOUISE: [*Surprised and really hurt.*] Constance, how can you say such things to me? I think it's terribly unkind of you. I thought you liked me.

CONSTANCE: I do. I think you a liar, a humbug and a parasite, but I like you.

MARIE-LOUISE: You can't if you think such dreadful things about me.

CONSTANCE: I do. You're good-tempered and generous and sometimes amusing. I even have a certain affection for you.

MARIE-LOUISE: [*Smiling.*] I don't believe you mean a word you say. You know how devoted I am to you.

CONSTANCE: I take people as they are and I dare say that in another twenty years you'll be the pink of propriety.

MARIE-LOUISE: Darling, I knew you didn't mean it, but you will have your little joke.

CONSTANCE: Now run along, darling, and I'll break the news to John.

MARIE-LOUISE: Well, good-bye, and be gentle with him. There is no reason why we shouldn't spare him as much as possible. [*She turns to go and at the door—stops.*] Of course I've often wondered why with your looks you don't have more success than you do. I know now.

CONSTANCE: Tell me.

MARIE-LOUISE: You see—you're a humourist and that always puts men off. [*She goes out. In a moment the door is cautiously opened and* JOHN *puts his head in.*]

JOHN: Has she gone?

CONSTANCE: Come in. A fine night and all's well.

JOHN: [*Entering.*] I heard the door bang. You broke it to her?

CONSTANCE: I broke it.

JOHN: Was she awfully upset?

CONSTANCE: Of course it was a shock, but she kept a stiff upper lip.

JOHN: Did she cry?

CONSTANCE: No. Not exactly. To tell you the truth I think she was stunned by the blow. But of course when she gets home and realises the full extent of her loss, she'll cry like anything.

JOHN: I hate to see a woman cry.

CONSTANCE: It is painful, isn't it? But of course it's a relief to the nerves.

JOHN: I think you're rather cool about it, Constance. I am not feeling any too comfortable. I shouldn't like her to think I'd treated her badly.

CONSTANCE: I think she quite understands that you're doing it for my sake. She knows that you have still a very great regard for her.

JOHN: But you made it quite definite, didn't you?

CONSTANCE: Oh, quite.

JOHN: I'm really very much obliged to you, Constance.

CONSTANCE: Not at all.

JOHN: At all events I'm glad to think that you'll be able to set out on your holiday with a perfectly easy mind. By the way, do you want any money? I'll write you a cheque at once.

CONSTANCE: Oh, no, thank you. I've got plenty. I've earned fourteen hundred pounds during this year that I've been working.

JOHN: Have you, by Jove! That's a very considerable sum.

CONSTANCE: I'm taking two hundred of it for my holiday. I've spent two hundred on my clothes and on odds and ends and the remaining thousand I've paid into your account this morning for my board and lodging during the last twelve months.

JOHN: Nonsense, darling. I won't hear of such a thing. I don't want you to pay for your board and lodging.

CONSTANCE: I insist.

JOHN: Don't you love me any more?

CONSTANCE: What has that to do with it? Oh, you think a woman can only love a man if he keeps her. Isn't that rating your powers of fascination too modestly? What about your charm and good humour?

JOHN: Don't be absurd, Constance. I can perfectly well afford to support you in your proper station. To offer me a thousand pounds for your board and lodging is almost insulting.

CONSTANCE: Don't you think it's the kind of insult you could bring yourself to swallow? One can do a lot of amusing things with a thousand pounds.

JOHN: I wouldn't dream of taking it. I never liked the idea of your going into business. I thought you had quite enough to do looking after the house and so forth.

CONSTANCE: Have you been less comfortable since I began working?

JOHN: No, I can't say I have.

CONSTANCE: You can take my word for it, a lot of incompetent women talk a great deal of nonsense about housekeeping. If you know your job and have good servants it can be done in ten minutes a day.

JOHN: Anyhow, you wanted to work and I yielded. I thought in point of fact it would be a very pleasant occupation for you, but heaven knows I wasn't expecting to profit financially by it.

CONSTANCE: No, I'm sure you weren't.

JOHN: Constance, I could never help thinking that your determination had something to do with Marie-Louise.

[*There is a moment's pause and when* CONSTANCE *speaks it is not without seriousness.*

CONSTANCE: Haven't you wondered why I never reproached you for your affair with Marie-Louise?

JOHN: Yes. I could only ascribe it to your unfathomable goodness.

CONSTANCE: You were wrong. I felt I hadn't the right to reproach you.

JOHN: What do you mean, Constance? You had every right. We behaved like a couple of swine. I may be a dirty dog, but, thank God, I know I'm a dirty dog.

CONSTANCE: You no longer desired me. How could I blame you for that? But if you didn't desire me, what use was I to you? You've seen how small a share I take in providing you with the comfort of a well-ordered home.

JOHN: You were the mother of my child.

CONSTANCE: Let us not exaggerate the importance of that, John. I performed a natural and healthy function of my sex. And all the tiresome part of looking after the child when she was born I placed in the hands of much more competent persons. Let us face it, I was only a parasite in your house. You had entered into legal obligations that prevented you from turning me adrift, but I owe you a debt of gratitude for never letting me see by word or gesture that I was no more than a costly and at times inconvenient ornament.

JOHN: I never looked upon you as an inconvenient ornament. And I don't know what you mean by being a parasite. Have I ever in any way suggested that I grudged a penny that I spent on you?

CONSTANCE: [*With mock amazement.*] Do you mean to say that I ascribed to your beautiful manners what was only due to your stupidity? Are you as great a fool as the average man who falls for the average woman's stupendous bluff that just because he's married her he must provide for her wants and her luxuries, sacrifice his pleasures and comfort and convenience, and that he must look upon it as a privilege that she allows him to be her slave and bondman? Come, come, John, pull yourself together. You're a hundred years behind the times. Now that women have broken down the walls of the harem they must take the rough-and-tumble of the street.

JOHN: You forget all sorts of things. Don't you think a man may have gratitude to a woman for the love he has had for her in the past?

CONSTANCE: I think gratitude is often very strong in men so long as it demands from them no particular sacrifices.

JOHN: Well, it's a curious way of looking at things, but obviously I have reason to be thankful for it. But after all you knew what was going on long before it came out. What happened then that made you make up your mind to go into business?

CONSTANCE: I am naturally a lazy woman. So long as appearances were saved I was prepared to take all I could get and give nothing in return. I was a parasite, but I knew it. But when we reached a situation where only your politeness or your lack of intelligence prevented you from throwing the fact in my teeth, I changed my mind. I thought that I should very much like to be in a position where, if I felt inclined to, I could tell you, with calm and courtesy, but with determination—to go to hell.

JOHN: And are you in that position now?

CONSTANCE: Precisely. I owe you nothing. I am able to keep myself. For the last year I have paid my way. There is only one freedom that is really important and that is economic freedom, for in the long run the man who pays the piper calls the tune. Well, I have that freedom, and upon my soul it's the most enjoyable sensation I can remember since I ate my first strawberry ice.

JOHN: You know, I would sooner you had made me scenes for a month on end like any ordinary woman and nagged my life out than that you should harbour this cold rancour against me.

CONSTANCE: My poor darling, what are you talking about? Have you known me for fifteen years and do you think me capable of the commonness of insincerity? I harbour no rancour. Why, my dear, I'm devoted to you.

JOHN: Do you mean to tell me that you've done all this without any intention of making me feel a perfect cad?

CONSTANCE: On my honour. If I look in my heart I can only find in it affection for you and the most kindly and charitable feelings. Don't you believe me?

[*He looks at her for a moment and then makes a little gesture of bewilderment.*

JOHN: Yes, oddly enough, I do. You are a remarkable woman, Constance.

CONSTANCE: I know, but keep it to yourself. You don't want to give a dog a bad name.

JOHN: [*With an affectionate smile.*] I wish I could get away. I don't half like the idea of your travelling by yourself.

CONSTANCE: Oh, but I'm not. Didn't I tell you?

JOHN: No.

CONSTANCE: I meant to. I'm going with Bernard.

JOHN: Oh! You never said so. Who else?

CONSTANCE: Nobody.

JOHN: Oh! [*He is rather taken aback at the news.*] Isn't that rather odd?

CONSTANCE: No. Why?

JOHN: [*Not knowing at all how to take it.*] Well, it's not usual for a young woman to take a six weeks' holiday with a man who can hardly be described as old enough to be her father.

CONSTANCE: Bernard's just about the same age as you.

JOHN: Don't you think it'll make people gossip a bit?

CONSTANCE: I haven't gone out of my way to spread the news. In fact, now I come to think of it, I haven't told anyone but you, and you, I am sure, will be discreet.

> [JOHN *suddenly feels that his collar is a little too tight for him, and with his fingers he tries to loosen it.*

JOHN: You're pretty certain to be seen by someone who knows you and they're bound to talk.

CONSTANCE: Oh, I don't think so. You see we're motoring all the way and we neither of us care for frequented places. One of the advantages of having really nice friends like ours is that you can always be certain of finding them at the fashionable resorts at the very moment when everybody you know is there.

JOHN: Of course I am not so silly as to think that because a man and a woman go away together it is necessary to believe the worst about them, but you can't deny that it is rather unconventional. I wouldn't for a moment suggest that there'll be anything between you, but it's inevitable that ordinary persons should think there was.

CONSTANCE: [*As cool as a cucumber.*] I've always thought that ordinary persons had more sense than the clever ones are ready to credit them with.

JOHN: [*Deliberately.*] What on earth do you mean?

CONSTANCE: Why, of course we're going as man and wife, John.

JOHN: Don't be a fool, Constance. You don't know what you're talking about. That's not funny at all.

CONSTANCE: But, my poor John, whom do you take us for? Am I so unattractive that what I'm telling you is incredible? Why else should I go with Bernard? If I merely wanted a companion I'd go with a woman. We could have headaches together and have our hair washed at the same place and copy one another's nightdresses. A woman's a much better travelling companion than a man.

JOHN: I may be very stupid, but I don't seem to be able to understand what you're saying. Do you really mean me to believe that Bernard Kersal is your lover?

CONSTANCE: Certainly not.

JOHN: Then what *are* you talking about?

CONSTANCE: My dear, I can't put it any plainer. I'm going away for six weeks' holiday and Bernard has very kindly offered to come with me.

JOHN: And where do I come in?

CONSTANCE: You don't come in. You stay at home and look after your patients.

JOHN: [*Trying his best to control himself.*] I flatter myself I'm a sensible man. I'm not going to fly into a passion. Many men would stamp and rave or break the furniture. I have no intention of being melodramatic, but you must allow me to say that what you've just told me is very surprising.

CONSTANCE: Just for a moment, perhaps, but I'm sure you have only to familiarize yourself with the notion in order to become reconciled to it.

JOHN: I'm doubtful whether I shall have time to do that, for I feel uncommonly as though I were about to have an apoplectic stroke.

CONSTANCE: Undo your collar then. Now I come to look at you I confess that you are more than usually red in the face.

JOHN: What makes you think that I am going to allow you to go?

CONSTANCE: [*Good-humouredly.*] Chiefly the fact that you can't prevent me.

JOHN: I can't bring myself to believe that you mean what you say. I don't know what ever put such an idea into your head.

CONSTANCE: [*Casually.*] I thought a change might do me good.

JOHN: Nonsense.

CONSTANCE: Why? You did. Don't you remember? You were getting rather flat and stale. Then you had an affair with Marie-Louise and you were quite another man. Gay and amusing, full of life, and much more agreeable to live with. The moral effect on you was quite remarkable.

JOHN: It's different for a man than for a woman.

CONSTANCE: Are you thinking of the possible consequences? We have long passed the Victorian Era when asterisks were followed after a certain interval by a baby.

JOHN: That never occurred to me. What I meant was that if a man's unfaithful to his wife she's an object of sympathy, whereas if a woman's unfaithful to her husband he's merely an object of ridicule.

CONSTANCE: That is one of those conventional prejudices that sensible people must strive to ignore.

JOHN: Do you expect me to sit still and let this man take my wife away from under my very nose? I wonder you don't ask me to shake hands with him and wish him good luck.

CONSTANCE: That's just what I am going to do. He's coming here in a few minutes to say good-bye to you.

JOHN: I shall knock him down.

CONSTANCE: I wouldn't take any risks in your place. He's pretty hefty and I'm under the impression that he's very nippy with his left.

JOHN: I shall have great pleasure in telling him exactly what I think of him.

CONSTANCE: Why? Have you forgotten that I was charming to Marie-Louise? We were the best of friends. She never bought a hat without asking me to go and help her choose it.

JOHN: I have red blood in my veins.

CONSTANCE: I'm more concerned at the moment with the grey matter in your brain.

JOHN: Is he in love with you?

CONSTANCE: Madly. Didn't you know?

JOHN: I? How should I?

CONSTANCE: He's been here a great deal during the last year. Were you under the impression that he only came to see you?

JOHN: I never paid any attention to him. I thought him rather dull.

CONSTANCE: He is rather dull. But he's very sweet.

JOHN: What sort of a man is it who eats a fellow's food and drinks his wine and then makes love to his wife behind his back?

CONSTANCE: A man very like you, John, I should say.

JOHN: Not at all. Mortimer is the sort of man who was born to be made a fool of.

CONSTANCE: None of us know for certain the designs of Providence.

JOHN: I see you're bent on driving me to desperation. I shall break something in a minute.

CONSTANCE: There's that blue-and-white bowl that your Uncle Henry gave us as a wedding present. Break that, it's only a modern imitation.

> [*He takes the bowl and hurls it on the floor so that it is shattered.*

JOHN: There.

CONSTANCE: Do you feel better?

JOHN: Not a bit.

CONSTANCE: It's a pity you broke it then. You might have given it away as a wedding present to one of your colleagues at the hospital.

> [*The butler shows in* MRS. CULVER.

BUTLER: Mrs. Culver.

CONSTANCE: Oh, mother, how sweet of you to come. I was so hoping I'd see you before I left.

MRS. CULVER: Oh, you've had an accident.

CONSTANCE: No, John's in a temper and he thought it would relieve him if he broke something.

MRS. CULVER: Nonsense, John's never in a temper.

JOHN: That's what you think, Mrs. Culver. Yes, I am in a temper. I'm in a filthy temper. Are you a party to this plan of Constance's?

CONSTANCE: No, mother doesn't know.

JOHN: Can't you do something to stop it? You have some influence over her. You must see that the thing's preposterous.

MRS. CULVER: My dear boy, I haven't the ghost of an idea what you're talking about.

JOHN: She's going to Italy with Bernard Kersal. Alone.

MRS. CULVER: [*With a stare.*] It's not true; how d'you know?

JOHN: She's just told me so, as bold as brass, out of a blue sky. She mentioned it in the course of conversation as if she were saying, Darling, your coat wants brushing.

MRS. CULVER: Is it true, Constance?

CONSTANCE: Quite.

MRS. CULVER: But haven't you been getting on with John? I always thought you two were as happy as the day is long.

JOHN: So did I. We've never had the shadow of a quarrel. We've always got on.

MRS. CULVER: Don't you love John any more, darling?

CONSTANCE: Yes, I'm devoted to him.

JOHN: How can you be devoted to a man when you're going to do him the greatest injury that a woman can do to a man?

CONSTANCE: Don't be idiotic, John. I'm going to do you no more injury than you did me a year ago.

JOHN: [*Striding up to her, thinking quite erroneously that he sees light.*] Are you doing this in order to pay me out for Marie-Louise?

CONSTANCE: Don't be such a fool, John. Nothing is further from my thoughts.

MRS. CULVER: The circumstances are entirely different. It was very naughty of John to deceive you, but he's sorry for what he did and he's been punished for it. It was all very dreadful and caused us a great deal of pain. But a man's a man and you expect that kind of thing from him. There are excuses for him. There are none for a woman. Men are naturally polygamous and sensible women have always made allowances for their occasional lapse from a condition which modern civilisation has forced on them. Women are monogamous. They do not naturally desire more than one man and that is why the common sense of the world has heaped obloquy upon them when they have overstepped the natural limitations of their sex.

CONSTANCE: [*Smiling.*] It seems rather hard that what is sauce for the gander shouldn't also be sauce for the goose.

MRS. CULVER: We all know that unchastity has no moral effect on men. They can be perfectly promiscuous and remain upright, industrious and reliable. It's quite different with women. It ruins their character. They become untruthful and dissipated, lazy, shiftless and dishonest. That is why the experience of ten thousand years has demanded chastity in women. Because it has learnt that this virtue is the key to all others.

CONSTANCE: They were dishonest because they were giving away something that wasn't theirs to give. They had sold themselves for board, lodging and protection. They were chattel. They were dependent on their husbands and when they were unfaithful to them they were liars and thieves. I'm not dependent on John. I am economically independent and therefore I claim my sexual independence. I have this afternoon paid into John's account one thousand pounds for my year's keep.

JOHN: I refuse to take it.

CONSTANCE: Well, you'll damned well have to.

MRS. CULVER: There's no object in losing your temper.

CONSTANCE: I have mine under perfect control.

JOHN: If you think what they call free love is fun you're mistaken. Believe me, it's the most overrated amusement that was ever invented.

CONSTANCE: In that case, I wonder why people continue to indulge in it.

JOHN: I ought to know what I'm talking about, hang it all. It has all the inconveniences of marriage and none of its advantages. I assure you, my dear, the game is not worth the candle.

CONSTANCE: You may be right, but you know **how** hard it is to profit by anybody's experience. I think I'd like to see for myself.

MRS. CULVER: Are you in love with Bernard?

CONSTANCE: To tell you the truth I haven't quite made up my mind. How does one know if one's in love?

MRS. CULVER: My dear, I only know one test. Could you use his tooth-brush?

CONSTANCE: No.

MRS. CULVER: Then you're not in love with him.

CONSTANCE: He's adored me for fifteen years. There's something in that long devotion which gives me a funny little feeling in my heart. I should like to do something to show him that I'm not ungrateful. You see, in six weeks he goes back to Japan. There is no chance of his coming to England again for seven years. I'm thirty-six now and he adores me; in seven years I shall be forty-three. A woman of forty-three is often charming, but it's seldom that a man of fifty-five is crazy about her. I came to the conclusion that it must be now or never and so I asked him if he'd like me to spend these last six weeks with him in Italy. When I wave my handkerchief to him as the ship that takes him sails out of the harbour at Naples I hope that he will feel that all those years of unselfish love have been well worth the while.

JOHN: Six weeks. Do you intend to leave him at the end of six weeks?

CONSTANCE: Oh, yes, of course. It's because I'm putting a limit to our love that I think it may achieve the perfection of something that is beautiful and transitory. Why, John, what is it that makes a rose so lovely but that its petals fall as soon as it is full blown?

JOHN: It's all come as such a shock and a surprise that I hardly know what to say. You've got me at a complete disadvantage.

[MRS. CULVER, *who has been standing at the window, gives a little cry.*

CONSTANCE: What is it?

MRS. CULVER: Here is Bernard. He's just driven up to the door.

JOHN: Do you expect me to receive him as if I were blissfully unconscious of your plans?

CONSTANCE: It would be more comfortable. It would be stupid to make a scene and it wouldn't prevent my going on this little jaunt with him.

JOHN: I have my dignity to think of.

CONSTANCE: One often preserves that best by putting it in one's pocket. It would be kind of you, John, to treat him just as pleasantly as I treated Marie-Louise when I knew she was your mistress.

JOHN: Does he know that I know?

CONSTANCE: Of course not. He's a little conventional, you know, and he couldn't happily deceive a friend if he thought there was no deception.

MRS. CULVER: Constance, is there nothing I can say to make you reconsider your decision?

CONSTANCE: Nothing, darling.

MRS. CULVER: Then I may just as well save my breath. I'll slip away before he comes.

CONSTANCE: Oh, all right. Good-bye, mother. I'll send you a lot of picture post-cards.

MRS. CULVER: I don't approve of you, Constance, and I can't pretend that I do. No good will come of it. Men were meant by nature to be wicked and delightful and deceive their wives, and women were meant to be virtuous and forgiving and to suffer verbosely. That was ordained from all eternity and none of your new-fangled notions can alter the decrees of Providence.

[*The* BUTLER *enters, followed by* BERNARD.

BENTLEY: Mr. Kersal.

MRS. CULVER: How do you do, Bernard, **and good**-bye. I'm just going.

BERNARD: Oh, I'm sorry. Good-bye.

[*She goes out.*

CONSTANCE: [*To* BERNARD.] How d'you do? Just one moment. [*To the* BUTLER.] Oh, Bentley, get my things downstairs and put them in a taxi, will you?

BENTLEY: Very good, madam.

BERNARD: Are you just starting? It's lucky I came when I did. I should have hated to miss you.

CONSTANCE: And let me know when the taxi's here.

BENTLEY: Yes, madam.

CONSTANCE: Now I can attend to you.

[*The* BUTLER *goes out.*

BERNARD: Are you looking forward to your holiday?

CONSTANCE: Immensely. I've never gone on a jaunt like this before, and I'm really quite excited.

BERNARD: You're going alone, aren't you?

CONSTANCE: Oh, yes, quite alone.

BERNARD: It's rotten for you not to be able to get away, old man.

JOHN: Rotten.

BERNARD: I suppose these are the penalties of greatness. I can quite understand that you have to think of your patients first.

JOHN: Quite.

CONSTANCE: Of course John doesn't very much care for Italy.

BERNARD: Oh, are you going to Italy? I thought you said Spain.

JOHN: No, she always said Italy.

BERNARD: Oh, well, that's hardly your mark, is it, old boy? Though I believe there are some sporting links on the Lake of Como.

JOHN: Are there?

BERNARD: I suppose there's no chance of your being anywhere near Naples towards the end of July?

CONSTANCE: I don't really know. My plans are quite vague.

BERNARD: I was only asking because I'm sailing from Naples. It would be fun if we met there.

JOHN: Great fun.

CONSTANCE: I hope you'll see a lot of John while I'm away. I'm afraid he'll be a trifle lonely, poor darling. Why don't you dine together one day next week?

BERNARD: I'm terribly sorry, but you know I'm going away.

CONSTANCE: Oh, are you? I thought you were going to stay in London till you had to start for Japan.

BERNARD: I meant to, but my doctor has ordered me to go and do a cure.

JOHN: What sort of a cure?

BERNARD: Oh, just a cure. He says I want bucking up.

JOHN: Oh, does he? What's the name of your doctor?

BERNARD: No one you ever heard of. A man I used to know in the war.

JOHN: Oh!

BERNARD: So I'm afraid this is good-bye. Of course, it's a wrench leaving London, especially as I don't expect to be in Europe again for some years, but I always think it rather silly not to take a man's advice when you've asked for it.

JOHN: More especially when he's charged you three guineas.

CONSTANCE: I'm sorry. I was counting on you to keep John out of mischief during my absence.

BERNARD: I'm not sure if I could guarantee to do that. But we might have done a few theatres together and had a game of golf or two.

CONSTANCE: It would have been jolly, wouldn't it, John?

JOHN: Very jolly.

[*The* BUTLER *comes in.*

BENTLEY: The taxi's waiting, madam.

CONSTANCE: Thank you.

[*The* BUTLER *goes out.*

BERNARD: I'll take myself off. In case I don't see you again I'd like to thank you now for all your kindness to me during the year I've spent in London.

CONSTANCE: It's been very nice to see you.

BERNARD: You and John have been most awfully good to me. I never imagined I was going to have such a wonderful time.

CONSTANCE: We shall miss you terribly. It's been a great comfort to John to think that there was someone to take me out when he had to be away on one of his operations. Hasn't it, darling?

JOHN: Yes, darling.

CONSTANCE: When he knew I was with you he never worried. Did you, darling?

JOHN: No, darling.

BERNARD: I'm awfully glad if I've been able to make myself useful. Don't forget me entirely, will you?

CONSTANCE: We're not likely to do that, are we, darling?

JOHN: No, darling.

BERNARD: And if you ever have a moment to spare you will write to me, won't you? You don't know how much it means to us exiles.

CONSTANCE: Of course we will. We'll both write. Won't we, darling?

JOHN: Yes, darling.

CONSTANCE: John writes such a good letter. So chatty, you know, and amusing.

BERNARD: That's a promise. Well, good-bye, old boy. Have a good time.

JOHN: Thanks, old bean.

BERNARD: Good-bye, Constance. There's so much I want to say to you that I don't know where to begin.

JOHN: I don't want to hurry you, but the taxi is just ticking its head off.

BERNARD: John is so matter-of-fact. Well, I'll say nothing then but God bless you.

CONSTANCE: Au revoir.

BERNARD: If you do go to Naples you will let me know, won't you? If you send a line to my club, it'll be forwarded at once.

CONSTANCE: Oh, all right.

BERNARD: Good-bye.

> [*He gives them both a friendly nod and goes out.* CON-STANCE *begins to giggle and soon is seized with uncontrollable laughter.*

JOHN: Will you kindly tell me what there is to laugh at? If you think it amuses me to stand here like patience on a monument and have my leg pulled you're mistaken. What did you mean by all that balderdash about meeting you by chance in Naples?

CONSTANCE: He was throwing you off the scent.

JOHN: The man's a drivelling idiot.

CONSTANCE: D'you think so? I thought he was rather ingenious. Considering he hasn't had very much practice in this sort of thing I thought he did very well.

JOHN: Of course if you're determined to find him a pattern of perfection it's useless for me to attempt to argue. But honestly, speaking without prejudice for or against, I'm sorry to think of you throwing yourself away on a man like that.

CONSTANCE: Perhaps it's natural that a man and his wife should differ in their estimate of her prospective lover.

JOHN: You're not going to tell me he's better-looking than I am.

CONSTANCE: No. You have always been my ideal of manly beauty.

JOHN: He's no better dressed than I am.

CONSTANCE: He could hardly expect to be. He goes to the same tailor.

JOHN: I don't think you can honestly say he's more amusing than I am.

CONSTANCE: No, I honestly can't.

JOHN: Then in Heaven's name why do you want to go away with him?

CONSTANCE: Shall I tell you? Once more before it's too late I want to feel about me the arms of a man who adores the ground I walk on. I want to see his face light up when I enter the room. I want to feel the pressure of his hand when we look at the moon together and the pleasantly tickling sensation when his arm tremulously steals around my waist. I want to let my hand fall on his shoulder and feel his lips softly touch my hair.

JOHN: The operation is automatically impossible, the poor devil would get such a crick in the neck he wouldn't know what to do.

CONSTANCE: I want to walk along country lanes holding hands and I want to be called by absurd pet names. I want to talk baby-talk by the hour together.

JOHN: Oh, God.

CONSTANCE: I want to know that I'm eloquent and witty when I'm dead silent. For ten years I've been very happy in your affection, John, we've been the best and dearest friends, but now just for a little while I hanker for something else. Do you grudge it me? I want to be loved.

JOHN: But, my dear, I'll love you. I've been a brute, I've neglected you, it's not too late and you're the only woman I've ever really cared for. I'll chuck everything and we'll go away together.

CONSTANCE: The prospect does not thrill me.

JOHN: Come, darling, have a heart. I gave up Marie-Louise. Surely you can give up Bernard.

CONSTANCE: But you gave up Marie-Louise to please yourself, not to please me.

JOHN: Don't be a little beast, Constance. Come away with me. We'll have such a lark.

CONSTANCE: Oh, my poor John, I didn't work so hard to gain my economic independence in order to go on a honeymoon with my own husband.

JOHN: Do you think I can't be a lover as well as a husband?

CONSTANCE: My dear, no one can make yesterday's cold mutton into to-morrow's lamb cutlets.

JOHN: You know what you're doing. I was determined in future to be a model husband and you're driving me right into the arms of Marie-Louise. I give you my word of honour that the moment you leave this house I shall drive straight to her door.

CONSTANCE: I should hate you to have a fruitless journey. I'm afraid you won't find her at home. She has a new young man and she says he's too divine.

JOHN: What!

CONSTANCE: He's the A.D.C. of a Colonial Governor. She came here to-day to ask me to break the news to you that henceforth everything was over between you.

JOHN: I hope you told her first that I was firmly resolved to terminate a connection that could only cause you pain.

CONSTANCE: I couldn't. She was in such a blooming hurry to give me her message.

JOHN: Really, Constance, for your own pride I should have thought you wouldn't like her to make a perfect fool of me. Any other woman would have said, What a strange coincidence. Why it's only half an hour since John told me he had made up his mind never to see you again. But of course you don't care two straws for me any more, that's quite evident.

CONSTANCE: Oh, don't be unjust, darling. I shall always care for you. I may be unfaithful, but I am constant. I always think that's my most endearing quality.

[*The* BUTLER *opens the door.*

JOHN: [*Irritably.*] What is it?

BENTLEY: I thought madam had forgotten that the taxi was at the door.

JOHN: Go to hell.

BENTLEY: Very good, sir.

[*He goes out.*

CONSTANCE: I don't see why you should be rude to him. Bernard will pay the taxi. Anyhow I must go now or he'll begin to think I'm not coming. Good-bye, darling. I hope you'll get on all right in my absence. Just give the cook her head and you'll have no trouble. Won't you say good-bye to me?

JOHN: Go to the devil.

CONSTANCE: All right. I shall be back in six weeks.

JOHN: Back? Where?

CONSTANCE: Here.

JOHN: Here? Here? Do you think I'm going to take you back?

CONSTANCE: I don't see why not. When you've had time to reflect you'll realise that you have no reason to blame me. After all, I'm taking from you nothing that you want.

JOHN: Are you aware that I can divorce you for this?

CONSTANCE: Quite. But I married very prudently. I took the precaution to marry a gentleman and I know that you could never bring yourself to divorce me for doing no more than you did yourself.

JOHN: I wouldn't divorce you. I wouldn't expose my worst enemy to the risk of marrying a woman who's capable of treating her husband as you're treating me.

CONSTANCE: [*At the door.*] Well, then, shall I come back?

JOHN: [*After a moment's hesitation.*] You are the most maddening, wilful, capricious, wrong-headed, delightful and enchanting woman man was ever cursed with having for a wife. Yes, damn you, come back.

> [*She lightly kisses her hand to him and slips out, slamming the door behind her.*

THE END

THE BREAD-WINNER

A COMEDY
in One Act

CHARACTERS

CHARLES BATTLE
MARGERY, *his wife.*
JUDY, *his daughter.*
PATRICK, *his son.*
ALFRED GRANGER
DOROTHY, *his wife.*
DIANA, *his daughter.*
TIMOTHY, *his son.*

The action of the play is continuous, and takes place in the drawing-room of the Battles' house at Golders Green. In order to rest the audience the curtain is lowered twice during the performance.

THE BREAD-WINNER

SCENE I

A well-furnished drawing-room, in the modern style but without excess, an airy, sunny room looking on to the handsome suburban garden.

When the curtain rises JUDY *and* PATRICK *are discovered.* PATRICK *is in flannels. He is a nice-looking boy of eighteen. He is lying on the sofa very comfortably, reading an illustrated paper; others are scattered about him on the floor.* JUDY *is seventeen. She is pretty, blond and self-possessed. She also is dressed in tennis things. She is standing at the gramophone, and has just put on a new record. However brusquely* PATRICK *and* JUDY *talk, and however frank they are in expressing their opinions, they remain engaging and delightful. The same applies to their friends* DIANA *and* TIMOTHY.

PATRICK: [*Without looking up from his paper.*] Aren't you sick of that yet?

JUDY: My dear child, it's absolutely new. It was only written last week, and the record came out yesterday morning.

PATRICK: Rot. I was weaned on it. I vividly remember mother turning it on to get me to take the bottle quietly.

JUDY: Liar! It's rather jolly to dance to. Come on.

PATRICK: [*Without moving.*] Oh, God!

JUDY: Slacker.

PATRICK: I wish Tim and Dinah would hurry up.

JUDY: What's the time? She said they'd come immediately after lunch.

PATRICK: Ring them up and tell them to hurry up.

JUDY: [*Amiably.*] Ring them up yourself.

PATRICK: Lazy hound.

JUDY: Tim's going back next term after all. He wanted to go up to Cambridge with you, but Alfred said he must stay at school another year.

PATRICK: He's only seventeen.

JUDY: He'll be eighteen in December.

PATRICK: There's all the difference between being eighteen now and eighteen in December. I should have thought that was obvious to the meanest intelligence.

JUDY: Here they are. [*She goes to the door and opens it.*] Dinah!

DIANA: [*Outside.*] Hullo!

JUDY: We're in here. Bring your rackets along.

DIANA: Right-ho.

> [*She comes in, a dark pretty girl of eighteen and a bit, with fine eyes and a fresh colour. She has a racket in her hand. She is followed by her brother* TIMOTHY. *He is a year younger than she, and, as we have heard, will not be eighteen till December. He is a slim, tall, dark youth wearing a gay blazer and a muffler, and he carries two rackets.* PATRICK *gets up from the sofa.*]

PATRICK: Hullo, Dinah.

DIANA: Hullo.

PATRICK: I forget, do we kiss?

DIANA: Only at dances under the influence of claret cup.

PATRICK: Hullo, Tim. How are you?

TIMOTHY: All right. How are you?

PATRICK: [*Pointing to the two rackets.*] I say, what's the idea?

TIMOTHY: I've come on in my game a bit lately. One must have two rackets, you know.

PATRICK: Wimbledon. Eh, what?

DIANA: Tim is now a blood.

PATRICK: I hear you're going back next term.

TIMOTHY: Rotten, isn't it? Alfred's being frightfully tiresome.

PATRICK: How is your respected parent?

TIMOTHY: Very facetious.

DIANA: Few people know how exhausting it is to have a humorist in the family.

PATRICK: I'm thankful to say that's not one of our troubles. You'd have to get an axe to get father to see that you're making a joke.

JUDY: Poor Daddy, no one could say that he has a sense of humour.

TIMOTHY: Have you plied him with liquor?

PATRICK: It has no effect, it's constitutional.

DIANA: When did you get back, Pat?

PATRICK: Just before lunch.

TIMOTHY: We broke up the day before yesterday.

DIANA: Are you glad to have left school?

PATRICK: Rather! I didn't have a bad time, you know. But I want to go up to Cambridge now. I think it'll be rather fun.

JUDY: I think he's grown since Easter, don't you, Dinah?

PATRICK: I'm sure I have. I can tell by my dinner-jacket. I'm going to order some new tails to-morrow.

TIMOTHY: Who are you going to?

PATRICK: Well, I don't know. I suppose Daddy'll want me to go to his tailor as usual. But I'm going to tell him that of course he's all right for him, but honestly he's not smart enough for me.

DIANA: I shall take off my hat. [*She does so, and shakes her shingled head.*] Lend me your comb, Tim.

TIMOTHY: [*Looking in his pocket.*] Oh damn, I left it at home.

JUDY: Pat'll lend you his.

PATRICK: [*Taking a comb out of his pocket.*] Here you are.

> [*He gives it to her, and taking a little glass from her bag she combs her hair. Then* JUDY *takes the comb from her and runs it through her hair.*

TIMOTHY: Are you still going in for the Bar, Pat?

PATRICK: Oh, yes. I think so. After all, it's the only profession that really gives you a chance. It'll be rather fun coming up to town to eat my dinners.

TIMOTHY: Let me have the comb a minute.

> [*He takes it and combs his perfectly ordered hair. He returns it to* PATRICK, *who mechanically does the same, and then puts it back in his pocket.*

PATRICK: Of course I shall go in for politics.

DIANA: Which side?

PATRICK: Well, I haven't really made up my mind yet. Daddy's always been a liberal, but there's nothing to be got out of being a liberal now. *I* think the only thing now is labour.

DIANA: I'm labour. I always have been.

PATRICK: They want people like us, public school and varsity, and that sort of thing.

TIMOTHY: Of course you're lucky, you can go in for anything you like. I've got to go into Alfred's rotten old business.

DIANA: You can't blame Alfred. It's an old-established firm, and he wants his only son to follow in his footsteps.

TIMOTHY: Can you see me as respectable family lawyer?

PATRICK: Perfectly, and I can see you giving me **fat briefs**.

TIMOTHY: I'll tell you one thing, I'm not going to live at home.

PATRICK: They couldn't expect you to do that. I don't mind coming here during the vac. for a bit when I haven't got anywhere better to go, but as soon as I settle down in London I'm going to tell Daddy that I must have a flat.

TIMOTHY: We might share one.

PATRICK: That's not a bad idea. I've got rather a fancy for Albemarle Street personally.

TIMOTHY: That would do me all right. As long as it's absolutely central I don't care where I live.

PATRICK: It's a damned good address. And one must have that.

TIMOTHY: Absolutely.

DIANA: I'm simply fed up with the suburbs.

PATRICK: So am I. Fed to the teeth.

JUDY: I can't imagine why they want to live out in the wilds like this.

PATRICK: Poor Mummy thinks this is such a nice neighbourhood.

JUDY: It was all very well when we were kids. We had to have fresh air and all that sort of rot. But now we're grown up I can't see the point of it.

DIANA: Would you believe it? Dorothy thinks it's central. When I tell her it's the back of beyond, she says, My dear, what are you talking about? It's only twelve minutes by tube from Piccadilly Circus.

PATRICK: One's people are really extraordinary. You know, ours haven't begun to realise that we are grown up.

JUDY: Mummy still wants to buy my clothes for me. I had to make the devil of a row before I could get my own dress allowance.

TIMOTHY: I will say that for Alfred, he's given us an allowance ever since we were fifteen.

PATRICK: I'm expecting to have a bit of a dust up with father over my allowance at Cambridge. I'm going to ask for five hundred.

TIMOTHY: Do you think he'll give you that?

PATRICK: No, but I think he'll give me four. If I ask for four he'll try and get off for three-fifty.

TIMOTHY: He oughtn't to kick at that.

PATRICK: He oughtn't to kick at anything. After all, I didn't ask to be brought into the world. He did it entirely for his own amusement, and he's had a lot of fun out of me. He must be prepared to pay for it.

TIMOTHY: That's fair enough.

PATRICK: When I settle down in London he'll have to give me at least five hundred a year. Everybody knows that you can't earn a living at the Bar till you're thirty.

TIMOTHY: If Alfred gave me the same, we ought to be able to do ourselves pretty well in a flat.

DIANA: It makes me perfectly sick when I hear you two talk of having a flat in town. I'd love to have one of my own. Wouldn't you, Judy?

JUDY: Simply love it.

DIANA: I'm sick of living at home.

PATRICK: Why don't you marry?

DIANA: Oh, I'm not going to marry for years yet. I want to marry when I'm twenty-four. I want to have a good time first.

JUDY: Oh, I think that's rather old. I want to marry when I'm twenty-one.

PATRICK: Why don't you tell Alfred that you want your own flat?

DIANA: Can you see his face? [*Imitating her father.*] I've made a jolly good home for my kiddies, old boy, and between you and I, I don't mind telling you they think there's no place like it.

PATRICK: [*With a smile.*] Poor Alfred.

DIANA: Alfred's all right. He means well.

TIMOTHY: Only he's so terribly hearty.

DIANA: I think it's rather pathetic sometimes, his delusion that one's really going to look upon one's parents as friends.

TIMOTHY: It's so shy-making, his one boy to another stunt.

DIANA: Well, you know, it's got its advantages. Call him old bean, and you can get anything you want out of him.

PATRICK: It's so damned humiliating having to play up to one's people all the time.

DIANA: What else can you do? They have an idea about you in their heads and you have to live up to it. They're incapable of understanding that you're not in the least what they think you are.

TIMOTHY: I shall never forget when I was leaving my prep school, and Dorothy told Alfred he must tell me what she called the facts of life.

PATRICK: Oh, God!

TIMOTHY: I've never seen Alfred in such a twitter. He was trying to be terribly hearty, and he got as red as a turkey-cock. I could see the sweat simply pouring down his face.

PATRICK: What did you do?

TIMOTHY: What could I do? I couldn't very well say to him, Look here, Alfred, you're about three years too late with all this, there's not much you can tell me I don't know.

DIANA: Our dear little innocent Timothy.

TIMOTHY: So I just did the little blushing boy stunt, and let him get it off his chest. And then he gave me a pound and said, You'd better take your sister to a matinée.

PATRICK: How is our respected parent these days, Judy?

JUDY: Oh, I don't know, same as usual.

DIANA: Of course you haven't seen him yet?

PATRICK: No. I suppose he'll be getting back from the City presently. I was only asking because I've been wondering if there was any chance of getting a car out of him.

TIMOTHY: I say, that would be grand.

PATRICK: Well, now I've left school I ought to have a car of my own. It's absurd that I should have to go about in the family bus. [*To* JUDY.] Have you said anything to Mummy about it?

JUDY: She says it all depends on how things are on the Stock Exchange.

PATRICK: They're all rolling on the Stock Exchange. As long as the world is full of mugs, stock-brokers are bound to make money.

DIANA: You know, *I* like your father, Pat.

JUDY: Very dull, poor darling.

DIANA: I'm not sure that I wouldn't rather have a dull father than a funny one.

PATRICK: Fortunately we don't see much of him except at dinner. And that's pretty ghastly, isn't it, Judy?

JUDY: Ghastly isn't the word.

PATRICK: Daddy sitting at one end of the table never opening his mouth, and mother improving our minds with bright chat about art and literature.

DIANA: That's home life.

PATRICK: Well, I've had about enough of it, I can tell you. D'you think that when *we're* their age we shall be as boring as they are?

JUDY: Oh, I don't see why we should for a moment.

TIMOTHY: How old is your father, Pat?

PATRICK: I think he's forty-two, isn't he, Judy?

JUDY: Yes, he was comparatively young when he married Mummy. Twenty-three.

DIANA: One of those awful war marriages, I suppose. Like Alfred and Dorothy.

JUDY: Oh, no. They must have been married before that. Pat's eighteen.

DIANA: Well, when was the war?

TIMOTHY: Oh, don't let's talk of that old war. I'm fed to the teeth with it.

JUDY: What a bore the people are who went through it.

PATRICK: Crashing.

JUDY: When they get together and start talking about their experiences I could scream.

DIANA: I know. As if anyone cared.

TIMOTHY: They were a dreary lot, that war generation.

DIANA: Well, don't forget that except for the war there would have been a lot more of them.

TIMOTHY: They don't amount to anything any more. They're finished and done with, thank God.

DIANA: Unfortunately some of them don't know it.

JUDY: Well, I'm going to make it my business to tell them whenever I have an opportunity.

PATRICK: After all, let's face it, people aren't any good after forty, are they? They're only in the way, and life can't be any pleasure to them.

DIANA: I don't suppose it is much, but what are you to do with them? You can't drown them like puppies.

TIMOTHY: It's obvious that people live much too long now.

PATRICK: If nature were properly organised they'd just drop off quite quietly at the age of forty.

DIANA: D'you think they'd like it?

PATRICK: I don't see why they should mind. They've had their day. They've done everything they're capable of doing. Look at all the poets and painters and so on. What on earth have they done that was worth while after they were forty? What's the good of hanging on, a burden to yourself and everyone connected with you? It would be much better if they just passed out quietly, like the mayflies when they've had their little bit of nonsense.

JUDY: Of course, I don't expect to live till I'm forty. Fancy being thirty-six. I shall die when I'm twenty-nine.

DIANA: Have you made your will?

JUDY: No, but I've been thinking about it.

TIMOTHY: You might leave me those jade buttons of yours. They'd make rather nice links.

JUDY: Oh, I'm going to be buried with all my jewellery. I made up my mind about that years ago.

PATRICK: Don't talk rot. I'm being serious. In a well-regulated state at a certain age everyone should be put painlessly out of existence.

DIANA: Without exception?

PATRICK: Of course.

DIANA: It would be rather a wrench when it came to one's own people.

PATRICK: Of course, it would be a wrench. But one would have to sacrifice one's private feelings to the common good. Take our case, for instance. Judy and I are quite fond of father and mother. Aren't we, Judy?

JUDY: Yes. We're as fond of them as anyone can be of their people.

PATRICK: But we're not blind to their defects. Mummy is terribly arty and highbrow. And poor Daddy has no sense of humour.

JUDY: Absolutely.

PATRICK: They've always been very nice to us. They've sent us to decent schools and given us a good time in the holidays. And we've always been very decent to them. We've never given them any trouble. I think we've been rather a credit to them.

DIANA: On the whole.

PATRICK: But now it's quite obvious that their use is ended. They can only hamper us in future. We're grown up and we want our freedom.

TIMOTHY: You're absolutely right, Patrick.

PATRICK: Of course, I'm right. I'm not just talking through my hat. I've thought about this a great deal. We've arrived at an age now when we ought to be on our own. We've got the whole world before us. We can't afford to be. . . . What's the word I want?

DIANA: Footled about.

JUDY: Tied.

PATRICK: Trammelled, that's it. Trammelled by domestic ties.

TIMOTHY: It is damned unfair, there's no doubt about that.

PATRICK: Unfair isn't the word. It's damned unjust. That's what it is. They've had their fling and now they want to prevent us from having ours. After all one must have money. And one wants it when one's young. What's the good of money to middle-aged people?

DIANA: They do spend it in the most idiotic way. One can't deny that.

PATRICK: Daddy's been on the Stock Exchange for a good many years and he must have made a packet. It does seem a bit thick that Judy and I should have to wait for it till we're too old to spend it.

DIANA: Of course, all that's true. But it does seem rather drastic to kill the poor old things off.

JUDY: I don't believe you'd have the heart to do it, Pat?

PATRICK: I daresay when it came to the point I should hesitate. One has one's feelings. After all, it's a rotten thing having to put an old dog out of its sufferings.

JUDY: Don't speak of it. God, how I cried when we had to send poor old Bonzo to the vet.'s to have him destroyed.

PATRICK: It made *me* feel a bit funny, I don't mind telling you.

JUDY: I shall never have a dog I love so much.

PATRICK: I don't want to be cruel. I merely said that in a well-regulated state when people have outlived their utility, say at forty, they ought to be put out of their misery. But we don't live in a well-regulated state, and I don't suppose we ever shall.

TIMOTHY: I don't know about that. Our generation hasn't had a chance yet.

PATRICK: Personally I'd be quite willing to compromise.

DIANA: How'd you mean?

PATRICK: Well, at forty I'd make people retire and hand over all their property to their children. If they hadn't any property the state would support them and, of course, if they had, their children would make them an allowance.

TIMOTHY: That's not a bad idea.

PATRICK: Judy and I would give our people two hundred and fifty a year. That would be quite enough. They could have a little cottage in the country. Mother could keep chickens and Daddy could potter about the garden. I think they'd be awfully happy.

JUDY: Mummy always has said that's just the sort of thing she'd love.

DIANA: Do you think two hundred and fifty would be enough?

PATRICK: Oh, quite. You see, they'd grow their own vegetables and then there'd be the eggs.

JUDY: I say, what a lark we could have.

DIANA: What would you do?

PATRICK: The first thing would be to sell the house and take a flat in town. Judy and I could live together till she married.

JUDY: I know the first thing I'd do. I'd join every night club in London.

PATRICK: I'd hunt. We could probably run to a little hunting-box somewhere in my constituency. And I could kill two birds with one stone that way.

TIMOTHY: I'd have the fastest car made and my own aeroplane.

DIANA: I don't know what I'd do. Of course, I'd get all my clothes in Paris.

JUDY: I think we'd make things hum.

PATRICK: There's no doubt in my mind we'd run the world a damned sight better than it's ever been run before. Why should the old think that they know better than we do? They belong to the past. We're the future and the future's ours. Why shouldn't we do what we like with our own property?

DIANA: You have come on since last holidays, Pat.

PATRICK: Three months is a long time. I've been thinking a lot about things in general.

TIMOTHY: I wish I had your gift of the gab.

PATRICK: It's not necessary for you. You're only going to be a solicitor. You must have it at the Bar.

JUDY: There's Mummy.

PATRICK: Oh, let's go and play tennis then.

TIMOTHY: Come on.

JUDY: How are we going to play?

> [*As they get up,* TIMOTHY *taking his rackets, the door is opened and* MARGERY *and* DOROTHY *come in.* MARGERY *is a pretty, slightly faded blonde, and*

DOROTHY *is dark, like her daughter, and rather alluring. Her pose is suppressed passion. They are both under forty, smartly dressed and a good deal made up. Neither is the decrepit old creature you might have suspected from listening to their children's conversation, and neither has the slightest idea that her day is over.*

MARGERY: You lazy people, why aren't you playing tennis?

JUDY: We're just going to, Mummy.

PATRICK: Hulloa, Aunt Dorothy.

DOROTHY: You've grown, Pat.

MARGERY: Isn't he enormous?

[DOROTHY *kisses* PATRICK *on the cheek.*

DOROTHY: [*Archly.*] I'm not quite sure if Alfred would approve of my kissing such a grown-up young man.

PATRICK: After all, you are my aunt.

DOROTHY: Not really, of course. Your mother and I are only first cousins.

DIANA: She means that except for Alfred you and she could marry.

DOROTHY: Don't be so silly, Dinah.

TIMOTHY: It's not a bad idea. If Alfred's run over by a motor-bus you shall marry Dorothy, Pat. I think you'd make me a very good father.

PATRICK: I wouldn't let you call me by my Christian name. I should insist on your calling me Papa.

MARGERY: Run along, you idiots. Dorothy and I want to talk.

TIMOTHY: Come on, you kids.

PATRICK: [*Going out.*] No rest for the weary.

[*The four young things go.* MARGERY *and* DOROTHY *settle themselves down for a gossip by getting their lip-sticks and mirrors out of their bags and starting to paint their lips.*

DOROTHY: What a nice-looking boy Pat is growing. You'll have to keep an eye on him, darling. You know what women are.

MARGERY: Oh, I'm not frightened. He's absolutely innocent. And he tells me everything.

DOROTHY: They talk a lot of nonsense about the young nowadays. I don't believe they know half as much as we did at their age.

MARGERY: I wish they wouldn't grow up quite so quickly. When Pat came back from school this morning, it gave me quite a shock.

DOROTHY: I don't care. It's not like before the war. People don't grow old like they used to. When Dinah and I go out together we're always taken for sisters.

MARGERY: I honestly don't think you look a day older than she does. But then you're dark. That gives you such an advantage. When you're blonde like me you fade.

DOROTHY: You haven't. Why, I was only thinking at dinner last night how lovely your hair looked.

MARGERY: It's several shades darker than when I was a girl. I was wondering if anyone would notice if I had it touched up a little.

DOROTHY: Of course, it does make the face look harder.

MARGERY: Oh, I wouldn't have it dyed. I'd only just have a few *reflets d'or* put in. Ernest said he could do it so that not a soul would know it wasn't natural.

DOROTHY: Well, I know someone who likes you very much as you are.

MARGERY: Dorothy! As a matter of fact I don't know what you're talking about.

DOROTHY: Come off it, Marge. Do you think I haven't got eyes in my head? Why, it was obvious last night.

MARGERY: You don't think it was, really?

DOROTHY: Well, it was obvious to me. I've been dying to know what he said to you.

MARGERY: I suppose those children really are playing tennis?

DOROTHY: Oh, yes. I'm simply thrilled, Marge.

MARGERY: Well, he said he was quite crazy about me. He said he'd been wanting to tell me for a long time, but knowing Charlie on the Stock Exchange and all that sort of thing, he hadn't liked to. But he simply couldn't help himself.

DOROTHY: During dinner, was that, or afterwards?

MARGERY: Well, he began during dinner, but not seriously, you know. Lightly. He didn't really get serious till afterwards when we'd been dancing.

DOROTHY: Does he dance well?

MARGERY: Divinely.

DOROTHY: I suppose he wanted to see how you'd take it. Men are rather cautious. I suppose they don't want to get snubbed. Tell me what you said to him.

MARGERY: Well, of course, I laughed. I said, Do you realise that I have two children who are practically grown up? He said he didn't believe it. He said he'd bet a monkey that I wasn't a day more than twenty-five. What is a monkey, darling?

DOROTHY: A thousand pounds and a pony's five hundred. I can't think why men don't say five hundred pounds when they mean five hundred pounds.

MARGERY: It does seem silly, doesn't it?

DOROTHY: Go on, dear.

MARGERY: Then I said, I've got a girl of seventeen. I didn't say anything about Pat. I thought if he liked to think he was younger he could.

DOROTHY: I don't blame you.

MARGERY: Then he said, Well, all I can say is, you must have been married out of your cradle. So then I gave

him a look and I said, Well, I wasn't very old, I
admit.

DOROTHY: I know exactly how you said it. Sweeping the
floor with your eyelashes so to speak. I've seen you do it
dozens of times and it always gets them.

MARGERY: It's quite unconscious. I never mean to. Then
he took my hand and said, I wonder if you know how
much more attractive it is to be a grown woman than a
silly slip of a girl.

DOROTHY: Men always say that. And I'm sure it's true. Men
don't fall in love with girls. They're not interesting
enough.

MARGERY: I suppose there's something in that.

DOROTHY: And what happened next?

MARGERY: He asked me what Charlie does on Sundays.
Oh, I said, he goes and plays golf. Good old
Charlie, he said. Then he asked me if I wouldn't go
motoring with him in the country.

DOROTHY: And are you going?

MARGERY: Of course not. Why, I hardly know the man.

DOROTHY: You can't expect to get to know the man if you
never see him.

MARGERY: It wouldn't be fair to the children.

DOROTHY: Charlie goes and has a good time playing golf.
I don't see why you shouldn't go motoring if you want
to.

MARGERY: You know what I am, Dorothy.

DOROTHY: I don't believe you're as cold as you pretend.

MARGERY: Perhaps not. But Charlie's never looked at
another woman since he married me. I shouldn't like to
do anything to hurt his feelings.

DOROTHY: It wouldn't hurt his feelings if he didn't know. I
don't say go too far, but a flirtation can do no one any

harm. And everyone knows there's nothing like having a man pay her a little attention to make a woman look young.

MARGERY: Of course, there's something in that.

DOROTHY: You know as well as I do that in all the time we've been married I've never been unfaithful to Alfred. But I've had scores of beaux. That's what's kept me fresh and alert and up to date.

MARGERY: It's true that one wants something to make up for married life.

DOROTHY: No one could want a better husband than Alfred, and I'm sure he's always been absolutely faithful to me, but I could never have stood his heartiness for all these years if I hadn't had my little flirtations on the side.

MARGERY: What a mercy it is that men have to go to business every day. What would one do if they were about the house all day long?

DOROTHY: How has Charlie been lately?

MARGERY: Well, you've seen him. Just the same as ever. He never changes.

DOROTHY: Of course, I've seen for ages that he rather bores you.

MARGERY: Nineteen years is a long time to be married.

DOROTHY: Too long, if you ask me.

MARGERY: I suppose I've got nothing to complain of really. He gives me everything I want.

DOROTHY: And you never quarrel, do you?

MARGERY: Oh, never. And he never fusses. But, of course, he *is* limited.

DOROTHY: Men are. I've noticed that often.

MARGERY: He isn't interested in art and literature like I am. When I have intellectual people up at the house he always seems rather out of it.

DOROTHY: Yes, I've noticed that. Of course, he's awfully nice, but he's not exactly what you'd call brilliant, is he?

MARGERY: No, I'm afraid he isn't, poor darling. I suppose one can't have everything, and he's just as much in love with me to-day as the day we were married. It's rather beastly of me to find fault with him.

DOROTHY: That's not finding fault. One can't be married to a man all those years without knowing what he is and what he isn't.

MARGERY: I shudder to think what would happen if he ever suspected that for years now I haven't cared for him; I mean, really cared.

DOROTHY: That's one advantage we have; men don't see things.

MARGERY: Of course, I like him, you know, and I wouldn't do anything to wound him. But I am an intelligent woman, and I can't help seeing he's a bit of a bore.

DOROTHY: If you don't mind my saying so, darling, the fact is, he has no sense of humour.

MARGERY: I know. It's tragic. I'm going to say something dreadful to you, Dorothy. Have you ever asked yourself what you'd do if you were a widow?

DOROTHY: What woman hasn't?

MARGERY: Of course, I'd be dreadfully upset if anything happened to poor Charlie. I'd simply cry my eyes out, and at first I'd miss him dreadfully.

DOROTHY: That's only natural. I don't know anyone who's got so much heart as you have.

MARGERY: But when once I'd got over the shock I believe I'd be very happy, you know.

DOROTHY: I'm sure you would. With your fair hair you'd look too lovely in mourning.

MARGERY: I'd never marry again. I think every woman should marry, but once is enough.

DOROTHY: Oh, I like having a man about the house. I think I'd be dreadfully lost without one.

MARGERY: Well, I have so many resources in myself. It would be lovely to be able to do exactly as you liked without consulting anybody. And having your own friends. And being free to run over to Paris or down to the Riviera without thinking. Of course Charlie can't get away and the poor old thing'll be so lost without me. And then there's one's own self-development. You can't really develop your personality properly when you're married.

DOROTHY: Speaking of the Riviera, have you said anything to Charlie about the summer?

MARGERY: It's rather difficult. Charlie wants to go on the river like we always do, so that he can go up to the city when he wants to.

DOROTHY: Why shouldn't Alfred and Charlie go on the river together? It's so silly of husbands and wives always to take their holidays together. It's no change for either of them.

MARGERY: It would be lovely for the children.

DOROTHY: They wouldn't interfere with us at all. They'd be bathing and boating all the time and they're too young to go into the Baccarat rooms. My dear, we'd have the time of our lives.

MARGERY: It sounds too divine.

DOROTHY: I saw some lovely pyjamas in Bond Street the other day. You know they wear pyjamas all day long in summer.

MARGERY: I know. I suppose it would be frightfully expensive.

DOROTHY: What *is* the use of money if you don't spend it? And you can always tell Charlie it would be such an education for the children.

[PATRICK *appears, followed immediately by the others*

PATRICK: I say, Mummy, it is disgraceful, the court wasn't marked out.

MARGERY: Oh, I am sorry.

PATRICK: I've given the gardener hell. He had the damned cheek to say he hadn't had any orders.

MARGERY: How stupid of him. I know I meant to tell him.

PATRICK: The moment my back is turned everything goes wrong in this house.

MARGERY: Is he doing it now?

PATRICK: Yes, but it won't be ready for a quarter of an hour. I don't know why Judy couldn't see about it. What's she there for?

JUDY: You seem to think I have nothing to do. I was fearfully busy this morning, and I forgot.

PATRICK: Well, you shouldn't forget.

MARGERY: Don't be disagreeable the moment you get back, darling. There's lots of time.

DIANA: Let's go and have a glass of lemonade. Tim and I are simply parched.

MARGERY: It's in the dining-room. You'll find it on the sideboard.

PATRICK: I don't know why we can't have a hard court. It's absurd to ask people to play on grass now.

TIMOTHY: I've told Alfred that we absolutely must have one at our place. I mean, you can't expect to improve your game if you have to play on grass all the time.

PATRICK: You might talk to father, Mummy. After all, if he wants us to live at home the least he can do is to provide us with the ordinary necessities of existence.

MARGERY: It would be an awful expense.

TIMOTHY: You can get a very decent hard court for about four hundred pounds.

PATRICK: That's nothing. Daddy couldn't jib at that. He hasn't got anything to do with his money except spend it on us.

MARGERY: That's true.

DIANA: How about this lemonade?

JUDY: Come on.

[*A ring at the door is heard.*

Hullo, who's that? Oh, God, I hope it's not callers.

MARGERY: I said I wasn't at home to anybody to-day.

PATRICK: Fancy living in a place where people pay calls. This *is* the back of beyond all right.

MARGERY: Don't be so silly, Pat. There are a lot of very intelligent people who live here, and it's a treat when they drop in for a chat over a cup of tea.

[*The front door is opened, and a voice is heard asking for* MRS. BATTLE.

DOROTHY: Why, it's Alfred.

MARGERY: Open the door, Judy. [*As* JUDY *does this she calls.*] Alfred!

ALFRED: [*Outside.*] Hullo, hullo, hullo.

MARGERY: Come in. Dorothy's here.

[ALFRED *breezes in. He is a tall, well set up, middle-aged man, with a red face and a hearty, blustering, jovial manner. He laughs a great deal at everything he says.*

ALFRED: [*Taking* MARGERY'S *hand.*] Hullo, popsy-wopsy. [*Seeing* PATRICK.] And look who's here. When did you breeze in, old bean?

PATRICK: [*Shaking hands with him.*] I got back just before lunch.

ALFRED: Trust you for that. And I bet you walloped into the fatted calf.

PATRICK: [*With hauteur.*] I managed to swallow a morsel of cold chicken.

ALFRED: And how does it feel to have left school for good, eh, young-feller-me-lad?

PATRICK: Oh, all right.

ALFRED: Best days of your life, you know, old boy. And when they're gone they're gone. Can't put the clock back if you try till doomsday. That's the way of the world. Well, it's not a bad old place if you have a front seat and take care that no one diddles you out of it.

TIMOTHY: You do talk the most footling rot, Alfred.

DOROTHY: Tim, you mustn't be so rude to your father.

ALFRED: Let the little blighter say what he likes. Respect be damned. Tim and I are a couple of pals, aren't we, old boy?

TIMOTHY: Rather. I say, old cock, what about the hard court? You said you'd think about it.

ALFRED: It's a devil of a lot of money.

TIMOTHY: It's not as if you couldn't afford it. Come on, old bean, be a sport.

ALFRED: [Beaming.] Well, if you put it like that, I'll tell you what I'll do, I'll give it my favourable consideration.

TIMOTHY: Good.

ALFRED: And how are you, Judy, old gal? Bit on the quiet side to-day, aren't you?

JUDY: I don't think so.

ALFRED: Love?

JUDY: No.

ALFRED: When are you going to get married?

JUDY: I'm not thinking of getting married.

ALFRED: And why not, if you please?

JUDY: Well, for one reason nobody's asked me.

ALFRED: What? Why, my little early-girlie has three proposals a week. Don't you, Dinah?

DIANA: No, Alfred, I don't.

ALFRED: Don't you believe her. I know. And when I say I know, I know. Paterfamilias. But we can't have little Judy-pudy neglected. [*To* TIMOTHY.] Come along, young pie-face, you propose to her and then she can say she's turned down a blood.

TIMOTHY: I'm not going to take a chance, like that, Alfred.

JUDY: Owl.

DOROTHY: Why have you left your office so early, Alfred?

ALFRED: A sudden desire to see my old Dolly-polly.

DOROTHY: Don't be funny, Alfred.

ALFRED: I can't help it, my dear. I've tried, but it's no good. It's my nature. But, joking apart, as a matter of fact I came along to see Charlie.

MARGERY: He's not here. He's in the city.

ALFRED: No, he isn't. At least I can't get hold of him. He hasn't been at his office all day.

MARGERY: That's funny.

ALFRED: No, it isn't. To tell you the truth I'm just a teeny-weeny bit anxious.

MARGERY: [*Surprised.*] Why?

ALFRED: Hasn't he told you anything?

MARGERY: No, what? Has something happened?

ALFRED: I suppose he thought if it came out all right there was no use bothering you, and if it didn't you'd know quite soon enough.

MARGERY: But what is it?

ALFRED: Perhaps I oughtn't to have said anything about it.

PATRICK: Father hasn't gone bust, Uncle Alfred?

ALFRED: I think you kiddie-widdies had better go out into the garden. Dorothy, you stay.

PATRICK: If anything's the matter you may just as well tell us too. Mummy will anyway, the moment you've gone.

DIANA: Come along, Tim. We'll go. Shout when you're through.

[DIANA *and* TIMOTHY *go out into the garden.*

MARGERY: This isn't another of your jokes, Alfred?

ALFRED: I wish it were. No, this is serious. Did you happen to notice that a fellow called Tommy Avon shot himself last Friday?

MARGERY: Yes. Dreadful, wasn't it? We knew him. We went to Ascot with him last year.

PATRICK: Who was Tommy Avon?

ALFRED: He was very well known in the city. He was one of your father's clients. Good fellow and all that. One of the best. But I'm afraid he's let your governor down badly.

MARGERY: But I always thought Charles had such a high-class business. He never went in for anything speculative.

ALFRED: That's why it's such tough luck on him. I flatter myself I'm about as shrewd as they make 'em, and I wouldn't have hesitated to trust Tommy Avon with a million if I'd had it.

JUDY: But what's actually happened?

ALFRED: You wouldn't understand if I told you. But the long and short of it is that it's settling-day to-day, and if your father hasn't been able to get his pals to come to the rescue he'll be hammered.

JUDY: What does that mean?

ALFRED: Ruin.

MARGERY: [*With a cry of dismay.*] Oh! What shall we do?

DOROTHY: Don't give way, Marge. It's not certain yet.

ALFRED: Luckily for him he's got some very good friends. Of course, his whole private fortune will have to go in.

But if he's able to raise a substantial sum outside he can weather the storm.

PATRICK: Shall we have to leave this house and give up the car?

ALFRED: I don't know about that. If he pulls through I daresay it won't make much difference to his income. He's got a very sound business and a very good reputation.

PATRICK: Oh, then things aren't as bad as all that.

ALFRED: Except that all his savings are gone down the drain.

MARGERY: Then if anything happened to him we'd be penniless?

PATRICK: He's as strong as a horse, Mummy. I was only telling Judy just now that I thought he'd probably live to a hundred. He'll make another fortune all right.

MARGERY: But what does it depend on, his pulling through?

ALFRED: Well, to put it shortly, it depends on whether Arthur Letter was willing to back him or not.

PATRICK: Who's Arthur Letter?

ALFRED: He's the chairman of your father's bank. He was to give your father his decision last night.

MARGERY: Oh, that's why he only got in just in time to dress for dinner. We were dining at the Savoy.

ALFRED: How did he seem?

MARGERY: Just about as usual.

ALFRED: He can't have been quite the same as usual. At that moment it had just been decided whether he would have to file his petition in bankruptcy or could start with more or less of a clean slate.

MARGERY: I didn't notice anything. I was afraid we'd be late for dinner.

ALFRED: How about this morning?

MARGERY: I had breakfast in my room. Judy and he had breakfast together.

ALFRED: Did he seem up or down?

JUDY: To tell you the truth I didn't pay any attention. I always read The Mirror at breakfast.

ALFRED: That's a wash-out then. He had an appointment with me at ten, but he never kept it. It was damned important too. That's what puzzles me.

JUDY: He left here about half-past nine.

MARGERY: Do you mean to say he hasn't been at his office all day?

ALFRED: No.

PATRICK: [With a gasp.] I say . . .

[The thought occurs to them simultaneously that CHARLES may have killed himself.

MARGERY: [With agitation.] Oh, no, no, it's impossible. He couldn't do anything so cruel to me.

JUDY: I wonder if he was rather strange this morning. Oh, Uncle Alfred, it would be too awful if while we were eating kedgeree he was—he was making up his mind to——

MARGERY: Judy, Judy. No. No. He couldn't do anything so cowardly.

PATRICK: D'you think it's possible, Uncle Alfred? I say, it would be rotten.

ALFRED: Well, old boy, I don't mind telling you that was in my mind when I got here. I tried to be hearty like I always am, but between you and I and the gatepost it was a bit of an effort. I daresay you noticed it. Charlie's the most punctilious fellow. I've never known him cut a date in my life.

MARGERY: [Becoming a trifle hysterical.] No, no, no, no! I'm so frightened.

DOROTHY: Darling, don't. After all, there's no reason why you should believe the worst at once.

MARGERY: But why wasn't he at his office? On this day when it was so essential?

ALFRED: If anything was to be saved from the wreck at all.

DOROTHY: Perhaps he was knocked down by a taxi and is lying unconscious in some hospital.

MARGERY: That wouldn't be much consolation either.

PATRICK: But can't we do something?

JUDY: I think we ought to drag the Thames.

PATRICK: You fool, one can't drag the Thames.

JUDY: Well, we can drag the ponds on the Heath.

MARGERY: Oh, don't, don't. He's so proud. He's so sensitive. I've got an awful fear that sooner than face us and tell us he's ruined . . . he's . . .

DOROTHY: Don't say it, Marge. It's so unlucky.

PATRICK: Oughtn't we to go to the police?

ALFRED: Not yet. We should look such fools if he suddenly turned up.

DOROTHY: I'm all for telephoning round to the hospitals.

MARGERY: We must do something. I shall go mad.

ALFRED: If he doesn't turn up to-night, of course, we'll get in touch with the police-stations.

PATRICK: Couldn't we send out an S.O.S. on the wireless? It's what people generally do when someone disappears.

JUDY: That wouldn't do much good if he's lying at the bottom of Whitestone Pond.

MARGERY: What a stigma on the children.

DOROTHY: Oh, darling, don't make things out worse than they are. Alfred could always get the jury to bring in a verdict of temporarily insane.

PATRICK: Of course it may be that he's only lost his memory and he'll turn up somewhere in a few days.

JUDY: Bournemouth. That's where they're generally found.

DOROTHY: But, Alfred, why can't you ring up that man who was going to back him? Then we shall know if Charlie had any reason to do anything desperate or not.

ALFRED: Arthur Letter? It's not so easy as all that to get hold of the chairman of a great London bank. I don't suppose he'd tell me anything if I did.

DOROTHY: Well, you can try.

MARGERY: Please, Alfred. I'm so terribly anxious.

ALFRED: All right. I'll see if he'll speak to me. He can't eat me.

[He goes out.

MARGERY: The suspense is too awful.

PATRICK: Did father go out in his top-hat this morning?

MARGERY: Oh, Pat, don't be so silly. This isn't the moment to think of top-hats.

PATRICK: I don't agree with you. I particularly want to know.

JUDY: I think so. I should have noticed it if he hadn't.

PATRICK: Then he can't have been meditating suicide when he left this house.

MARGERY: Why not?

PATRICK: Mummy darling, no man in his senses would commit suicide in a top-hat.

JUDY: But if he was temporarily insane he wasn't in his senses.

PATRICK: Don't be idiotic, Judy. What can you know about men? A chap who was going to commit suicide would naturally put on a cap or at the outside a bowler.

MARGERY: Oh, no, Pat, your father was always so particular. He would never have gone out in a tail coat and a cap, whatever he was going to do. Never. Never.

PATRICK: That's what I say, if he went out in a topper he hasn't committed suicide.

JUDY: I don't see why not. Supposing he jumped in the river, he could always have left it on the tow-path.

PATRICK: And have people come along and say, Hullo, what's a bran-new topper doing on the tow-path?

DOROTHY: What *is* Alfred doing?

MARGERY: Isn't it awful to think that only a few minutes ago we were all so happy. We were talking of going down to the Riviera for the summer. We hadn't a care in the world. And now this terrible thing has happened.

JUDY: Life is like that.

PATRICK: Oh, God, you are a gloom, Judy. If you haven't got anything cheerful to say, for God's sake shut up.

JUDY: I don't see any object in not facing facts. I'm psychic. I'm absolutely convinced that Daddy's lying at the bottom of Whitestone Pond.

[ALFRED *comes in.*

ALFRED: Well, boys and girls, it's all right. Good news.

MARGERY: Alfred!

ALFRED: I just mentioned my name, and they put me through to Sir Arthur at once. I didn't give anything away. Trust your Uncle Alfred for that. He told me he'd seen Charlie last night at his private house and in consideration of Charlie's personal character he'd agreed to let him have enough money to meet all his obligations.

MARGERY: Oh, my dear, how awfully nice of him.

ALFRED: When old Charlie-parlie left Sir Arthur's sumptuous mansion, he had a whacking fat cheque in his pocket.

MARGERY: What a relief!

DOROTHY: But why hasn't he been at his office to-day?

ALFRED: Oh, that's a minor point. I suppose he's been

tearing round and hadn't any time. He'll tell us that when we see him. The great thing is that he's weathered the storm.

PATRICK: Then we're not ruined after all?

ALFRED: No. Your father's taken a toss, but he's in the saddle again, and there's no reason why in a few years he shouldn't be where he was. Of course, he'll have to work like blazes.

JUDY: Daddy loves work. That's one thing.

ALFRED: He'll have to keep his nosy-posy to the grindstone.

PATRICK: Oh, well, there's no harm in that. At Daddy's age there's nothing much for a chap to do except work.

MARGERY: I used to be sorry that he had no outside interests, but as things have turned out, I daresay it's all for the best.

ALFRED: You kiddie-widdies mustn't be extravagant, you know. For some time your father won't have any spare cash to throw about.

PATRICK: I've thought of that. I'm willing to do my bit. We shall have to make do with the family bus for a bit longer, Judy old girl.

JUDY: It is sickening, isn't it? I suppose it can't be helped. And we shan't be able to have a hard court either.

MARGERY: Call the others in, Judy. There's no reason they should stay out any longer.

JUDY: All right. [*At the window.*] Dinah, Tim! Come in.

MARGERY: And then you'd better play tennis if you want to.

JUDY: After all this excitement I couldn't hit a ball.

ALFRED: Are you going to play tennis? I'll just nip over the garden wall and change. I don't mind showing you young things that there's life in the old dog yet.

[DIANA *and* TIMOTHY *stroll in.*

T

JUDY: Oh, my dear, we've had such a thrill. Daddy's vanished and we all thought he'd committed suicide. And we were ruined and everything had to be sold, and now it's all right and Daddy hasn't committed suicide after all.

DIANA: If you were going to tell us all about it, it seems hardly worth while to have turned us out of the room.

JUDY: I didn't want you to go. It was grand. Mummy was in hysterics. And Pat was keeping a stiff upper lip, and I was being the brave little woman.

DIANA: Do you mean to say it was all a false alarm?

TIMOTHY: You know Alfred and his little jokes. You oughtn't to let him get away with them. He only gets above himself.

ALFRED: Now then, young feller-me-lad, not so much of your lip. We're not out of the blooming old wood yet.

PATRICK: We're ruined all right.

JUDY: But the only difference it'll make is that Pat can't have a car of his own, and we shall have to go on with the old court until Daddy makes some more money.

TIMOTHY: I say, that's a bit thick.

PATRICK: If they can play on grass at Wimbledon I suppose on a pinch we can too.

ALFRED: That's the spirit, old bean. I'm jolly glad to see that you're taking it like a sportsman.

DIANA: And where's Uncle Charlie?

PATRICK: We don't know that.

MARGERY: We wish we did. We wish to God we did.

JUDY: We think he's lost his memory and is sitting on a bench at Bournemouth in a top-hat.

PATRICK: He's much more likely to be at Southend.

MARGERY: Oh, no. Even if your poor father had lost his memory it would never occur to him to go to Southend.

[*The door is opened and* CHARLES *strolls amiably in. He is a man in the early forties, quiet and of rather distinguished appearance; he is very neat in his black coat and grey striped trousers. He wears a top-hat.*

MARGERY: Charlie!

THE CURTAIN FALLS

SCENE II

The curtain rises. All are present but CHARLES.

PATRICK: If they can play on grass at Wimbledon, I suppose on a pinch we can too.

ALFRED: That's the spirit, old bean. I'm jolly glad to see that you're taking it like a sportsman.

DIANA: And where's Uncle Charlie?

PATRICK: We don't know that.

MARGERY: We wish we did. We wish to God we did.

JUDY: We think he's lost his memory and is sitting on a bench at Bournemouth in a top-hat.

PATRICK: He's much more likely to be at Southend.

MARGERY: Oh, no. Even if your poor father had lost his memory it would never occur to him to go to Southend.

> [*The door is opened, and* CHARLES *strolls amiably in.*

MARGERY: Charlie!

CHARLES: [*Taking off his hat.*] Hullo.

MARGERY: [*Much agitated.*] Where have you been? Oh, we've been so anxious. It's too bad of you.

CHARLES: What have I done?

MARGERY: The suspense has been too awful.

CHARLES: [*Coolly.*] Why, what's the matter? Hullo, Pat. Home for the holidays?

PATRICK: Hullo, Daddy.

CHARLES: You look all right. Had a nice time your last term at school.

PATRICK: Yes, grand.

CHARLES: How's everybody? Back from the city early, Alfred? Don't tell me you're idling.

ALFRED: I say, old boy, where the devil have you been? I've been trying to get hold of you all day long.

CHARLES: I? I've been for a walk on Hampstead Heath.

ALFRED: A walk?

MARGERY: All day?

CHARLES: No, I found rather a jolly little pub and had lunch there. A cut off the joint and a bottle of beer. Very nice.

ALFRED: Why didn't you go to your office?

JUDY: We were sure you'd committed suicide.

PATRICK: Judy wanted to have Whitestone Pond dragged.

MARGERY: We've been so frightfully anxious, Charlie.

CHARLES: I may be very dense, but I don't quite understand what you're all talking about.

ALFRED: Well, old boy, I had to tell them. You see, you didn't keep your appointment with me, and you hadn't turned up at the office.

CHARLES: Oh, I see. [*Amiably.*] Well, now you know, don't you?

PATRICK: We know it's all right, Daddy.

ALFRED: They were all so upset they persuaded me to call up Arthur Letter. He told me what he'd done.

CHARLES: Sporting of him, wasn't it?

JUDY: Were you absolutely broke, Daddy?

CHARLES: I couldn't comply with my bargains.

JUDY: What does that mean?

CHARLES: Well, when a broker can't comply with his bargains he's hammered.

ALFRED: And then he can't trade any more.

CHARLES: How are you, Dorothy? You've got a new hat on.

DOROTHY: [*Alluringly.*] D'you like it? How clever of you to notice.

ALFRED: Look here, Charlie, we must have a talk. Tim, you and Dinah had better make yourselves scarce.

TIMOTHY: All right.

PATRICK: Sorry, old man. I'm afraid tennis looks like being a wash-out.

TIMOTHY: Oh, that's all right. I know what these domestic upsets are.

PATRICK: It's one of the penalties of having a family.

CHARLES: Why don't you and Dinah go and have a knock-up? Pat and Judy can join you presently.

TIMOTHY: I don't mind.

CHARLES: I shan't keep them long.

TIMOTHY: Oh, that's all right. There's no hurry.

CHARLES: [*With a tinge of irony.*] Thanks.

DIANA: Come on, then.

[DIANA *and* TIMOTHY *saunter out.*

DOROTHY: Do you wish me to go, too?

MARGERY: No, stay, Dorothy. I've got a presentiment that something is rotten in the state of Denmark.

ALFRED: My dear, I'm afraid that this is no time for culture.

MARGERY: I know. That is why I want Dorothy to stay There are moments when a woman wants another woman's support.

ALFRED: Where have you been all day, Charlie? I rang up every place I could think of.

CHARLES: I told you. I've been for a walk on Hampstead Heath.

ALFRED: But you had an appointment to see me at ten.

CHARLES: [*Smiling.*] I can't tell you how excruciatingly the idea of seeing you at ten bored me.

ALFRED: Thank you. You made the appointment yourself.

MARGERY: What did you do on the Heath?

CHARLES: I walked. I thought. I admired the scenery.

ALFRED: When every minute was of vital importance?

CHARLES: That, too, added to the charm of the prospect.

PATRICK: I don't wish to cast a gloom on the party, but it sounds to me as though father were trying to be facetious.

MARGERY: Don't be silly, Pat. You know your father isn't like that.

ALFRED: [*Shrewdly.*] There's more in this than meets the eye. I have no hesitation in saying that whatever.

CHARLES: It was a bad blow for me, you know, when Tommy Avon shot himself. [*He makes this remark conversationally, with deliberation, but not as though he attached great importance to what he was saying.*]

ALFRED: It was the best thing he could do. If he hadn't he'd have got fourteen years.

CHARLES: It cost me a packet.

ALFRED: And you're not the only one. A lot of my clients have been hit. Damned scoundrel.

CHARLES: I was proud of my firm. I took a harmless vanity in the fact that my name stood so high on the Stock Exchange. It was a source of a good deal of satisfaction to me to know that people pointed me out and said, Good fellow, Charlie Battle, safe as the Bank of England.

ALFRED: That's why Arthur Letter was willing to help you when you were up against it. Character is the best asset any man can have in the City.

CHARLES: When the crash came my first thought was to save the firm. I was prepared to sacrifice every bob I had to keep my head above water. By George, there wasn't a stone I left unturned.

ALFRED: You don't have to tell me that. No one could have done more.

CHARLES: And last night, at the eleventh hour, you might say, I did the trick. I was saved. I don't mind telling you it was a relief.

ALFRED: I'll bet it was.

CHARLES: You know, this is settling-day. It had been a nightmare. Last night I knew I could comply with my bargains. All my savings had to go down the drain, but I didn't care a damn. The old firm was saved and my reputation was all right. Funny thing, honour, isn't it? And the importance we attach to it. I suppose it's the force of habit.

JUDY: You've been rather wonderful, Daddy. No one could have guessed anything particular was happening, could they, Mummy?

MARGERY: No, dear, I never dreamt anything was wrong.

CHARLES: I'm glad of that. I was afraid I'd been a trifle disagreeable.

JUDY: [*Quite pleasantly.*] No, not more than usual.

CHARLES: I was in great spirits when I left the house this morning. You'd have thought I'd made a fortune instead of lost one. I walked to the tube as I've walked every morning, more or less since I was demobbed. I nodded to one or two people I knew. All going down to the City just as I was. I got to the station. There was the usual crowd hurrying in. . . . Suddenly my heart sank.

JUDY: Why?

CHARLES: Well, my dear, you know, once or twice during these last days it looked as though I couldn't pull through. And as I lay awake at night turning things over, I thought of what I'd do if I went broke. I made pretty elaborate plans. It relieved me. I didn't see why

I shouldn't make the best of a bad job. Well, I weathered the storm and I was in a position to start all over again. I could go on quite quietly to the end of my life doing what I'd done every day for the last twelve years, going down to the City and studying the markets, buying and selling stock. Suddenly it seemed to me that for me ruin meant life and liberty—and that tube, with all those people hurrying to catch their train, led to slavery and death. So I went for a stroll on Hampstead Heath.

MARGERY: But, Charlie, my dear, that was only nerves. I mean, that's the sort of thing we're all liable to since the war. All of us who went through that awful experience bear its mark. I know I do. And I expect to bear it always.

JUDY: But, Mummy, you had the time of your life when you were working in your canteens.

MARGERY: Oh, Judy, how can you say anything so beastly? I was on my feet for hours on end. I could never have stood it except that I was determined to do my bit.

ALFRED: You know, Judy old gal, you were only a baby. You don't know what we went through during that terrible time, and, please God, you never will know.

JUDY: Well, I'll tell you what I think. Except when you were actually under fire you had more fun than you've ever had before or since. My belief is that if there was another war the greatest majority of you would just jump back into it with a whoop.

ALFRED: We answered the call when it came, and if it came again we'd answer it again.

MARGERY: But not with a whoop, darling. With death in our hearts.

ALFRED: Do you realise how great a sacrifice we made then? And we made it for you.

PATRICK: For us?

ALFRED: Yes, for you and Judy and Dinah and Tim. For your generation.

PATRICK: You make me laugh. Why, we're the sacrifice you made.

JUDY: And if you think we like it, Uncle Alfred, you're mistaken.

ALFRED: Well, upon my word. You were only just born when it started. I really can't see that it affected you much.

PATRICK: Don't you? Whichever way we turn it's there facing us. It's been like a great weight round our necks all our lives. We have the right to live like every other generation, and you've crabbed our pitch before we start.

ALFRED: But we didn't want the war. It was forced on us.

JUDY: No, you didn't want the war. You just muddled into it, and then you muddled through it, and then you muddled out of it. You muddled your lives and you've muddled ours.

MARGERY: That's so ungrateful, Judy. You've always had the best of everything. I'm sure no one could have had better chances than you've had.

PATRICK: But you don't understand, Mother. All our lives we've been surrounded by depression and anxiety, and, of course, it's had its effect on us. You've sapped our vitality. You've made a mess of the world and you've taken away our power to put it right.

JUDY: If a man can't get a job, it's the war. If he's slack and incompetent, it's the war. If he forges a cheque or commits bigamy, it's the war. If the roads are bad and the trains rotten, it's the war. If we're crippled with debts and taxes, it's the war.

ALFRED: Everyone knows it left behind it a long train of problems and difficulties. We've got to face that.

JUDY: But why should *we?* Why should we suffer for your stupidity?

CHARLES: You know, there's some truth in what the child says about the war. We weren't always frightened, we weren't always cold, we weren't always hungry. There were times when it was no end of a lark.

ALFRED: To me it was unmitigated horror.

CHARLES: Oh, come off it. We talk a lot of bunk to the younger generation in order to show them what stern stuff we're made of, but, damn their eyes, they don't believe us. Let's face it. You loved being a temporary gent. A good deal of authority and no responsibility to speak of. There were long periods when one could be thoroughly idle without one's conscience reproaching one. And there was a lot of excitement. All I got out of the war was pneumonia, a wound in the hip, a cracked skull and a temporary captaincy. But it's an experience I wouldn't have missed.

MARGERY: It's a miracle that you returned at all.

JUDY: Wasn't it an awful let-down when you came back, Daddy?

CHARLES: You know, I got a lot of fun out of thinking I was alive. I was thirty. I said to myself, Well, I've lost the five best years of my youth, but it's no good grousing; let me make the best of what remains. That was twelve years ago. And now my youth has gone.

ALFRED: No one can say you haven't made good use of it. Like a great many others at the end of the war you had to start again at the beginning. You haven't done so badly. You've had a nice house and a car and you've kept your wife in the sort of way your position required. You've sent your children to first-rate schools. You had saved a bit of money.

CHARLES: Fifty thousand pounds, roughly.

ALFRED: It's true that through no fault of your own that's gone, but all the rest remains. You've still got your position and you can make more money. I don't think you've got much to complain of.

CHARLES: [*Reflectively.*] Of course, it's not out of his solid clients that a broker makes his money. He makes it out of the speculator. Whether he's a gambler who wants a flutter for the excitement of it, or a fool who thinks he can make money without working for it, the result is always the same. It's only a question of time before the whole of his money finds its way into the broker's pocket.

ALFRED: That's the speculator's look-out.

CHARLES: Of course. But sometimes I couldn't help asking myself if it was to spend my life so tamely that I'd escaped death a score of times by a hair's-breadth.

PATRICK: I shouldn't have thought it was tame.

CHARLES: You've never been in the Stock Exchange, have you? Pity I didn't take you in one day. It would have interested you.

JUDY: I thought strangers couldn't get in.

CHARLES: No, they're not allowed, and if they're caught they must expect to be hustled a bit. They'll probably want a new hat.

ALFRED: You could have smuggled him in as one of your clerks. No one would have taken any notice of him. It's an amazing sight.

CHARLES: It's indescribable. There's a hell of a row, you know.

ALFRED: Deafening.

CHARLES: Everyone's yelling at the top of his voice, and men are rushing about like mad. I must say, at first there's something rather exhilarating about it. That frantic activity does give you a thrilling sensation of life.

ALFRED: By Jove, it does.

CHARLES: You've never heard a man hammered, have you, Alfred?

ALFRED: No, I haven't.

CHARLES: It's impressive. At three o'clock, for instance, as the hour strikes. [*The clock in the drawing-room strikes three.*] Just as that clock is striking now, the two waiters appear on the stands and take off their hats, as if to a corpse. They beat with a wooden mallet three times. Fellows look up and that deafening row stops. Suddenly, as though it had been cut with a knife. And it's so still you really could hear a pin drop. However often you've heard it, the sound of that mallet ringing through the deathly silence is frightening. The waiter at the Consol Market end reads out a notice, and the waiter at the Mining Market end repeats it. "Gentlemen, Mr. Charles Laurence Battle, trading as Wargrave, Battle & Co., is unable to comply with his bargains." They read in a loud, hoarse voice, without any expression in it, they've read the same sort of things so often, and then they shuffle off the stands. There's a moment's pause, and however hardened you are, there's something tragic in it. They're good fellows on the Stock Exchange most of them, and a bit sentimental, and it gives one a pang to think someone's beaten. It may have been just bad luck. It may have been that one bit off more than one could chew. If you're up, you can afford to be sorry for the man who's down, and if you're shaky, you wonder if it'll be your turn next. Yes, just for a moment dismay fills every heart, and then, before you can say Jack Robinson, as suddenly as the row stopped, the row begins again. Pandemonium. Charles Laurence Battle, trading as Wargrave, Battle & Co., is forgotten. The world has passed him by.

[*Suddenly there is a ring on the telephone in the hall.*

MARGERY: See who it is, Judy.

CHARLES: If it's anyone for me I'm not at home. Never mind how urgent.

JUDY: All right.

[She goes out.

ALFRED: Well, old boy, I'm glad you've escaped that. It's true you've lost a packet, but you'll make it again. While there's life there's hope.

DOROTHY: Have you been terribly anxious all these days, Charlie?

CHARLES: I have a bit.

MARGERY: Why didn't you tell me?

CHARLES: Oh, my dear, there didn't seem any object in worrying you.

[JUDY comes in again.

JUDY: It's Mr. Turner. He wants awfully to speak to you, Daddy, and when I said you were out he seemed all fussed and bothered.

CHARLES: That's nice of him. I hope you lied like my own daughter.

JUDY: He asked me if I knew where he could get hold of Uncle Alfred, and I told him he was here. He's holding the line.

ALFRED: I wonder what he wants me for?

DOROTHY: You'd better go and see, Alfred.

[ALFRED gets up and goes out.

MARGERY: Will this interfere with our summer holiday, Charlie?

DOROTHY: Marge and I were thinking it would be so good for the children if we went down to the Riviera for a change.

MARGERY: I like the river, but I do realise that it would be

much more of an education for them to take them to
France. And everyone's going to Antibes now.

JUDY: Oh, Mummy, that would be too divine. And Tim
and Dinah too?

DOROTHY: Well, I haven't spoken to Alfred about it yet.
Your mother and I have been putting our heads
together.

MARGERY: Of course, before all this happened.

DOROTHY: [*To Judy.*] I suppose your father couldn't get away,
but I'm sure he wouldn't mind your going. We'd go
to some cheap pension, and really I don't suppose it
would be any more expensive than staying in England.

MARGERY: Naturally we'd have to be frightfully economical.

JUDY: Oh, Daddy, do say yes. It would be awful fun.
Wouldn't it, Pat?

PATRICK: Not so dusty.

[ALFRED, *distraught, bursts into the room.*

ALFRED: Charlie, he says you're hammered.

CHARLES: [*Coolly.*] Well, what of it?

ALFRED: He's frightfully upset. He said he understood
everything had been arranged. Charlie, it's not true,
is it?

CHARLES: [*Sardonically.*] Yes, my boy, the waiter went
knocky-knocky with his little mallet and poor old
Charlie-parlie was blown sky high.

ALFRED: It's not true, Charlie. You don't know what
you're saying. For God's sake pull yourself together,
old bean.

MARGERY: Oh, Charlie, what has happened?

ALFRED: [*Emphatically.*] What do you mean, Charlie?

CHARLES: Only that at the very moment that I was so
dramatically describing to you what happens when a
man is hammered on the Stock Exchange, I was actually

being hammered. Don't you remember, I called your attention to the clock striking three?

PATRICK: I hate these cheap theatrical effects.

CHARLES: I have a simple mind. They get me every time.

JUDY: If one didn't know Daddy had no sense of humour one would think he'd just been pulling our leg.

CHARLES: You see, as three o'clock approached and I knew what was going to happen, I felt a trifle lonely on Hampstead Heath. I suddenly craved for the society of my fellows.

MARGERY: I can't believe it. It's so fantastic.

CHARLES: They say that when the dying buffalo feels his end approaching, he leaves his herd and retires into solitude. In that respect I am unlike the dying buffalo.

ALFRED: It's not often I'm puzzled. But I am now, and I don't mind admitting it. You could have complied with your bargains perfectly well.

CHARLES: I didn't choose to.

ALFRED: You had Arthur Letter's cheque in your pocket.

CHARLES: I have it still. [*He takes a cheque out of his pocket and hands it to* ALFRED.] Perhaps you wouldn't mind sending it back to him and telling him that I made up my mind not to avail myself of his kindness.

ALFRED: There's more in this than meets the eye. I have no hesitation in saying that.

MARGERY: But then we're ruined.

DOROTHY: Oh, Margery, how awful!

ALFRED: You cut along, Dorothy.

DOROTHY: All right. [*To* MARGERY.] I'll be in the garden in case you want me, dear.

MARGERY: All right, dear.

[DOROTHY *goes out.*

JUDY: D'you want us to go, Uncle Alfred?

CHARLES: Oh, I think you'd better stay. I have one or two things to say that a good deal concern you.

PATRICK: But if you're hammered we're in the soup, Daddy.

CHARLES: Up to the neck, my boy.

PATRICK: I don't know what there is to be so damned cheerful about.

ALFRED: Neither do I, believe me. Your father has let himself be hammered when he actually had in his pocket the means of saving himself.

PATRICK: But what's the big idea?

ALFRED: Of course, he'd had a knock. But he isn't the only one. Why, I know brokers who've made and lost half a dozen fortunes in their time. On the Stock Exchange you have to take the rough with the smooth.

PATRICK: That's when a fellow shows his grit, when he's down and out.

CHARLES: [*With a smile in his eyes.*] True, my son. You're presently going to have an opportunity of showing yours.

ALFRED: But how did you have the heart to let an old-established business like yours go to blazes?

CHARLES: I steeled it. I don't deny that when the clock struck three just now it gave me a funny little feeling in the pit of my stomach.

MARGERY: Your poor father was so proud of the business, Charlie. He always said there wasn't a more respectable firm in the city of London.

ALFRED: What are you going to do now?

CHARLES: [*Casually.*] I'm going abroad.

MARGERY: [*In sudden agitation.*] Charlie, you haven't done anything dreadful? They're not going to issue a warrant?

CHARLES: No, no, my dear. However dishonourable my

conduct may be, I have done nothing that the law can take exception to.

MARGERY: [*Helplessly.*] One never knows with brokers. It's such a funny profession.

ALFRED: My God, this is a pretty kettle of fish. For goodness' sake, explain yourself, Charlie. A man doesn't commit suicide for fun.

CHARLES: The explanation is very simple. This morning I came to the conclusion that it wasn't worth it.

ALFRED: What?

CHARLES: This life I've been leading. For twelve mortal years I've been going down to the City in the same tube, I've spent the day buying and selling shares; for twelve mortal years I've come home every evening in the same tube. And the world was rolling on and on. I'm fed up. Fed to the teeth. I'm not going to be the drudge of respectability any longer. I'm through. Look. [*He takes his glistening topper.*] Here is the badge of my office. This is the symbol of my position and my respectability. Sleek, shining, new and rakish. Look at it. It represents the potentiality of wealth beyond the dreams of avarice. To hell with it. [*He flings it down on the floor, stamps on it and kicks it away from him.*]

MARGERY: Charlie, Charlie, Charlie. And you who were always so particular about your hats. Oh, what is going to become of us now?

PATRICK: Are you obliged to be so melodramatic, father?

CHARLES: In moments of emotion we're all apt to fall into it, my dear boy.

JUDY: And what about us, Daddy?

CHARLES: I'm going to leave you.

PATRICK: How long for?

CHARLES: For good.

PATRICK: [*With the utmost surprise.*] Why?

CHARLES: [*Very naturally.*] Because I'm bored with you.

PATRICK: Bored with us? Bored with me and Judy?

CHARLES: Yes, bored with you and Judy. Aren't you bored with me?

PATRICK: That's different. You're our father.

CHARLES: How is it different?

PATRICK: People are always rather bored with their parents. That's human nature.

CHARLES: Is it?

PATRICK: After all, they belong to a different generation. The middle-aged are naturally tedious.

CHARLES: [*Smiling.*] Has it never struck you that the middle-aged find the young tedious too?

PATRICK: It certainly hasn't.

CHARLES: They do.

PATRICK: But why? They're not tedious.

CHARLES: Oh, aren't they?

PATRICK: How can they be? They've got youth and high spirits. They're brimming over with ideas. Aren't they, Mummy?

MARGERY: Yes, darling, of course.

PATRICK: It's absurd to say that Judy and I are boring. What would this house be without us? A mausoleum. At meals we're the life and soul of the party. Aren't we, Judy?

JUDY: Rather.

PATRICK: Ask anyone you like and they'll all tell you the same thing. We've got the reputation all over the place for being unusually brilliant. If you find us boring it can only be on account of your own stupidity.

MARGERY: Oh, that is rude, Pat. You shouldn't talk to your father like that.

PATRICK: He asked for it, and, damn it all, what other explanation is there?

MARGERY: I don't know, darling.

PATRICK: It's so ungrateful.

CHARLES: I don't suppose you're more boring than most young things of your age. I daresay it's only because I know you better that you bore me more.

PATRICK: But isn't youth enough in itself? You can't be so unintelligent as not to realise that nowadays the only thing that counts is youth. And it's because we've discovered that, that our generation is so much ahead of every other. You know what I mean, Judy, don't you?

JUDY: Of course I do. In Daddy's time when they were young they just wanted to be older.

PATRICK: That's right. And we don't. We're young and we want to enjoy our youth. For the first time in the world's history we've realised the immense value of it.

MARGERY: Of course, it's lovely to be young.

PATRICK: Your lives would be nothing without us. Think of the exhilaration we bring and the vitality and go. I mean, to say we're boring is perfectly outrageous. I don't want to blow my own trumpet, but I can honestly say that's the last thing anyone could call Judy, and I think I can safely say that she'd say the same about me.

JUDY: Absolutely.

CHARLES: [*Amiably.*] I wonder if it has ever occurred to you how tiresome the conversation of the young is to the middle-aged. Chatter, chatter, chatter about nothing at all. Just to hear yourselves speak. And you take yourselves with such appalling seriousness. You know nothing, and you haven't the sense to hold your tongues. You utter the most obvious commonplace with the air of having made a world-shaking discovery. You're so solemn. You're so self-satisfied. You're so dogmatic. You're inane. The only excuse for you is that you're very young. One tries to have patience with you. But, my God, don't think we find you amusing. We find you quite incredibly dull.

[JUDY *gives a smothered chuckle.*

PATRICK: Shut up, Judy. This is no laughing matter. I can tell you this, Daddy, this is the last time I take any trouble to be gay and jolly and amusing in this house. God knows, it's been an uphill job, but I've done my best. I've just sweated my guts out. But now I'm through, definitely and absolutely through.

JUDY: But have you no affection for us, Daddy?

CHARLES: No, I haven't.

MARGERY: Oh, Charlie, what a cruel thing to say. How can you help loving your children?

CHARLES: I rather liked them when they were kids, but now they're grown up I don't find them very interesting.

PATRICK: [*Outraged.*] But that's simply unnatural.

CHARLES: D'you think it is? I don't. Of course, when they're small one's fond of one's children. One likes them as one likes puppies or kittens. They're dependent on you, and that's rather touching. They think you're very marvellous, and that's rather flattering. But almost before you know where you are, they're young men and women with characters of their own. They're not part of you any more. They're individuals. They're strangers. Why should you care for them?

PATRICK: Do you mean to say that Judy and I mean no more to you than if we were puppies or kittens?

CHARLES: No, I mean that you don't mean very much more to me than puppies mean to their father when they're grown into fine healthy young dogs.

JUDY: But you'd be sorry if we died, Daddy?

CHARLES: Wretched. I've been frightfully worried when either of you has been ill. I was devoted to you then. Perhaps it's unfortunate that on the whole you've both had robust health.

PATRICK: You can hardly expect us to have a series of illnesses just to excite your parental affection.

CHARLES: You're right, Pat. I should certainly congratulate myself on the excellent physique I was able to endow you with.

PATRICK: I should have thought you'd be so proud of us. I've always been in the first five in all my forms, and I was head of my house. I was captain of the first eleven, and in the first fifteen. Any unprejudiced person would say I was rather a credit to you.

CHARLES: You know, to be proud of one's children is really and truly only to be proud of oneself. I'm not a vain man.

PATRICK: Well, I'm dished.

CHARLES: Do you care very much for me, Pat?

MARGERY: Of course he does, Charlie. I've never known two more affectionate children.

CHARLES: Let him answer for himself.

PATRICK: I don't know what you mean. I like you as a chap naturally likes his father. You're not going about it exactly the right way to make me crazy about you.

CHARLES: I suppose if *I* died you'd cry a bit. That would be nice of you and very proper. But I'm all alive and kicking. Don't you find me rather a nuisance? Don't you resent having to come to me for money, and my wanting to know how you're going to spend it?

PATRICK: Well, naturally, any fellow of my age wants to be his own master.

CHARLES: Hasn't it ever struck you that it would be grand to have a flat of your own?

PATRICK: I don't see what that's got to do with it.

CHARLES: It doesn't suggest that you find the family circle precisely thrilling.

PATRICK: But you can't alter the facts of life. It's human nature that parents should be frightfully fond of their children. But they can't expect their children to be frightfully fond of them.

MARGERY: Oh, Pat.

PATRICK: Well, ask Uncle Alfred. He's a man of the world. He doesn't expect Tim and Dinah to be as keen on him as he is on them.

ALFRED: There you're very much mistaken, young feller-me-lad. I flatter myself that there's nowhere in this country a more united family than ours. But then I admit my kiddie-widdies weren't brought up as you were. Dorothy and I have made friends of our children. That's why we've always made them call us by our first names. Our family life is just a grand lark. You know how we chaff one another. They look upon me as their great big brother. Why, they just roar with laughter at my jokes.

[PATRICK *and* JUDY *exchange a look.*

CHARLES: I've come to the conclusion that such clever and intelligent children as you are can get along quite comfortably without me. And as that suits my convenience, I'm going to give you the opportunity of doing so.

PATRICK: But how are we to live? It means that Judy will just have to go on the streets.

JUDY: Don't be so silly, Pat. You boys are so ignorant.

PATRICK: Well, if father leaves us without a bob, there's nothing else you can do.

JUDY: Don't you know that since the war the amateurs have entirely driven the professionals out of business? No girl can make a decent living now by prostitution.

MARGERY: Judy, Judy, what are you talking about? Really, a girl of your age. I don't know what the world is coming to.

PATRICK: How am I to go up to Cambridge and read for the Bar?

CHARLES: Are you still proposing to enter Parliament in the Labour interest?

PATRICK: That's the idea ultimately, of course.

CHARLES: Don't you think the Labour Party are beginning to fight a trifle shy of the people like you, who only joined them when it looked like a good thing, and now grab all the plums?

PATRICK: They want people of our class.

CHARLES: Have you ever reflected upon St. Paul? He was a tent-maker, you know. He got a lot of kudos out of it.

PATRICK: Damn it all, Father, we're talking seriously now, don't bring in religion.

CHARLES: You know, I believe it would pay you to become a working man. A stoker, for instance, or a dustman.

PATRICK: Me?

CHARLES: Get to know the proletariat from the inside, my dear boy, and when you're all fighting for the spoils of office you'll have the bulge over the Eton boy and the Oxford graduate.

ALFRED: You're talking through your hat, Charlie. It's just when children are growing up and entering the world that they need a father's guidance. You can't leave them in the lurch like that.

CHARLES: Oh, can't I? You wait and see.

ALFRED: Penniless?

CHARLES: No, not exactly penniless. That would require more fortitude than I possess.

PATRICK: But haven't you lost everything?

MARGERY: Most brokers have something tucked away somewhere, Pat, that their creditors can't get at.

CHARLES: I'm afraid *I* haven't. Until to-day I've been what I can only describe as the soul of honour.

PATRICK: Well, then, you haven't a bob.

CHARLES: In order to comply with my bargains, I should have had to throw into the hole my private fortune. But I'm hammered. I happen to have twenty thousand pounds worth of bonds in a New York bank.

PATRICK: Oh!

CHARLES: I must tell you that in honour I should hand it over to my creditors. They have a moral right to it.

ALFRED: I'm afraid they have.

CHARLES: You see, my solicitor agrees with me. There is no doubt in my mind that to keep it is a most ungentlemanly proceeding. I propose, however, to do so.

ALFRED: Oh, Charlie, you can't.

CHARLES: Legally?

ALFRED: Legally, of course you can. But not morally. I mean, it would be frightfully bad form. Your friends will think you a dirty dog.

CHARLES: And with justice. But after mature reflection I've come to the conclusion that that won't impair my appetite or disturb my night's rest.

[JUDY *again gives a little laugh*.

MARGERY: Don't giggle, Judy. This is frightfully serious. Your father's honour is at stake.

CHARLES: There are two courses open to me. The twenty thousand pounds I've saved from the wreck will bring in roughly about a thousand a year. I can keep that for myself, and subsist modestly on the income. But I think it would be rather selfish.

MARGERY: My poor children. They can't beg their bread in the streets of London.

CHARLES: I have a very sensitive conscience, and I'm not quite sure that I should be entirely happy if at moments the thought crossed my mind that my wife and children were in want.

> [MARGERY *gives a start and looks at him with perplexity and consternation.*

MARGERY: But Charlie . . .

CHARLES: [*Interrupting her.*] The other course is to hand the entire amount to them and go out into the world alone and destitute. The gesture would be romantic, but to my mind absurd. I propose, therefore, to leave you fifteen thousand pounds and keep five thousand for myself. The income from that will always prevent me from starving.

MARGERY: But aren't I to come with you?

CHARLES: Oh, no, dear, that would be an awful bore for you.

MARGERY: [*Gasping.*] Oh! It never occurred to me for a moment you meant that.

CHARLES: Didn't it? I thought I made it quite clear.

MARGERY: It never dawned on me. Was it clear to you, Alfred?

ALFRED: Don't ask me, Margery. I don't know if I'm standing on my head or my heels.

MARGERY: But I don't understand. It's the most ridiculous thing I ever heard in my life. You can't tell your wife that you're going to leave her just like that, in the course of conversation. Without a row or a scene or anything. Like a chauffeur giving notice because he wants to better himself.

CHARLES: No, not like that. Like an old family retainer

breaking it gently to his employers that advancing years oblige him to take a well-earned rest.

MARGERY: Oh, it's absurd. You've got no reason to leave me and the children.

CHARLES: I've been a husband and a father long enough. I think one should always abandon an occupation when it has ceased to be a source of pleasure and profit.

MARGERY: But do *I* bore you, Charlie?

CHARLES: A bit. No, that's a lie. To extinction.

MARGERY: He's not sane, Alfred.

ALFRED: Well, that's what I've been thinking myself. My belief is, Charlie, that you're completely potty.

CHARLES: Don't you think I'd know if I were?

MARGERY: Even their nearest and dearest don't know sometimes. Thank God, it's never been in my family. [*A ring on the telephone is heard.*] Oh, bother!

CHARLES: See who it is, Pat. If it's anyone for me I'm out.

[PATRICK *goes without a word.*

MARGERY: I thought you meant me to come with you. I thought your idea was that we should settle down in some place in France or Italy where we could live cheaply and play golf.

CHARLES: You'd have hated that, Margery.

MARGERY: I shouldn't have liked it, but I *am* your wife and if I'd really thought it my duty I'd have consented. And, of course, we might have got to know some very nice people.

CHARLES: I would never dream of asking you to make such a sacrifice.

[PATRICK *comes in.*

PATRICK: It's Mr. Turner. I told him you were here, and he's holding on.

CHARLES: Oh, damn!

[*He goes out quickly.*

MARGERY: Oh, Alfred, what shall we do?

ALFRED: Well, my dear, I think you'd better let me have a talk to Charles alone. I'm used to dealing with matters of this sort, and my experience is that it's much better for a friend of both parties to step in before anything irreparable is said on either side.

MARGERY: I'm so flabbergasted, Alfred. I mean, it's so strange that Charlie should turn after all these years.

JUDY: Come on, Mummy. If Uncle Alfred wants us to get out we'd better nip before Daddy comes back.

ALFRED: I'm sure it's wiser. I can find out exactly how the land lies.

MARGERY: If he'd made a point of my going with him I should have said to him, Charlie, I am not only a wife, but a mother. I cannot leave my children. And if you feel that I mean nothing to you any more, then you must go. And we might have arranged an amicable separation. But if he doesn't want me, the situation is entirely different.

ALFRED: At the first glance I don't quite see how.

MARGERY: It's obvious. I won't let myself be treated like that for a moment. I have my woman's dignity to think of.

ALFRED: Oh, yes, of course. I'd forgotten that. Now you popoffski, my dear.

MARGERY: Very well.

PATRICK: Of course, I think he's off his chump. I mean, to say that we're dull, why it doesn't begin to have any sense.

MARGERY: I wonder if it would be wise to send for a doctor. [*To* JUDY.] Give me your father's hat, darling.

JUDY: [*Picking it up.*] Here you are.

MARGERY: [*Pressing it to her bosom.*] It's like a poor little baby brutally done to death. It reminds me of those Armenian folk-songs.

> [*They go out, leaving* ALFRED *alone.* CHARLES *re-enters.*

CHARLES: Hullo, where are the others?

ALFRED: I packed them off. I wanted to have a word with you alone.

CHARLES: That was Bertie Turner on the 'phone.

ALFRED: What did he want?

CHARLES: [*With a little smile.*] H'm. Good chap. He and some of the lads have got together and they've offered to put up all the money to settle so that I can get back into the House.

ALFRED: By jingo!

CHARLES: J. C. was a good judge of character, wasn't he? It's so much harder to resist kindness than brute force.

ALFRED: [*Eagerly.*] Have you accepted?

CHARLES: No, I couldn't. But I was so shaken I had to be a bit short with him. I told him to mind his own damned business and rang off.

ALFRED: Oh, Charlie, how could you be such a damned fool?

CHARLES: Don't nag me now, Alfred. I'm a bit shattered.

ALFRED: I'm not going to nag you, old boy. But now that we're alone, let's get down to brass tacks. Gloves off and cards on the table, and all that sort of thing. What's the little game?

CHARLES: [*Recovering himself.*] I wonder what you're talking about now, Alfred?

ALFRED: [*Very hearty.*] Go on with you, Charlie. Now you tell your Uncle Alfred the truth. There's a woman in this. Deny it if you can.

CHARLES: I do.

ALFRED: You can't throw dust in Uncle Alfred's eyes like that. Uncle Alfred wasn't born yesterday. If you've let your business go to old billy-o and you're leaving your wife and family, it's for a woman or I'll eat my hat.

CHARLES: [*Good-naturedly.*] Eat it then.

ALFRED: Oh, come off it. You can trust an old friend. I'm a man of the world. I know you've been married nineteen years. A chap wants a change now and then. I'm not going to blame you if you've got stuck on a little bit. Have your fun if you want to. Life is short and we're dead a long time. But be reasonable about it. One doesn't break up a happy home for a little bit of fluff. I mean. Well, you know what I mean. The game isn't worth the candle. Don't do it, old boy; don't do it.

CHARLES: My dear Alfred, you know more about little bits of fluff than I do.

ALFRED: [*Archly.*] My business brings me in contact with them now and then. And I'm human. But I never let them interfere with my home life. No, sir.

CHARLES: Have you ever met a little bit of fluff who was prepared to share the life of a middle-aged man with two hundred and fifty pounds a year?

ALFRED: I wondered at the time if Margery hadn't hit the nail on the head when she hinted that you had a tidy little sum tucked away somewhere.

CHARLES: Not a bob.

ALFRED: Do you mean to tell me that you expect to live on five quid a week?

CHARLES: It's enough to provide me with the necessities of existence. The good thing about luxury is that when you've had it, you can so very easily do without it. If I'd never had a car I should always have hankered after one. I've had one for twenty years, and now I'm perfectly willing to walk on my flat feet. But I don't want to waste my time on work whose only object is to keep body and soul together.

ALFRED: Well, if you're not going off with a woman I'm blowed if I see why you are going off?

CHARLES: I'm not prepared to waste the rest of my life doing things that bore me for people in whom I take no interest. I hanker after my own company. You see, I think I've done all that I'm called upon to do for those dependent on me. I want the future for myself.

ALFRED: What are you going to do with it?

CHARLES: I haven't a notion. I'm going to see.

ALFRED: You must have some idea at the back of your head.

CHARLES: I have only one life. When I look back and think of all the fellows who were killed in the war, I think I'd like to make more use of it than just buy and sell shares and make or lose a fortune.

ALFRED: Oh, my dear boy, you're just talking through your hat. We hear a lot about women leading their own lives. I think it's all tommy-rot myself, but there it is, and we've got to put up with it. But whoever heard of a man leading his own life? It's not done.

CHARLES: Don't you think it's rather a pretty compliment we pay the other sex if we sometimes take a leaf out of their book?

ALFRED: Do you think I don't get a bit restless sometimes? Dorothy's the best woman in the world, but now and again she's rather tiresome. Women are, you know. And sometimes on Monday morning I don't much want to go down to the office. But I say to myself, now then, Algy-palfy, this won't do, you know, shoulder to the wheel, old boy.

CHARLES: And your reward is the esteem of your wife and the respect of your fellow-citizens.

ALFRED: What do you suppose would happen to society if everybody behaved like you? I mean, it would be the end of progress and civilisation and the whole bag of tricks.

CHARLES: I think it's very silly to say that you should only do the things that you think everyone else should do. The great majority are quite content to travel in the same old rut from the cradle to the grave. Well, let them. I don't blame them.

ALFRED: It's such madness to change your whole way of life and break up your home on a moment's impulse. You've only thought about it for a few hours.

CHARLES: I've only thought about it for a few hours with my head. I've thought about it for twelve years with my belly.

ALFRED: You'll regret it. You'll never stop regretting it.

CHARLES: One has to take that risk. Who'd marry if he was afraid he'd regret it later? What is life, old boy, but a leap in the dark?

ALFRED: You'll never be happy, you know.

CHARLES: I don't see why not. I have a capacity for enjoyment, a placid disposition and an absence of wants.

[DOROTHY *comes to the garden window and looks in.*

DOROTHY: I'm sorry to interrupt you. Margery wants to know what is happening.

CHARLES: Come in. Alfred and I have been having a little chat, but we've finished.

ALFRED: Has Margery told you?

DOROTHY: Yes. Can she come now?

CHARLES: I shall be ready in a few minutes. I'm just going upstairs to change and pack.

DOROTHY: [*Taken aback.*] You're not going now?

CHARLES: Yes. When you've made up your mind to do a thing it's only a waste of time not to do it quickly.

ALFRED: But you can't go to-day, Charlie.

CHARLES: Why not? I'm only taking a handbag.

ALFRED: Your affairs are in a god-awful mess. There are a thousand things to arrange.

CHARLES: Nothing that I can't leave in your hands, Alfred. You're a highly competent solicitor.

ALFRED: It looks so damned fishy, your running away like this. I mean, there's sure to be a bit of a rumpus. It's only decent for you to stay and face the music.

CHARLES: [*Gaily.*] I don't agree with you at all. I think it's much more elegant to slip out quietly through the artists' entrance.

[CHARLES *goes quickly and*

THE CURTAIN FALLS

SCENE III

When the curtain rises CHARLES, ALFRED *and* DOROTHY *are discovered.*

ALFRED: But you can't go to-day, Charlie.

CHARLES: Why not? I'm only taking a handbag.

ALFRED: Your affairs are in a god-awful mess. There are a thousand things to arrange.

CHARLES: Nothing that I can't leave in your hands, Alfred. You're a highly competent solicitor.

ALFRED: It looks so damned fishy, your running away like this. I mean, there's bound to be a bit of a rumpus. It's only decent for you to stay and face the music.

CHARLES: [*Gaily.*] I don't agree with you at all. I think it's much more elegant to slip out through the artists' entrance.

[CHARLES *goes out quickly.*

DOROTHY: Can *you* make head or tail of it, Alfred?

ALFRED: I think I know a thing or two about human nature, and I'm convinced there's a woman in it.

DOROTHY: [*With a quick look at him.*] Have you told him that?

ALFRED: Yes. He denies it.

DOROTHY: [*Smiling a little.*] Of course, he'd do that.

ALFRED: How have he and Margery been getting on lately?

DOROTHY: Oh, all right, like they always have. Of course, she had her own interests and he was in the City all day. I shouldn't call either of them very passionate people.

ALFRED: Well, just the ordinary typical married couple, I suppose. I don't see that either of them had anything to complain of.

DOROTHY: I shouldn't have thought so.

ALFRED: Has he been going about with anybody?

DOROTHY: I haven't heard of it.

ALFRED: You'd better ask Margery. If a man's in love with somebody else, his wife generally has some suspicion.

DOROTHY: I'm sure if she had, she'd have told me. We tell one another everything.

ALFRED: If a fellow is prepared to chuck everything, his business and his family and the whole bag of tricks, it must be for some reason.

DOROTHY: Oh, yes, I don't suppose he'd do it just for fun.

ALFRED: I've been a solicitor for a good many years, and my experience is that there are only two things that matter to a normal man. One's money, and the other's women.

DOROTHY: If anyone knows, you ought to, Alfred.

ALFRED: Well, I mean, what else is there?

DOROTHY: You don't think he might have some spiritual motive, if you know what I mean?

ALFRED: Of course, there's a possibility of that. He may not be quite right in his head.

DOROTHY: I didn't mean that exactly. I was wondering if he isn't doing this on account of some ideal.

ALFRED: Come off it, popsy-wopsy. You've been reading too many novels; business men don't do things for an ideal.

DOROTHY: He's never been quite normal since the war.

ALFRED: He's a thundering good chap, and I hate to see him make a damned fool of himself.

DOROTHY: Well, what's to be done?

ALFRED: I think the only person who can do anything is Margery. Pity she isn't a bit more intelligent.

DOROTHY: It's not easy for a woman to be intelligent with a man who isn't in love with her.

ALFRED: Charlie's an emotional fellow, and, hang it all, she's a woman. She ought to be able to get round him somehow.

DOROTHY: Five o'clock in the afternoon isn't a very good time for emotion.

ALFRED: If you'd been mixed up in as many divorce cases as I have you wouldn't say that. Look here, you have a talk to her. You can give her a lead. I'll go along and send her in. It's a bit awkward for me.

DOROTHY: I'll do what I can.

ALFRED: I know you will, old gal.

[ALFRED *goes out.* DIANA *comes in.*

DIANA: Hullo, Dorothy! Are you alone?

DOROTHY: Is there anything you want?

DIANA: I was looking for Uncle Charlie.

DOROTHY: Why?

DIANA: I just wanted to say good-bye to him.

DOROTHY: Oh, are you going?

DIANA: No, but I thought he was.

DOROTHY: Run along, darling, I'm busy. If there's anything to tell, I'll tell you later.

[MARGERY *comes in quickly, and with her first words* DIANA *slips out.*

MARGERY: Alfred says you've got something to say to me.

DOROTHY: He thought I'd better speak to you before you saw Charlie.

MARGERY: Where is Charlie?

DOROTHY: Upstairs. He's packing.

MARGERY. [*Dumbfounded.*] Packing? He isn't really going?

DOROTHY: I'm afraid so.

MARGERY: To-day?

DOROTHY: Now.

MARGERY: [*With a gasp.*] Oh! I never thought for a moment that he meant it. I thought he was hysterical and just making a scene.

DOROTHY: Don't take it too tragically, darling. He'll come back.

MARGERY: What to? He won't have any business. We shan't have anything to live on.

DOROTHY: Had you no suspicion that anything was wrong?

MARGERY: With the business? No, he never talked to me about it. He knew I hated shop.

DOROTHY: No, I meant at home.

MARGERY: No, he always seemed just the same. I never paid much attention to him. Why should I?

DOROTHY: That's true.

MARGERY: I think it's so frightfully selfish of him. If a man's lost his money, it's his duty to work hard and make some more.

DOROTHY: D'you think he's in love with someone else?

MARGERY: Oh, no, I should have noticed that at once. I gave him everything he wanted in that way.

DOROTHY: That's wasn't very much, was it?

MARGERY: We were very good friends. We didn't interfere with one another. I should have called it an ideal marriage.

DOROTHY: Men are very funny. You never really know what they want. I don't believe they know themselves.

MARGERY: What do you mean by that?

DOROTHY: Well, I always had an idea that Charlie hankered after something different.

MARGERY: I don't know what. I've been a perfect wife.

DOROTHY: Perhaps you didn't bring enough beauty into his life.

MARGERY: Dorothy, how can you be so unkind? Oh, I think it's dreadful to say a thing like that when I'm so upset. I surrounded him with beauty. Everyone knows how much beauty means to me. Painting and books and all that sort of thing. How about the Czecho-Slovak peasant industries? I organised them. It was a revelation of beauty. And the Armenian folk-songs. Who'd heard of Armenian folk-songs until I discovered them? No one's keener about beauty than I am. I'm crazy about it. I practically made beauty in Golders Green.

DOROTHY: [*Soothingly.*] I'm dreadfully sorry, darling. I didn't mean to hurt your feelings.

MARGERY: I may not be clever, but if there's one thing I do know something about, it's beauty.

DOROTHY: You've taught me a lot, darling.

MARGERY: What's wrong with Charlie is that he's got no sense of humour. And I can't do anything about that.

DOROTHY: It's a pity Alfred can't give him some of his. Alfred has almost too much.

MARGERY: Life's so complicated.

DOROTHY: Alfred says you're the only person who can do anything now.

MARGERY: I'm in a frightful position, Dorothy. You know how spiteful people are. When a woman leaves her husband they say it's because he was a brute, but when a man leaves his wife they say it's because she couldn't hold him. It's so frightfully humiliating.

DOROTHY: What are you going to say to him?

MARGERY: I shall just appeal to his better nature. After all, he's a reasonable man. He must see that he can't leave the children just when they're entering the world and need his help and guidance more than ever.

DOROTHY: Oh, my dear, men aren't reasonable. They're not like women. You surely know that by now. The only way you can influence them is through their emotions. I mean, the great advantage we have over them is that they're weak and sentimental. In your place I'd just be terribly pathetic. I'd cling to him and just cry like a child.

MARGERY: I've never been able to cry when I wanted to. You know that. It's always been a handicap. I hate slush.

DOROTHY: It's no good saying that now. It's the only thing that gets a man every time. You know what I mean. Flatter him. Be soft and loving and tender. Oh, my dear, I could do it on my head.

MARGERY: It's so difficult after all these years. I'm afraid he'd laugh.

DOROTHY: Ah, there we come back to the old trouble. It is so hard to know how to take a man who has no sense of humour.

MARGERY: I almost think it would be better if you saw him first, Dorothy. I think it would be easier for you.

DOROTHY: But, darling, I can't be loving and tender for you. I mean, that's the kind of thing you must do for yourself.

MARGERY: Yes, I know, but you can prepare him. I mean, you can tell him that, of course, I'm reserved and don't show my feelings, but you know for a fact that I'm frightfully in love with him.

DOROTHY: Yes, I could do that.

MARGERY: I daresay you're right. I suppose I haven't flattered him enough. One always forgets how vain men are.

DOROTHY: It's fatal when one does. All right, I'll see what I can do. I'll call him.

MARGERY: You're a brick, Dorothy. I shall be in the garden.

[MARGERY *goes out through the french window and* DOROTHY *goes to the door. She opens it for a moment, and is lost to sight.* DIANA *slips into the room and tiptoes across it, but she hears her* MOTHER'S *voice, and slips quickly away.*

DOROTHY: [*Outside.*] Charlie! Charlie! Will you come down? I've got something to say to you.

[SHE *comes back into the room. She takes out her mirror and her lipstick and paints her lips. The door opens, and* CHARLES *comes in. He has changed into a lounge suit.*

CHARLES: Here I am.

DOROTHY: [*A trifle solemnly, as though she were speaking of a corpse.*] I've just been talking to Margery.

CHARLES: Yes?

DOROTHY: She's dreadfully unhappy.

CHARLES: [*Coolly.*] Peeved and exasperated. Not unhappy.

DOROTHY: You don't know her.

CHARLES: After nineteen years of marriage? Don't be silly. I know Margery as well as it's possible for one human being to know another.

DOROTHY: She's very reserved.

CHARLES: A trifle phlegmatic even.

DOROTHY: What a cruel thing to say, Charlie!

CHARLES: Not at all. It's not an unpleasant trait in a wife. It makes for peace in the home.

DOROTHY: I wonder if you realise how deeply attached to you Margery really is.

CHARLES: You wouldn't say she was madly in love with me, would you?

DOROTHY: Yes, I would. I really would. She adores you.

CHARLES: Don't talk such rubbish. You know just as well as I do that Margery doesn't care two hoots for me.

DOROTHY: No, no, no! She loves you. Oh, Charlie, it's such a serious step you're taking.

CHARLES: [*With a slight change of tone.*] And I'm taking it seriously. Believe me, my dear, nothing that you can say is going to have any effect on me. You're only wasting your breath and my time.

DOROTHY: I should never forgive myself if I didn't do everything I could to stop you.

CHARLES: Pardon me, but exactly what business is it of yours?

DOROTHY: [*With a little helpless gesture.*] Well, you see, I happen to know why you're going.

CHARLES: I'm not surprised, considering that I took the greatest pains to explain it to Margery and Alfred.

DOROTHY: Oh, all that about freedom and not wanting to be a broker? You don't suppose I believe that?

CHARLES: All the same it's the truth.

DOROTHY: [*Softly.*] D'you think I haven't got eyes in my head?

CHARLES: Very handsome ones, and you make excellent use of them. But what have they got to do with it?

DOROTHY: [*With a certain coyness.*] Well, it's me, isn't it?

CHARLES: [*Astounded.*] You?

DOROTHY: [*With self-satisfaction.*] I thought it was.

CHARLES: Why?

DOROTHY: D'you think I haven't noticed how you looked at me? D'you remember kissing me the other night?

CHARLES: Not particularly. I've kissed you a thousand times.

DOROTHY: Not like that. You may have thought you were kissing me the same as always. But you weren't. I know. After all, it was me you kissed.

CHARLES: It was quite unintentional.

DOROTHY: I know. That's why it gave you away.

CHARLES: My dear Dorothy . . .

DOROTHY: [*Interrupting.*] No, no, no, don't. Don't speak. Let me speak. I know so well what you've got to say. There's Alfred, your oldest friend, and Margery, my first cousin, and the children—your children and my children. Oh, it's all hopeless, hopeless. I've seen you brooding over the misery of it, and my heart has bled for you. Oh, Charlie, Charlie, you don't have to tell me. I know everything.

CHARLES: Look here, Dorothy, you put me in a very awkward position.

DOROTHY: [*Acting so well that for the moment she believes every word she says.*] And d'you think you haven't put me in an awkward position? What do you think I've been feeling all this time? I'm not a stick or a stone. Do you think I could sit there and know that those great, sad, tragic eyes of yours were resting upon me without being stirred to the depths of my soul? Of course, I know that Margery never understood you. Oh, my dear, my dear, I've been so sorry for you. But, Charlie, we can do nothing. What can we do?

CHARLES: We can talk not quite so loud.

DOROTHY: Oh, damn! As a matter of fact there's nobody about.

CHARLES: But in point of fact why are you saying all this?

DOROTHY: Don't you know?

CHARLES: I haven't a notion.

DOROTHY: Oh, Charles, Charles, what a fool you must think me. I know you love me.

CHARLES: How?

DOROTHY: Intuition. D'you think that ever fails a woman in a matter like this?

CHARLES: Ah, I'd forgotten that.

DOROTHY: [*Persuading herself that it is all true.*] I've seen your face grow pale with desire when you touched my hand. I've seen you bite your tongue in order to prevent yourself from speaking. Oh, I know, of course you couldn't speak, it was so brave of you, don't think I didn't realise how brave you were, but this last moment does it matter? I can't let you go without telling you that I know. Don't ask me to tell you that perhaps I love you too. No, no, no.

CHARLES: I don't for a moment think you do.

DOROTHY: I don't know. Don't ask me. Don't force me to say more than I want to. Oh, Charlie, when they came and told me you were going away and in a flash I knew that it was on account of me—oh, what shall I do, I cried to myself. It's awful that you should make such a sacrifice for me. I can't bear it! I can't bear it!

CHARLES: You know, one finds after a time that one *can* bear the sacrifice that other people make for one.

DOROTHY: I *must* bear it. Oh, but you don't know what bitterness it is. I know if I were a brave woman I would throw everything to the winds and come with you. Don't ask me to do that, Charlie. Don't tempt me.

CHARLES: No, no.

DOROTHY: You're so wonderful. It's no good pretending to be something I'm not. I haven't the courage. After all I've got a husband who loves me and two children who worship the ground I tread on, and then there's my position in Golders Green. I know I'm weak. I know you'll despise me, but perhaps also some day you'll find room in your heart for a little pity.

CHARLES: I'm sure you're very happy with Alfred.

DOROTHY: Happy! Happy! Who is happy? Oh, I think life is so sad .

CHARLES: It has moments when one seems justified in taking a moderately cheerful view of things.

DOROTHY: Oh, you're bitter. I've disappointed you. It's no good, Charlie. I can't run away with you. Be sensible, old boy, what should we live on? Is it true that you'll only have five pounds a week?

CHARLES: Quite true.

DOROTHY: It's no good, darling. I know you'll think me hard and worldly, I'm only being cruel to be kind. Love can't live on five pounds a week. It would be criminal to put it to such a test. You do understand, don't you?

CHARLES: Quite.

DOROTHY: It would be different if you had a hundred thousand pounds tucked away in a Swiss bank.

CHARLES: Quite, quite.

DOROTHY: I'm not really cynical, you know. Only I am a woman, and I know what money means.

CHARLES: I always think that is one of the most delightful characteristics of your sex.

DOROTHY: Don't feel hardly towards me, Charlie. Don't make my suffering still harder to bear.

CHARLES: I'm sure you're right.

DOROTHY: I know I'm right, and one of these days you'll realise it. Perhaps in years to come we shall meet again, in Paris or somewhere, and then, who knows? Perhaps you will have forgotten me.

CHARLES: Oh, no.

DOROTHY: And perhaps, perhaps I shall say to you, God knows I've suffered, God knows I've tried to do my duty, but there are limits to human endurance. Perhaps

I shall say, Charlie, Charlie, we've waited long enough, we have such a little time before us, let us accept the happiness that chance has so mysteriously thrown in our way.

CHARLES: Now, I think, if you don't mind, I'll just go up and finish my packing.

DOROTHY: I can't let you go without giving you something to remember me by. Charlie, kiss me on the mouth.

> [CHARLES *looks round the room with embarrassment; he is very nervous in case someone should come in by the door or the french window. Then he kisses* DOROTHY *full on the lips. She flings her arms round his neck. He takes her hands and releases himself.*

DOROTHY: I have given you more than my body, Charlie, I have given you my soul. Good-bye. Good-bye for ever.

> [SHE *walks swiftly out into the garden, with heroic courage mastering her emotion.* CHARLES *stands for a moment, smiling wryly after her; he passes a finger round his collar, which seems rather tight for him, and then, smiling a little still, walks towards the door to go upstairs. Just as he is about to turn the handle the door is opened; he starts as* DIANA *comes in and almost treads on him.*

CHARLES: Hullo, what are you doing there?

DIANA: I've just been hanging about till Dorothy was out of the way. I've got something I want to say to you.

CHARLES: Fire away.

DIANA: Has she been trying to vamp you?

CHARLES: It would be rather late in the day for that.

DIANA: I bet she thinks you're leaving Aunt Margery on her account.

CHARLES: You've been listening, Dinah, my dear. Not a very pretty trick.

DIANA: Don't be stuffy, darling. I don't have to listen at doors to know what Dorothy's saying.

CHARLES: Mutual sympathy, I suppose. One of the disadvantages of a united family.

DIANA: Poor Dorothy has reached the age when women think every man they meet is in love with them. It's such a bore when they get like that. It makes them so unpunctual.

CHARLES: Oh, why?

DIANA: You see, they start doing their face and they say, Oh, my God, my face is awful to-day, and they start again; and they go on and on, and by the time they've given it up as a bad job they've kept you waiting for hours.

CHARLES: My dear, I've still got a few things to pack. What was it exactly you wanted to say to me?

DIANA: Oh, don't you like general conversation?

CHARLES: Is that what it was? I thought you were making a few tart remarks on your mother.

DIANA: I adore Dorothy. I'm sorry for her. You know, I think it's so pathetic her gratitude when she can persuade herself she's got off with somebody.

CHARLES: It's nice of you to be so sympathetic. I must bolt now. Good-bye, my dear. We've had a jolly little chat.

DIANA: Oh, but I haven't started yet. I've been trying to get you alone for the last hour.

CHARLES: You know, I'm going away to-night.

DIANA: Yes. Would you like me to come with you?

CHARLES: What for?

DIANA: Company.

CHARLES: That's awfully sweet of you, but I shall manage all right by myself.

DIANA: Won't you be awfully lonely by yourself?

CHARLES: After being married nineteen years I'm used to loneliness

DIANA: A girl's different from a wife, you know.

CHARLES: Quite. Even more of a nuisance.

DIANA: I'd look after myself. I wouldn't be any trouble to you.

CHARLES: Whatever put such an idea into your head, Dinah?

DIANA: I'm so bored at home. After all, I'm eighteen, and the time's just flying, and I'm getting nowhere. I want to get out into the world and do something.

CHARLES: That's all right, but a married gentleman in the early forties is hardly the best companion for such an adventure.

DIANA: Why not?

CHARLES: My dear, ancient as I am, I'm afraid it would be difficult to persuade the people we ran across that my relation towards you was simply paternal.

DIANA: I'm not a damned fool, darling. Of course I'd come as your mistress.

CHARLES: Oh, I see. It hadn't occurred to me that you meant that.

DIANA: I think you must be rather stupid, darling.

CHARLES: To tell you the truth I don't want a mistress.

DIANA: Why not? You're not so old as all that.

CHARLES: I should prefer any attachments I make to be of a strictly temporary nature.

DIANA: You could always chuck me if you got sick of me.

CHARLES: Women are so clinging.

DIANA: Don't you think I'm attractive?

CHARLES: Very.

DIANA: And I am a virgin, you know.

CHARLES: *I* guessed that.

DIANA: [*Somewhat hurt.*] I don't know why. It's just an accident. Lots of girls of my age aren't.

CHARLES: I think it's a pleasing trait in the young unmarried female.

DIANA: That's rather middle-aged of you, darling.

CHARLES: I am rather middle-aged, my pet.

DIANA: Tim is, too.

CHARLES: What? Middle-aged?

DIANA: No, a virgin. I think it's rather chic in a boy.

CHARLES: It doesn't interest me so much.

DIANA: He says he's going to wait for Potiphar's wife to make the usual advances to him, and then it'll be such a pleasant surprise for her.

CHARLES: Or contrariwise. Innocence is charming in theory, but in practice experience has many advantages.

DIANA: You're not going to turn me down?

CHARLES: You bet your life I am.

DIANA: You needn't hesitate because you're afraid I don't realise what I'm up against. I should go into it with my eyes open, you know.

CHARLES: I wasn't thinking of you. I was thinking entirely of myself. I should be a fool to jump out of a tepid frying-pan into a red-hot fire.

DIANA: It would be such a lark.

CHARLES: It wouldn't really. I haven't a bean, you know. Love can't live on five pounds a week.

DIANA: Hullo, that sounds like Dorothy. Have you been asking her to run away with you?

CHARLES: Certainly not.

DIANA: Swear to God?

CHARLES: Cross me heart.

DIANA: All right. As a matter of fact, I've thought of that. You wouldn't have any silly prejudices about my keeping you, would you?

CHARLES: Not at all. I trust that in the well-regulated society of the future that will be the universal practice. Women with their executive ability and natural industry will toil from blushing dawn to dewy eve and leave men free to devote themselves to art and literature and the less violent form of athletics.

DIANA: Don't talk. Listen to what I've thought. You know everyone says I dance divinely. I can easily get up stage dancing and then I'll get engagements at the Casinos in France and Italy.

CHARLES: I don't believe there's much money in that, do you? I've always said that if I was kept by a woman I'd want to be kept in style.

DIANA: No, but wait. That's why I said I'd get engagements at Casinos. A lot of rich men go to them and when I see that there's one attracted to me I can lure him on, and then at the psychological moment you can come in and say, What are you doing with my daughter? D'you see what I mean?

CHARLES: Yes, that's all right in the pictures, but in real life it always ends you up in jug. It's no good, Dinah, I'd never have the nerve for that.

DIANA: I suppose that means that you don't want me at any price?

CHARLES: To be frank with you, it does. [SHE *gives a deep sigh.*] Oh, come on, don't sigh.

DIANA: I'm so frightfully disappointed.

CHARLES: You'd be bored stiff with me in a month. And where would you be then?

DIANA: I could always have left you. After all, you're not the only man in the world. I don't suppose it would have lasted for ever, but while it did, it might have been rather lovely.

CHARLES: I think in your place I'd wait till some suitable young man comes along, and marry him. You can always see then, you know.

DIANA: I can't understand why you hesitate. I should have thought it such a snip.

CHARLES: To run away with you? No, it's not my idea of a snip at all.

DIANA: You haven't got moral scruples, have you?

CHARLES: Do you think it would be very nice of me to bolt with the daughter of an old friend and she only just out of the schoolroom, so to speak?

DIANA: Everybody's the daughter of someone, and surely it's better to run away with a girl than with an old hag.

CHARLES: I imagine it's more agreeable.

DIANA: If you won't have me because you think it's dishonourable or rot like that, I think it's simply foul of you. I mean that's just stuffy and frightfully middle-class.

CHARLES: Oh, d'you think it is?

DIANA: Of course. I'd never forgive you if it was that.

CHARLES: I'm sorry.

DIANA: But if it's just that I don't appeal to you sexually, then I don't mind a bit. I mean, it's rotten for me, of course, but that's the sort of thing you can't help, and I must lump it. Is that it?

CHARLES: My dear, that's not a very nice thing for a man, even a middle-aged one, to say to a girl of eighteen.

DIANA: Oh, shut up! It never occurred to me that you might . . .

[SHE *stifles a little sob.*

CHARLES: Good God! What are you doing? You're not crying? What on earth are you crying for?

DIANA: You see, I'm so frightfully in love with you.

CHARLES: [*With astonishment.*] With me? You never said that before.

DIANA: I didn't want to appeal to your emotions. I wanted to make it practically a business proposition. I'm simply crazy about you.

CHARLES: [*Angrily.*] You damned little fool, what rot is this you're talking now?

DIANA: It isn't rot. I'm madly in love with you.

CHARLES: Well, you jolly well stop it. I never heard such nonsense.

DIANA: I can't help it.

CHARLES: Yes, you can help it. You're just a silly, hysterical, sloppy schoolgirl. What you want is a thorough spanking, and by George, if I weren't in such a hurry, I'd damned well give it you myself.

DIANA: [*Smiling through her tears.*] You are rather sweet, you know.

CHARLES: Upon my soul. [*Changing his mood and laughing.*] Don't be a little idiot, Diana. Fancy falling in love with a funny old thing like me. You ought to be ashamed of yourself.

DIANA: I'm not. And I can't help it. I've got an awful thing about you. I think you're so frightfully attractive.

CHARLES: Why?

DIANA: Well, you have no sense of humour.

CHARLES: You're not going to tell me that you fell in love with me because I had no sense of humour.

DIANA: Yes, madly. You knew you had no sense of humour, didn't you?

CHARLES: I didn't, to tell you the truth.

DIANA: People who haven't seldom know it. Funny, isn't it? You see, all my family have so much, sometimes it's almost unbearable. I love you for not having it. You can understand that, can't you?

CHARLES: Perfectly. But what a bore it would have been if you'd discovered you'd made a mistake when it was too late?

DIANA: How d'you mean?

CHARLES: Well, you see, our happiness might have been shattered if I'd made a joke.

DIANA: [*Tenderly.*] Perhaps I shouldn't have seen it. You know, one often doesn't see the jokes of people who have no sense of humour.

CHARLES: I think it's just as well not to have taken the risk.

DIANA: You might kiss me once, will you?

CHARLES: Of course, and then I really must see about my packing.

> [HE *goes to her, and is about to put his arms round her. She looks at his lips, peering a little, then she passes her forefinger over them and smells it.*

DIANA: I wish Dorothy wouldn't use such beastly lip-stick. Wipe your mouth, darling.

> [SHE *takes his handkerchief out of his pocket and wipes his lips. She throws her arm round his neck and offers him her lips, but he takes her head in his hands and kisses her good-humouredly first on one cheek and then on the other. She sighs as he releases her.*

DIANA: Lend me your comb, will you?

CHARLES: My comb? I haven't got one.

DIANA: Then what do you do when you're out somewhere and want to comb your hair? All the boys I know carry one. Darling, I could have taught you so much.

CHARLES: [*With a glance at his watch.*] Where do you suppose Pat and Judy are?

DIANA: Judy's in the garden. I don't know where Pat is.
[CHARLES *goes to the french window and calls.*

CHARLES: Judy. [*To* DIANA.] I wish you'd ask Margery to come here.

DIANA: All right. I don't care if you are angry, I think you're terribly attractive.

CHARLES: Go to hell.

[*As she is going out,* JUDY *enters.*

JUDY: Did you call me, Daddy?

CHARLES: Yes. I'm just going to have a little chat with your mother. I wish you'd go upstairs and see that Johnston is packing my things all right. I put everything I wanted on the bed.

JUDY: Right-ho!

CHARLES: And when the bag is ready tell her to put it in the car.

JUDY: D'you want me to drive you down to the station?

CHARLES: No, better let the chauffeur. Where's Pat?

JUDY: He's locked himself up in his room. He's eating butter-scotch. He's sulking.

CHARLES: If butter-scotch makes him sulk, why does he eat it?

JUDY: He isn't sulking because he's eating butter-scotch, he's sulking because you said he was a bore.

CHARLES: I didn't blame him for it. I merely stated it as an interesting fact.

JUDY: You couldn't expect him to like it. I didn't either. I've been thinking it over. Do you know, I've got rather a ghastly suspicion about you, Daddy?

CHARLES: Oh! What is it?

JUDY: Well, I've got a ghastly suspicion that perhaps you've got more sense of humour than any of us quite realised.

CHARLES: I? Oh, my dear, what makes you think that?

JUDY: I don't know. It's made me rather uneasy. I mean, it would be rather comic if all this time you'd been laughing at us up your sleeve. Isn't it funny? I like you better now than I've ever liked you before.

CHARLES: I don't know why.

JUDY: Well, I suppose the fact is that now you're doing the dirty on us you seem so much more human.

CHARLES: H'm!

JUDY: Do I surprise you? You see, you don't know me, Daddy. I suppose it's impossible for a father to know his daughter.

CHARLES: Do people ever know one another?

JUDY: I think when they're in love they think they do.

CHARLES: And are never more mistaken.

JUDY: Were you in love with Mummy when you married her?

CHARLES: Oh yes. Crazy about her.

JUDY: I suppose love can't be expected to last for ever.

CHARLES: I suppose not. I think that's the only real tragedy in life. Death? Well, one expects death. But when one's in love, one never expects love to die. It makes life look such a sell.

JUDY: I wonder why it doesn't last?

CHARLES: Habit kills it.

JUDY: Dinah and I have often discussed whether it wouldn't be better to have affairs than to marry.

CHARLES: There's not much in it. An affair is just as tiresome and more inconvenient.

JUDY: Pity you're going just now. There are a lot of things I should have liked to ask you.

CHARLES: Why have you never asked me before?

JUDY: One can't talk to one's father. It's only because I don't look upon you as my father any more that I can treat you as a human being. Of course, parents and children bore one another. They never talk to us of the things that interest them, and we never talk to them of the things that matter to us.

CHARLES: If we ever meet again we must try to forget our unfortunate relationship. You will be an engaging young woman I've run across by chance, and I shall be an elderly gentleman in reduced circumstances who once knew your mother.

JUDY: I daresay we shall find we have quite a lot to say to one another.

CHARLES: For my part I should like to tell you that I shall be delighted to renew the acquaintance we've so unexpectedly made. It's been charming to meet you.

JUDY: Daddy, why are you going away? It's for your soul's sake, isn't it?

CHARLES: That sounds rather pretentious and high-falutin', doesn't it?

JUDY: Does that matter? Just for once and within these four walls.

CHARLES: Well, perhaps it is. I have so few years before me. It seems a pity to waste them. Have you ever had an awful lot of letters to write and only ten minutes to catch the post? You don't write the most important ones from the standpoint of eternity, but only the important ones to you. Perhaps they're quite trivial, making a date or answering an invitation, but they are all you have time for. The others must go to the devil. I only have time now to do what I urgently want to do.

JUDY: You've got your chance. You'd be a fool not to take it. I don't blame you. In your place I'd do what you're doing.

CHARLES: You're a good girl, Judy.

JUDY: You've given me my chance, too. I never wanted to be a young lady. Coming out and going to parties, getting married and going to parties. I want to go on the stage.

CHARLES: Are you prepared to work? It isn't just doing your bit in a play and then going to supper at the Savoy. It's a whole time job.

JUDY: Oh yes, I'll work.

CHARLES: Well, be natural, that's the chief thing.

JUDY: That ought to be easy.

CHARLES: It isn't. It's the result of infinite pains. It's the final triumph of artifice. And remember that society only looks upon you as a freak and the moment you're out of fashion drops you like a hot potato. Society has killed more good actors than drink. It's only your raw material. Let the footlights, at least spiritually, always hold you aloof. These are the last solemn words that a father whispers in his daughter's shell-like ear as he is about to leave her for ever.

JUDY: Why for ever? When I'm a celebrated actress with a princely salary and you a broken-down old reprobate, I shall be always pleased to offer you a home in my palatial flat.

CHARLES: That's sweet of you. Here is your mother. Nip along, darling, and when my packing's finished come and tell me.

JUDY: Right-ho! Bless you, Daddy. Have a good time.

CHARLES: Same to you, my pet.

[SHE *slips out of the door as* MARGERY *comes in from the garden.* CHARLES *goes towards her and takes her hand.*

Come and sit down, Margery.

MARGERY: Is it true you're going away to-day?

CHARLES: Yes.

MARGERY: You're deliberately breaking my heart.

CHARLES: My dear, for the first time in our lives we're going to have a serious talk. It'll be so much easier if we say nothing that we don't mean.

MARGERY: But I love you, Charlie.

CHARLES: No, dear, that's not true. If you still had for me that hungry craving of the soul they call love, I think it's possible I shouldn't have the courage to leave you.

MARGERY: I've never loved anybody in my life but you.

CHARLES: I daresay not, but that isn't quite the same thing.

MARGERY: I don't know what you mean by love.

CHARLES: I think you do. You were in love with me once just as I was in love with you, and one doesn't forget.

MARGERY: You can't expect me to be the same as I was nineteen years ago. It would be absurd if I were still the love-sick girl I was then.

CHARLES: And extremely tiresome.

MARGERY: Love isn't everything. I mean, there's companionship and mutual confidence and all that. I've always had a great affection for you. I often thought what a picture we made of a happy and domestic couple. Why, I don't believe we've even had a squabble for ten years.

CHARLES: I wonder it didn't make you a little uneasy. Doesn't it strike you that two people must be profoundly indifferent to one another if they never find occasion to disagree?

MARGERY: I don't know how you can be so ungrateful. Don't you realise that if we got on so well it was entirely due to my wonderful tact? Believe me, it wasn't always so easy. You were very different when you came back from the war.

CHARLES: We were both very different. Or perhaps we weren't different at all, but we'd been separated for five years and we saw one another for the first time as we really were.

MARGERY: I don't know what you mean by that. I'd developed a lot during the war. I wanted to do my bit, and I don't see how anyone can deny that I did it. Most people thought I was so much improved.

CHARLES: Out of all recognition, my dear. We were strangers to one another. We had to start making one another's acquaintance all over again from the beginning. I don't think we liked one another very much.

MARGERY: I was a little disappointed in you, I don't mind admitting it. Fortunately I have imagination. I remember how disgusted I was when once you dropped a piece of bread and butter on the ground and picked it up and ate it as though nothing had happened. But I said, that's the war, and I made allowances.

CHARLES: It's very difficult for two people who are not in love with one another to live together. It's funny what trivial things get on their nerves.

MARGERY: It wasn't trivial at all. It was deeply significant of the change that had taken place in you. You'd lost all your beautiful idealism. Why, you weren't even patriotic any more. You drank too much and your language was filthy.

CHARLES: I suppose my nerves were a bit groggy. You were very patient with me.

MARGERY: I made up my mind that I must be. When the Armistice came, the war was over for you, but I had to go on doing my bit just the same. And there were thousands of women in England like me. I've been a good and faithful wife to you. I think I have the right to some consideration.

CHARLES: Perhaps we've both been too good and faithful. You know, of course, that the Tasmanians, who never committed adultery, are now extinct.

MARGERY: No, I didn't. And I'm not interested in the Tasmanians. I think it's frightfully callous of you to mention them when I'm so upset.

CHARLES: You mustn't think I'm not sorry to cause you annoyance.

MARGERY: Did you say annoyance?

CHARLES: I did. I think your vanity is hurt by my leaving you. I don't believe your heart is much concerned.

MARGERY: What's the good of my telling you I love you if you don't believe a word I say?

CHARLES: I shall believe you if you speak the truth.

MARGERY: How can I speak the truth when I'm taken by surprise like this. I don't know what the truth is. The whole thing has come as such a shock to me. It never occurred to me that you weren't absolutely satisfied. I always looked upon ours as an ideal marriage. I don't know what more you wanted.

CHARLES: Like Queen Victoria I was not amused.

MARGERY: You can't expect marriage to be amusing. If it were, the law wouldn't protect it and the church wouldn't sanctify it. Do you think women find marriage amusing? They've been bored stiff by it for a thousand generations. Half the women I know are so bored by their husbands that they could scream at the sight of them.

CHARLES: Why do they stick it?

MARGERY: Because everybody else sticks it. Because marriage is like that. They get used to it. Because it always has been and always will be their only respectable means of livelihood. And because of the children. I think it's awful that you should condemn your innocent children to poverty just because you want to have a good time.

CHARLES: I'm giving you fifteen thousand pounds.

MARGERY: It isn't even yours to give.

CHARLES: Morally, of course, it belongs to my creditors, but they have no legal claim to it.

MARGERY: How can tainted money bring one any enduring benefit?

CHARLES: If you feel uneasy about it, you are at perfect liberty to hand it over to them, but I tell you frankly that I shall stick to the five thousand I'm keeping for myself.

MARGERY: Are you sure your creditors couldn't get it by going to law?

CHARLES: Quite.

MARGERY: If I only had myself to think of, for the sake of your honour I would give it to them without a moment's hesitation. But my children have a prior claim on me. For their sake I shall certainly keep it.

CHARLES: I think you're very sensible.

MARGERY: But how you expect me to live on seven hundred and fifty a year, less income tax, I can't imagine.

CHARLES: I don't see why you shouldn't be very happy.

MARGERY: The position of a woman whose husband has run away from her isn't very nice.

CHARLES: Tell your friends that I've had a nervous breakdown, and had to go abroad.

MARGERY: You know what people are. They always think the worst. They'll say there's a warrant for your arrest, or that you've gone off with a chorus girl. You can't blame them. It's natural they should. And I almost wish it were true. That would at least be normal. I could understand that.

CHARLES: Do you really think that I'm called upon to go on working indefinitely in order, not to provide my wife and children with the necessities of existence, but with luxuries they can very well do without?

MARGERY: It's what one naturally expects a man to do.

CHARLES: And what about life? Where does that come in?

MARGERY: I don't understand what you mean. That is life. The ordinary man gets his pleasure by providing his family with the things they want. I mean, that's his normal existence.

CHARLES: And do you think it's worth while?

MARGERY: Why, of course it is. Otherwise everybody wouldn't do it. After all, it's no hardship to work. It's the only thing that brings enduring happiness. There's beauty in doing your duty in that state of life in which a merciful Providence has been pleased to place you. And after all, beauty is the thing that counts. There's beauty in the commonplace round of every day.

CHARLES: Not much in selling stocks and shares.

MARGERY: Oh, yes, there is. I mean, we must take a spiritual view of things. I've always been frightfully keen on that, and it's been a bitter disappointment to me that you were incapable of entering into that side of my life. My Czecho-Slovak peasant industries and the Armenian folk-songs and so on. Dorothy was only saying to me just now, I practically made beauty in Golders Green.

CHARLES: You're a remarkable woman, Margery.

MARGERY: No, I'm not, but I'm not a fool, and no one has ever called me a prig. I daresay I've thought about these things a little more deeply than you have. I'm an idealist. I think it's so ugly to be selfish. You can only get permanent satisfaction from life if you live for others. I mean, it's only by forgetting yourself and living only for Pat and me and Judy that you can hope to achieve any real happiness. I don't suppose you'll listen to me, there are none so deaf as those that won't hear, but one day you'll confess I was right. It's in self-sacrifice that a man fulfils himself. It's in giving all he has to those who are near and dear to him that he solves the riddle of life and makes out of his poor little existence a thing of beauty.

CHARLES: Margery, you're priceless.

[JUDY *comes in.*

JUDY: Daddy!

MARGERY: Run along, darling. Your father and I are talking.

JUDY: I only came to say that everything was packed, Daddy. Johnson is putting your bag in the car.

CHARLES: Oh, good. Then nothing remains but for me to say good-bye.

MARGERY: But you're not going now?

CHARLES: Yes.

MARGERY: But you can't. I haven't said half the things I wanted to say. I haven't begun yet. We must thresh the matter out.

CHARLES: My dear, we've discussed love, beauty, work and the economic situation. What else is there?

MARGERY: It's not fair. I mean, it's so fearfully sudden. If I'd only had time to get used to the situation, perhaps I shouldn't have minded so much.

CHARLES: My dear, you must look upon me like a fellow-passenger on a ship that you've seen a lot of during the trip. But the ship reaches port and you and he go your separate ways.

MARGERY: Oh, don't talk like that. I always think ships are so terribly pathetic. I shall cry.

JUDY: Yes, have a good cry, Mummy, it'll do you good.

MARGERY: I know I could get you to stay if I could only think of the right things to say. I was so unprepared.

CHARLES: My dear, you'd never think of the right things to say, because in your heart you don't want me to stay. I shouldn't go with such a kindly feeling towards you if I didn't feel that there's somewhere stirring in you the thrill of a new adventure.

MARGERY: It's no good crying over spilt milk, is it?
CHARLES: Good-bye, Margery.

> [*He kisses her on the cheek. She gives it to him listlessly, as she has done for years.*

MARGERY: It seems so strange your going like this. I simply don't know what to make of it.

JUDY: Johnston said you didn't want your tails, but I told her to pack them.

CHARLES: Oh, why? They'll be quite useless to me.

JUDY: You never know. You might want to be a waiter.

CHARLES: Thoughtful child. That had never occurred to me.

MARGERY: Charlie! You can't be a waiter.

CHARLES: Why not? When I'm up against it I'll take any job I can get. I'm prepared to be a bar-tender, a mason, a house-painter or a steward on a ship.

MARGERY: How can you? Think of the people you'll have to mix with.

CHARLES: I have in point of fact a particular fancy to be a commercial traveller.

MARGERY: Oh, Charlie, how *infra dig*. What will you travel in?

CHARLES: Romance.

MARGERY: How unpractical.

JUDY: But what fun.

CHARLES: Good-bye, Judy.

JUDY: Good-bye, darling. Bless you!

> [*He kisses her and goes out quickly.*

MARGERY: Judy, I don't feel at all well.

THE END